HE FU...

ALLOUT, A

HER EPISO...

RADIOAC...

ORLD-MA...

FUTURE O

LOUT, AN

R EPISOD

DIOACTIV

LD MAKIN

Duke University Press *Durham and London* 2021

THE FUTURE OF FALLOUT, AND OTHER EPISODES IN RADIOACTIVE WORLD-MAKING

JOSEPH MASCO

© 2021 Duke University Press. All rights reserved.
Printed in the United States of America on acid-free paper ∞
Designed by Courtney Leigh Richardson. Typeset in Warnock Pro
and Flama by Westchester Publishing Services.

Library of Congress Cataloging-in-Publication Data
Names: Masco, Joseph, [date] author.
Title: The future of fallout, and other episodes in radioactive
world-making / Joseph Masco.
Description: Durham : Duke University Press, 2020. | Includes
bibliographical references and index.
Identifiers: LCCN 2020018847 (print)
LCCN 2020018848 (ebook)
ISBN 9781478010081 (hardcover)
ISBN 9781478011149 (paperback)
ISBN 9781478012665 (ebook)
Subjects: LCSH: Threats of violence. | National security. |
World politics—21st century. | Nuclear warfare. | Emergency
management. | Terrorism—Prevention.
Classification: LCC HV6431 .M3725 2020 (print) | LCC HV6431
(ebook) | DDC 355/.033073—dc23
LC record available at https://lccn.loc.gov/2020018847
LC ebook record available at https://lccn.loc.gov/2020018848

Cover art and frontispiece: Kenji Yanobe, *Atom Suit Project:
Desert*, 1998 (courtesy Kenji Yanobe).

CONTENTS

CELLULOID NIGHTMARES

IV

AFTER COUNTERREVOLUTION

On January 13, 2018, at 8:07 a.m., on an otherwise picture-perfect Pacific island morning, the outdoor Emergency Alert and Wireless Emergency Alert systems for the state of Hawaii lit up and blasted out the following message: "Ballistic missile threat inbound to Hawaii. Seek immediate shelter. This is not a drill" (figure P.1). The emergency alert activated smartphones, radio, and television—instructing the 1.4 million inhabitants of the Hawaiian Islands to stay indoors and, implicitly, to wait for the bombs to drop (FCC 2018). On television, the alert message read:

> The U.S. Pacific Command has detected a missile threat to Hawaii. A missile may impact on land or sea within minutes. THIS IS NOT A DRILL. If you are indoors, stay indoors. If you are outdoors, seek immediate shelter in a building. Remain indoors well away from windows. If you are driving, pull safely to the side of the road and seek shelter in a nearby building or lay on the floor. We will announce when the threat has ended. Take immediate action measures. THIS IS NOT A DRILL. Take immediate action measures. (CBS News 2018)

This is not a drill. For the next thirty-eight minutes Hawaiians lived inside the opening moments of a likely nuclear war, seeking shelter, sending hurried last notes to loved ones, and anxiously scanning the horizon for the first signs of the "inbound threat," which might come in the form of the contrail of an intercontinental ballistic missile or the mushroom cloud of a nuclear detonation. It was the terrifying global promise of the nuclear era, the decades of end-times rehearsals and apocalyptic potentials, played out in miniature. The "this is not a drill" language of the alert also mirrored the official emergency

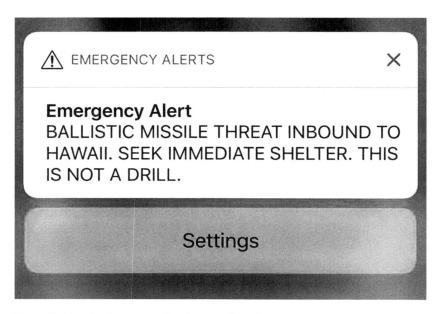

Figure P.1. Hawaiian Emergency Alert System universal text message broadcast on January 13, 2018.

response to the Japanese surprise attack on Pearl Harbor some seventy-seven years earlier (FCC 2018, 3), creating an uncanny resonance for many on the islands with the historical start of that world war (see Dower 2010). Since 1941, the United States has maintained a permanent wartime mobilization relying on national security affects (Masco 2014) to enable a vast set of foreign and domestic projects, hinging the stability of everyday American life on the possibility of an impossibly sudden and total form of violence.

Indeed, a surprise nuclear attack has served as the formal authorizing nightmare of the U.S. security state since the U.S. atomic bombings of Hiroshima and Nagasaki in 1945, an anticipated existential danger (in this case, also a projective counterformation) that energized the building out of the intelligence agencies (now seventeen strong), a permanent military commitment (now more than $1 trillion a year in "defense" spending), and the ongoing mobilization of a counterterror state (with simultaneous war activities involving more than a third of all countries in 2017; see Savell 2019).[1] The United States not only remains the only country to have engaged in nuclear warfare; it has also pioneered and maintained cutting-edge nuclear weapon technologies since 1945, while cultivating a national security culture organized by nuclear fear, a perverse orchestration of international and domestic politics through visions of an abrupt collective end. The Hawaiian missile alert came only days after a highly controversial new U.S. president promised to deliver "fire and fury like the world has never seen" to the North Korean government if they did not acquiesce to his inchoate demands to "denuclearize" (Baker and Sang-Hun 2017). At the time, Donald Trump, like George W. Bush before him, was a president who did not win the popular vote, and thus came into political power without the most basic democratic mandate. Trump, like Bush before him, also foundationally rejected the existential dangers raised by environmental scientists about petrochemical emissions and a warming planet. And Trump, like Bush before him, also issued nuclear threats at will while removing the United States from international arms control treaties, reveling as president in his sole control of the U.S. nuclear arsenal. In this heated international confrontation over nuclear weapons, the missile alert was immediately understood by many Hawaiians as a North Korean nuclear attack (although no missile source or type of warhead was named in the emergency message). In jumping to this conclusion, citizens intuitively activated a well-publicized U.S. geopolitical scenario involving a North Korean intercontinental nuclear attack on Hawaii or Alaska (which were believed to be just within reach of North Korea's longest-range missile technology in 2018). This attack scenario was immediately available to many in Hawaii because of the official orchestration of nuclear fear within the United States, the decades of nation building through images of the end and through extending military programs and geopolitical ambitions via rehearsing imagined attacks by enemies armed with nuclear weapons (see Masco 2014). But of course, this alert, though terrifying for Hawaiian residents, proved ultimately to be a phantom, a ghost in the machine of the nuclear state, an awful mistake, fully retracted some thirty-eight minutes later by officials. Indeed, a recall message was sent out by emergency managers across all media, appearing even on highway road signs, declaring "THERE IS NO THREAT" (see figure P.2).

As luck would have it, I was in Hawaii when the missile alert was issued, having just arrived for a much-needed vacation, actively seeking a rest from contemporary crisis politics. But there is no escape from collective problems such as these, for we are always already inside them: my intended reprieve was instead abruptly interrupted by neighbors frantically shouting about incoming missiles and the need to shelter in place with terrified voices and panic in their eyes. A profound sense of the "nuclear uncanny" emerged on our street, as people experienced a world that from every sensory perspective seemed perfectly calm and normal but was simultaneously infused with invisible forms

Figure P.2. Hawaiian Emergency Alert System retracting the missile attack warning on January 13, 2018 (photograph by Jhune Liwanag).

of totalizing danger (see Masco 2006, 27). While surrounded by incredible flowering plants in January and looking out at a pristine beach and ocean, it was impossible to reconcile the "ballistic missile threat inbound" message with the peaceful calm of the island on a beautiful clear blue day. Both time and space became out of joint, and different generational responses to the alert were immediately on display: older Americans revisited a fear that had been a structuring principle in their lives since childhood (leading to later discussions of duck-and-cover drills and the "where were you" question of other nuclear scares), while younger residents sought to gain more information and distinguish this emergency from all the other ones that compete for their urgent attention in the twenty-first century (from economic collapse, to resurgent racisms and xenophobia, to radically changing environmental conditions—each operating on its own frequency of collective danger). The official alert thus not only activated an emergency response communication system that was a key achievement of Cold War technopolitics (one recently upgraded in Hawaii in light of the heightened U.S.–North Korean tensions); it also activated a range of national security affects built up by generations of nuclear nation building in the United States (Masco 2014). The nervous systems of the U.S. nuclear state were instantly on display—connecting the infrastructures of command and control and warning with the negative affects of nuclear terror in citizens, mobilizing (or in many cases immobilizing) individuals in different ways as they confronted a long-fantasized imminent obliteration.

But if the first emergency message of nuclear attack was officially in error, so too was the second, that there was no threat. Since the invention of intercontinental missiles and nuclear submarines, one might always already be under attack, with each citizen-subject living simply in the lag between the missile launch and its detonation. All residents of planet Earth reside somewhere within a fifteen-minute window of nuclear warning, a condition not changed by the end of the Cold War, or the dissolution of the Soviet Union, or nearly two decades of the War on Terror. This lag between industrial capability and embodied experiences of injury informs numerous other domains of life today. Indeed, the accumulating force of historical greenhouse gas emissions is shifting all ecosystems and climatic potentials, creating planetary conditions that are increasingly both hypervolatile and violently in motion.

Thus, the politics of lag—what I call in this book the fallout—of the military industrial petrochemical age are vitally important to understand, as they are playing out now in a wide range of violences that operate over different time-space dimensions and with radically different tempos.[2] Life on a Pacific island (under nuclear threat and facing both ocean rise and intensifying storms from global warming) amplifies these understandings, as there is literally nowhere to run, no safe space to retreat to in troubled times. The missile alert was ultimately attributed to human error, produced when an unannounced training exercise was mistakenly understood by a key member of the emergency response team as a real attack (FCC 2018, 14). Mistakes in the nuclear age—accidents, malfunctions, human errors, unintended effects—are as much of a danger as nuclear war, as the always-on, 24/7, U.S. nuclear triad of missiles, submarines, and bombers is the center of a global nuclear war infrastructure involving a vast set of machines, people, and contingencies. The nuclear age is already filled with the near misses of accidental cataclysm (see Hoffman 2010; Schlosser 2013) and the slower violences created by the nuclear production complex itself.[3] A radically destabilizing climate is also the unintended outcome of a petrochemical-based global economy, the side effect of an energy regime promising security and safety but only at the expense of future ecological conditions. These two existential dangers—nuclear weapons and climate disruption—are industrially manufactured problems that now colonize the future in different ways but also draw on each other (in technoscientific, affective, and imaginary registers) in increasingly complex configurations.

I was visiting the Pacific Islands to explore coral ecologies, to experience the remarkable intensity and diversity of marine life informing reef ecosystems.

Taking refuge from the missile alert by diving into the ocean, I could see not only a fantastic range of life—continually surprising in its diversity and beauty—but also the mounting evidence of bleaching, of coral killed by the cumulative effects (of both chemicals and warming) on the ocean, a direct but slow-moving effect of a petrochemical-based global economy. Endangerment, as Tim Choy (2011) has shown, is a future anterior subject position, a way of looking back from a not-yet-existing future to create urgency in the present for an imagined loss. In the age of nuclear weapons and climate disorder, endangerment is increasingly a planetary formation, a multivector problem set that threatens the biosphere with different temporalities and forms of violence. Thus, the issue in any given moment is not whether or not the "threat is real" but to identify the specific material intensities (radioactive, greenhouse gases, synthetic chemical) that matter in the moment, as well as the linked practices of psychosocial erasure that structure environmental awareness across the radically different ways of living on Earth. Put more directly, the imbrication of nuclear nationalism and petrochemical capitalism over the past seventy-five years has produced a world that no longer has natural disasters. Rather, life in the twenty-first century is structured by violent events formed, over different tempos of time, by the increasingly dangerous fusion of consumer activities, technological revolutions, aging infrastructures, and earthly conditions.[4] Is there a place on planet Earth that has not already been altered by radioactive fallout, petrochemical emissions, synthetic chemicals, and plastics? What storm, heat wave, flood, or famine is not today affected by modes of carbon-intensive living distributed unequally across the globe? Similarly, what war or refugee crisis is not in part a result of a competition for petrochemical resources or based on projections of future environmental scarcity? These questions are at the center of this book, as is another: What if our inherited language and social theory fail precisely when confronted by these embedded forms of violence, forms that have become so large, so long-lived, varied, and embedded that they exceed human sensory perception as well as the reach of existing governmental administrative instruments and social theory?

The chapters in this book were written in an effort to assess the strange conceptual reliance on existential danger in the United States after 1945. I am interested in how the language of imminent existential danger has been, and continues to be, linked to disavowals of actually existing forms of violence and mobilized to create new forms of war. I track the historical development and contemporary consequences of a perverse mode of necropolitics (Mbembe 2003) across these chapters, analyzing an American style of living that focuses so intently on one kind of manufactured danger (consolidated in the image of "the bomb") that all others can be dismissed or de-prioritized by a state that is both an economic and military superpower. I am interested in showing how technological revolution is both world-making and world-breaking, installing new capacities in everyday life but also new forms of violence that can both become a norm and create new conceptual blockages to peace and collective safety. In the United States, technological revolution over the past century rides on top of, and often works to reinforce, the foundational violences of a settler colonial society (founded in indigenous dispossession, antiblackness, immigrant exclusions, and related forms of environmental extraction) while also simultaneously promising that the future can be endlessly reengineered, perfected through technoscience, markets, and war.

In these chapters, I am interested in engaging (ethnographically, historically, and in terms of social theory) the psychosocial project of living within a violent technopolitical order that could always have been, or could still be, otherwise (see Povinelli 2012), one that claims to value democracy and nonviolence while at the same time practicing atrocities at home and abroad. That is, I assess the mechanisms of recognition and misrecognition, indoctrination and recruitment, desire and dehumanization that naturalize nuclear weapons and climate disorder as foundational conditions of life within a nation-state that spends so much on defense that it has literally attempted to garrison the world via military bases and activities. I am interested in how, over only a few decades, in the life span of many living people, it is possible that multiple problems literally the size of the planet could emerge via the technoscientific intensities of military-industrial capitalism and how such problems are mediated politically and imaginatively in relation to one another. I consider how human senses (affects, imaginaries, nervous systems) are remade via industrial living and the types of futurity that are both conceivable and rendered inconceivable in any given moment. The crisis of contemporary life, across war, economy, and environment, is not then a recent invention but a long-standing structural achievement, a multigenerational project that continues. This raises vital questions about the logics and languages of emergency, crisis, and apocalypse and the ways these idioms come to structure specific political moments as defensive, even counterrevolutionary, forms. As I explore in the final chapter, one consequence of the "crisis in crisis" today is the loss of a range of social imaginaries and positive ideas about the future, a key attribute of the fusion of nuclear nationalism and petrochemical capitalism in the United States.

This is to say that the atomic bomb offers a particularly salient mirror to American society, as it took a multidisciplinary scientific effort, a wide political consensus, and an industrial society to build a nuclear arsenal, a military-political culture, and the supporting national security affects in citizens.[5] In my first book, *The Nuclear Borderlands*, I examined how the Manhattan Project remade northern New Mexico across multiple domains, proliferating kinds of insecurity for populations marked by class, race, and radically different understandings of nature. I argued that, after 1945, the United States built itself via the bomb, remaking its political, industrial, military, and academic institutions around the nuclear revolution while distributing nuclear injury domestically with a wide range of intensities. In this way, the atomic bomb has always presented a foundational challenge to democratic order, as it was made in secret, relies on the production of existential enemies, provokes a genocidal imaginary, and locates sole authority to launch a nuclear war in a single individual, the president (see Wills 2010). Maintaining the atomic bomb thus requires a new kind of radically undemocratic social contract, one that is negotiated only through fear: the early Cold War state taught U.S. citizens to engage the bomb in a particular way, establishing nuclear fear as a new terrain of nation building and thereby opening up the emotions of citizens in unprecedented ways. The U.S. nuclear project rides on a set of foundational contradictions, promising a superpowered relationship to other states while colonizing American life across multiple vectors of materiality and imagination. In New Mexico this means that nuclear politics fundamentally matter but not in the same way for everyone, linking concerns about employment to scientific research to environmental and health issues to matters of religion, ecology, ethics, and futurity in powerful and often incommensurable ways across communities. In *The Nuclear Borderlands*, I sought to show how the bombs built in Los Alamos remade everyday life for everyone but not in the same way or with the same consequences, fusing basic questions about settler colonialism, environmental justice, worker rights, and radically different ideas about security within U.S. nuclear nationalism.

Right from the start, the U.S. nuclear state sought to unify American experience via depicting a collective future of unlimited technological revolutions across medicine, engineering, and society or a world that would end suddenly, and finally, in a nuclear flash. This split view of the future—either purely utopian or purely apocalyptic—was promoted via state propaganda about both progress and existential danger, ideological projects that have now been weaponized across generations of U.S. statecraft. The chapters in this book are efforts to understand how nuclear fear was crafted and mobilized in the United States across a variety of these registers, connecting the countercommunism of the Cold War to the counterterrorism of the War on Terror while always negotiating the fundamental violence of American inclusion, exclusion, and extraction. I also consider the legacy of these core projects of U.S. state- and nation building for collective thought today, tracking the political impasses and conceptual restrictions produced by national security in an age of planetary-scale environmental disruption. For despite an unprecedented investment in defense, the U.S. security state cannot today address a wide range of dangers that impact everyday life (across health, economy, and the environment), which makes national security a form that colonizes everyday life in the twenty-first century rather than protects it.

Much of this book was written in an effort to understand, and respond to, the George W. Bush administration's declaration of a war on terror in 2001, after the suicide-hijacker attacks on New York and Washington, DC, and the coterminous, but much less publicized, Bush administration war on environmental science. The Bush administration immediately claimed that American history was starting over in light of the suicide attacks, that the U.S. needed to create a vast new security apparatus to fight a new kind of enemy, and that many of the normative tools of international order (the Geneva Conventions, arms control treaties, the sovereignty of state borders, democratic modes of accountability, citizen privacy, to name but a few) could no longer be maintained in the face of unprecedented danger. But in making this argument for a hegemonic counterterror state unrestrained by law, norms, or democratic order, U.S. officials often used language citational to that deployed fifty years earlier at the start of the Cold War orchestration of nuclear fear—thus, Bush's program was as much a repetition as a reinvention of the security state. In my second book, *The Theater of Operations*, I sought to understand precisely how the countercommunist state focused on nuclear weapons of the twentieth century was converted (at the level of affect, imagination, and infrastructure) into a counterterror state focused on the phantasmatic figure of the terrorist with a weapon of mass destruction (WMD) in the twenty-first century. The notable lack of content in either the figure of the terrorist or the WMD constitutes a radical expansion in the concept of threat, one that makes the future itself an unending field of existential danger subject to an equally unending militarization (while allowing older forms of racism to be resanctioned and expanded).[6] I identified the national security affects that support these historical forms of American militarism, theorizing the affective, imaginary, and material infrastructures that inform a national security society focused on different kinds of existential dangers. Few remember today that the Bush administration declared war not only on "terror" but also on environmental science, limiting the work of climate researchers, downplaying or denying the evidence of global warming while working at every stage to promote the very petrochemical industries shifting the chemical composition of both atmosphere and biosphere. The politics of both lag and terror, here, are complicated, recursive, and competing; they also draw on a set of logics, imaginations, and affects built up over generations of nuclear governance. I came to understand that nuclear danger and climate danger were competing forms in the Bush years because one enabled a superpowered state sovereignty while the other required a new planetary political order (see Masco 2010).

The paradox (if not to say incoherence) of declaring a war on terror was evident from the start: it was a renewal of a long-standing form of military-industrial power but also one no longer tied to a specific state or enemy configuration, and, of course, it was bound to fail: for when will there be no more terror in the world or an end to the possible emergence of new technologies that might become frightening to someone? Thus, this new type of war was conceived from the start to be endless and unwinnable, a project not limited to the danger posed by any specific state, group, or individual (although in practice it often reinforced existing racisms and ethnic demonizations). In this sense, it was a perfection of the Cold War state apparatus that was limited only in its ties to a specific enemy formation that could, and did, disappear. The Bush administration also sought explicitly to control which terrors mattered and which did not, and it used nuclear fear aggressively at home and internationally to bypass democratic and international norms and law. Thus, an expansive global campaign against future terror was accompanied by a near-total rejection of the dangers documented with increasing precision and urgency by climate science, dangers that will affect literally every region of the world in the decades to come with ever-amplifying violence, constituting a direct and serious threat to life as it currently exists.

The Future of Fallout, and Other Episodes in Radioactive World-Making considers how the two existential dangers of our collective moment—nuclear war and climate disorder—emerged in the mid-twentieth century together and are entangled at the levels of scientific infrastructures, imaginaries, and affects in the United States. I also evaluate the code shifts at the level of national security discourse and culture that render certain threats hypervisible and urgent while others become disavowed, are rendered invisible, or are simply ignored.[7] My core question has to do with normalized violence in the U.S., with the mechanisms by which technological, political, and imaginative infrastructures built in the name of security and prosperity install violent conditions in the world in such a manner that requires constant psychosocial and affective support to maintain as unchallenged forms. Thus, this book is an effort to unpack how national culture functions in the nuclear age, literally colonizing bodies and minds in ways that drastically curtail democratic potentials and collective futures.

This is another way of saying that existential dangers are conceptual formations that are constantly in motion, changeable over time and subject to reevaluation, and thus are always political. The nuclear referent, for example, has never been stable and requires enormous cultural work to maintain (see Masco 2006; Hecht 2012). Consider these quite recent articulations of the nuclear problem: the United States has formally committed to rebuilding its nuclear triad and warheads by the mid-twenty-first century, effectively giving up on its legal commitments to the Nuclear Nonproliferation Treaty to pursue universal nuclear disarmament while reinvesting American geopolitical power in the ability to launch a nuclear war and destroy any location on the globe in less than thirty minutes (U.S. Department of Defense 2018). Simultaneously, 122 nonnuclear states passed a Treaty on the Prohibition of Nuclear Weapons at the UN General Assembly (United Nations 2017), which when fully ratified will add the atomic bomb to the list of illegal weapons (thereby rendering all existing nuclear powers, including the United States, rogue states from the point of view of international law).[8] Meanwhile, geologists looking for a planetary-scale sign of human activity on the earth that could be the basis for designating a new geological epoch concluded that the plutonium distributed by atmospheric nuclear detonations in the mid-twentieth century meets the criteria for starting what they are calling the Anthropocene, thereby rendering the nuclear age a distinct chapter not only in geopolitics but also in the material composition of the earth (Waters et al. 2016). These are radically different acts of radioactive world-making, in the sense that each articulates a different kind of collective order and projects different conditions of futurity and injury via the bomb.[9] They also do not easily align. The nuclear age is therefore still emerging, still highly contested, and changeable, informing simultaneously a new arms race, a new international antinuclear legal regime, and a new earth science periodization. The atomic bomb remains an affectively charged technology that is at the center of global politics. It is also woven so deeply into U.S. statecraft and institutions that it is infrastructural in American life, holding a tenacious grip on definitions of power in ways that restrict action on other planetary-scale problems. This book ultimately then seeks to historicize and theorize a mode of thinking that blocks both thought and action, one that functions to maintain and exacerbate collective danger rather than working to reduce it. It is a study of the multiple modalities of radioactive world-making in the United States—of thinking life, politics, and futures via the uncanny logics of nuclear technoscience.

The first chapter introduces the major concerns of the book, theorizing the material legacies of twentieth-century nuclear national security regimes that will continue to colonize life well beyond the twenty-first century, unfolding violent relations in increasingly complicated and unpredictable ways. It considers the emergence of planetary-scale dangers by revisiting the history of radioactive fallout and mobilizing it as a model for a wide range of toxic problems that operate at maximum scale and on a wide range of temporalities. "The Age of Fallout" pays particular attention to the politics of lag as a form of violence, one that opens up conceptual problems for evaluating terms like progress, profit, and security. It then moves past the nation-state form to see nuclear effects as a planetary-scale formation, one that unsettles perspectives on security via consideration of the multigenerational legacies of environmental injury. It calls for an entirely new definition of security, one that operates outside the nation-state and that sees collective life as simultaneously integrated, connected, and exposed.

Part I, "Dreaming Deserts and Death Machines," then gathers a set of chapters around technoscience and claims made on the modernist desert, where settler colonial visions of an empty space fuse directly with nuclear nationalism in a violent formation. Written as the post–Cold War era (1991–2001) became the War on Terror era (2001 to today), these chapters ethnographically engage the psychosocial spaces of insecurity produced by U.S. militarism inside the United States, attending to the politics of erasure, imagination, and fantasy in the U.S. Southwest. Each chapter considers the mechanisms (imaginary, mass mediated, infrastructural) of creating a phantasmatic relationship to technoscience and history, finding in military machines modes of self-fashioning that constitute the grounds for power but only via new forms of dispossession, toxicity, and collective endangerment.

Part II, "Bunkers and Psyches," brings together genealogical studies of infrastructures and affects that are key to maintaining a highly militarized, nuclear society, focusing on how the imaginary space of the bunker was crafted as a site of power, pleasure, desire, and escape. These chapters address the psychosocial preconditions for some of the most violent aspects of the War on Terror, written as preemptive war, rendition, torture, and illegal surveillance were publicly revealed to be tools of a new counterterror state focused on eliminating imaginary WMDs in Iraq and beyond. These chapters work to unpack the ways that Cold War officials crafted existential danger as a perverse space of nation building while promoting military technoscience as the means to perfect, and perfectly secure, the collective future. I am interested here in a set of pivot points between citizens and the state that open up modes of internal escape, encouraging a retreat into the bunkers of the psyche while also creating and/or reinforcing long-standing forms of internal exclusion across race and class. These pivot points are mechanisms of insulating the self from state violence in both its international and domestic forms, enabling, for example, the United States to become the most nuclear-bombed country on the earth, all in the name of national defense.

Part III, "Celluloid Nightmares," continues this exploration of a specifically American form of necropolitics by looking at the cinematic building blocks of nuclear fantasies and fears. For despite the fact that millions of Americans have worked within the U.S. nuclear complex over the past seven decades, relatively few understand or have witnessed the power of the exploding bomb. In this lacuna, film has always filled the educational gap, with documentaries made for political, military, scientific, and public audiences. The midcentury effort to craft the bomb on film created the visual vocabulary for the nuclear age, generating a set of images and ideas that have been continuously repurposed since the 1950s in both documentary and Hollywood productions. These forms also come to play a huge role in how collective danger itself is understood and inform debates about rival existential dangers such as global warming in complicated ways. This part of the book consequently asks how images of collective danger change over time, and how the countersubversive imagination, in Michael Rogin's (1988) sense of the term, could become so powerful that it cannot be challenged, or corrected, by documented facts or monumental failures in policy and action. "Celluloid Nightmares" follows Derrida's (1984) insight that until existential danger is realized, it is "fabulously textual"—that is, one can only tell stories about it. Thus, the stories people tell—in print and, I would argue even more powerfully, on film—matter to the conceptual space that is understood to be collective danger, installing a fundamental weakness in the ongoing challenge of reconceptualizing nuclear and climate dangers.

The final part, "After Counterrevolution," brings together a range of chapters exploring the resetting of American sensibilities of existential danger after 2001, tracking the excitable subjects and technoscientific revolutions that inform national security in the twenty-first century. Here, I am interested in the ways that certain political and conceptual impasses are constructed and maintained, even when challenged by factual evidence, historical distance, or the recognition of unexpected forms of violence caused by official action. The question of how a political culture or governmental apparatus deploying a language of security creates its own future crises informs these chapters, which also ask where revolutionary energies are located today (see Siegel 1998). Motivating this section is the foundational challenge of understanding how the War on Terror with its now well-documented illegality, immorality, and immense body count exists without formal modes of accountability in the United States. Nearly two decades into this new form of war, there is both no end in sight to counterterror and also no formal effort inside the United States to hold anyone accountable for spectacular forms of mass violence, strategic deception of the public, or even financial fraud committed in the name of U.S. national security. I consider how it is that two decades into the War on Terror, formal U.S. policy is set to expand military budgets and activities globally (including new nuclear weapons) while simultaneously rejecting environmental science and the ever-amplifying physical evidence of global warming (revealed in almost daily environmental emergencies). I ask how it is, given the historical record, that a presidential administration can reject both nuclear arms treaties and international climate change mitigation protocols while promoting both petrochemical industrial expansion and next-generation nuclear weapons. I ask how, in other words, the U.S. has come to officially embrace and promote the very counterrevolutionary forms—nuclear weapons and petrochemical capitalism—that threaten its future in the most immediate, visceral, measurable, and documented ways.

The book concludes with an epilogue looking back across my research on national security sciences and the constitution of the two linked existential dangers in the United States, underscoring the loss of once-vital demilitarized concepts and commitments to social welfare. In the end, this book seeks to unpack a particular American investment in military-industrial capitalism (relying on existential enemy formations, threat escalations, and a belief in constant technological revolution) that increasingly has blocked attention to health, welfare, and a demilitarized collective future. This form of nuclear nationalism has been literally world-making, informing all major institutions of society today. But it also remains equally world-breaking, as nuclear nationalism is pursued regardless of outcomes, enables antidemocratic and inhumane policies, functions with indifference to the collective costs of permanent war, and has been used to block action on global warming and other forms of industrial toxicity. Seventy-five years of nuclear nationalism combined with nearly two decades of counterterror have profoundly altered democratic order in the United States, evidenced by the inability to respond, despite vast institutions and resources, to lived forms of violence that operate in unrelentingly slower registers (such as toxicity, financial precarity, dispossessions, and racisms) or existential dangers that exceed the space of the nation-state (such as climate disruption). But then, a society that has forgotten the concept of peace, exchanging it for a limited universe of imagined dangers with which it can forever be at war, cannot ever be safe, let alone secure.

The Future of Fallout, and Other Episodes in Radioactive World-Making seeks then to interrupt the normative forms of security culture in the United States, to explore moments when alternative political paths were available, and to mobilize a critical mode of assessment for multigenerational forms of violence that continue to unfold without much serious debate. My goal is to activate the positive world-making attributes of society by resisting calls to American exceptionalism or pure crisis or permanent war. It is to foment critical and collective assessment of a mode of living—call it national security or petrochemical capitalism—that has remade material, psychic, and political orders so profoundly that the ongoing transformation of the conditions of possibility for life on the planet—what biologists call the sixth great planetary extinction—can be experienced as unremarkable, inevitable, and nonurgent. The project of this book, then, is to call for a foundationally different concept of security, to imagining and enabling a radically different, culturally and ecologically diverse, planetary future.

1

THE AGE OF FALLOUT

Being able to assume a planetary, as opposed to a global, imaginary is a surprisingly recent phenomenon. Although depictions of an earthly global sphere are long-standing and multiple, the specific attributes of being able to see the entire planet as a single unit or system, I would argue, is a Cold War creation.[1] This mode of thinking is therefore deeply imbricated not only in nuclear age militarism but also in specific forms of twentieth-century knowledge production, as well as a related proliferation of visualization technologies (see Haffner 2013; Kurgan 2013). A planetary imaginary includes globalities of every kind (finance, technology, international relations) but also the earth system (geology, atmosphere, glaciers, oceans, and biosphere) as one totality. What is increasingly powerful about this point of view is that it both relies on the national security state for the technologies, finances, and interests that create the possibility of seeing in this fashion, but also, in a single gesture, exceeds the nation-state as the political form that matters. A planetary optic is thus a national security creation (in its scientific infrastructures, visualization technologies, and governing ambitions) that transcends these structures to offer an alternative ground for politics and future making. Proliferating forms of globality—including the specific visualizations of science, finance, militarism, and environment—each achieve ultimate scale and are unified at the level of the planetary, which raises an important question about how collective (in)security problems can, and should, be imagined.

In the early twenty-first century, there are unprecedented technical optics for assessing large-scale problems, allowing scientists to identify with increasing precision the as yet uncontrolled impacts of nuclear nationalism and petrochemical capitalism on Earth. However, there are not yet political systems operating on the right scale to address truly planetary problems. This conundrum—that people now possess a kind of technical awareness that exceeds the scope of political institutions—can be profitably interrogated through an examination of the conceptual history, technoscience, and psychosocial effects of fallout. In the twenty-first century, a radically changing environment is the unintended achievement of the imbrication of specific forms of capitalism, militarism, and industrialism. A critical theory of fallout allows us to contemplate industrial effects as a cumulative form of planetary engineering, a remaking of earthly domains that becomes visible only at certain scales and over certain temporalities.

Attending to fallout draws attention to emerging forms of violence across the Global North and South divide while challenging the temporal logics of settler colonialism and postcoloniality (Chakrabarty 2012; Parenti 2011; Rivkin 2017). This also means moving well past the logics of the nuclear state, a political form that has dominated international politics since 1945. For even as earth scientists generate increasingly precise and vivid depictions of ecological precarity on planet Earth, the ongoing political challenge is to achieve a form of governance that can recognize, let alone seriously respond to, escalating planetary-scale fallout. As we shall see, the Age of Fallout is a way of recasting historical categories and periodizations to recognize the future-oriented planetary environmental consequences of historical and ongoing industrial activity. Rather than a bounded period, the Age of Fallout is thus an open-ended concept of futurity, a historical transformation unfolding on the scale of the total environment (linking sociopolitical orders, multispecies relations, and cellular health), one that requires new logics and optics to enable a not yet achieved but increasingly necessary planetary process.

Figuring Fallout

"Fallout" is a relatively recent term in the English language designating an unexpected supplement to an event, a precipitation that is in motion, causing a kind of long-term and unexpected damage: it is the aftermath, the reverberation, the negative side effect. The term is used today to talk about the fallout of the mortgage crisis or of official action or inaction, or of drone strikes and preemptions across the field of counterterrorism. Fallout comes after the event. It is the unacknowledged until lived calamity built into the infrastructure of a program, project, or process. Fallout is therefore understood primarily retrospectively but lived in the future anterior—a form of history made visible in negative outcomes. People live today increasingly in the Age of Fallout, inheriting from the twentieth century a vast range of problems linking ecologies with national security with science, technology, and finance in an ongoing negative aftermath. For example, the nuclear disaster at the Fukushima Daiichi plant in March 2011 produced literal fallout in the form of cesium-137 contamination but also was the combined result of a technoscientific, financial, and regulatory failure.[2] Industrialism, militarism, and capitalism are each massive fallout-generating practices, producing reverberating dangers, now consolidated in wide-ranging collective insecurities, on issues ranging from energy to finance to war, each of which operates in a specific register of globality.

Fallout, the noun, derives from the verb "to fall out," which since the sixteenth century has designated a social break or conflict. It is thus the fight that separates comrades, marking the end of intimacy, shared purpose, and social pleasure. Military personnel also fall out from being at attention, a marker of a return to individual activities after a collective review, a relaxing of the conditions of formal militarism. Falling out thus involves individual actions and lived consequences, a postsociality, lived in isolation from the collective action of society or the war machine. To fall out is both to break with a friend and to relax from formal review; it is to burn a bridge and to be off duty all at the same time. Being off duty matters today, as so many regulatory institutions are not doing their stated jobs, short-circuited by political agendas, lack of funding, or more generally misguided priorities. For example, in response to major reports from the Intergovernmental Panel on Climate Change and the U.S. Climate Assessment detailing a disturbing future of ecological instability on an unprecedented scale, the U.S. House of Representatives passed a bill prohibiting the Department of Defense from using any funds to respond to the vast range of security problems documented in these scientific studies. By banning both science and the environment from U.S. defense policy, the House voted to protect short-term petrochemical profits over collective security (Koronowski 2014). In the United States, citizens are living within an increasingly post-Foucauldian kind of governmentality, in which the project of improving and securing life is being overrun by a narrowly construed notion of profit, one that functions in the ever-shorter lag between the engineered event and its fallout. Contemporary notions of globality are thus also increasingly tied to tracking negative rather than positive outcomes, as global flows of money, carbon, and information tend not to be recognized as infrastructural creations until they emerge as planetary-scale dangers.

Fallout, the noun, is of course an invention of the nuclear age, appearing in the English language soon after the U.S. atomic bombings of Hiroshima and Nagasaki in 1945 (see Boyer 1998, xiii). Formally, fallout refers to the radioactive debris put into the atmosphere by a nuclear explosion, designating an atmospheric event with far-reaching consequences (see Glasstone and Dolan 1977). Marked as a precipitation, it involves a gradual settling of radioactive materials and effects over a wide area. Fallout thus formally links human actions, technological capabilities, atmospheres, and ecologies in a new configuration of contamination.[3] Radioactive fallout also consists of a wide range of possible nuclear elements—cesium, strontium, plutonium, iodine, to name but a few—all with specific radioactive half-lives and environmental effects. As a process, fallout operates on a vast spectrum of temporal frames: it poses an immediate threat to health through radiation illness while installing the longer-term threats of cancer, shortened life, or intergenerational genetic change (see also Brown 2019; Jain 2013; Nixon 2011). Fallout is, thus, always an act of coproduction, a simultaneous remaking of environment and society via collective, if unequally distributed, injury.

With this complexity in mind, consider how fallout was first presented to U.S. citizens, not long after the invention of the concept, in the largest propaganda campaign to date in American history, known as atomic civil defense. In reaction to the first Soviet nuclear test in 1949, a new U.S. Federal Civil Defense Administration (FCDA) was created. The FCDA worked to transform U.S. citizens into cold warriors by saturating the public sphere with nuclear narratives, images, and themes (Masco 2014). Inaugurating an unprecedented effort to reorient American society around the dangers of a new technology, the FCDA sought to create a productive fear of the nuclear age in order to achieve a permanent war posture (Oakes 1994). Figure 1.1 offers an emblematic illustration of the atomic civil defense campaign of the 1950s, presenting fallout not simply as a new wartime threat to domestic life but as a new structuring principle of American modernity.

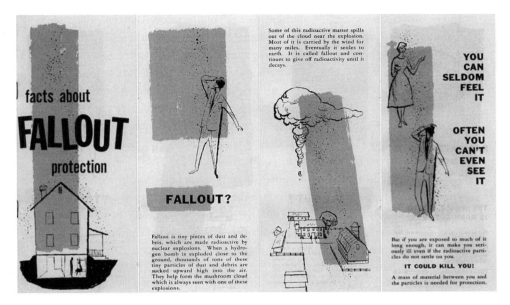

Figure 1.1. "Facts about Fallout Protection," 1958 civil defense handout (Federal Civil Defense Administration).

In "Facts about Fallout Protection," citizens learn that at home as well as on the street they are vulnerable to a new kind of invisible injury. Urban populations are no longer even the specific target of military attack; it is the environment itself that has been transformed into a potentially toxic space, remaking clouds and air as dangerous entities. The atomic bomb transforms the atmosphere on which living beings depend, converting it from a vital life support system into something now suspect, potentially loaded at any moment with invisible and harmful elements.

Part of a larger Cold War recalibration of American society through nuclear fear, the FCDA campaign attempted to shift responsibility for injury from the security infrastructures themselves to the individual citizen, now positioned as properly informed about everyday risk via civil defense programs and expected to be both alert and resilient in a minute-to-minute confrontation with nuclear war. After 1945, Americans were increasingly recruited to normalize unprecedented danger within an industrial atmosphere also undergoing radical change across a vast set of chemical trajectories.[4] "Facts about Fallout Protection" illustrates this new kind of industrial awareness, offering a cloud that no longer brings the sustenance of rain but rather delivers deadly particulates that "you can seldom feel or see." Fallout is thus an environmental flow that matters to health and safety but that also demands a new form of everyday perception and governance. Fallout, here, also implicitly positions the citizen less as national subject than as earth dweller, increasingly at risk, as Tim Choy (2011) would put it, simply for being a "breather." This conversion of atmosphere from the most rudimentary domain of life into an uncertain circulation also directly challenges the territorial vision of the national security state system, as international borders and security states are rendered irrelevant by windborne industrial effects within changeable earth systems (see Sloterdijk 2009; also Beck 2007).

How many cumulative toxic industrial processes fall into this similar category of the unseen but cumulatively damaging or deadly? How many issues of toxicity are now also issues of scale and perspective—raising questions not only about visualization but also about how to conceptualize danger across raced, classed, gendered, and regional dynamics? Fallout—in the form of radioactivity, synthetic chemicals, or the impacts of the carbon cycle—produces cumulative effects that only become visible in the destabilized organism or ecological relation. The temporality of injury thus becomes central to the assessment of danger itself, as the industrial age generates products that install injuries incrementally into the future, colonizing an ever-deeper time horizon.

In U.S. Cold War practice, fallout was initially constituted as the bomb's lesser form. This approach allowed a strange and perverse splitting of the nuclear event itself into the expected and planned detonation and its lingering atmospheric effects (see Eden 2004; van Wyck 2004). Though it was understood in 1945 that the irradiated particulate matter that travels on wind patterns constituted a kind of weapon, enabling a new form of atmospheric terrorism, it was the explosive power of the bomb that was fetishized by the U.S. military and became the basis for nuclear war planning. A fundamental part of any nuclear event, fallout was nonetheless coded within U.S. military-industrial practice as a side effect. Much as pharmaceutical companies today split the desired from the undesired effects of a molecule—the political economy of the side effect here has huge consequences, installing bizarre metrics and significant misrecognitions throughout nuclear national security logics—allowing certain forms of destruction to be recognized while others are marginalized. For example, while potentially deadly on a mass scale and constituting a radically new kind of chemical-biological weapon all in one, radioactive fallout was officially crafted as a secondary formation to the exploding bomb during the era of atmospheric nuclear testing.

The official project of producing a "safe" nuclear detonation involved evaluations of wind patterns and weather, as well as efforts to target radioactive fallout at unpopulated geographical regions. The unpopulated area, as history has repeatedly shown, was rarely so, creating vast exposures that quickly undermined any notion of national security as a protection of populations.[5] Indeed, physicians and environmental scientists led a media crusade to publicize the health effects of atmospheric nuclear testing in the 1950s, directly challenging the logics of civil defense and national security. In the process, they helped mobilize peace, justice, and environmental social movements (see Commoner 1958; Fowler 1960a). The first decades of the nuclear age were thus filled with both hemispheric exposures and new forms of social protest based on an emerging planetary consciousness. These social movements were met by an unsuccessful, if highly publicized, official effort to build a "clean bomb" at the U.S. weapons laboratories—a bomb, that is, which could explode without producing fallout.

A crucial development in the Cold War nuclear system was the move to underground nuclear testing. The 1963 Limited Test Ban Treaty (LTBT)— which stands as simultaneously the first nuclear weapons treaty and the first global environmental treaty—both recognized the planetary-scale health consequences of nuclear testing and worked to preserve the global nuclear arms race. By consolidating their energetic experimental test regimes underground, the U.S., Britain, and the USSR eliminated nuclear tests in the atmosphere, outer space, and the ocean while continuing to detonate nuclear devices feverishly for decades. The LTBT also had the important effect of shifting the environmental register of nuclear test programs from atmospheric fallout to a different plane of ecological damage—one not borne on wind patterns but connected to underground seepage and flow.

The move to underground testing also significantly changed the visual politics of the nuclear age during the Cold War, allowing a shift from the iconic image of the mushroom cloud to diverse data sets produced by new technologies of global surveillance (devoted, for example, to detecting seismic signatures of nuclear tests and to testing atmospheric chemistry). By the end of the 1960s, images from outer space, produced first by satellites and then by piloted space missions, provided photographic images of planet Earth as a singular totality.[6] These emerging visualization infrastructures were tied in direct and indirect ways to U.S. efforts to monitor foreign nuclear test regimes, as well as to develop more powerful infrastructures (from missiles to early warning systems, to satellite-based command and control technologies) for fighting nuclear wars.

The environmental legacy of Cold War nuclearism (from fallout, to environmental contamination, to nuclear waste) stands as an iconic illustration of toxic industrialization, fomenting an emergent planetary politics of harm assessment. In what follows, I want to make a case for radioactive fallout as an emblem of industrial modernity but also invite you to think with it as a model for a larger set of processes now collectively gathered together under a popular rubric of climate change. The historical development of nuclear danger and climate danger is complexly intertwined at the level of environmental conditions, knowledge systems, and public perceptions (Masco 2010). The cumulative toxic fallout of the twentieth century continues to shift global politics and earth systems, requiring a new politics of air, soil, water, energy, and finance while also demanding new concepts of planetary security. Toxicity is an amplifying planetary force, a realization that requires new critical theory as well as different concepts of the political (see Clark 2014; Murphy 2017a). For the remainder of this chapter, just to be clear, "fallout" is therefore meant to be both material and conceptual, a way of talking about legacies and futures, toxics and natures, perceptions and misrecognitions.

A Planetary Stratum

It is easy to forget today just how radical the U.S. nuclear program was right from the beginning. Founded in secrecy, the emerging program quickly turned the entire planet into an experimental theater for nuclear science. The politics of radioactive fallout were central to the first efforts to regulate the bomb, contributing to a wide-ranging social revolution, linking issues of war and peace to those of the environment and public health in entirely new ways (see Egan 2007). Just consider the territorial scope of the nuclear complex for a moment, for as an ever-emerging global infrastructure, its fallout exceeds any existing map. Figure 1.2 shows a U.S. Department of Energy (DOE) map that details the geographical reach of its core facilities at the end of the Cold War. But even as it documents the formal U.S. nuclear weapons production complex at its height, this map barely gets at the true scope of U.S. nuclearism, as it leaves out nuclear power plants as well as sites of environmental contamination and nuclear waste storage across the continental United States. Nonetheless, the DOE map does suggest that, as infrastructure, the nuclear complex has always strained to achieve a kind of globality. This effort to achieve maximal scale assumed several forms; first, via the reach of nuclear weapons—including intercontinental missiles, nuclear submarines, and bombers—and second, through the extensive network of production and testing sites (Brown 2013), which link a global uranium industry (Hecht 2012), vast experimental laboratories (Gusterson 1996, Masco 2006), and numerous test sites with military support and delivery systems.

If one were to consider nuclear detonations in their totality—undoubtedly the single most destructive human enterprise to date—one would start with a map like that shown in figure 1.3, which also illustrates how the atomic bomb continually remakes relations between the Global North and South. Constituting a new form of radioactive colonization, the build-out of nuclear infrastructures and experimental regimes regularly impacted minority populations most directly while also generating collective fallout effects. One of the most important aspects of fallout is that it can be both collectively and asymmetrically distributed, marking everyone to a degree while having an intensified effect on specific communities, ecologies, and bodies. But even this map, with its global frame, is radically incomplete: one must add the wartime atomic bombings of Hiroshima and Nagasaki in 1945, as well as a half century of underground nuclear explosions at test sites around the world, including those of newer nuclear powers—India, Pakistan, and North Korea. Think of each of these sites as a node in a global nuclear network of technologies, experiments, waste, and fallout—each radiating on a distinct frequency.

Fallout—in the form of accidents, contamination, and waste—has always been retrospectively diagnostic; it forces us to pay attention to how connected humans, nonhumans, technologies, and environments have become in the industrial era. What emerged in the first decades of the nuclear age was a powerful new vision of the biosphere as an integrated ecological space of complex interactions. But this scientific vision was only made possible by tracking radioactive contamination through both bodies and biosphere (Masco 2010). Indeed, earth scientists used the radioactive signatures of strontium-90 and cesium-137 to map a vast range of processes, including weather systems, food chains, and environmental complexity in the early Cold War period (see Odum and Odum 1955; as well as Hagen 1992). The planetary is emergent in these processes as the radioactive signatures of fallout offered a new way of documenting ecological flows of every kind— connecting local exposures to regional contamination to global distributions of atmospheric endangerment.

Consider the first U.S. hydrogen bomb experiment in 1952. Code-named Mike, the detonation was conducted in the Marshall Islands as part of the Ivy test series. It produced a mushroom cloud that rose to over 120,000 feet and stretched over sixty miles wide. The resulting fallout cloud was quickly transformed by environmental scientists into a new kind of experimental lens,

The U. S. Nuclear

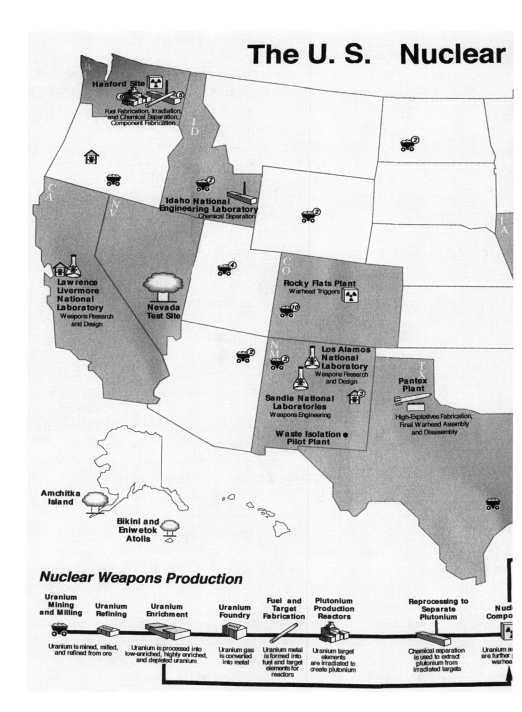

Hanford Site
Fuel Fabrication, Irradiation, and Chemical Separation; Component Fabrication

Idaho National Engineering Laboratory
Chemical Separation

Lawrence Livermore National Laboratory
Weapons Research and Design

Nevada Test Site

Rocky Flats Plant
Warhead Triggers

Los Alamos National Laboratory
Weapons Research and Design

Sandia National Laboratories
Weapons Engineering

Waste Isolation ●
Pilot Plant

Pantex Plant
High-Explosives Fabrication, Final Warhead Assembly and Disassembly

Amchitka Island

Bikini and Eniwetok Atolls

Nuclear Weapons Production

Uranium Mining and Milling	Uranium Refining	Uranium Enrichment	Uranium Foundry	Fuel and Target Fabrication	Plutonium Production Reactors	Reprocessing to Separate Plutonium	Nuclear Compo
Uranium is mined, milled, and refined from ore	Uranium is processed into low-enriched, highly enriched, and depleted uranium	Uranium gas is converted into metal	Uranium metal is formed into fuel and target elements for reactors	Uranium target elements are irradiated to create plutonium	Chemical separation is used to extract plutonium from irradiated targets	Uranium a are further warhea

Weapons Complex

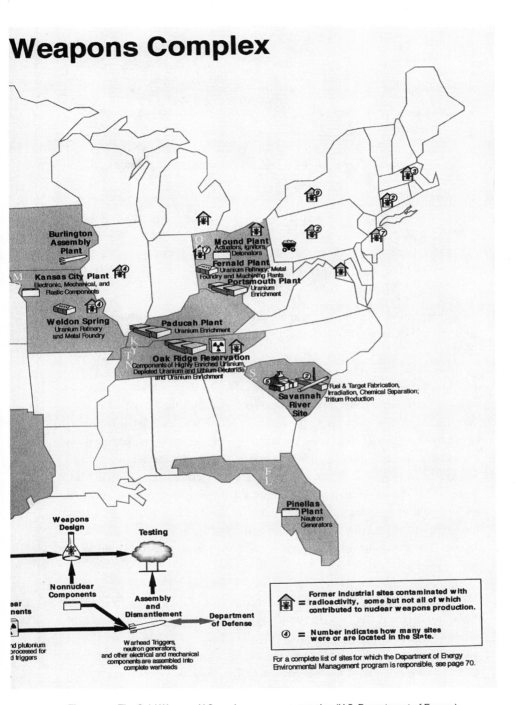

Figure 1.2. The Cold War–era U.S. nuclear weapons complex (U.S. Department of Energy).

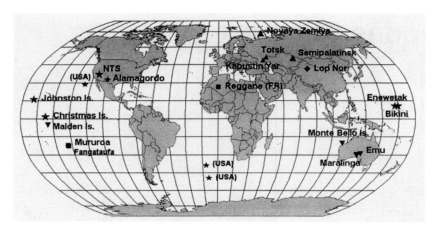

Figure 1.3. Locations of aboveground nuclear test detonations (from Beck and Bennett 2002).

becoming a primary means of empirically documenting stratospheric flows, ultimately revealing with a new specificity how earth, ocean, and atmosphere interact.

The fallout produced by the Ivy Mike detonation was tracked by Lester Machta, Robert J. List, and L. F. Hubert (1956) in their foundational study of the stratospheric transport of nuclear materials (see figure 1.4). This work was among the first in a series of studies that followed the global transport of nuclear materials produced by atmospheric detonations, offering increasingly high-resolution portraits of atmospheric contamination within an integrated biosphere. These wide-ranging studies directly challenged a national security concept that was no longer able to protect discrete territories. Fallout studies began generating, in Ulrich Beck's (2007) terms, new "risk societies" united not by territory, national identity, or language but rather by airborne environmental and health risks increasingly documented to be global vectors of differentially timed injury.

Indeed, radioactive fallout studies helped to foment a new kind of planetary vision in several ways across the second half of the twentieth century. Most importantly, the effort to understand fallout involved the creation of new surveillance systems and comprehensive data sets across the earth sciences, generated in the name of understanding nuclear environmental effects and tracking the Soviet nuclear program. The Cold War produced a massive investment in air, ocean, geology, ice cap, and, eventually, outer space research. This was an unprecedented effort to track and investigate every

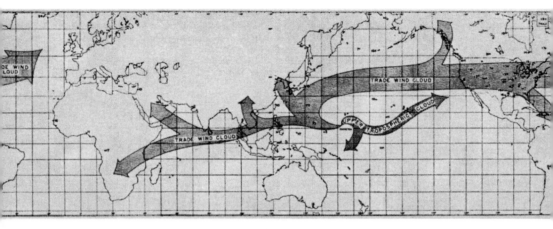

Figure 1.4. Global fallout study of Ivy Mike fallout cloud (from Machta, List, and Hubert 1956).

possible kind of nuclear event both as a mode of self-defense and to militarize nature for national advantage (see Fleming 2010; Hamblin 2013). In each case, nuclear injury was both the motivating logic and the experimental lens for producing a new set of national security earth sciences. These data sets become, as Paul Edwards (2010) has shown, a kind of global infrastructure; they enabled new portraits of planetary process to be possible, particularly global warming. The effort to understand nuclear injury (for both war fighting and national defense) thus generated a conceptual frame for engaging a planetary space that was simultaneously being transformed by nuclear industry. As Peter Sloterdijk (2009) has argued, a militarization of the environment in the twentieth century also enabled new forms of environmental thinking, which in turn produced a scalar multidisciplinary commitment to connecting locality to global infrastructures and ultimately to planetary processes.

By 1960, for example, Machta and List were exploring a more expansive vision of fallout, pulling the reader's field of view increasingly off planet in their effort to illustrate the scale and scope of nuclear effects. Figure 1.5 is an illustration from John M. Fowler's (1960a) important edited collection *Fallout: A Study of Superbombs, Strontium 90, and Survival*, published at the height of the public health debate over atmospheric nuclear testing. In it Machta and List (1960) document the stratospheric height of fallout and its ability to travel on wind patterns for great distances, connecting the Global North and South as irradiated space. The development of U.S. national security in the form of the hydrogen bomb was thus linked to the production of (1) an

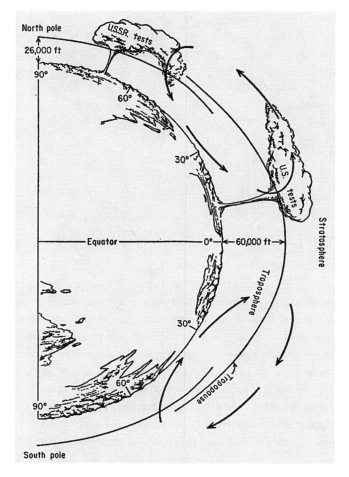

Figure 1.5.
Visualizing the global travel of fallout, circa 1960 (from Machta and List 1960).

entirely new global ecological danger and (2) a new technoscientific and environmental investment in understanding integrated environmental spaces and ecological transport. The earth sciences become a national priority in this early Cold War moment, as efforts to study the bombs' material effects connected researchers to the Department of Defense in a major new way, leading to revolutions in biomedicine, computing, geology, oceanography, and atmospheric sciences.

The dangerous uncertainties of fallout danger led to the creation of many research programs that continue to this day, including biomedical studies of exposed populations in areas such as Hiroshima and Nagasaki, the U.S. Southwest, and the Marshall Islands, in addition to the vast population of workers within the nuclear complex itself.[7] These forms of internal and external sacrifice became embedded within Cold War national security practices, raising basic questions about what kind of human population was emerging via the encounter with nuclear technologies and accumulating forms of fallout. In "Radiation and Future Generations," James Crow's (1960) contribution to Fowler's *Fallout* anthology, readers are asked to contemplate the genetic consequences of atmospheric nuclear explosions for as yet unborn men and women. Crow underscores the uncertainty in measuring the relationship between radioactive fallout and mutation rates across generations and species (e.g., flies, mice, humans), and he projects alternative futures of genetic damage across species based on different amounts of nuclear testing. Thus, as Machta and List consider the atmospheric and territorial reach of nuclear events, Crow investigates the accumulating force of exposure itself within the human genetic pool. Space and time are thus radically reconfigured in these fallout studies, enabling a vision of a collective future that is incrementally changing in unknown ways through cumulative industrial effects. The logics of a national security state (with its linkage of a discrete territory to a specific population) become paradoxical in the face of mounting evidence of genetic damage on a collective scale, not from war but rather from atomic research and nuclear weapons development programs. It is important to recognize that while cast as experiments, Cold War atmospheric detonations were nothing less than planetary-scale environmental events.

Fowler (1960b), for example, was able to calculate the amount of strontium-90 from nuclear testing in the Pacific and Nevada within the New York food supply, indexing measurable amounts in milk, cereal, fruits, vegetables, and meat. This is a remarkable moment in an emergent planetary consciousness: the nuclear age was only fifteen years old in 1960 and already understood to be transformational in terms of global ecology and public health. Fowler, and the many natural scientists tracking similar radioactive flows, documented how military science, atmospheric conditions, plants, animals, and people were connected both systemically and increasingly via military-industrial toxicity. Put differently, by 1960 radioactive fallout was recognized as a planetary industrial signature, one being inscribed at different levels, and in different ways, into every living being on Earth.

Figure 1.6 is a National Cancer Institute chart of the iodine-131 contamination from Cold War–era nuclear tests conducted at the Nevada Test Site. This county-by-county chart remakes the continental United States—the territorial space usually thought to be secured by nuclear defense—as a new kind of sacrifice zone, with citizens remade by varying degrees of exposure (see also Beck and Bennett 2002). Fallout exposure from the atmospheric

Per capita thyroid doses resulting from all exposure routes from all tests

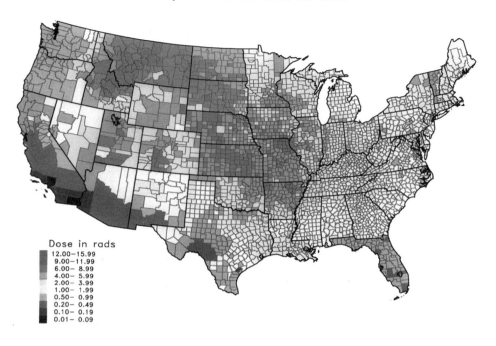

Dose in rads
12.00–15.99
9.00–11.99
6.00– 8.99
4.00– 5.99
2.00– 3.99
1.00– 1.99
0.50– 0.99
0.20– 0.49
0.10– 0.19
0.01– 0.09

Figure 1.6. Cumulative iodine contamination by county from nuclear detonations at the Nevada Test Site (U.S. National Cancer Institute).

Figure 1.7. Background radiation sources for U.S. populations (from National Research Council 2006).

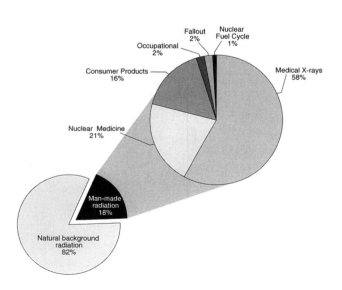

nuclear weapons tests is measurable and remains an environmental fact so ever-present as to become a literal biological stratum in the human population (Bennett 2002). Such strata are not recognized as a health risk today, although the National Academy of Sciences has concluded that there is no safe level of radiation exposure (National Research Council 2006; Simon, Bouville, and Land 2006). Consider figure 1.7, a chart of the background radiation rate, judged by medical science and the nuclear industry to be the baseline exposure rate for contemporary human populations (see Cram 2015, 2016). This nominal exposure rate (involving a small but measurable contribution from atmospheric nuclear testing and nuclear accidents) constitutes in its ubiquity a new form of industrial nature.

In other words, since 1945 people have become postnuclear creatures, marked with the signatures of nuclear nationalism and weapons science (Masco 2006, 294). What is in question is not the material fact of radioactive fallout or mass exposure but rather collective perceptions of its effects and implication. This lag between the environmental event and the recognition of its long-lasting effects is a major psychosocial achievement of the industrial age, where in the name of commerce or security consequences are loaded into an uncertain future and thus expelled from the realm of political discourse until they resurface as injury at a later date. Starting in 1945, fallout constitutes a new kind of global process, one that brings the planetary into view across a variety of scientific disciplines. This makes the nuclear age the era in which the planet, in its earth system totality, first becomes an object of comprehensive scientific study and the moment when people become an existential threat to themselves. Due to the scale and scope of industrial activities (both nuclear and petrochemical), and their cumulative negative impact on the environment, atmospheric chemist Paul Crutzen (2002) has argued that the Holocene geological epoch has concluded, advocating instead the designation of a new epoch, the Anthropocene, to acknowledge that people have gained the collective force of an earth system. With this in mind, geologists have suggested that July 16, 1945, the date of the first nuclear detonation, could be the start of a new planetary ecological regime (see Steffen et al. 2011). Other geologists have determined that the distinct signature of plutonium from atmospheric nuclear tests, beginning with the Ivy Mike detonation on November 1, 1952, is a more technically accurate date for the start of the Anthropocene, as it is an artificial signal that will be clearly legible in the earth system for hundreds of thousands of years, and its fallout remains literally planetary in scope (Waters et al. 2016).[8] In these technical debates within geology, one can see how life has become increasingly structured by the literal and conceptual fallout of human industry, amplified across nuclear, petro-chemical, and synthetic chemical regimes. These material effects claim an ever-deeper future, making industrial fallout an ever-unfolding temporal as well as physical force.

Nuclear Testing as Geoengineering

In the early twenty-first century, rising ocean levels, shifting weather patterns, and intensifying storms are generating wide-ranging problems, across food production, public health, and urban spaces (see, e.g., Costello et al. 2009). In the face of these emerging dangers, various schemes for geoengineering a way out of global warming have been proposed.[9] Geoengineering is an effort to consciously shift the dynamics of earth systems, and as a conceptual enterprise it often draws on imaginative schemes to "terraform" another planet—that is, create an atmosphere on another world capable of supporting human life. Geoengineering envisions a profound understanding of planetary-scale ecological relations even as its proponents negotiate the cumulative unintended environmental consequences of human industry (across nuclear, energy, and capitalist-consumption regimes) on Earth. Ideas for massive carbon capture (underground and in the oceans) compete with imaginative proposals to shift the composition of the atmosphere by injecting sulphate particles into the upper stratosphere or by changing the composition of clouds to reflect back heat from the sun. Other proposals look to space, to create mechanical means of diffusing sunlight and cooling the planet. In all, these proposals consider reengineering the oceans, air, forests, ice caps, and outer space to handle carbon dioxide and heat differently, in hopes of cooling the planet, imagined as a complex thermostat that needs to be adjusted (see Hamilton 2013; Robock et al. 2009; Schneider 2008). What is implicitly attractive to many about these schemes is the idea of correcting an atmospheric imbalance caused by industrial activity, of now consciously treating the biosphere as a mechanism that can be tuned to optimal human outcomes. This would allow some control over weather (a long-dreamed-of capacity; see Fleming 2010) while allowing petrochemical capitalism to continue unimpeded. It promises a perfect engineering fix to a world undone by petrochemical technologies and practices.

For those versed in the history of the U.S. nuclear program, these projects sound eerily familiar, as they mirror the scientific efforts to understand nuclear effects on land, sea, and air during the long Cold War (see Hamblin 2013). Each of these experiments was a de facto form of geoengineering; they produced environmental problems of a new kind and scope and ultimately new planetary optics to understand those effects. The nuclear state has been geoengineering since 1945, remaking both atmospheres and ecologies, creating problems impossible to remediate or clean up. The Nevada Test Site today (see figure 1.8) contains valley after valley of radiating nuclear test craters—a monumentally changed environment visible in its entirety only from a stratospheric point of view (Coolidge 1996). Here, industrial injury demands a new planetary vision, one that sees cumulative environmental effects over and against national boundaries and short-term profit making.

Fallout—now operative across nuclear and extractive energy regimes—has proliferating forms as well as temporalities (see Brown 2013; Masco 2006). The 1986 Chernobyl accident offered an iconic image of industrial disaster, a failed technology that created an airborne global environmental danger but also created an ongoing regional transformation across ecology and social order.[10] Today, a gigantic engineering effort is underway to build a new containment vessel for the damaged reactor, one that hopes to prevent further radioactive releases for the next one hundred years (the expected life of the containment facility). Chernobyl illustrates the profound consequences of technological failure in the nuclear age, but it is only one permanent danger zone among many ongoing nuclear disaster sites around the world. Hanford, for example, is devoted in the twenty-first century not to producing fissile materials for U.S. nuclear weapons (as it did from World War II through the end of the Cold War) but rather to observing the accumulated radioactive sludge of the twentieth century both age and chemically transform into novel substances. Hanford engineers devote each day to managing holding tanks of Cold War–era radioactive waste that resists both chemical assessment and full containment. As these holding tanks leak, a slow-moving transformation of the Columbia River region is underway, derived from Cold War–era American commitments to the bomb. The Fukushima Daiichi nuclear power plant disaster in 2011 presents a similarly long-lived problem, as the combined effects of earthquake, tsunami, and fire overwhelmed the security measures at the plant and revealed how few technical options there are for undoing the fallout of failed nuclear technologies. Industrial failure on this scale is a form of geoengineering, just one operating without a planetary plan, joining the cumulative planetary force of petrochemical greenhouse emissions.

In applying the lessons of the twentieth-century nuclear complex to contemporary expectations about overcoming global warming via geoengineering, it is important to question (1) the narrative of a newfound crisis that installs a state of emergency and suspends normal forms of law and regulation;

Figure 1.8. Underground nuclear detonation craters at the Nevada Test Site
(U.S. Department of Energy).

(2) a process that rhetorically reproduces the split between the event and its fallout so completely; and (3) the assumption that geoengineering is a future activity, that it is not an ancient practice with many examples to think with in assessing the current moment. Scholars might also interrogate how the past half century of multidisciplinary work to create detailed visualizations of the planet now installs a dangerous confidence in globality itself, as increasingly high-resolution visualizations come to stand in for both objectivity and sovereignty (see Daston and Galison 2010). Aestheticized visualizations can enable psychosocial feelings of mastery over vastly complex and dynamic earth systems that remain, at best, only partially understood.

Geoengineering emerges in the twenty-first century as a frequently evoked alternative to green energy conversion, as those committed to petrochemical capitalism choose to approach earth systems as machines that can be tuned by people to better outcomes. This high modernist position, which assumes an external relation to nature, is the same one that created the nuclear infrastructure in the twentieth century and that continues to generate new forms of fallout well into the twenty-first century. It refuses to acknowledge the logic or history of fallout or to accept that in the era of big-data analytics there is not a single planetary vision but rather a proliferation of planetary optics tied to specific sciences and projects, visions that may not align, may be incomplete, or may mask data frictions. The conceptual pull of the Anthropocene—which attempts to articulate the scale and scope of industrial change on planet Earth—can also be used to argue that human agency is all that is involved in producing the increasingly complex world of organisms, ecological flows, technologies, and toxics. The term flattens the complexity of human/nonhuman interactions, as well as natural systems, even as it recognizes the planetary scale of cumulative industrial effects. One unintended but pernicious effect of the enthusiasm for these visions of planetary process is the suggestion that as a species people are now living in an entirely human-made ecology, or alternatively that a stable state of nature could be recovered through a reverse geoengineering. Narratives such as these could only find purchase in an increasingly antiscientific era, denying the coevolution of human and nonhuman systems, and by ignoring the many alternate ways people live on the planet. Rejecting a self-reflexive critique of nuclear nationalism or petrochemical capitalism, they instead offer a set of false promises about the management of radionuclides, greenhouse gases, and synthetic chemicals as they work through, and transform, earthly conditions.

Hugh Raffles (2002), for example, has documented that what appears today to be giant tributaries of the Amazon River are in fact the collaborative work of people and river ecologies, as small canals cut by people for easier canoe navigation have grown to become massive waterways over time, now only visible in their entirety from outer space. The first satellite images of North America revealed ancient road systems connecting what is today the U.S. Southwest to Mexico, etched into the landscape. Similarly, modern concrete and steel cities are geoengineering projects of the most direct kind, foundationally effecting landscapes, ecologies, weather patterns, and resources. The current problem is thus less the fact of human agency as a geological force (which has many historical forms) than the cumulative scale and scope of industrial toxicity, which changes the composition of ecology and biology as they unfold through time. The seven billion people on Earth, most of whom are living in megacities, are increasingly enmeshed in nuclear, petrochemical, and synthetic chemical regimes. Toxicity, the cumulative fallout of the industrial age in all its myriad forms, has now achieved multiple vectors of planetary agency. As awareness of these collective environmental concerns scales up past the nation-state form to, and beyond, the global, a new threshold is being reached for visualizing a planetary environment. Consider, for example, the Science on a Sphere project run by the National Oceanic and Atmospheric Administration (figure 1.9), an educational program that projects complex big-data visualizations of earth systems onto a six-foot sphere. This project makes the unit of analysis the planet itself but with an added temporal dimension coded into each visualization.[11] This is one example of how planetary optics are proliferating in the twenty-first century and taking on new forms, as big data sets, emerging visualization technologies, and the cumulative force of toxicity in all its forms generate both the need and the capacity for new visions of ecological process.

Terraforming Planet Earth

Current geoengineering discourse emerges from a consideration of how to build an atmosphere capable of supporting human life on another planet, terraforming for human survival and comfort a previously uninhabitable environment. Mars is often the center of these imaginative efforts, but they are also often motivated by the idea that environmental damage on Earth—the end of fossil fuel, a destabilized climate, nuclear war, overpopulation, disease, or food scarcity—will drive interplanetary research (see, for example, Pixar's WALL-E from 2008 or Christopher Nolan's *Interstellar* from 2014). The escape pod to Mars has a long history in science fiction and as an imaginative project is intellectually stimulating, and often quite entertaining.[12] But

Figure 1.9. Science on a Sphere visualization of sea temperatures and currents (National Oceanic and Atmospheric Administration).

this idea rehearses the American modernist story of self-invention via settler colonialism, the ability to always start over somewhere else, to break with the past and begin anew, to escape fallout by simply relocating to a newly exciting frontier. Here, nature once again becomes a lived-in experimental laboratory, of the kind that once supported nuclear weapons tests, a denial of coconsititution that enables visions of exoplanetary industry and potentially endless colonial space projects.[13] Before such an endeavor is launched even conceptually, it is important to interrogate the ecological and health impacts of the introduction of synthetic chemicals and other long-lived toxins into the biosphere since 1945 (see Murphy 2008; Orff and Misrach 2012). In short, through the combined efforts of the petrochemical industry and the nuclear state, people have been feverishly terraforming planet Earth for generations, creating an atmosphere increasingly precarious for human life, rather than one tuned to its creature comforts. This means that people are living in the unintended aftermath of cumulative industrial, military, and financial projects, remaking bodies, ecologies, and atmospheres differentially on a planetary scale, enduring unfolding forms of violence that have yet to be fully accounted for, let alone governed.

On this difficult point, which asks individuals to think on scales and in temporalities that are radically different from everyday embodied experience, consider Isao Hashimoto's remarkable visualization of the nuclear age, *1945–1998* (see figure 1.10 and Hashimoto 2003). His video animation shows in chronological order the 2,053 nuclear detonations on Earth between 1945 and 1998. The video is straightforward: it offers a global map and a chronological sequence of nuclear detonations, each marked by a white flash and beeping noise, with the date recorded in the upper right corner. In the margins, counters tally the detonations for each nuclear state, as well as the total count. In the thirteen minutes it takes to move month by month from 1945 to 1998, Hashimoto offers viewers an extremely precise illustration of nuclear politics in the twentieth century, documenting the expansion of both nuclear industry and national power. In certain years—1957, 1962, or 1984, for example—it appears that nuclear explosions are the only things happening on planet Earth, with multiple continents flashing white and beeping at a feverish pace. The disturbing power of the video is that it both recognizes the nation-state form and renders it irrelevant to the cumulative, ongoing planetary force of the bomb.

Hashimoto shows us the planetary logics of the nuclear complex and allows us to reconsider the temporality of nuclear war itself. In the Cold War competition between the U.S. and Soviet Union, nuclear war was conceived of as brutal and short. It was a matter of hours and minutes, as always-on-alert weapons systems (still active today) made war possible every second of the day. Thus, the current inherited portrait of nuclear war imagines it as extremely short, fast, and totalizing—the end of everything. But Hashimoto reorients one's point of view, showing that a nuclear war was fought in the twentieth century: it started in the summer of 1945 with three explosions— in New Mexico, Hiroshima, and Nagasaki—and then was fought vigorously in test sites around the world. Hashimoto's video is elegantly devastating in its display of the planetary politics of the bomb. He gives us access to the long-term violence that amplifies over decades; this new temporal politics of

Figure 1.10. Still from Isao Hashimoto's video art installation *1945–1998* (courtesy of Isao Hashimoto).

environmental crisis allows a new perspective on a national security industry that—in the name of energy, protection, and profit—has acted as radioactive geoengineer.

Given the ever-present material reality of environmental toxics, there is no need to project geoengineering with its specific planetary ambitions into a distant future or to travel to other worlds to experience terraforming. One can look closer to home for an example of an industrially transformed atmospheric planetary politics. A terraforming project has already been conducted on planet Earth, one drawn from the cumulative and recursive effects of nuclear nationalism and petrochemical capitalism. That global warming—despite such imaginative industrial activity and scientific insight across generations—was not planned or intended is precisely the point. Constituted as a side effect of the industrial age, climate disruption articulates the ongoing challenge to conceptualizing an ecological security not based on the split between the engineered event and its aftermath, between the boom and the bust of capital, between the preemptions and blowbacks of counterterror. Such a project requires instead many new planetary optics as well as a politics of complexity capable of assuming a postnational form of security and new understandings of the collective planetary future. A recognition of the accelerating environmental changes brought on by decades of human industrial activity destabilizes existing notions of bounded technological ages or historical periods or bounded territorial units. To the contrary, to collectively engage radically changing earthly conditions in the twenty-first century, along the lines I have outlined here, inaugurates the Age of Fallout.

I

DREAMING DESERTS AND DEATH MACHINES

IN THIS FIRST PART of *The Future of Fallout, and Other Episodes in Radioactive World-Making*, I explore how nuclear nationalism in the U.S. relies on a vision of the desert as empty, a space capable of absorbing any degree of violence in the name of a technoscientific self-fashioning. Such a vision relies on the very practices of erasure that inform the foundational American logics of indigenous dispossession, constituting a pristine nature only through violent removal. The chapters that follow trace the politics of indigenous resistance to nuclear nationalism in the 1990s around Los Alamos, focusing on the way that tribal sovereignty became a kind of extractive resource for potential nuclear waste storage projects rejected in nonnative communities. Including indigenous governments and Nuevomexicano interests in the nuclear frame fundamentally changes the logics, dynamics, and consequences of U.S. nuclear nationalism and also forces a fundamental critique of security studies as historically constituted in the United States as a means of establishing and expanding state power. Chapter 4 then explores the secrecy of the Nevada Test Site and the publicity of Las Vegas as dual sides of the same "desert modernism." It is an ethnographic effort to capture the historical fusion of technoscience and frontier masculinities that informs nuclear nationalism, one that brings nuclear detonations and gaming into the same regional space via advanced practices of risk and amnesia. Finally, chapter 5 concludes with an innovative peace activist project to use highway billboards to force the nuclear economy and tourist economy of New Mexico into the same frame. Critiquing the U.S. invasion of Iraq over WMDs by revealing the number of nuclear weapons in New Mexico, the Los Alamos Study Group's "billboard campaign" sought to disrupt the normative everyday within U.S. nuclear nationalism. The goal of "Dreaming Deserts and Death Machines" is to explore how practices of erasure and reinvention inform the U.S. nuclear economy and how American self-fashioning through violence against people and ecologies continues unabated, and with entirely new forms of ferocity, in the twenty-first century.

2

5:29:45 A.M.

July 16, 2005, 5:29:45 a.m.—thousands of tourists assemble in the early morning hours at a remote desert location in the southwestern United States to bear witness to the sixtieth anniversary of the first atomic explosion. Located in the middle of the White Sands Missile Range (an active U.S. military test range located in central New Mexico), the Trinity test site is open to the public only two days a year and for special anniversaries. Getting to this open-air museum and historical monument (which gained National Historical Landmark status in 1975) requires a difficult journey: visitors commit to a minimum two-hour drive from the nearest big city, Albuquerque, and must negotiate military checkpoints, gates, and miles of barren desert road to arrive at the birthplace of the military atomic age. Once there, international tourists mix with past and present U.S. nuclear workers, military personnel, antinuclear activists, military history buffs, and the increasingly large number of Americans fascinated by the historic sites of the atomic age. But what of the first atomic bomb actually remains at this desert test site? And what is capable of drawing such an international and politically diverse audience to this remote piece of New Mexican desert minutes well before sunrise on a midsummer morning? Visitors expecting to encounter the great modernist accomplishment of the twentieth century—the start of a new age of military science, international relations, and everyday terror—instead discover a large patch of desert surrounded by a chain-link fence. There are no buildings at the point of detonation, only a simple historical marker, the empty metal casings of the bombs that destroyed Hiroshima and Nagasaki (devices code-named Little Boy and Fat Man by Manhattan Project scientists), and a photographic display.

Both a museum and monument to itself, the site is a near-total simulation: the closest visitors get to the first atomic blast is to view a long line of historical photographs strung on the chain-link fence, which document some of the personnel and equipment involved in the test, as well as a time-lapse sequence of the explosion. One photograph documents the ceremonial installation of the obelisk in 1965, offering an odd aboveground perspective on the site, noting the lack of a fence around ground zero (see figure 2.1). The photographic display ends with a photograph of the historical marker (see figure 2.2) with a caption that reads, "The Obelisk sits exactly at ground zero. It is made of Lava Rocks." The stupefying banality of this exhibit is enhanced by the fact that the obelisk actually sits some fifty yards behind the viewer and is the core object of public attention at the Trinity test site, providing the preferred snapshot souvenir for most visitors. The culminating photograph in the historical display thus introduces the viewer to the space that he or she actually inhabits— conveying nothing of the power of the nuclear age. For those interested in acknowledging the wonder or terror of the first nuclear explosion—a scientific accomplishment that revolutionized nearly every institution of American life, turned the surface of the earth into an experimental test range covered in radioactive fallout, and produced a new kind of state (the global nuclear superpower), as well as new kinds of world war (both cold and apocalyptic)— the bomb remains invisible in its site of origin. Visitors are presented instead with a hall of mirrors, a simulation that evacuates the nationalist fervor, the technoscientific accomplishment, and the terror of the first nuclear explosion through the deployment of neither firsthand experience nor expert knowledge nor realistic ambiguity but instead blindingly obvious factoids.

The Trinity Site is part of an evolving series of monuments and museums commemorating nuclear nationalism in the United States built after the dissolution of the Soviet Union in 1991 (e.g., Wray 2006). Since many of these sites were concealed by U.S. national secrecy practices for decades, the new Cold War museums and atomic monuments often represent not a commemoration of known history but rather the first public writing of it in the post–Cold War era. These new military museums and monuments strive to document the historical evolution of the nuclear security state on its own terms; consequently, they are also deeply embedded within the current U.S. national security project known as the War on Terror. Thus, while officially positioned as neutral histories of World War II and the Cold War, atomic history sites are nonetheless highly politicized spaces, ideologically charged in how they engage the past, present, and future of nuclear nationalism through practices of erasure and selective emphasis. A few years after the 2001 suicide-hijacker attacks on New York and Washington, DC, for example, the Bradbury Science Museum at Los Alamos National Laboratory pulled Little Boy, the bomb that destroyed Hiroshima, off display, citing new security concerns in a world once again officially organized by nuclear terror. Thus, despite years of public display in New Mexico, the empty casing of the first bomb used in atomic warfare became, at age sixty, once again a national security secret in Los Alamos, one of potential use to terrorists. Concurrently, the National Atomic Museum in Albuquerque (which houses the largest public collection of U.S. nuclear weapons casings in the world) staged a "blast from the past" fundraiser on July 15 in which participants were given secret identities for the evening and presented with a 1940s-era fashion show and a panel discussion with Manhattan Project personnel before taking an early morning bus to the Trinity test site for the sixtieth anniversary event. A coalition of antinuclear activist groups responded to this effort to romanticize the bomb as simply a fun part of midcentury modern aesthetic culture by flying a survivor of the atomic bombing of Hiroshima in from Japan to attend the event. Crashing the fundraiser with an alternative narrative of the nuclear age, activists also installed a sidewalk museum in front of the building detailing the destructive reality of the bomb. Presenting images of damaged bodies and the bombed cities of Hiroshima and Nagasaki, activists challenged not only the National Atomic Museum's effort to approach the atomic bomb as lighthearted popular culture, but also the continued U.S. investment in nuclear weapons in the twenty-first century.

Thus, despite official efforts to ideologically contain the Trinity test within New Mexican museums and memorials, public discourse around the sixtieth anniversary of the bomb proliferated conflicting interpretations. Nuclear activists—both pro and con—mixed with tourists (Japanese, German, American) on this anniversary, demonstrating that the bomb is not yet located in

Figure 2.1. Photographic display of the Trinity Site at the Trinity Site.

Figure 2.2. Photographic display of the Trinity Site obelisk at the Trinity Site.

a stable narrative of the past or present. Indeed, the nuclear public sphere in New Mexico revealed the atomic detonations in the summer of 1945—on July 16 in New Mexico, and three weeks later on August 6 in Hiroshima and August 9 in Nagasaki—to be fundamentally linked events, explosions that make the U.S. the only country in the world to have engaged in nuclear warfare. The more subtle transformation of the U.S. into a society that largely organized itself around the bomb in the second half of the twentieth century remains a more difficult and elusive narrative, one more easily encountered today in works of art than in official history.[1]

Patrick Nagatani's vision of the test site, for example, *Trinity Site, Jornada del Muerto, New Mexico* (figure 2.3), engages the nuclear revolution from a rather different vantage point than that offered by the official history sites. Part of a larger book-length photographic work, *Nuclear Enchantment* (Nagatani 1991), he directly challenges the silences, contradictions, and public romance with the bomb in New Mexico. In a state that is almost entirely supported by U.S. nuclear weapons research and tourism, Nagatani's beautiful photographic montages present philosophical statements on race, class, and nationalism, as well as childhood, militarism, and the processes of social normalization in a nuclear age. Nagatani recovers lost histories—not only of nuclear tests, accidents, and espionage in New Mexico, but also of the complicated racial context of the bomb, which connects indigenous populations, both Native Americans and Nuevomexicanos in New Mexico, to the Japanese through forms of nuclear victimization and American racial othering. His *Trinity Site, Jornada del Muerto, New Mexico* returns us to the Trinity Site but through the eyes of tourists who appear to be literally startled by the viewer. Under the wing of the Enola Gay, seemingly poised to drop another Little Boy bomb, the startled Japanese (or are they Japanese American?) expressions raise immediate questions about the normalization of the bomb and the economy of otherness that supports the U.S. nuclear arsenal. What, after all, is being commemorated by their tourist snapshots of the "obelisk made of lava rocks" at the Trinity Site—a scientific accomplishment, a new superweapon, the end of World War II, the destruction of Japan, the start of the Cold War, or merely some unarticulated collective pleasure in atomic kitsch?

The explosion at 5:29:45 a.m. on July 16, 1945, inaugurated an ongoing revolution in global affairs and began a process of transforming ecological relations on an equally vast scale. However, the Trinity Site, the precise spot of the detonation in the New Mexican desert, though promising visitors unmediated access to the bomb, actually denies entry into the event or its

Figure 2.3. *Trinity Site, Jornada del Muerto, New Mexico* by Patrick Nagatani (courtesy of Patrick Nagatani).

historical meaning. For that, one must turn to a more imaginative register, one that makes a claim not on the physical real, but on the complexity of the nuclear revolution itself in all its affective, imaginary, and ideological dimensions. As comparative modes of display, the physical site of the first atomic explosion pales in comparison to the photographic fantasy, as Nagatani's ambiguous challenge to the present articulates the vital need for critical public engagement—a sorting out of memory, history, and ideology—in a nuclear age still managed by partial memories and inchoate fear of the bomb.

3

STATES OF INSECURITY

Though a historic arena of anthropological inquiry, New Mexico is not often thought of as an important site in which to study geopolitical insecurity, or to assess the costs of American militarism more broadly. Within security studies, after all, the continental United States has traditionally been imagined to be the one stable entity in an anarchy-filled world, the one territorial space that can remain untheorized in the face of a volatile and dangerous international order (see Campbell 1992). The end of the Cold War in 1991 made this conceptual lacuna visible, just as the dissolution of the Soviet Union demonstrated the fragility of even superpowered nation-states. With this historical context in mind, it is important to consider how the end of the Cold War affected visions of security in the West, and within the United States in particular. For the political opening of the 1990s—the startling absence of a global enemy formation for the first time in generations—revealed that the dual-structured, oppositional nation building of the Cold War did not transmute insurgent regional identifications or ethno-nationalist desires.[1] Indigenous and regional ethnic identities were not unified or superseded by Soviet—or, as I argue here, U.S.—Cold War policies but were complexly and asymmetrically harnessed to them. Revisiting New Mexican politics in the decade between the end of the Cold War and the start of the War on Terror (1991–2001) not only enables a rethinking of the terms of scholarly inquiry into global order; it also reveals the complicated political and cultural legacies of nuclear nationalism under conditions of setter colonialism. In a post–Cold War, pre–War on Terror moment, diverse national communities could publicly express identities, ambitions, and fears once rendered invisible, kept secret, or subsumed under the Cold War dialectics of the nuclear age.

The end of forty-plus years of Cold War was of particular importance in New Mexico, as it was here that the very first atomic bomb, as well as the majority of nuclear weapons in the U.S. stockpile, were designed. In significant ways, New Mexico's two nuclear weapons laboratories (Los Alamos and Sandia) might even be said to have coauthored the Cold War with their scientific counterparts in the Soviet Union. Consequently, this chapter investigates how reorganizations in global political and economic structures since the end of the Cold War have affected regional articulations of self and nation in New Mexico—a central part of what I call the "nuclear borderlands" (Masco 2006). It does so by examining how the activities of the U.S. nuclear weapons complex are experienced by communities in New Mexico, by examining how diverse racial, (ethno)national, indigenous, and political groups who usually fall under the rubric "U.S. citizens" define and experience U.S. national security at home. Thus, this chapter explores the social imaginaries where concepts of national security meet with practices of national sacrifice, where the interests of the sole remaining global superpower collide with those of indigenous nations, and where U.S. national identity is complexly negotiated and challenged in the everyday life practices of local citizenry negotiating the continuing force of a nuclear-powered settler colonialism. By looking at how neighboring communities alternately experience the national security offered by the U.S. nuclear complex in New Mexico, the chapter reveals that the four-decade-long nuclear standoff of the Cold War precluded attention to another set of international relations internal to the U.S., complexly infused with settler colonial relations, environmental ruin, and radically different notions of collective security.[2] It also shows how the end of the Cold War, and the fragility of the nuclear complex itself, made visible new spectrums of insecurity that exceed the logics, affects, and imaginaries of nuclear nationalism within the United States.

As an ethnographic exploration of a post–Cold War public sphere in New Mexico, this chapter develops in three parts: The first section introduces New Mexico as a subaltern, international space, whose populations were complexly harnessed to a Cold War nation-building enterprise through the U.S. nuclear weapons complex; the second section explores how the quintessential commodity of the nuclear age—plutonium—generates widespread insecurities in New Mexico; and the concluding section mobilizes the New Mexico context to call for a significantly different notion of geopolitics, one that expands, and decenters, the very concept of security.

New Mexican Geopolitics

To investigate the terms of national security in New Mexico means engaging the complex histories and competing national identities that inform everyday life in the U.S. Southwest, which is among the most politically contested regions in North America. Consider for a moment the diverse claims made in New Mexico on historical presence, territorial identity, and legal status. The U.S. Southwest is a geographical area first inhabited by the scores of Native American nations that have maintained a territorial sovereignty there in legal terms "from time immemorial."[3] Seven indigenous languages are currently spoken by twenty-two nations inside the state of New Mexico. And in just the hundred-mile stretch of the Rio Grande River roughly bounded by Los Alamos National Laboratory (LANL, Los Alamos, New Mexico) to the north and Sandia National Laboratory (Albuquerque, New Mexico) to the south, sixteen Pueblo nations maintain territorial sovereignties manifested in their own tribal governments, police forces, courts, and legal codes.

This complex geopolitical reality is complicated by the fact that when the U.S. Declaration of Independence was signed in 1776, much of the Southwest (and notably what is today New Mexico) had already been an established part of the Spanish Empire for nearly two hundred years. After the war of independence with Spain in 1821, the region became the northern half of the United States of Mexico, before falling twenty-seven years later to the United States of America in the Mexican-American War. With the Treaty of Guadalupe Hidalgo in 1848 the United States gained over a million square miles, more than the Louisiana Purchase, and nearly doubled its total territory, thereby securing its control of North America (see Griswold del Castillo 1990; Meinig 1993). Most importantly for local communities, the U.S. Southwest was taken via a war with Mexico, providing distinct ethnic groups in New Mexico, identifying as indigenous, Spanish, and Mexican, with cultural memories, and ongoing political negotiations, of U.S. colonization. The extensive land grants given by the Spanish and Mexican governments to their citizens, which were reaffirmed by the U.S. government in the Treaty of Guadalupe Hidalgo, remain in legal dispute in the area and are a perennial source of regional tension.[4] For much of the Nuevomexicano (or Spanish-speaking population), New Mexico is alternately a Hispano homeland, a unique enclave of Spanish cultural identity, or Aztlan, the sacred homeland of the Aztec Empire, the geographical center of an indigenous Chicano/a nation.[5] A consistent theme within both contemporary Native American and Nuevomexicano experience is, therefore, the battle to overcome the historical amnesia in American political life and to communicate the continuing social impacts of being forcefully incorporated into the United States and then marked as minority communities at home.[6] Settler colonialism here is a multiple and differential formation in New Mexico, which fused in 1942 with the intensities of U.S. nuclear nationalism in Los Alamos.

Indeed, the same part of the north-central Rio Grande Valley that has been the epicenter of cultural resistance movements in New Mexico, from the Pueblo Revolt of 1680 through the Hispano land grant battles of the 1890s and the Chicano activism of the 1960s, has also been subject to U.S. government appropriations of land under national security guidelines since the atomic bomb project came to Los Alamos in November 1942 (see Garcia 2010; Kosek 2006; Rothman 1992; Trujillo 2009). Since the Cold War, New Mexico, like much of the Southwest, remains a crypto-U.S. military colony: it is the center of the U.S. nuclear weapons complex, where the first atomic bomb was developed and tested, home to two of the three U.S. nuclear weapons laboratories (LANL and Sandia), the only permanent repository for U.S. military nuclear waste (Waste Isolation Pilot Plant), the largest aboveground missile testing range in the U.S. (White Sands Missile Range), and other military installations.[7] In the immediate post–Cold War moment, New Mexico's military role only expanded in importance, with formal calls for the twenty-first-century U.S. nuclear weapons complex to be consolidated along the Rio Grande River (Secretary of Energy Advisory Board Task Force 1995). Over the next two decades, New Mexico nuclear weapons laboratories would retain higher than Cold War funding levels to scrupulously maintain Cold War nuclear weapons, to stay ready to resume nuclear testing and ultimately to develop designs for simplified and robust nuclear weapons that could support U.S. military interests through the twenty-first century (see U.S. Department of Energy 2018).

Each of these vibrant national imaginings—Native American, Nuevo-mexicano, and U.S. military-industrial—evokes a different sense of territorial identity as well as a different approach to national security. Traditional approaches to U.S. national security policy quickly become problematic if we acknowledge the complicated, power-laden, and historically suppressed international politics that surround national security institutions within the United States. A close analysis of how security issues are elaborated in a highly contested settler colonial space like New Mexico, in fact, demonstrates that the universalistic approaches to sovereignty, security, and citizenship that have typified security studies render invisible the political tensions and human experiences that structure everyday life in much of the world. For example, what conceptual space is there in security studies or international relations theory for the national security of a "domestic, dependent nation" (the official legal definition of Native American territories in the United States)? The ambiguous international legal standing of nations that are domestic and/or dependent has enabled ongoing violence throughout the Americas toward indigenous populations, yet these kinds of conflicts have rarely entered into the formal debates about geopolitics, international relations, or national security. Similarly, how should one talk about the security of the traditional Spanish-speaking populations in New Mexico, who have periodically taken to armed protest against the U.S. government to assert their ownership of land and to affirm cultural rights validated by the Treaty of Guadalupe Hidalgo (e.g., see Gardner 1970; Pulido 1996; Rosenbaum 1981)? It is within this ambiguous legal and national context that the U.S. nuclear weapons complex operates in New Mexico, folding the logics of U.S. national security back on themselves and requiring a more expansive conceptual approach to the production of (in)security. In fact, New Mexico might best be approached as a multinational, multicultural state, an arena of proliferating and contradictory visions of national identity, where the U.S. government is merely the current dominant sovereign entity.

What, then, is the correct way of describing a territorial space this complex, where the Cold War rhetoric of communist containment becomes eerily resonant with the reservation system in the U.S., or where Nuevomexicano residents will sometimes self-identify more with Palestinians negotiating a different settler colonialism than with other U.S. citizens, or where living next to a nuclear facility may present more immediate threats to personal health and safety than the thermonuclear arsenals of countries overseas? One answer is to decenter security studies, to explore how neighboring communities alternatively experience vulnerability and risk, and to investigate how they articulate experiences of danger in relation to one another. More specifically, my method has been to look at how local populations mobilize to strategically forward ethno-national identifications and/or U.S. citizenship in their engagements with state and federal authorities and with each other, and to search out those areas where contesting "national imaginaries" collide (see Anderson 1991). I explore geopolitics here in their local complexity, forwarding arenas of insecurity rendered invisible or produced by U.S. nuclear nationalism. By including indigenous sovereignties, acknowledging subaltern legal formations, and placing cultural logics in a comparative settler colonial perspective, one can not only appreciate how these diverse national-cultural imaginings in New Mexico are mutually dependent and interconnected, but also realize how people occupying the same territorial space can nevertheless live in ontologically different worlds. To illustrate the connections across these radically different local investments, I follow the path of plutonium as it circulates between communities in northern New Mexico. Tracing the local plutonium economy will help locate and identify the complex articulations of security and insecurity that structure everyday life in the U.S. Southwest and to see the geopolitics of nuclear fear in its fuller international intensity.

The Plutonium Economy

Plutonium is not, of course, an arbitrary choice for an analysis of (in)security; it is a material that has been crucial to definitions of U.S. national security since World War II and has been equally powerful in defining areas of national sacrifice within nuclear states.[8] In fact, one might argue that the unique capabilities of plutonium enabled the Cold War to take the shape that it did.[9] Plutonium remains instrumental in structuring global relations of power in the post–Cold War era and will be an ever-increasing presence in New Mexico as the U.S. nuclear complex returns to nuclear production in the twenty-first century (with Los Alamos tasked with making plutonium pits as well as designing a new generation of nuclear weapons), and as the decades of nuclear research continue to exact their environmental toll.[10] In fact, by tracing how plutonium, as a material commodity, moves in and out of different commodity phases and national regimes of value in the Rio Grande Valley, we can identify how competing national insecurities are articulated there and begin to appreciate how the legacies of the Cold War will continue to generate insecurity for generations to come.[11]

Consider the social contradictions plutonium evokes: First, plutonium-239 is a material that does not exist in nature, yet which by virtue of its quarter-million-year life span is now, for all practical purposes, immortal. Second, as a poison, it is a material whose production has inevitably produced ecological devastation, but it has, nonetheless, been the basis for definitions of national security since 1945.[12] Put differently, in the name of protecting territorial borders from attack, nuclear powers have practiced an internal cannibalism in the form of multiplying national sacrifice zones—areas that are too contaminated for human habitation. Indeed, nuclear states have pursued the security offered by plutonium production to the point of bankruptcy, mutual annihilation, and at an unforeseeable cost to future generations. This complex articulation of national identity through plutonium has also always hidden a colonial dynamic, for lost in the polarizing logics of the nuclear age have often been the most direct victims of nuclear proliferation, the indigenous nations around the globe who have predominantly borne the physical consequences of radioactive material production, weapons testing, and waste storage in their communities.[13]

This reality was implicitly acknowledged in New Mexico after the fall of the Berlin Wall in 1989. As officials at LANL watched with mixed emotions as the Soviet Union fell apart, they quickly turned their attention toward the nations within. After a half century of silence and in the context of growing public concerns about local cancer rates and environmental damage, LANL set up formal government-to-government relations with four neighboring Pueblo nations who by default have been intricately involved in the plutonium economy right from the very beginning of the nuclear age. The Pueblos of San Ildefonso, Santa Clara, Jemez, and Cochiti (who for fifty years have lived with the regular sound of explosions echoing off canyon walls and have wondered about the toxicity of the clouds that drift over their territories from Los Alamos) achieved a new, post–Cold War legal recognition of their sovereign status solely by virtue of their forced entry into the plutonium economy. This was not simply an altruistic move by LANL, however, as new environmental laws suddenly put these Pueblo nations in the legal position to set environmental standards for the air, water, and land they share with the laboratory. This meant that the United States' premier nuclear weapons facility was suddenly responsible to the environmental regulations of four sovereign indigenous nations after a half century of nuclear production in the region. This produced an entirely new political dynamic in New Mexico, one providing new legal power to some indigenous communities while energizing others, particularly Nuevomexicano and antinuclear groups, to mobilize in an unprecedented manner to formally engage the national security mission of Los Alamos National Laboratory.

The plutonium economy in northern New Mexico begins, of course, with the U.S. nuclear weapons complex and specifically at LANL, an institution with a complicated administrative structure. The laboratory is part of the Department of Energy (DOE) in Washington, DC, but it has been managed by the University of California since 1943; it is funded by Congress, yet for most of its history it has written its own mission statement. With its key regulatory structures on both coasts, LANL has enjoyed a remarkable autonomy in New Mexico (until the end of the post–Cold War era when its weapons programs were reorganized under a new DOE administrative unit called the National Nuclear Security Administration after a series of security scandals at the laboratory; see Masco 2006). Perched at 7,200 feet on the Pajarito Plateau above the Rio Grande Valley, LANL's central mission for over a half century now has been to pursue scientific answers to U.S. national security questions (see figure 3.1), with the unique explosive capabilities of plutonium the laboratory's raison d'être. For most of its history, national security at Los Alamos has meant deterring the Soviet nuclear threat through new and improved nuclear weapons. Thus, national security at LANL has traditionally been something that began first overseas; by the 1980s, for example, a Soviet thermonuclear missile could reach the U.S. with less than fifteen minutes' warning. Consequently, Los Alamos scientists developed a uniquely global plutonium-mediated vision: national security issues were everywhere, but the ones of most concern were outside U.S. territorial borders and far away from New Mexico, requiring a global surveillance system and a militarizing of earth, sea, and sky.

The foundational geopolitical mission of the laboratory, however, seemed to dissolve alongside the Soviet Union. In the immediate post–Cold War moment, as in any culture that has experienced the loss of a cosmology, elder nuclear bomb designers worried about how to preserve their cultural knowledge in the face of a rapidly changing world. Some at the laboratory began saying that "designing nuclear weapons is a folk art." Unable to perform underground nuclear tests after 1991, and with a significant weapons dismantling project underway around the country, weaponeers began archiving their nuclear weapon folk knowledge and pursuing a new set of high-tech facilities that will allow them to continue work on nuclear weapons without ever actually exploding one. Under the terms of the underground test moratorium, nuclear weapon scientists began working increasingly in the virtual worlds of computer simulation and less in the hard world of physical experimentation, a massive change in institutional culture.[14] Simultaneously, the U.S. nuclear weapons complex began slowly consolidating into New Mexico,

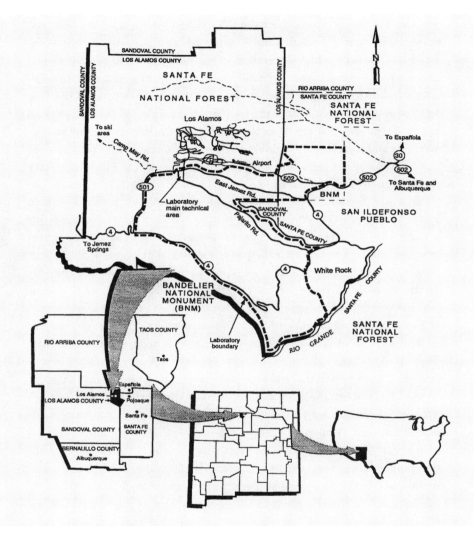

Figure 3.1. Los Alamos National Laboratory location map emphasizing New Mexican and U.S. national borders (U.S. Department of Energy).

as LANL is uniquely positioned by virtue of capacity to become the United States' centralized design and production facility. In the U.S. nuclear stockpile of the post–Cold War period, five of the seven nuclear weapon systems were LANL designs, and the laboratory begun to produce the plutonium pits that are the core components in U.S. nuclear weapons for the first time since the late 1940s. In post–Cold War Los Alamos, national security is defined less through actual deterrence—who exactly is there to deter?—and more through maintaining the ability to resume nuclear weapons production should a new Cold War arise. The laboratory's revised post–Cold War mission is officially to "Reduce the Global Nuclear Danger" (LANL 1994), an expansive project that attempts to recenter the institution around nuclear weapons and materials on a global scale, even though no new weapons are (officially) being designed, and while money for cleanup of Cold War military production sites here in the United States has been repeatedly cut back.

This new mission, however, still has not provided the laboratory with an identity or motivation equal to that of the Cold War arms race. Weapons scientists say privately that "reducing the global nuclear danger" could mean anything and is therefore an inadequate mission statement for an institution long motivated by geopolitical urgency, except for those few working directly on the nonproliferation of nuclear materials and technologies (see U.S. General Accounting Office 1995a). They yearn for a giant organizing structure, a scientific project on the scale of the Manhattan Project, the Strategic Defense Initiative, or the technical and strategic targeting problems of the Cold War. These projects presented massive technological challenges, required unprecedented financial backing, and assumed the need to produce constant technological revolution. The Brookings Institution, for example, estimates the Cold War costs of the U.S. nuclear weapons arsenal (including development, delivery systems, and cleanup) at over $4 trillion—roughly the total U.S. national debt in 1995 (Schwartz 1995). Security expenditures on this scale were a reaction to the perception of a massive external threat to the nation. What could fill this void in the post–Cold War era? In the immediate scramble to justify the laboratory's continued presence, the Soviet nuclear threat was soon replaced in Los Alamos by talk of giant killer space asteroids that might need to be pulverized with thermonuclear weapons to protect Earth from the kind of catastrophe that ended the dinosaur age. This was, however, merely a transitional effort in oppositional mission building, for the Persian Gulf War soon provided a more terrestrial threat, that of the now ubiquitous rogue or terrorist state, a precursor to the formal constitution of a counterterror state in 2001 (see Masco 2014). This conceptual innovation has proven to be a remarkably successful logic, effectively institutionalizing military expenditures above the Cold War level in the U.S. for the foreseeable future (Klare 1995).

One nuclear weapons scientist described the post–Cold War challenges to the laboratory to me in this way:

> The problem is, we've overdesigned our weapons for safety reasons. It's part of the craziness surrounding nuclear weapons, and there is a lot of that. For example, we were ordered to take beryllium out of nuclear weapons because it's a poison. Now think about it—you're worried about the health effects of a bomb that's in the megaton range! Today you could shoot a bullet through a weapon, light it on fire, drop it out of a plane, and it still won't go off or release its nuclear components. We developed a form of high explosive that will just barely go off as well. We also worried about how to prevent a weapon falling into the wrong hands, so we designed elaborate security systems and codes on each device that prevent that. Today these weapons will just barely detonate, they're so complicated. Since the end of the Cold War we have had what you call a paradigm shift. We used to think that all the weapons being designed were as complicated as ours, so you would want to track specific nuclear materials associated with those designs. Now we realize that if you aren't concerned about the safety of your troops or about containing nuclear fallout, and if you just want one bomb, you can do it very quickly. Now some of us have been thinking about how someone might use fertilizer to set off an atomic yield. We've seen what could be done with that in Oklahoma City. We now realize that it's much easier to build a single bomb than we ever thought before. So, the question we are asking about proliferation today is: Do you monitor materials or people? I say people, because there is too much nuclear material floating around out there to ever effectively monitor it. You've got to track the people with the know-how.

These weapons will just barely detonate. Thus, Los Alamos, a techno-scientific community that prides itself on having saved the free world from both fascism and communism, and believes it prevented a third world war by implementing a global targeting system for mutually assured destruction, has been reduced to trying to figure out just who might have the technical knowledge to set off an atomic bomb with fertilizer. This is a far cry from the 1980s in the heady days of the Strategic Defense Initiative when quite literally weapon designers were working on a space-based technological revolution in planetary security (see Broad 1992; Gusterson 1996; Rosenthal 1990).

Although the laboratory has developed skills suited to global nuclear threats—those presented by governments with huge military capabilities or involving the spread of nuclear materials and weapons components—it has stumbled in dealing with the concerns of local populations in New Mexico, for local populations do not fit any of the categories developed during the Cold War for international relations. Local populations include indigenous nations who have no standing army, only a few thousand citizens, whose political leadership changes every year, and who have a sudden ability to directly affect research activities at the laboratory. Similarly, the laboratory has struggled to negotiate the activities of local nongovernmental organizations (NGOs) who are part of a global antinuclear and peace movement and are thus not only unwilling to accept LANL's vision of security at face value, but also quite interested in focusing global attention and applying legal pressure on LANL activities. Thus, while laboratory officials justify the institution's purpose to Congress by talking about intercontinental threats, this kind of national security discourse does not necessarily elicit the support of local communities, who, in some cases, are either diametrically opposed to the laboratory's interests or find themselves to be only marginal U.S. citizens.

A thousand feet below Los Alamos at San Ildefonso Pueblo, for example, national security is a much more immediate business than it is on "the hill," and of foremost concern is protection against the social and environmental impacts of LANL (see figure 3.2).[15] Government officials at San Ildefonso Pueblo self-identify as the only Native American nation whose recognized territory borders directly on a DOE site. The pueblo also has an aboriginal land claim standing in the courts for return of the entire Pajarito Plateau, which Los Alamos has occupied since 1943. For San Ildefonso, national security is a brutally local affair: in addition to the perceived health effects of living next to a nuclear facility and recovering the land lost to the Manhattan Project in 1942, national security for the pueblo involves protecting the local ecosystem as well as the thousands of religious sites on the plateau from ongoing laboratory activities. It means engaging the present with a long-term view of the future. Having already outlived the Spanish and Mexican territorial governments, Pueblo leaders assume their nation will also outlive the United States, and today must wonder about the environmental conditions they will inherit when the laboratory finally closes down. In the future, the most serious environmental impacts may derive from the nuclear waste dump that the laboratory has installed on a plateau directly above the pueblo. The accumulation of radioactive waste buried in shafts and pits at what is known as Area G has made it a national sacrifice zone: an important unresolved question, however, is for whose nation?

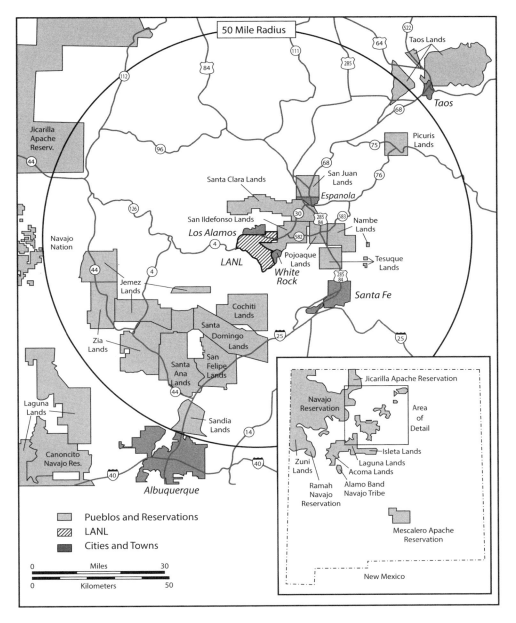

Figure 3.2. Location of Los Alamos National Laboratory in relation to federally recognized Native American territories.

San Ildefonso's forced entry into the plutonium economy now presents a national security problem of indefinite longevity for the pueblo. Pueblo leaders are responding to these millennial problems by working to train a new generation of Pueblo youth as environmental scientists. The future of the pueblo will increasingly involve monitoring LANL activities and mobilizing environmental laws to protect the physical, spiritual, and financial security of the tribe from the local effects of U.S. national security policy.

The unique legal status of Pueblo nations in North America infuses such negotiations with a complicated international context. Pueblo communities were incorporated into the U.S. in the Treaty of Guadalupe Hidalgo in 1848. Unlike many indigenous nations, they did not enter into individual treaties with the U.S. government but were incorporated as Mexican citizens. Their aboriginal status, however, was debated for the next sixty years, during which many Pueblo communities lost much of their land base before the U.S. government took up formal trust responsibility in 1913 (Ortiz 1980; Simmons 1978, 213–15). Though the Treaty of Guadalupe Hidalgo theoretically made all citizens of Mexico in the ceded territories U.S. citizens in 1848, and the U.S. Congress theoretically granted all Native Americans full citizenship in 1924, Pueblo members did not actually achieve the right to vote in either state or federal elections until 1948 (Sando 1992, 102). Moreover, Native American nations in the U.S. are legally designated as "domestic, dependent nations," an ambiguous status that allows state and federal bureaucracies to redefine indigenous sovereignty rights on an issue-by-issue basis (Cohen 1941; see also Richland 2008). This relegates Native American communities to the paradoxical position of being, as John Borneman (1995) puts it, entities that are "simultaneously domestic and foreign" to the United States. Today, Pueblo members maintain a dual citizenship with the United States and their respective nations.

It is important to acknowledge that the people who arguably paid the most immediate local price for the Manhattan Project in the 1940s did not at the time even have the right to vote in New Mexican or federal elections.[16] Many of the shrines and pilgrimage sites that Pueblo members identify as having been spiritually important "since time immemorial" were destroyed by laboratory installations, roads, weapons tests, and the town of Los Alamos.[17] Moreover, post–Cold War revelations about LANL's environmental impacts and the amount of nuclear materials on the highways have alerted Pueblo leaders to the frightening possibility that one nuclear accident on the highways crossing Pueblo land could potentially destroy their entire nation. I asked one Pueblo member about the environmental justice implications of nuclear weapons work at LANL:

What your people have done here is more than racism or environmental racism. It's genocide against my people. It's part of the system of apartheid in America. South Africa is not the only place with apartheid you know. It's part of a system where Europeans came to this area and because we didn't have a written system, a written title, took the land and placed us on reservations. Little areas of land that restrict our movement and culture. I thought in the 1940s we were fighting against Nazi experiments on humans and the creation of a Nazi "superman." That's why we helped the government at Los Alamos. But now with all the revelations about human experimentation here, the U.S. government was doing the same things. There's no difference.

There's no difference. The reference to human experimentation here is a pointed one. Many in northern New Mexico fear that the laboratory has poisoned the land and people. This concern is exacerbated by the fact that current epidemiological models are unable to evaluate statistically the cancer rates in the small-scale communities of northern New Mexico, leaving these fears on an ambiguous scientific terrain. Los Alamos's technoscientific approach also falters when confronted with Pueblo cultural and religious concerns. In response to Pueblo demands to protect the undisturbed religious sites on the forty-three square miles of what is now laboratory territory, LANL officials offered to map these sites and design future construction projects around them. However, the strict prohibitions within Pueblo societies about speaking to the noninitiated about religious matters, a tactic developed to fight the missionary zeal of seventeenth-century Spanish officials and reinforced by the aggressive ethnographic collecting of early twentieth-century anthropologists, made this approach untenable. Thus, Pueblo negotiations with LANL and DOE officials have been historically fraught over two very crucial national security issues: the health and religious rights of Pueblo nations. In the end, Pueblo governments who believe their health, territorial borders, and spiritual security have been compromised by U.S. national security work at Los Alamos must face the reality of fighting an institution with a $1 billion annual budget (which is vital to the national security of the world's sole remaining superpower) and of doing so in U.S. courts.[18]

If we follow the plutonium economy one community farther to the east in the New Mexico landscape, to Pojoaque Pueblo, which lies immediately adjacent to San Ildefonso and fifteen miles north of Santa Fe, we find a very different articulation of a plutonium-mediated national security. Pojoaque is a pueblo with a difficult history. It has, as its governor says, "died twice" due to epidemics in the eighteenth and nineteenth centuries, and was only reconstituted in the 1930s. Pojoaque entered the plutonium economy in 1996 with a public announcement that it was going to pursue nuclear waste storage as a form of economic development. Pojoaque has taken only the first steps in this process, a series of conceptual studies, but their national security strategy shows how mediated by energy and waste issues indigenous politics in New Mexico have become (e.g., see Powell 2018). In the late 1980s, the DOE began a process of soliciting all indigenous nations about nuclear waste storage projects on tribal lands (Hanson 2001; Stoffle and Evans 1988). This was an explicit attempt to break the gridlock around nuclear waste caused by suburban American fears of living near nuclear materials. For many tribes, new recognition as a sovereign nation is quickly followed by invitations from federal bureaucracies and corporations for lucrative nuclear waste storage projects. In the post–Cold War era, the outlines of a transnational Native American nuclear waste storage economy were beginning to take shape in New Mexico: the Mescalero Apache began work on a short-term nuclear waste storage facility in southern New Mexico and signed agreements with an association of northern Canadian Cree nations for permanent storage of U.S. nuclear waste. The North American Free Trade Agreement explicitly marked radioactive waste as a nontariff item, paving the way for this kind of transnational indigenous nuclear waste infrastructure.

Pojoaque's nuclear waste storage project was, however, also a political tactic designed to underscore what was at stake for the pueblo in debates over casino gaming. National security for the few hundred people that make up Pojoaque Pueblo today means economic independence. The government at Pojoaque Pueblo has been among the most vocal supporters of Indian gaming in New Mexico, and today the pueblo has one of the most successful casinos in the state. Its City of Gold casino plays off the ancient myth of the seven golden cities of Cibola that energized the Spanish conquest of the Southwest, and today it extracts money, with almost surgical irony, from tourists and residents of the mostly Spanish-speaking counties of northern New Mexico. In the mid-1990s, the legality of Pueblo gaming operations in U.S. courts remained in doubt, even though compacts had been signed by the governor of New Mexico and approved by the U.S. secretary of the interior. The consequences of these negotiations could not be more serious; as few industries are more profitable than casino gaming or nuclear waste, quite literally millions, and possibly billions, are at stake in these decisions (cf. Cattelino 2008). It is hardly surprising, then, that in response to a steady stream of new legal roadblocks on gaming from state and federal officials, a coalition of nine Pueblo nations in 1996 repeatedly threatened to shut down the highways in northern New Mexico (all of which cross Pueblo lands) if the gaming compacts were not honored.[19]

In their public announcement, Pojoaque representatives specifically stated that they were interested in storing high-level nuclear waste—that is, plutonium—from dismantled U.S. nuclear weapons, precisely the weapons that were designed a few miles up the road at LANL. The plutonium economy has come back to Los Alamos, as has the role of nuclear materials in defining national security. Pojoaque's leadership played off fears of nuclear waste in Santa Fe to press their claims about tribal gaming. Pojoaque Pueblo's tactical consideration of placing a nuclear waste site on tribal lands, however, is not only an example of the high-stakes international politics that have taken place around nuclear materials in New Mexico for over fifty years; it also suggests a strategy that privileges an economics-based national security over all other concerns. Thus, as the national security of San Ildefonso is compromised by the environmental and social costs of the laboratory's nuclear waste dump, neighboring Pojoaque, a community that has already died twice in its history, can forward nuclear waste storage as the ultimate means of achieving its own national security. Pojoaque's strategy is, however, a direct consequence of the settler colonial dynamic between Native American communities and the United States. Thus, while no indigenous nation currently produces nuclear waste, all are potential candidates for the disposal of the nuclear materials produced by the U.S. nuclear complex.[20]

If we follow our plutonium economy ten miles north from Pojoaque along Highway 68 to the town of Española, a different, but equally charged, set of security issues is evoked. Española is the largest town in Spanish-speaking Rio Arriba County. Many Española residents are direct descendants of the first Spanish settlers in the region in 1598 and can self-identify as twentieth-generation New Mexicans. Accounting for roughly half of the jobs in greater Rio Arriba County, LANL is the area's largest single employer. Before Los Alamos was built in the 1940s, most Nuevomexicano families in the area lived on small-scale farms and spoke primarily Spanish (Forrest 1989; Weigle 1975). Many had to work as migrant laborers all across the Southwest to support their families. Currently, there are three generations of men and women from the tiny villages of northern New Mexico who have worked almost exclusively at the laboratory (see Garcia 2010; Kosek 2006). Traditionally they have been the security guards, laborers, and support staff. Although more Nuevomexicanos are now working in technical fields at the laboratory, in the early 1990s still very few had careers as scientists or project managers. Thus, an extreme cultural and economic, as well as geographical, divide separates Los Alamos from the valley: Los Alamos County is 94 percent white, with the highest number of PhDs per capita in the nation. Rio Arriba County is 75 percent Hispanic, with 10 percent of the population completing college degrees.[21] The average income in Los Alamos is three times that of Rio Arriba County. Unemployment is 2 percent on the hill while over 27 percent in the valley. Some describe the trip from small villages in the region to the laboratory as a kind of time travel, linking small-scale agricultural life to a high-tech world of big science, militarism, and space travel via two-lane roads. Figures 3.3 to 3.6 are national recruiting advertisements for Los Alamos Scientific Laboratory from the 1960s that play on the idea of offering future workers experiences of time travel, cultural exoticism, and outer space research in New Mexico. Since the 1940s, however, for most people in Rio Arriba County who desire a middle-class lifestyle, LANL remains the primary game in town.

One Hispano, who recently retired from a thirty-five-year career as a construction foreman at LANL, put it this way, jabbing his finger into my chest for emphasis:

> I'll tell you what to write in your book—you write that the lab saved everybody in this valley! Without Los Alamos all these little Spanish villages wouldn't exist. Everybody tries to work at the lab—because it's good steady work. Before the lab, all the men in the valley had to go all over the country trying to find work—they would see their families only once or twice a year. With the lab we have good jobs that allow us to stay with our families. People drive from all over New Mexico to work at the lab—from Albuquerque, from Tierra Amarilla—because it's such good work. People from the valley built Los Alamos and there are always big construction projects there. There's always work.

The lab saved everyone. This narrative of endless economic security, however, broke down in 1995 as the laboratory laid off over one thousand people, predominantly Nuevomexicanos from the valley, and forecast more post–Cold War layoffs to come. Within this political context, Nuevomexicanos began expressing long-standing concerns that LANL holds northern New Mexico hostage economically, that it is more responsible to officials in Washington, DC, than to local communities. Employees began to talk openly about racism at the laboratory, about a glass ceiling in promotions, and about how Nuevomexicanos do most of the dangerous and dirty work. Outside the laboratory, residents of the valley measured the effects of having to speak English at the laboratory on Nuevomexicano culture and noted when LANL employees start pronouncing their Spanish surnames with an English accent. Without the security of employment provided by an endlessly expanding national laboratory, the post–Cold War public sphere surrounding LANL in northern New Mexico was being radicalized and racialized, with an increasingly public portrayal of LANL as a colonial institution. The laboratory's post–Cold War layoffs, for example, were immediately interpreted by some in Española and neighboring communities as a federal declaration of war on northern New Mexico.

It is important to understand the historical context of such a conclusion. From the Nuevomexicano point of view, the 1848 Treaty of Guadalupe Hidalgo has never been honored by the United States (see Acuña 1988; Chavez 1984; Trujillo 2009). Explicit provisions in that treaty for the protection of the culture and land of Mexican citizens being incorporated into the United States were negotiated and then stricken by Congress at the last moment. The Mexican government demanded, and received, further assurances that its citizens' land rights would be protected in the United States (Griswold del Castillo 1990). The land grants that were the basis for both Spanish and Mexican social and economic organizations were, however, quickly broken apart by U.S. territorial judges who affirmed legal ownership of small plots of land to individuals but not the large collective landholdings that had traditionally been used for cattle grazing and that were the basis for communal life. Only a fraction of Nuevomexicano land claims were upheld by the U.S. courts in the late nineteenth century, and many were stolen outright by a corrupt legal system. Literally millions of acres changed hands, leaving almost every Nuevomexicano family in northern New Mexico with a story about how the U.S. government or someone manipulating the U.S. legal system took part of their land and impoverished their communities (see Briggs and Van Ness 1987; Ebright 1994). Consequently, much of the U.S. national forest land in New Mexico remains hotly contested to this day and is a perennial source of regional tension. In a discussion about California's Proposition 187, an act that would deny public services (including hospitals and schools) to undocumented Mexican immigrants in California (and matters locally, as the University of California manages LANL), one Hispano activist summed it up for me with a casual shrug: "The United States and Mexico never signed the same treaty in 1848—they are still at war."

For many Nuevomexicanos, and those who do not work at the laboratory in particular, there is bitter irony in the fact that New Mexico is now the center of the U.S. nuclear weapons complex. The U.S. government saturates everyday life in northern New Mexico, monitoring land and water use

Experimentation in nuclear particle motion and energy—one of our many probes into the future.

For employment information write:
Personnel Director
Division 59-94

los alamos
scientific laboratory
OF THE UNIVERSITY OF CALIFORNIA
LOS ALAMOS, NEW MEXICO

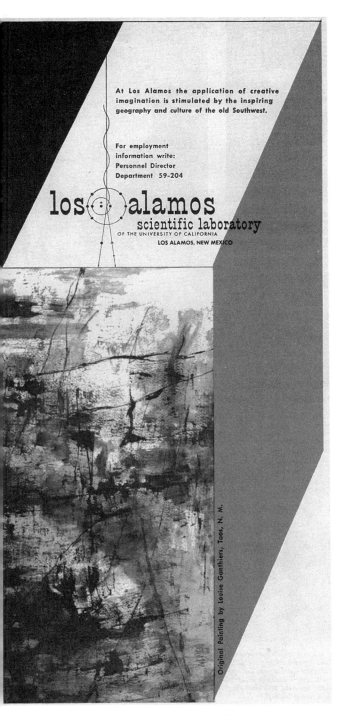

Figures 3.3 and 3.4. Los Alamos Scientific Laboratory advertisements promising work that "probes into the future" and is "stimulated by the inspiring geography and culture of the old Southwest," circa 1960.

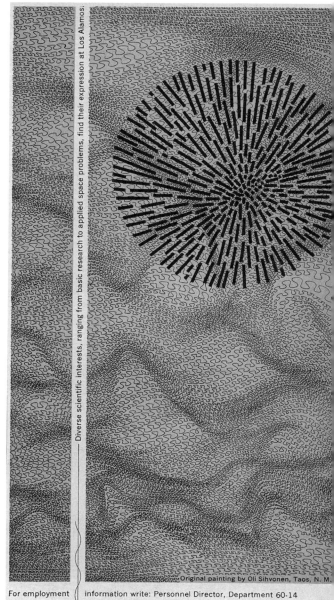

Diverse scientific interests, ranging from basic research to applied space problems, find their expression at Los Alamos.

Original painting by Oli Sihvonen, Taos, N. M.

For employment information write: Personnel Director, Department 60-14

los alamos
scientific laboratory
OF THE UNIVERSITY OF CALIFORNIA
LOS ALAMOS, NEW MEXICO

Figures 3.5. and 3.6. Los Alamos Scientific Laboratory advertisement recruiting workers for space programs—both subatomic and extraterrestrial, circa 1960.

Space Propulsion for the future . . .

from the **KIWI** family of Nuclear Reactors

Los Alamos Scientific Laboratory has the major responsibility for research, development and testing in the AEC-NASA Rover program . . . another of the many investigations at Los Alamos into peacetime uses of nuclear energy.

PHOTO: First field test of a KIWI nuclear propulsion reactor.

through the U.S. Forest Service and the Office of the State Engineer, housing and welfare through Housing and Urban Development and other agencies, and regulating employment through LANL. Thus, while the U.S. nuclear weapons complex provides an important job base in New Mexico, which perennially competes for the title of poorest state in the U.S., federal and state officials nonetheless practice a historical amnesia about treaty obligations and the long-standing land claims of Nuevomexicano residents. As one Chicano land grant activist put it to me:

> The real problem is dealing with white politicians, most of whom came to New Mexico very recently. You go to a public hearing and talk about land grants and the Treaty of Guadalupe Hidalgo, and they look at you like you're from another planet—they don't know what you are talking about. They treat you like you just got off the boat from Juarez and they want to see your green card. We've been here for hundreds of years. The real immigrants are all those people from New York, Boston, and California that come to live here and know nothing about us.

You're from another planet. This political dynamic is what anthropologist John Bodine (1968) has called a "tri-ethnic trap," a situation in which the legal and cultural position of Nuevomexicanos is doubly marginalized by white structures of power and by the cultural status of Native Americans as First Nations. Thus, while Pueblos as sovereign governments have gained a new post–Cold War legal discourse with the laboratory, equally affected Nuevomexicano communities have gained no such legal voice. In this context, Nuevomexicano concerns about the economic and environmental impacts of the laboratory can be dismissed, as they were following the 1995 layoffs by LANL leadership, as an expression of a welfare state mentality and not of legitimate political concern. Nuevomexicano participation in the plutonium economy is therefore double edged: through hard work it has allowed many access to a middle-class life, but it has also meant participating in an ongoing consolidation of northern New Mexico to Anglo-American and U.S. governmental interests. It is with new post–Cold War anxiety, then, that Nuevomexicanos continue to look to LANL as the future of northern New Mexico. Others, however, underscore their resistance by referring to the laboratory and town site simply as "Los Alamos, D.C." (Romero 1995), acknowledging that, even decades after the Manhattan Project, Los Alamos remains, in their eyes, more properly a suburb of Washington, DC, than a legitimate part of New Mexico.

NUCLEAR HIGHWAYS

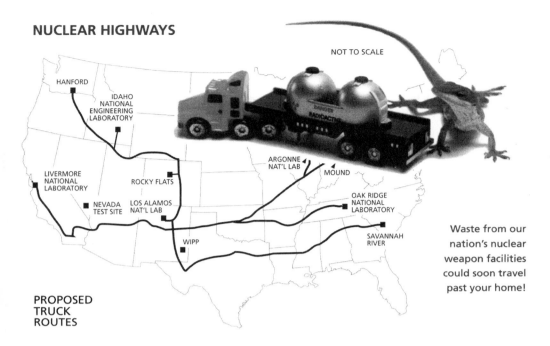

NOT TO SCALE

HANFORD

IDAHO
NATIONAL
ENGINEERING
LABORATORY

LIVERMORE
NATIONAL
LABORATORY

ROCKY FLATS

NEVADA   LOS ALAMOS
TEST SITE NAT'L LAB

ARGONNE
NAT'L LAB   MOUND

OAK RIDGE
NATIONAL
LABORATORY

WIPP

SAVANNAH
RIVER

Waste from our
nation's nuclear
weapon facilities
could soon travel
past your home!

PROPOSED
TRUCK
ROUTES

Figure 3.7. Early post–Cold War–era New Mexico activist map showing how all U.S. nuclear waste roads run through the state.

Our exploration of the plutonium economy concludes in Santa Fe, which is twenty miles equidistant from Española and Los Alamos and is home to several antinuclear NGOs that have been instrumental in organizing community debates about the laboratory in the post–Cold War era and raising awareness about the centrality of New Mexico within the U.S. nuclear complex. As figure 3.7 demonstrates, a key mission of these groups is to make visible the U.S. nuclear complex, including its transportation routes and waste storage plans—to show how all roads lead to New Mexico for things nuclear. The membership of these NGOs, notably the Los Alamos Study Group and Concerned Citizens for Nuclear Safety, is mostly Anglo, first-generation New Mexicans who self-identify as citizens of the United States. These antinuclear NGOs have become adept at utilizing environmental laws to gain a voice in nuclear weapons policy at LANL. In 1995, for example, they temporarily halted construction of the Dual Axis Radiographic Hydrodynamic Test Facility (DARHT), which the DOE has identified as the premiere post–Cold War facility for ensuring "the safety and reliability" of the U.S. nuclear weapons stockpile (U.S. Department of Energy 1995). They did so by forcing LANL, through U.S. courts, to do an environmental impact study of DARHT and to publicly justify the need for the project. Since the end of the Cold War, NGOs have provided consistent, technically and legally informed, public critique of U.S. nuclear weapons work at LANL. They have also sought to provide technical information about the laboratory and its environmental impacts to a fragile coalition of diverse Pueblo, Nuevomexicano, and Anglo interests.

For many in these organizations, the real achievement of the Manhattan Project was not the atomic bomb, but the institutionalization of a system of government secrecy and with it the curtailing of democratic process when it comes to U.S. national security policy (see Masco 2002). They view their work as combating the secrecy and public manipulation of an insurgent military-industrial complex and, more specifically, as exposing the environmental, social, and global security impacts of nuclear weapons work at LANL. As one Anglo peace activist put it: "Everything having to do with nuclear weapons is born secret in the United States—and the division between what is secret and what is not secret is also secret." Thus, for antinuclear activists, U.S. citizens are eliminated from the decision-making process because federal authorities can argue that by definition citizens never have the information necessary to make informed statements about U.S. national security policy.[22] Consequently, antinuclear NGOs in Santa Fe initiated an early post–Cold War project to lobby the World Court to outlaw nuclear weapons globally (a project that only reached a degree of formal success in 2017 with the passage of a prohibition on nuclear weapons at the United Nations).[23] By appealing directly to a global legal body, NGOs not only call into question the legality of U.S. national security policy in New Mexico but also dramatically demonstrate that the federal government does not represent their national security interests. This act not only underscores a profound distrust of the United States when it comes to nuclear weapons policy; it also exemplifies how the local is now intersecting the global, how individuals are beginning to imagine their community as part of a post-nation-state world order. Through such actions, antinuclear NGOs publicly challenge and reject the state's right to define authoritatively the meaning of security and danger for their communities (see figure 3.8).

For members of these groups who fear environmental contamination from the laboratory and identify nuclear weapons as the greatest threat to their personal security, the U.S. government remains the most immediate danger in the region. For many, LANL is both the symbol for, and the real-

Figure 3.8. Antinuclear peace protest at Los Alamos National Laboratory.

ization of, a society in love with violence. As another Anglo Santa Fe peace activist put it to me, the central question is:

> How are we going to put an end to this monstrous development of weapons? How are we going to put an end to an institution which so far has existed, as far as I can see, primarily as an institution developing means of threat, an institution which works to instill fear in people, an institution basically which has devoted itself for over fifty years now to violence? We're all very aware of the violence that we have around us. What is it like for young people to grow up in this city and to look out and see those lights every night and know what's going on up there, that [LANL] is an institution devoted to violence . . . that Los Alamos is a place of death?

Those lights. Antinuclear NGOs critique LANL, therefore, on moral and ethical, as well as on environmental, grounds. They point out that the majority of the nuclear weapons in the current U.S. stockpile were designed after the United States signed the Nuclear Nonproliferation Treaty in 1968, in which government leaders promised to "achieve at the earliest possible date the cessation of the nuclear arms race and to undertake effective measures in the direction of nuclear disarmament" (United Nations 1968, 1). In 1996, as a comprehensive test ban was being negotiated by the Clinton administration, activists feared that the arms race was simply going into a new phase, emphasizing the design and testing of nuclear weapons in virtual reality. This is a major structural change in the nuclear complex, one that will generate few environmental impacts, thus eliminating one of the primary legal tools NGOS have for influencing U.S. nuclear weapons policy. These are not unfounded concerns, for U.S. weapons laboratories have been promised tens of billions of dollars' worth of new facilities for their "science-based stockpile stewardship programs" (Zerriffi and Makhijani 1996). The DOE claims these facilities are necessary to ensure the safety and reliability of nuclear weapons in a world without underground nuclear testing, but these programs will also provide a state-of-the-art complex (with the world's fastest computers, as well as numerous new nonnuclear testing facilities) as capable of designing new nuclear weapons as testing old ones (see Gusterson 1995; Masco 2006; Zerriffi and Makhijani 1996). Thus, the post–Cold War period has produced unexpected, and new, forms of insecurity for local antinuclear NGOS as the U.S. has rejected the opportunities for large-scale disarmament, renewed its commitment to a plutonium-mediated national security, and begun retooling for a new generation of nuclear weapons work.

Anthropology in an Insecure State

What I have tried to demonstrate in this chapter is that national security in post–Cold War New Mexico is not simply a question of how to defend the territorial borders of the United States; it evokes the contradictory and competing worldviews currently attached to military-industrial, indigenous, subaltern, and antinuclear subject positions in North America. Moreover, each of these ideological positions involves a specific constellation of racial, ethnic, national, and territorial identities while maintaining distinct internal politics as well. Communities in New Mexico, in a post–Cold War moment, are mobilizing historical identities and pursuing new forms of subaltern nation building by challenging U.S. national security policy in international forums, in U.S. courts, and in the everyday life, settler colonial context of living next to a major nuclear facility. So, what does this political fragmentation surrounding the plutonium economy in New Mexico tell us about the new global context or insecurities in the post–Cold War era?

The end of the Cold War inaugurated a reorganization of global political and economic structures generating new internal and external pressures for many regional populations. New Mexico, for example, is now part of a transnational economic arena in which the sovereignty of Native American nations has become an attractive means through which corporations can manipulate legal restrictions on dangerous substances like nuclear waste. Current DOE regulations for burying nuclear waste, for example, require that permanent storage facilities have a ten-thousand-year operative plan, an unprecedented legal requirement that is still just a momentary blip in the social life of plutonium. Here, the dilemma of the national sacrifice zone is finally revealed: how to designate which nations—past, present, and future—must bear the costs of the Cold War nuclear economy. I have argued here that the Cold War reliance on a plutonium-mediated national security has already surpassed the ability of the United States to control its fallout, unleashing materials and social logics that will be generating diverse insecurities for generations to come. Concurrently, the post–Cold War effort in Congress to do away with unifying national programs and policies in favor of individual state programs, what might be called a national unbuilding project, promises to put poor states like New Mexico, which rely on federal dollars for basic services, at ever greater risk. This dynamic is exacerbated by the marginalizing of local ethnic groups in New Mexico, many of whom were instrumental in fighting the Cold War and who are now being targeted by corporate and U.S. national interests. U.S. national security policy has, therefore, produced a wide range of effects in the Southwest over the last half century, leaving many in the post–Cold War era now to search out their own forms of security.

To understand these realities, we might now consider the advantages of a decentered scholarly approach to the production of (in)security. "Decentered" means moving beyond the nation-state to a nation-state dynamic that has in different ways dominated both security studies and anthropology, to pursue projects that investigate multiple subject positions and that explore how specific experiences of place are constructed in the tension between the global and the local and, increasingly, the planetary. As I have sought to demonstrate in this chapter, approaching the production of insecurity with universalistic definitions of sovereignty, security, or citizenship means erasing the cultural and political complexity of many areas of the world, like northern New Mexico, and rendering invisible the long-standing and emerging forms of conflict. The post–Cold War period has demonstrated this over and over again. In the early 1990s, for example, it was still possible to describe the former Yugoslavia as an example of a working multiethnic, pluralistic society. And who could have predicted the eruption among indigenous communities in Chiapas over the terms of the 1994 North American Free Trade Agreement? In both of these situations, the relationship of memory to land and to race and ethnicity has combined with historical shifts in geopolitical relations to produce regional volatilities that challenge Cold War assumptions about the foundational bases of security and national stability.

To understand these forms of (inter)national conflict in the post–Cold War era, I suggest we need to move beyond a model of security studies based primarily on alignments of weapons and armies to include investigations of how people experience insecurity across a broader sphere of relationships, from those of economic exploitation to environmental degradation to racial conflict and geopolitical marginalization to the ongoing force of settler colonialism. This poses several distinct disciplinary challenges. For anthropology, it means moving beyond the implicit Cold War emphasis on using one's home nation-state as the ultimate point of reference for identifying difference. As John Borneman (1995) has argued, anthropology has always been involved in a subtle form of foreign policy, in that by exploring the boundaries of otherness, anthropologists have also been implicitly reinforcing national borders. This is most clearly evidenced in the long-standing requirement for entry into anthropology as a profession: the completion of an ethnographic project that takes place outside the territorial borders of the nation-state one was born in. From this perspective, anthropology has been involved, however obliquely, in a particular state- and nation-building project right from the very beginning, and consequently it is quite likely that in the future we will look back on the anthropology of the Cold War as a distinctive global project (see Nader 1997). Post–Cold War efforts to examine global processes from an ethnographic point of view have produced a number of initiatives to expand the possibilities for ethnographic research (see Appadurai 1991; Friedman 1994; Marcus 1995). However, since the Cold War provided much of the energy and funding for the development of area studies programs, the challenge that remains is to articulate a compelling new understanding of the value of cross-cultural research, one that is not tied to the kind of state- and nation-building projects of the Cold War (or the War on Terror).[24]

Decentering security studies is a more profound challenge, given that it is largely a creation of the Cold War and because of the close interactions many security scholars maintain with government policy makers, creating in some cases a revolving door between government and the academy. Here, we might locate one conceptual blind spot in Cold War security studies by reviewing institutional responses to the national security debates in New Mexico I have detailed in this chapter. With one notable exception, security studies agencies in the mid-1990s found the security issues raised in this work to be literally unrecognizable. Two issues seem to inform readings that positioned the debates in and around Los Alamos outside the purview of U.S. security studies: (1) the ambiguous legal standing of indigenous nations within international relations theory, and (2) the absence of an area studies category devoted to investigating security issues internal to the United States. These conversations, at times, provoked curious results. In one multiyear discussion over funding, for example, I was informed that if I could demonstrate that the political context around Los Alamos had international implications—something that might affect arms control agreements, for instance—then this project might be considered a contribution to security studies. Then, while readily acknowledging the territorial sovereignty of Pueblo nations in New Mexico and thus an international context, this same funding agency concluded that, since the Pueblos were unlikely to "break away" from the United States, New Mexico (and thus this research) lacked the criteria to be relevant to security studies. A paradoxical vision of sovereignty was revealed in these exchanges, one defined by an ability to threaten the United States. Since Pueblo nations do not have standing armies, and cannot militarily challenge the United States, this agency saw no security concerns in the region. Within such a schema, indigenous nations can only enter the world of security studies by taking military action, and even then, they would enter it only as a threat to U.S. national security, not as national entities with security concerns unique and valid unto themselves. The broader security implications of building (and after the Cold War, consolidating) the U.S. nuclear weapons complex in an area of New Mexico that is territorially contested (with sixteen indigenous nations and numerous land grant controversies), racially and ethnically unique (a majority Nuevomexicano and Native American region), and poor (one in three people around Los Alamos live below the poverty line) were rendered invisible, in this case, by devotion to a specific Cold War–era internationalism. Thus, it proved impossible for me in this post–Cold War moment to argue that settler colonialism has a geopolitics, and one relevant to nuclear studies within the United States.

Undoubtedly the end of the millennium will witness new parameters for what counts as security as well as for whose insecurity is important to understand (as the inauguration of a war on terror would ultimately show in 2001). I suggest that one test of the institutional ability to disengage with Cold War structures (including both their priorities and occlusions) is whether North

America, and the United States in particular, is included within a revised security studies topography. Certainly the kinds of issues being debated in post–Cold War New Mexico—which involve state and quasi-state entities, asymmetrical legal structures, complex settler colonial dynamics, alternative definitions of citizenship, and fundamental questions of environmental justice—argue for a move away from a strict focus on state-to-state interactions to enable investigations into how people actually experience insecurity in everyday life. Given the embedded cultural and institutional legacies of the Cold War, however, it may well be that in order to study insecurity at the end of the twentieth century, we may all have to embrace it as well.

DESERT MODERNISM

*Too much of a good thing
is wonderful.*
—Liberace

The modern American desert is a place where curious things seem possible. It exists as (post)modernist frontier and as sacrifice zone, simultaneously a fantasy playground where individuals move to reinvent themselves on their own terms and a technoscientific wasteland where many of the most dangerous projects of an industrial, militarized society are located. Since the mid-twentieth century, the desert Southwest has become a space of modernist excitement, where the challenge of an expansive wildness has been met by monumental efforts to dislocate its indigenous inhabitants, to redirect its rivers, to populate its interior with cities and roads, and to fill its airspace with jet and missile contrails. Part neon oasis, the modern desert now dazzles with a phantasmagoria of electric lights, presenting monuments of distraction that offer up the wonder of the built for intimate comparison with that of the natural.

At the turn of the century, Las Vegas was the fastest-growing city in the United States, consuming water as if it were surrounded by an ocean of fresh water. It is also a desert island within a military-industrial crypto-state, a place where secret military machines are designed, where atomic bombs are detonated, and where chemical weapons and nuclear waste are stored; it is a home, in other words, to all the national security technoscience supporting a superpowered military state founded in settler colonialism. Nevertheless, for those caught under the spell of American desert modernism, the desert can still take on the appearance of a pristine possibility, an existential blank page awaiting a script to provide it with an essential meaning. This ability to reinscribe the desert West requires constant imaginative work, as the pursuit of utopian potential relies on a continual emptying out of the dystopian projects of settler colonialism and the nuclear security state. It is this capacity to invest in monumental projects through practices of cognitive erasure that I call desert modernism, a conceptual enterprise that perennially reinvents the desert as dreamspace for a hyperviolent idea of progress.

The desert has always captivated American imaginations by offering settlers the hope of leaving the past behind in favor of an endlessly renewable frontier, forever open to new possibilities. But this migration away from self and nation is now doubly fraught, as refugees to the interior run headlong into an equally imaginative military-industrial economy that constructs the desert as a hyperregulated national sacrifice zone, a proving ground for the supersecret, the deadly, and the toxic. A national-cultural excess is evident in the shared nature of this desert modernism, visible not only in the official images of nuclear nationalism, but also in the afterimages of American Cold War culture. In the slippages between the form and content of American desert modernism, we can see how a careful crafting of appearances has been mobilized to endow everyday life with an epic quality that denies an ongoing commitment to regeneration through violence (see Slotkin 2000). In the desert West, both citizens and officials have come to rely on tactical amnesias and temporal sutures to enable a precarious—if addictive—cosmology of progress, one fueled by high-octane combinations of risk, secrecy, utopian expectation, and paranoid anxiety in everyday life.

During the Cold War, desert modernism took on a decidedly masculine form, combining military science with corporate capitalism in a highly gendered national performance. What follows is a reflection on this particular blending of utopian desire and toxic practice in American culture, a narrative experiment provoked by a post–Cold War research tour of Nevada. Presented in the form of an ethnographic notebook, the following four biographical sketches offer up a dialectical image, a composite portrait of the masculinist afterimages of Cold War culture. What is at stake in these distinct articulations of male mastery (each linked through practices of mirror imaging or inversion in an overarching attempt to define and control the future) is the nature of modernity itself as a knowable enterprise. For we can see in the American desert today a national-cultural arena in which the high modernism of the Cold War—sustained by a powerful belief in an unlimited possibility for self-reinvention and an unending technological progress fueled by ideologies of a manifest destiny—circles back to confront itself in the everyday lives of nuclear weapon designers, tunnel engineers, conspiracy theorists, and sequined entertainers. As survivors of that expressive national performance known as the Cold War, which offered these figures the delirious rush of participating in a universe-making or universe-breaking cosmology, desert dwellers are left now to negotiate the accumulating residues of desert modernism in the here and now, even as they mobilize to reinvent the future once again. Indeed, we can see in the following fragmentary moments how the contradictions of a disabled master narrative of progress have come to saturate everyday life with unruly new forms of imaginative agency, simultaneously exhilarating, excessive, apocalyptic—American.

On Mythic Masculinity

Our guide is utterly charming.[1] A thirty-five-year career at the Nevada Test Site (NTS) building detonating mechanisms for nuclear weapons has obviously been good to him. [2] He carries himself today with the cool assurance of someone who has performed well at the center of an important national project, a Cold Warrior in the truest sense of the term. Even after the demise of the Soviet Union and while in retirement, he upholds the mission of the test site, educating the public about "what really went on," articulating the continued need for weapons of mass destruction, and reiterating the critical role the NTS plays in managing a global order of proliferating danger and constant threat. Physically strong, crystal clear in thought, and with a great sense of cowboy humor, our guide's manner is, in and of itself, a political counter to many of the popular images of weapons scientists, the NTS, and the nuclear security state. This is no Dr. Strangelove but more like a very favorite storytelling uncle.

Driving us through the NTS, he relates stories of Cold War excitement, pointing out project details: "That's Sedan Crater (second biggest crater in the U.S.—part of the nonmilitary use of nuclear explosives program—astronauts trained there before going to the moon); that's the Chemical Spill Test Facility (the only place in the country where you can create a major toxic accident to study how to clean it up); that's the new Device Assembly Facility (it's got miles of underground tunnels—*we* can't go there)." He presents a seamless history of work at the test site, mediated by an understated, if undeniable, patriotism. I asked him when, in his experience, was the best moment to be working on nuclear weapons at the test site. "From 1962 to 1988," he replies without hesitation. This is the period from the implementation of the atmospheric nuclear test ban to the near collapse of the nuclear narrative in 1988, when revelations about the scope of environmental damage at places like Hanford, Washington, Rocky Flats, Colorado, and Fernald, Ohio, brought heightened public suspicion and new regulatory restraints on work at the test site. During this twenty-six-year period, the only pause he mentions in a narrative of pure techno-national progress was for President John F. Kennedy. "He was assassinated on a test day," he tells us. "We postponed the 'shot' for twenty-four hours in his memory, but then got back to work."

For our guide, working at the test site provided access to the very best minds in the world, the weapons scientists at the national laboratories (Los Alamos, Livermore, and Sandia), but it also demanded a constant negotiation of the military mindset. He confides that he had to put an army colonel or two in his place who did not understand the technoscientific logistics of the test site. During one such confrontation, he simply pulled the detonating mechanism out of the nuclear device, placed it in the trunk of his car, and drove away—putting the whole multimillion-dollar test on hold until he felt confident in its success. In the realm of Cold War masculinity, the buck stops here. But it was also obviously so much fun. Our guide populates his stories with tales of adventure, of midnight helicopter rides across the desert test site, hints at secrets he's not allowed to share, and reiterates the pleasures of commanding earth-shaking techno-science. "I could wreck twenty thousand marriages," he proclaims, the isolation and excitement of nuclear science at the NTS creating a culture of hard work, drink, and play. His commentary constantly registers the pleasure of the Cold War, the satisfaction of having a significant job, all the resources the nation-state could muster to support it, and a race with a real enemy to give military science meaning in everyday life.

Much of our tour focuses on remnants of the weapons effects tests from the 1950s, consisting of tanks, bridges, and buildings that were placed near a nuclear blast to see what would happen to them (see figure 4.1). The torn wreckage that remains documents a particular moment in the Cold War, when in order to understand how to fight a nuclear war with the Soviets, U.S. military officials actually waged one at the NTS. We look at twisted steel girders, whose original shape has been lost to the bomb and the shifting sands of the desert, and learn about kilotons and blast effects. But our guide continually emphasizes moments of survival over all. Ignoring that which was vaporized by the nuclear blast, he shows us a safe, which was filled with money and used in a 1957 nuclear effects test called Priscilla (see figure 4.2). The building was completely destroyed by the thirty-seven-kiloton explosion, but the safe and the money inside it, he notes with clear satisfaction, came through just fine. This was an important discovery in the early days of the Cold War, suggesting the monetary system might just survive a nuclear exchange after all.

Next, we visit the nuclear waste storage site at the NTS, which consists of an enormous trench filled with neatly stacked wooden boxes and metal drums filled with radioactive refuse (see figure 4.3). In the accompanying office building, we immediately encounter a poster-board presentation detailing how site workers mobilized to relocate a family of foxes that were living inside the nuclear waste dump. Thus, while asking questions about radioactive waste and pondering the 100,000-year threat posed by some nuclear materials at the NTS, we are presented with images of baby foxes and overtly documented signs of worker environmentalism. When we ask about radiation contamination, our guide steps in to say that he has walked "every inch of this site" and suffered "no ill effects." Here his own vitality is used as vibrant political commentary: thirty-five years at the test site without a cancer. Yes, there is some contamination at the test site, he acknowledges, but it is readily contained by the desert and poses no risk to the public.[3] He soon counters the reference to radioactive contamination with a story about a rattlesnake that attacked him one day while he was wandering the test site. It bit into his cowboy boot and would not let go. He fought back and then had the boots—snake included—bronzed. Dangers at the test site, in his presentation, are natural or international but not radioactive or technoscientific—*that's* well under control.

Our final stop on the tour is the Apple II site, where the U.S. military built a typical American suburb in 1955 for the sole purpose of detonating a nuclear bomb on it (see figures 4.4–4.8). A fire station, a school, a radio station, and a library, as well as a dozen homes, were built and furnished with everyday items (televisions, refrigerators, furniture, carpets, and linens). They were then stocked with food, populated with white mannequins, and neatly incinerated. Two remnants of the test remain: a brick ruin and what looks like an abandoned wooden house. Our guide describes the latter as "a real fixer-upper," but soon suggests that it wouldn't take much work to bring the house back to life after all (see figure 4.9). This is a curious place. The only real sign that something dramatic happened here is that the brick chimney

Figure 4.1. Railroad bridge section, Nevada Test Site (U.S. Department of Energy).
Figure 4.2. Priscilla detonation, June 24, 1957 (U.S. Department of Energy).
Figure 4.3. Nevada Test Site radioactive waste disposal facility (U.S. Department of Energy).

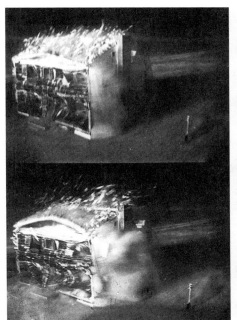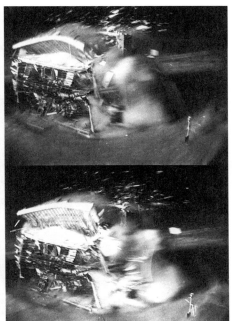

Figures 4.4–4.8. Nuclear blast effect sequence on test house at Nevada Test Site (U.S. Department of Energy).

Figure 4.9. Survival Town house today (U.S. Department of Energy).

is significantly cracked and off center, suggesting a powerful blast but only hinting at the force of the twenty-nine-kiloton bomb that was detonated one mile away, which vaporized the rest of "Survival Town." After the explosion, scientists held a feast in which they ate the food that survived the test, again, as our guide informs us, "suffering no ill effects." The food had been flown into the NTS by special military charter from Chicago and then cooked after the explosion. In the serious play of the test site, this was a kind of reverse last supper, where any signs of life after the nuclear explosion were celebrated as an absolute victory.

I ask our guide if the U.S. could survive a nuclear war. "Oh yes, I believe we could," he replies confidently, but at another moment he seems unsure, stating that a nuclear war would be, of course, an "act of insanity—the end of everything." This is the only ambiguity in a nearly perfect performance, a slight slippage about what the end would look like. The seamlessness of his narrative, in fact, is a register of his Cold War discipline: he neither confirms nor denies anything that makes work at the NTS suspect. To that end, he focuses on certain historical events in our tour while scrupulously avoiding others. His history of the test site, for example, is largely restricted to the era of aboveground nuclear testing (1951–62), after which U.S. nuclear detonations—and most of the visual consequences of nuclear explosions—went underground. This was, however, also the era of the most extreme environmental damage, when studies of nuclear blast effects included experiments not only on banks, tanks, houses, and airplanes, but also on soldiers (ordered to march toward the mushroom cloud) and on civilians (hit by the fallout). We know now that much of the continental U.S. was covered with radioactive fallout from aboveground testing at the NTS, contributing significantly to national thyroid cancer rates. But when I ask about fallout, he simply states, "That was before my time," and moves on in his narrative.

But isn't this simply desert modernism in its purest form, a profound belief in the possibility of an unending and conceptually clean progress, but one made possible only by tactical amnesias and sublimated technophilia? The Cold War nuclear complex required a constant regulating of discourse to retain its narrative purity. For just as the desert constantly threatens to overrun the activities of the test site, introducing sage and blowing sand where shiny metal should be, the cosmology of the Cold Warrior requires a constant self-monitoring, a patrolling of the cognitive field, to prevent multiplicity or ambiguity from taking root. As we leave the NTS, I ask our guide about the future of nuclear weapons after the Cold War. He states unequivocally that the U.S. will need to return to nuclear testing, that a world without an active NTS producing new and improved nuclear weapons is a more dangerous and uncertain world. "The Soviets," he begins, then corrects himself with a private half-smile that we hadn't seen previously, "I mean Russians," are still unpredictable and dangerous.

Our guide reiterates that developing nuclear weapons is a means of protecting the "free world," a means of producing stability and security in everyday life. However, his narrative does not acknowledge the local consequences of nuclear testing or assess the legacy of nuclear waste produced by that mission, for in a perceived fight to the death one does not have time to think about such things. Historical displacement and tactical erasure enable a strategic renarration of America's nuclear-powered national security in his presentation. Thus, the signs of nuclear nationalism revealed to us in our tour are not drawn from the current nuclear complex, which is busily reinventing itself and prospering after the Cold War, but are instead a displaced and carefully edited reiteration of 1950s nuclear culture. By the end of our visit to the NTS, it's difficult not to conclude that nuclear weapons, despite our guide's proclamations about the future, are now located in the far distant past, part of an abandoned project soon likely to be completely reclaimed by the desert sands. We have seen no real evidence that nuclear weapons remain the foundation of U.S. national security or a multibillion-dollar-a-year operation in the U.S., with budgets exceeding the height of the Cold War levels. The vast desert landscape of the test site, combined with the aged quality of the buildings we visit and the lack of any substantive sign of ongoing nuclear science, reduce the scale of the nuclear project at the NTS and, seemingly, its claim on the future.

In the end, this may be a public relations tactic (a strategy to reduce public concern about activities at the test site during a time of institutional change), but it might also be one structural effect of desert modernism. For it might well be that those inhabiting the center of this kind of technopolitical project cannot assess their own history, or terms for being, nor recognize their own historical excess. For that we might have to look more closely at the borders, look to neighboring communities that live with the effects of nuclear nationalism but are excluded from the internal logics of the national security state. In other words, we might have to turn to those who reflect back the mission of the NTS but who do so from radically different perspectives, revealing nuclear weapons science at the NTS to be productive of far more than a particular form of international relations.

On the western periphery of the NTS, overlooking the desert proving grounds where nuclear devices were detonated throughout the Cold War, is Yucca Mountain, which since the 1980s has been in preparation to become the principal nuclear waste storage site in the United States (see figure 4.10).[4] If the narrative of weapons scientists at the NTS presents desert modernism in its positive form (that is, still invested in a conceptually pure narrative of progress), then the Yucca Mountain Project represents its flip side, an arena where the dream space of absolute technical mastery and control of nature slips out of joint. For in this mountain, a spiritual center for the displaced indigenous nations of the desert region, the industrial waste of a nuclear-powered state proves to be uncontainable, exceeding the power of the nation-state that produced it to predict its future effects. From a distant Atlantic coast, the DOE has ruled that any permanent nuclear waste depository in the U.S. must have an operative plan that would make it safe for ten thousand years. Such a plan is unprecedented in human history, though still accounting for only a fraction of the life span of the most dangerous nuclear materials, which will remain radioactive for hundreds of thousands of years. Nevertheless, a ten-thousand-year safety plan—consider the astonishing confidence this regulation reveals, as well as the certainty it registers about the future and the near-eternal reliability of the U.S. nation-state.

We arrive at Yucca Mountain from Las Vegas at midmorning, just in time for a safety lecture before plunging into the thirty-foot-diameter cave that U-turns in a great arch through the center of the mountain (see figure 4.11). We don red hard hats, put on huge fluorescent orange earplugs and eye protection, and strap an emergency breathing filter around our waists. We have been told to wear long-sleeve shirts and good shoes. In our briefing on emergency procedures, we are told that in case of a fire we should use our breathing filters even though they might scorch our lungs. Weighted down with our awkward new gear, we move slowly past the work trucks and walk single file along the railway tracks into the darkness of the tunnel. Deafening machine noise mixed with the long shadows produced by artificial light and the smell of stale earth greet us. We walk about seventy-five yards into the mountain and move into a large chamber off the main tunnel.

Here, we meet the tunnel engineer, a middle-aged man who wears his protective gear with practiced ease, and learn about the technical aspects of the Yucca Mountain Project. He explains to us how the waste is to be shipped to the site in barrels and where and how it will be stacked within the mountain,

Figure 4.10. Yucca Mountain (U.S. Department of Energy).

Figure 4.11. Entrance to the Yucca Mountain Project (U.S. Department of Energy).

Figure 4.12. Yucca Mountain Project tunnel interior (U.S. Department of Energy).

as well as contingencies for retrieving specific barrels once stored. Our tunnel engineer is nervous talking with us, the intense politics around the Yucca Mountain Project having undoubtedly brought many confrontations to his workplace. He immediately has my sympathy, for he is not a public relations expert or a nuclear policy maker; he builds things, tunnels to be precise (see figure 4.12). Shouting over the machine noise echoing through the mile-long project, he seems to be most comfortable providing technical information about the tunnel itself, which he does in great detail. Eventually, our attention moves to the chamber walls and ceiling, which are covered with countless metal spikes, secured by netting. It looks as though project engineers feared that the entire surface of the cave might crumble and sought to shore it up with hundreds of metal spikes each set about a foot apart. A strange place for a public conversation about nuclear safety, the overwrought performance of the cave surface begs immediate questions about the nature of its technology as well as its long-term stability.

The engineer, who has seemed tentative up to this point in our conversation, lights up with newfound enthusiasm at our questions. "Well you see, there are two kinds of rock: good rock and bad rock. *This* [he says, looking around] is bad rock." We learn that bad rock is that which crumbles and needs mechanical reinforcement, while good rock is internally stable and reliable from an engineering point of view. Yucca Mountain, he tells us, has both good and bad rock, and the tunnel has been engineered through use of rock bolts to compensate for both. "There are three different kinds of rock bolts," the tunnel engineer offers, and then, in a moment of pure techno-scientific reverie, proceeds to introduce us to the engineering cosmology of the rock bolt. In the next few minutes, we learn that rock bolts differ by length, thickness, head type, and means of insertion. Some can be removed; some cannot. Some are stronger than others and are used on certain kinds of rock but not on others. We learn that rock bolts are a very important technology and that this tunnel is largely dependent upon them. With alarming ease, in fact, all the debates about the scientific viability of Yucca Mountain as a nuclear waste site, the twenty-plus years of acrimonious technical and political debate, the hundreds of thousands of pages of technical reports that argue with specificity the potential risks and advantages of the site, the entire ten-thousand-year modernist plan for ensuring safety at the site are reduced to the (conceptual and engineering) power of the rock bolt. Rock bolts, a brilliantly simple technology, present desert modernism in its primordial form, for they seem to offer the possibility of holding Yucca Mountain together, of disciplining the earth itself through the millennia.

I ask the tunnel engineer if the ten-thousand-year safety plan required by federal law for the Yucca Mountain Project has affected his engineering in any way, if it has made this tunnel different or more difficult than other tunnels he has built. "No, it hasn't," he replies testily. Startled by his answer, I continue, "Do you ever feel like you are building something for the ages here, like the pyramids in Egypt, because it will last for thousands of years?" "I don't like to think about those kinds of things," he replies. Then, looking me directly in the eyes, he says, "I'll guarantee this tunnel for one hundred years. After that I hope they'll have someplace else to put this stuff." *After that I hope they'll have someplace else to put this stuff.* It soon becomes clear that the tunnel engineers do not believe the ten-thousand-year plan is attainable. In fact, they readily dismiss the ten-thousand-year program as a product of a political, not a technoscientific, process. We also learn from our guide that Yucca Mountain is on top of several major fault lines and that the underground water supply for much of the Southwest runs underneath the project. Neither our guide nor our tunnel engineer will say that Yucca Mountain is a good place to permanently store nuclear waste; they just say it will happen and that much of the reason for it is politics: there is simply nowhere else to put the nation's Cold War–era radioactive waste. As the zeros drop off the ten-thousand-year master plan, the Yucca Mountain Project assumes for many of us the appearance of a national hoax, and its desert modernism once seemingly perfected fractures irredeemably.

We leave Yucca Mountain knowing that the ten-thousand-year safety plan enables a very public secret.[5] The narrative of absolute technical mastery and control of nature, propagated by work on nuclear weapons at the NTS and now necessary to legitimate the power of the state to deal with its nuclear waste, is revealed to be a political tactic at Yucca Mountain and not a technoscientific reality. The excesses of nuclear nationalism, the tons of nuclear waste located all around the country, thus remain unpredictable despite the rhetorical effort by the state to contain them within a ten-thousand-year institutional plan. What will happen a thousand years from now at Yucca Mountain, and who will be around to watch over the radioactive waste of the twentieth century? Can we imagine a nation-state that lasts a thousand years, let alone ten thousand?

Leaving the Iron Age technology of the rock bolt to grapple with the unpredictable products of the nuclear age, the future is being reinvented at Yucca Mountain through a condition of unending fallout. The nuclear apocalypticism of the Cold War, the fear of a sudden fiery end that propelled nuclear weapons science and the creation of deterrence theory, assumed that the nation was going to end abruptly with a nuclear flash, requiring radical action in the here and now. The Yucca Mountain Project, however, now assumes an eternal nation-state, one that will diligently uphold twentieth-century laws, and watch over twentieth-century nuclear waste, across the millennia, in perpetuity. Thus, the nuclear waste storage project at Yucca Mountain is where the desert modernism of the NTS formally confronts its own apocalyptic excess and, in an effort to control that excess, is expanded—exponentially— to the point of self-contradiction and failure. The same modernist logic that made the nuclear complex blind to its own fallout in the first place, to nuclear contamination in all its material and settler colonial forms, continues to inform the Yucca Mountain Project, which is now attempting a massive compensation for the unprecedented physical effects of the Cold War nuclear complex by maintaining the fiction of a ten-thousand-year operative plan.

But in this American desert, reality is mandated not only by modernist planning and official discourse, but also by wild processes. Over the millennia,

Yucca Mountain is in motion, literally a living being, subject to tectonic shifts, erosion, and vast planetary forces. In the Yucca Mountain Project, we see desert modernism transformed into a kind of mystic vision, an arena in which human control is assumed to be eternal, even as our tunnel engineer articulates the tenuous power of the rock bolt as emblem, exemplar, and limit of modernity. The poetic call of the rock bolt may be the conceptual limit of Yucca Mountain, but the logic that supports it—the search for a master narrative that denies the uncontainability of the future—proliferates in modern American life and, like the unpredictable course of nuclear materials, radiates, catching individuals outside the center in its mutating glow.

Paranoid Surveillance

If nuclearism at the NTS represents the center of a certain kind of modernist planning, of big science protected and enabled by government secrecy, what is it like to be removed, displaced, or disappeared, or to live just on the outside, to be surrounded by nuclear nationalism but denied access to its internal logics or lines of power?[6] One need drive only ninety minutes north of Las Vegas to find just such an outpost on the frontier of desert modernism. In the little town of Rachel, which consists of a dozen or so mobile homes parked on the side of a two-lane desert highway, one encounters an important cultural side effect of Cold War military technoscience (see figure 4.13). Apparently surrounded by wilderness, the desert calm of Rachel—population one hundred—is broken primarily by the military aircraft that fly overhead from Nellis Air Force Base, the NTS, and the mysterious Area 51, also known as Dreamland, where stealth fighter technology was covertly invented, some locals say, by a process of reverse-engineering crashed UFOs. On the outer periphery of military-industrial airspace, Rachel is a center for conspiracy theorists and UFO believers, a point of pilgrimage for those caught up in another aspect of American desert modernism. In Rachel an important cultural legacy of the Cold War intermingling of secrecy, security, and science at the NTS becomes visible. Indeed, we can see in Rachel how a century of revolutionary technological progress has combined with a half century of intense government secrecy to permeate everyday life, encouraging those on the periphery of national security to assume the existence of a secret master narrative that controls everything, one that is busy regulating and reinventing the terms of existence from a hidden center of power.

We go into the Little A'Le'Inn Café, where you can buy conspiracy theory and a hamburger. The walls are covered with hundreds of photographs of

Figure 4.13. Highway to Rachel, Nevada.

Figure 4.14. Photographs of UFOs on the wall of the Little A'Le'Inn Café in Rachel, Nevada.

fuzzy disk-shaped things that might be space ships (see figure 4.14), and talk here frequently turns to tracking the signs of cover-up, of misinformation, of why "they" are here and "what's going on." Here you can discuss government black budgets and black helicopters: are they disguised UFOS or part of a covert military project? You can explore the latest theories on cattle mutilations in the desert West or on human abductions, covert genetic experimentation, and the coming New World Orders. Who is secretly behind the United Nations, the International Monetary Fund, and the Trilateral Commission, and when will they reveal their true purpose? Was the Cold War really a battle with the Soviets or merely a way for both countries to secretly arm themselves against an invading extraterrestrial source? Is the current fascination with UFOS a giant misinformation campaign to hide The Truth or is the government slowly preparing us for news that They have been here for a long, long time? Whose soldiers are training under the cover of the desert night and using that vast underground network of tunnels connecting

U.S. military sites to stay hidden during the daytime? Why did JFK need to be silenced, and which government entity invented HIV-AIDS? And above all—what's coming next?

While we eat lunch in the café and discuss the strange desert context of life in Rachel (a curious mix of pure western Americana and paranoid utopia), a conspiracy theorist takes center stage, literally. He begins singing country western songs through a microphone while playing an electric organ. One of the two waitresses joins him for a song. They are having a good time, and the public space has been made sweetly intimate by their performance. Between tunes, he introduces himself and spins a conspiracy.

I recognize him, having seen one of his self-financed videos on UFOS. On tape he argues that all UFO sightings are masterminded by an "international cabal" of men who are planning to take over the world. He believes UFOS are human-made, a ruse to distract people from the real conspiracy, from the men who are positioning themselves to take control of everyday life and implement a "new world order." He warns that sometime in the near future a "major UFO incident" will be staged at Area 51, a carefully planned media distraction to enable the global takeover. Today, he has some new information he wants to share, identifying perhaps the first salvo in this upcoming campaign of public misdirection and conspiracy. He holds up an enlarged color photograph, an aerial image of a parking lot, which is surrounded by trees and populated with several olive-green U.S. Army vehicles and one discordant bright yellow Ryder moving van. "This photograph was taken in April of 1995 at a military base near Oklahoma City a few days before the Oklahoma City bombing." Then he holds up another photograph of the same parking lot, same visual perspective, same olive-green army jeeps but no Ryder moving van. "This photograph was taken after the Oklahoma City bombing. Now, I think this is very interesting. Now what is a Ryder moving van doing in a military parking lot? I'm not saying the government was directly involved in the bombing of the Oklahoma federal building, but I think this is very interesting. Before the bombing of the Murrah Federal Building there is a Ryder van on the military base, and after, it is gone. I think this is very significant." Having set the conspiratorial narrative in motion, he returns to his music, leaving his audience to contemplate what it would mean to their everyday lives if a secret organization with access to U.S. Army facilities had bombed a U.S. federal building and implicated a white supremacist group for the crime as part of a calculated plan to take over the world.

Conspiracy theorists are one of the unexpected side effects of the desert modernism pursued at the NTS and Area 51. Excluded from the internal logics of state power, but well aware of the effects of these military sites—radioactive fallout, a militarized space, lights in the night sky—conspiracy theorists mobilize to fill in the gaps in their knowledge. The conspiracy theorist patrols everyday life for the signs of a hidden master narrative, a master narrative that he endlessly constructs out of the strange details of modern life, attempting to make visible that which is hidden, making rational the national cultural excesses within desert modernism. The very lack of proof becomes evidence of conspiracy as the personal observations of a vast cross-section of America sees that which the government denies. The people of Rachel, for example, live only a few miles from Area 51, a military base that everyone knows about. Some residents have even worked at the base and trace their current health problems to toxic exposures on the job. For years, one of the best, and most readily available, photographs of Area 51 was made by a Cold War–era Soviet surveillance satellite (see figure 4.15). Yet despite the worker histories and the toxic lawsuits, the Soviet photographs and a significant presence in American popular culture (as, for example, in the film *Independence Day*), the U.S. Air Force will only acknowledge an "operational presence" in the Groom Lake area.[7] Officially, Area 51 does not exist.[8]

For citizens in Rachel, the engine of modernity has become a giant conspiracy, requiring those who want to "live free" in the desert West to track the signs of military-industrial life that impinge upon everyday life, and search for the truth behind the cover-up and misinformation. It should not be surprising that places like Rachel exist. A half century of government policy to "neither confirm nor deny" questions about nuclear nationalism has forced the question of security to remain open and unanswered. An ironic effect, the effort to control technical information about military science in a world of competing nation-states, has produced a proliferating discursive field where citizens who confront the effects of nuclear nationalism are left to rely on their own imaginations for information. The reality of black budgets and apocalyptic technologies, the possibilities of a ten-thousand-year safety plan and its obvious propaganda, the history of nuclear fallout and covert human plutonium experiments on U.S. citizens, and always the wild new technologies that arrive unannounced (especially during wartime)—all of these realities have demonstrated that government planning can indeed take the shape of conspiracy. The problem in Rachel is how to negotiate that knowledge, how to resolve the effects on everyday life of living side-by-side with covert and dangerous government projects, how to make sense of it all with only the peripheral effects and those strange lights in the night sky as muse. In this way, the citizens of Rachel present merely the displaced mirror image of nuclear

Figure 4.15. Satellite image of Area 51 (Terraserver.com and Spin-2).

nationalism, for the logics informing work at the N T S, Yucca Mountain, Area 51, and life in Rachel all assume that the world is ultimately knowable, that there are no coincidences in modernity, and that careful observation of the details of everyday life can reveal the hidden master narrative of existence. This fixation on the scripting of appearances in the desert West, however, now exceeds the logics of the national security state, evolving into a resilient new kind of American expressive culture—apocalyptic, narcissistic, sensational.

Delirious Excess

One of the most remarkable attributes of the N T S is its location.[9] Founded on the need for concealment (of military technoscience and environmental ruin), it is nonetheless bordered by the one city in the world most famous for its embrace of extravagant public display. Contrary to the N T S, where every act is supposedly regulated by a national security state, and where the foremost experience of place involves fences, gates, and guards, Las Vegas is known as the town where quite literally anything goes (gambling, prostitution, the Mafia), a place where there are few barriers to the imagination, and the nation-state is somehow conceptually absent. If there is a seam in the structure of desert modernity that links the introverted world of the N T S and the extroverted world of Las Vegas, it should be visible in any number of sites, but perhaps most powerfully in the cultural exemplars of Las Vegas itself. We enter just such a site on our tour through the afterimages of American Cold War culture, the Liberace Museum, which is located in a shopping complex just off Tropicana Avenue.[10] Inside this museum/shrine, one can move through room after room filled with the material traces of a Cold War life uniquely devoted to visual excess. Near the end of our visit, our senses increasingly dulled and bored with ostentatious display, we are nevertheless stopped dead in our tracks, caught in the shimmering reflection of a room filled with an entirely new form of desert modernism. Dazzled by the sheer visual power of tens of millions of glimmering sequins, we stare at Liberace's fantastic suits and are forced to contemplate how Liberace, and the broader Las Vegas culture of excess he embodies, participates in the desert modernism of the Cold War (see figure 4.16).

As one of the most popular attractions in Las Vegas, the Liberace Museum, which houses the entertainer's famous costumes, his jewel-encrusted pianos and candelabras, his custom-built cars, and other mementos from a career that resides within the temporal limits of the Cold War, provides a unique window into American Cold War culture. Indeed, Liberace, Las Vegas, and the N T S were structurally linked right from the very beginning. The N T S

Figure 4.16. Liberace in sequins (courtesy of the Liberace Foundation for the Performing and Creative Arts, https://liberace.org/).

opened in 1951, about the time Liberace first played Las Vegas, and by the mid-1950s the two biggest shows in Nevada were the nuclear explosions at the test site and Liberace, who by then was making $50,000 a week at the brand-new Riviera casino performing in a black tuxedo jacket studded with 1,328,000 shimmering sequins. We can begin to see here how the serious politics of concealment at the NTS and the seemingly frivolous politics of display in Las Vegas are mutually reinforcing, sharing in a common desert modernity. Indeed, a favorite pastime of that era was to take a cocktail to the top of a Las Vegas casino in the early morning hours, and from that vantage point search the northern horizon for a flash of light or the shape of a mushroom cloud emanating from the test site, and thereby offer a toast to America's ascendancy to superpower status. Could it possibly be that Liberace, whose career is a both a Cold War and a Las Vegas artifact, never partook in that premier spectacle of the nuclear age?

Whereas the public/secret world of the desert nuclear complex, as we have seen, denies its own excess, the public/private world Liberace created so successfully for himself delights in presenting a delirious excess. Linked with that other icon of Cold War masculinity, JFK, Liberace's fame was, in part, drawn not only from a public fascination with his sexuality but also from the explicit constructedness of his public persona, which constantly offered audiences the chance to participate in the act of its construction. Performing at a moment when to be gay was to occupy the structural position of the communist in the U.S. (and therefore to be subject to all the assaults of the McCarthy era), Liberace successfully sued newspapers that questioned his heterosexuality in print, even as he lived with male partners. (And we might note here that it was only in 1993 that U.S. security clearance guidelines for those working within the nuclear complex were revised to take homosexuality off the list of things that make a potential employee, by definition, a national security risk.) Liberace's over-the-top stage performances and fantastic costumes, however, constantly registered his acute awareness of the normalizing structures in Cold War life, and his charm was, in part, how explicit his scripting of appearance was, enabling audience after audience to enjoy his overt class transgressions and mimetic gender play without feeling in any way challenged by them.

In the realm of Cold War masculinity, Liberace's life reveals something important, both inverting an imagined white, heterosexual norm and, through expressive cultural performance, becoming a site of release, where the excesses of Cold War identity politics were put on stage and manipulated for pleasure. As an intensely private person, who paradoxically made a living displaying himself as spectacle, Liberace rejected the Cold War logics of white, middle-class masculinity that emphasized self-sacrifice and capitalist production above all. This is evident both in his stage persona and in the nature of his musical performance. Liberace comingled musical genres, high classical and contemporary popular music, in his stage show, cutting and pasting musical types as a gag. Mixing works by Liszt, Chopin, and Debussy with the "Beer Barrel Polka" and "Cement Mixer (Put-ti Put-ti)," Liberace played with the division between classical and popular music and showed a keen attention to the power of transgressing, and marking the artificiality of, such boundaries. In his early performances, one of Liberace's famous acts was to play duets with recordings of famous classical pianists on stage. His perfect bodily synchronization with the virtuoso recordings of Vladimir Horowitz, Arthur Rubinstein, and other classical artists demonstrated for all his musical technique, but also his ability to mimic official culture, thus drawing attention to the constructed discourse of high classical art. His fantastic financial success and his unrelenting public display of wealth cut against serious logics of Cold War consumption and suggested that money could be fun. Not tied to serious art production, mocking notions of class standing, rejecting the need to produce a traditional nuclear family (the most prominent woman in his life remained his mother, who was ritually evoked in every performance), while ridiculing Cold War notions of utilitarian consumption through his baroque lifestyle, Liberace offered relief from the seriousness of the Cold War nuclear standoff while nonetheless sharing in its (desert) modernity.

So, one need not be a conspiracy theorist to wonder today at the vast global intrigue that must have been in place to bring down two exemplars of Cold War masculinity on that same terrible November night in 1963. As news of John F. Kennedy's assassination swept the nation, Liberace promised to put special energy into that evening's performance to console his audience. However, his own life was soon put into jeopardy by his fabulous wardrobe—which, quite simply, tried to kill him. In the midst of that evening's memorial performance and while the nation mourned, Liberace collapsed, having been poisoned by the dry-cleaning chemicals used on his costumes. The toxic shock brought on by the chemicals sent Liberace into complete kidney failure. Unconscious, and on life support, he was eventually given last rites and thought lost.

In its pure form, I have suggested, desert modernism is necessarily blind to its own excess. And just as the toxins produced by the nuclear complex are somehow conceptually absent from the narrative of our nuclear weapons scientists at the NTS, so too was Liberace's brush with a toxic death taken by him not as an invitation for critique, requiring at least a moment of reflection,

Figure 4.17. Liberace on stage (courtesy of the Liberace Foundation for the Performing and Creative Arts, https://liberace.org/).

but instead as a new authorization of his act. Liberace claimed afterward that in a vision, a white-robed nun had not only healed him but had actually blessed his love of opulent display. After this near-death experience, his outfits only got more lavish, and he embraced his love of visual excess with no restraint. Indeed, Liberace sought to reinvent himself with each new costume and was soon fighting a Cold War of his own with entertainers like Elvis Presley and other Las Vegas superpowers for command of the most over-the-top performance. Liberace's love of sequins continued to escalate; by the 1970s, his sequined outfits had attained truly epic proportions—often weighing over two hundred pounds (see figure 4.17). Sequins serve no purpose other than to be pretty. But consider their power when sewn together in the hundreds of thousands: they shimmer brilliantly, becoming luminous. To achieve this visual effect, Liberace performed nightly in sequined suits that could, like his poisonous outfits, certainly kill him. The nature of this public display, its perilous tightrope act, was always a meta-commentary on Liberace himself, who was always on the verge of crashing, of turning into a spectacular ruin.

Figure 4.18. Underground nuclear test craters, Frenchman's Flat, Nevada Test Site (U.S. Department of Energy).

In this light, his Las Vegas career provides a distinctive index of American Cold War culture, in which the hyperproduction of nuclear weapons (seventy thousand in all, enough to destroy every major city on the planet dozens of times over) also registered a national fascination with excess and display, and involved a precarious dance with death. The shared nature of this desert modernism allowed Liberace's stage performances in Las Vegas and the technoscientific work at the NTS to mirror image each other, as both provided distractions from the desert landscape (and from each other) through specific forms of techno-social power. It is important to remember that (after Hiroshima and Nagasaki) the U.S. nuclear arsenal was officially designed never to be used; it was intended merely to display American might to the Soviets and thereby to be a tool in foreign relations. Thus, the Cold War nuclear explosions at the NTS were not merely tests, *they were the entire performance*, communicating to the world the U.S. possession of, and commitment to, weapons of mass destruction (see figure 4.18). From this perspective, the Cold War logics of containment that energized the U.S. nuclear economy also produced a powerful scripting of appearance that today can be read as a kind of expressive national cultural performance. To suggest that Liberace shared in the logic of this Cold War display, inverting and revealing its excess, making playful that which was so deadly serious (particularly in the 1950s when he began), and reinventing Las Vegas in the process is only to wonder at the danger and discipline required to perform in a life-threatening mass of sequins.

5

THE BILLBOARD CAMPAIGN

In the domestic realm of U.S. politics, the nuclear weapons complex has always maintained two extreme attributes: phenomenal cost and social invisibility. While seemingly opposed, these aspects are actually reinforcing, a structural effect of compartmentalized secrecy, patronage networks, and an implicit nuclear security consensus among U.S. policymakers. Stephen Schwartz (1998, 3) has documented that between 1940 and 1996 the U.S. spent at least $5.8 trillion on nuclear weapons. This makes the bomb the third largest federal expenditure since 1940, ranking just after nonnuclear military spending and Social Security—accounting for roughly eleven cents out of every federal dollar spent. Yet, despite this colossal investment, and the widespread distribution of nuclear production, testing, and waste sites across the continental United States, most Americans have little or no knowledge of the history or continuing investments in weapons of mass destruction by the United States. It remains a disturbing truth that most Americans can say more about North Korea's, Iran's, or Iraq's nuclear ambitions (which, in 2003, were the target of a public U.S. policy of preemptive warfare) than those of the United States. Most would be surprised to learn that the 1990s witnessed not a post–Cold War movement away from nuclear weapons, but rather the establishment of a new nuclear status quo in the United States, one requiring a massive reinvestment in the U.S. nuclear program. Nuclear weapons budgets at the national laboratories, for example, have exceeded their Cold War averages for decades, even though the mission is not to produce new nuclear weapons but to maintain existing ones. In short, the most active nuclear weapons program on the planet has always been, and remains, in the United States, and much of it is located in New Mexico. For New Mexicans committed to disarmament and peace activism, the dilemma of the post–Cold War period has thus been how to engage this resurgent U.S. nuclear project in a way that breaks the structures of silencing and patronage that keep America's investments in weapons of mass destruction from public view.

Beginning in 1998, visitors to New Mexico could encounter one of the most direct and imaginative efforts to engage New Mexico's nuclear economy simply by driving out of the Albuquerque International Sunport. Positioned on the main exit route from the airport, a large billboard confronted motorists with an image of a rainbow-enhanced desert and the words "Welcome to New Mexico: America's Nuclear Weapons Colony" (see figure 5.1). Seeking to defamiliarize the desert landscape through political shock, the billboard both evokes and inverts the familiar portrait of New Mexico as the Land of Enchantment, a zone of pristine nature and exotic multiculturalism. A website address on the billboard—www.lasg.org—serves as both signature and invitation for viewers to learn more about the scale of the U.S. nuclear project in New Mexico (which includes two of the three national weapons laboratories, the largest missile testing range in the continental United States, the largest arsenal of U.S. nuclear weapons, and the most active U.S. nuclear waste dumps). By repurposing a centrally located commercial space, the billboard challenges residents and visitors alike to recognize an invisible presence in New Mexico, one that colonizes the austere beauty of the high desert landscape with the nuclear science, toxicity, and militarism of a global superpower (see Masco 2006).

The welcome sign was merely the first salvo in an eight-year billboard campaign orchestrated by the Los Alamos Study Group (LASG), a nonproliferation and peace activism group formed in the waning days of the Cold War.

Figure 5.1. "Welcome to New Mexico: America's Nuclear Weapons Colony," Los Alamos Study Group billboard.

As one of the most vocal nuclear watchdog groups in New Mexico, the LASG has vigorously challenged post–Cold War nuclear weapons science at Los Alamos National Laboratory while promoting public education about the accruing environmental effects of the greater nuclear complex. Greg Mello, the cofounder and director of the LASG, explained to me that the billboards were a response to a lack of public conversation about the post–Cold War evolution of the nuclear complex in New Mexico. They were also a reaction to the high cost of advertising in newspapers, or on radio and television, all of which have an episodic nature. Billboards could make a long-term, highly visible statement at, as Mello calculates it, "one-tenth of a cent per viewer." Billboards thus offered a new kind of political space that could perform a complex set of ideological tasks in an economical manner. From the start, the goals of the LASG billboard project were to puncture the normality of the nuclear economy by linking New Mexico's two leading industries—tourism and nuclear weapons—and to present a stable and highly visible space for political dissent and nuclear critique. For Mello, the project was also intended to "slow down" the media space in order to encourage public contemplation in a largely commuter and tourist economy, thereby transforming New Mexico's unique road culture into a new conceptual space for political critique. As part of a larger activist effort in New Mexico to "use the tourists to get rid of the plutonium, or the plutonium to get rid of the tourists," the LASG project, as described by Mello, is interested in provoking a "more enlightened form of tourism," one that could ultimately contribute to the LASG's larger environmental and nonproliferation efforts.

Placed for maximum visibility along the main thoroughfares and highways that connect Albuquerque to Santa Fe and ultimately to Los Alamos, the LASG billboards speak directly to inhabitants of the 25,000 cars that travel Interstate 25 daily. Mello told me the LASG had specific audiences initially in mind for the billboard campaign, namely laboratory management, state and federal politicians, and particularly new recruits to the weapons program who might be visiting for job interviews. By visually disrupting the assumed social consensus over the role of the nuclear economy in New Mexico, the LASG seeks to document for policy makers and employees evidence of local resistance and hope for an alternative nuclear future. The billboard project is also a direct response to decreasing access to policy makers and laboratory personnel after a brief period of post–Cold War openness. After a series of security scandals at Los Alamos (see Masco 2002) and the start of the War on Terror, expanding secrecy within the nuclear complex forced activists to seek an alternative public sphere to mobilize for change.

Pursuing their political agenda in visual statements 48 by 18 feet wide, the billboard campaign has raised a wide range of provocative issues. The billboards provided a direct counterdiscourse to the U.S. nuclear project in New Mexico, while more recent efforts have responded to the expanding forms of U.S. militarism under the George W. Bush administration's War on Terror. Evoking the 1930s Works Progress Administration aesthetic that is featured in much of the tourist literature about New Mexico, the second LASG billboard asked, "New Mexico: #1 in Nuclear Weapons, #1 in Poverty— Coincidence?" (see figure 5.2). Here, the LASG challenges the primary local justification for the nuclear weapons complex—that it provides jobs for New Mexicans. But while Los Alamos National Laboratory currently maintains an annual budget of over $2 billion, New Mexico has for decades competed for the title of poorest state in America. Marshaling equally alarming statistics about violent crime, drug abuse, suicide, alcoholism, and the condition of the public school system in New Mexico, the LASG has argued that the nuclear economy has actually prevented other sustainable industries from developing, creating a highly distorted regional economy dangerously reliant on federal investments. For Mello, New Mexico is "held hostage" by Wash-

Figure 5.2. "New Mexico: #1 in Nuclear Weapons, #1 in Poverty—Coincidence?," Los Alamos Study Group billboard.

ington, DC, because of its poverty. Consequently, New Mexico is part of that rural American economic space that now relies on toxicity, vice, incarceration, and industrial livestock, or, as Mello puts it, the "four Ps—plutonium, poker, prisons, and pigs." By arguing that the nuclear complex prevents the development of a sustainable regional economy, the "Coincidence" billboard also moves the discussion of what constitutes security from the realm of geopolitics to the terms of everyday life.

The LASG billboard campaign has sought to reveal the linkages between global and local economies, and to provoke motorists to consider how nuclear nationalism participates in a larger political and moral sphere. For example, one billboard presented a color image of a mushroom cloud on a stark black background, declaring in bright orange letters: "New Mexico: World Capital of Weapons of Mass Destruction" (see figure 5.3). By identifying New Mexico as the center of the global nuclear complex, the billboard challenged the tourist portrait of the region as idyllic desert landscape and multicultural paradise. The LASG has also sought to link the local nuclear economy to the global nonproliferation project through direct actions. Sponsoring a citizens' inspection team modeled on the United Nations arms inspectors who worked in Iraq in the 1990s, the group has repeatedly demanded entrance to U.S. nuclear facilities in New Mexico in order to certify that the United States is living up to the terms of the 1968 Nuclear Nonproliferation Treaty

Figure 5.3. "New Mexico: World Capital of Weapons of Mass Destruction," Los Alamos Study Group billboard.

(in which all signatories agreed to pursue the end of the arms race and commit to eliminating nuclear weapons).[1] By drawing attention to the expanding U.S. commitment to nuclear weapons in the post–Cold War period, the LASG has argued for a coherent global policy for nuclear disarmament and peace-making, one that begins by rejecting the assumptions of American exceptionalism that currently support the U.S. nuclear arsenal.

The LASG billboard campaign sought not only to provide basic information about U.S. nuclear projects in New Mexico but also to ground that knowledge in a broader moral economy. Another early billboard presented a large white dove on a blood-red background alongside text declaring, "Nuclear Weapons are incompatible with the peace we seek for the 21st Century—The Vatican." By quoting the Vatican, the LASG sought to mobilize the largely Catholic population of northern New Mexico to consider the moral implications of participating in the production of weapons of mass destruction. More aggressively, the LASG has also sought to make New Mexicans uniquely responsible for the nuclear age itself. Another billboard, which also quickly became a popular bumper sticker in New Mexico, declared alongside a mushroom cloud, "It Started Here, Let's Stop It Here." In each case, the call is for New Mexicans to take responsibility for their participation in the production of nuclear danger—to replace the status quo logics of national security with an ethical investment in and commitment to a peaceful, nonnuclear future. The billboard campaign has also appealed directly to residents' fear of nuclear hazards. In 2002, a bright red billboard presented a leaking barrel of nuclear waste, declaring in large white letters, "Close Los Alamos Nuclear Waste Dump Now" (see figure 5.4). Here, the LASG provokes viewers to see Los Alamos National Laboratory not only as a regional employer and high-

Figure 5.4. "Close Los Alamos Nuclear Waste Dump Now," Los Alamos Study Group billboard.

tech research facility, but also as an industrial environmental hazard that is colonizing both land and the region's future with nuclear waste and the ever-present potential for nuclear accidents.

In linking the global and the local, the tourist and military-industrial, the environmental and the social, the billboard campaign has turned a purely capitalist and largely banal space—usually the stuff of accident lawyers, casinos, and car dealerships in the desert West—into a space of political mobilization and subversive critique, one literally integrated into the New Mexican landscape. In January 2003, the LASG expanded its efforts to provide a direct counterdiscourse to the George W. Bush administration's expanding War on Terror. The first billboard presented a terrifying image of an Air Force bomber releasing a load of cluster bombs beside the text, "Do Unto Others . . . ?" (see figures 5.5 and 5.6). Mello told me that this sign was directed at the conservative Christian coalition supporting the Bush administration. Seeking to remind the administration of biblical doctrine, the billboard asks if the Golden Rule is compatible with the evolving global military logics and counterterrorism of the United States. A subsequent billboard challenged an implicit rationale for the war, declaring, "No Blood for Oil" in white letters on a red background. Within weeks of the start of the 2003 Iraq War, the sign was vandalized, the heavy vinyl torn so that the previously posted advertisement was visible, adding an ironic "Cool Summer Idea" to the antiwar message (see figure 5.7).

Figures 5.5. and 5.6. "Do Unto Others . . . ?," Los Alamos Study Group billboard.

Figure 5.7. "No Blood for Oil," Los Alamos Study Group billboard.

Figure 5.8. "Weapons of Mass Destruction? Look Closer to Home," Los Alamos Study Group billboard.

Figure 5.9. "Weapons of Mass Destruction? Iraq: 0; Albuquerque: 2000," Los Alamos Study Group yard sign.

In May 2003, the first post–Iraq War billboard went up on the outskirts of Albuquerque asking provocatively, "Weapons of Mass Destruction? Look closer to home" (see figure 5.8). This billboard was not simply a reply to the official rationale for the U.S. invasion of Iraq (that Saddam Hussein was stockpiling nuclear, biological, and chemical weapons) or to the inability of U.S. authorities to find those weapons after occupying Iraq; the billboard was also a statement about the evolving shape of U.S. nuclear policy. In its 2002 Nuclear Posture Review, the U.S. Department of Defense expressed a desire for several new types of nuclear weapons and projected an increasing role for nuclear weapons in U.S. military planning in the twenty-first century.

The War on Terror has been constituted around fear of an unsourced atomic bomb but is also coterminous with increased U.S. nuclear investments and a massive rise in U.S. military spending: in the 2000s, the United States was responsible for almost half of all global military expenditures (see Masco 2014). The vast sums the U.S. now spends annually on its defense budget will likely support New Mexico's weapons scientists for another generation—reproducing the structures that the LASG has been mobilizing to critique. However, as the billboard campaign has argued from the start, escalating U.S. militarism can be answered only by a clear accounting of its social, environmental, economic, moral, and geopolitical costs. It is not surprising, then, that the billboard campaign took on a more intimate form, as yard signs began surreptitiously appearing throughout northern New Mexico asking rhetorically, "Weapons of Mass Destruction? Iraq: 0; Albuquerque: 2000 (at Kirtland Air Force Base)" (see figure 5.9). Consistent with their long-term antinuclear critique, the LASG underscores that for those seeking to reduce the global nuclear threat, New Mexico might be the best place to start.

II

BUNKERS AND PSYCHES

THE SECOND PART OF *The Future of Fallout, and Other Episodes in Radioactive World-Making* explores the relationship between psyches and infrastructures, tracking how the figure of the bunker came to be invested with strange new forms of desire in the nuclear age. It seeks to document how the U.S. nuclear state works to create new forms of interiority in citizens that mobilize older idioms of a settler colonial society—frontier mentalities and assumptions about American exceptionalism and a Manifest Destiny—to constitute the postnuclear as an imaginative space, one carrying the potential for positive self-fashioning and endless reinvention. These chapters thus explore a radical new relation to death in the nuclear age, where the fixation on nuclear warfare fuses with a consumer society to create a range of fantasies about invulnerable bodies, armored spaces, and reinforced social boundaries. Race, class, gender, and age were all redeployed and redefined by nuclear nationalism in profound ways in the twentieth century, creating a psychic space oriented toward existential danger, one that authorizes new codes of conduct, new social contracts, and new abandonments. The four chapters in "Bunkers and Psyches" ask, then, about how emotions and fantasies become as infrastructural in the nuclear age as missiles, plutonium, and command and control systems, and interrogates the perverse American pleasure in imagining not only the end but the aftermath.

6

REHEARSING THE END

"We don't strike first; we strike fast," says our guide, a former Cold War Titan missile commander now taking us through a simulated launch of a thermonuclear missile. We are standing in the control room of a Titan II missile silo, thirty miles south of Tucson, in Sahuarita, Arizona (see figure 6.1). We are buried deep underground, facing a wall of lime green computer terminals that look much too archaic and quaint to produce any substantial degree of violence. We play out the authorizing of fail-safe launch codes, the countdown and launch sequences for imaginary nuclear war. This act happens daily in this room just as it did for the two decades of the Cold War (1962–82), in which this Titan silo was a central part of the U.S. nuclear deterrent. Now presented as history, the nuclear war logics supporting mutual assured destruction and the necessity of the Titan missile system are visible

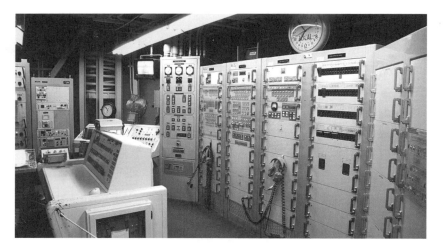

Figure 6.1. Titan missile control and launch center.

today only as relics, seemingly disconnected from the nuclear militarism of the contemporary United States, which endures.

The Titan Missile Museum is the only place in the world where you can see an intercontinental missile system on public display (see figure 6.2). It stands as both a museum and an archive of Cold War technology, presenting an all-too-rare chance to walk through the infrastructure of the nuclear balance of terror and interact with the former Titan missileers that once practiced mutually assured destruction and now staff the museum. A visit to the museum consists of viewing a small display of artifacts and narrative depiction of Cold War history, a film presentation that gives background on the Titan system (hosted by Chuck, a ponytailed narrator who looks more like a forest ranger than a Cold War veteran), and, in my case, a tour of the missile silo by a former Titan commander (see figure 6.3). The Titan missile was part of a global system for nuclear end times, linking the U.S. and the USSR in a shared technological apocalypticism (e.g., see Hoffman 2010). We learn, for example, that the Titan missile bases were located as close to the U.S.-Mexican border as possible to maximize the time available for radar to pick up incoming Soviet intercontinental missiles rising up over the North Pole in their deadly planetary arc, and thereby give the U.S. missile crews time to launch their retaliatory counterstrikes.

The Titan missile itself is over one hundred feet tall and protected by eight-foot-thick steel blast doors hardened against nuclear attack (see figure 6.4).

Figure 6.2. Titan Missile Museum exterior.

Figure 6.3. Titan Missile Museum interior exhibits.

The entire facility was built on giant springs to absorb the impact of nearby nuclear detonations. Even the electrical and plumbing systems were designed with enough slack to allow eighteen inches of bounce (see figure 6.5). The massive silo doors—now bolted open to allow ongoing satellite reconnaissance of the decommissioned missile—are the only visible aspect of the silo from ground level. However, an aboveground museum site is now populated with outdoor displays of the multiply redundant communication and security systems, as well as an exhibit on rocket engines and fuel management systems (see figure 6.6). Much of the tour, however, is spent underground rehearsing the security of the site (working through the multiple code words, safes, telephone checkpoints, and procedures for crews entering the facility and the various fail-safe mechanisms for preventing infiltration or an unintentional launch) and playing nuclear war (see figure 6.7).

We learn early in the presentation that crew members carried a pistol at all times while on duty, marked as a necessity for site security but also to ensure that a reluctant crewman "did his job properly in case of a launch order." They needn't have bothered with so overt a threat. The crew was not only highly trained but also preselected for the job, chosen precisely for their willingness to launch a thermonuclear missile on command. Our guide tells us, for example, about daily life in the missile silo: the four-person teams (two on duty, two off) would work twenty-four-hour shifts and spend each working minute on alert checking and double-checking the equipment. This constant rehearsal of maintenance and launch sequences served also to make the crews robotic in their actions and thoughts regarding the facility.

Our guide states repeatedly that the U.S. would never launch first—even though Air Force policy stated otherwise through much of the Cold War—underscoring the strange moral positioning that is required to be a cog within a larger nuclear war system (see Burr 2004). The one-shot Titan missile was, of course, pretargeted by U.S. military planners. The silo crew (which rotated shifts between multiple silos) never knew where any of the missiles they controlled would land: their job was simply to maintain the facility and to push the launch button without hesitation on order of the president. Crew members only knew that "58 seconds after the launch keys are turned the engines would ignite" and "thirty minutes later a target on the other side of the planet would be destroyed"—where, when, and why was someone else's responsibility.

Today the technology looks so archaic as to be incapable of being so fantastically violent. The computer controlling missile guidance—"state-of-the-art 1963 technology" we are told—has a total of one kilobyte of memory. "That 1K is less than the ring tone on your phone," says our guide in the best laugh line of the tour. But consider what this 1K memory system could unleash: Lifting off via a two-stage liquid fuel rocket, the Titan II ballistic missile could reach near space orbit and then send its heavy payload—in this case a nine-megaton thermonuclear warhead—back to Earth with enough precision to destroy an entire city six thousand miles away. Withstanding radical acceleration and vibration, as well as extremes of heat and cold, the Titan missile system was designed to launch within sixty seconds and to deliver absolute destruction over the horizon to the far side of the planet in under thirty minutes. Never before had the potential for mass death been rendered as automated, anonymous, or easy as in the Titan system.

The Titan II missile system was a central part of the technological, affective, and imaginative infrastructures of the nuclear age. Built in terrified reaction to the Soviet launch of Sputnik, the first artificial satellite, in 1957, the Titan missile was a response to the perceptions of a "missile gap." Top-secret reports at the time imagined the Soviet Union deploying hundreds and soon thousands of intercontinental ballistic missiles. John F. Kennedy was elected president in 1960 in part to solve this so-called missile gap through a massive arms buildup. Soon after his election, however, the new, top-secret Corona reconnaissance satellite provided proof that the Soviets had deployed fewer than ten missiles, not the hundreds imagined by U.S. planners. The phantom Soviet missiles of the 1950s that helped produce the Titan missile complex were very much like the phantom Iraqi weapons of mass destruction in 2003 that enabled the invasion of Iraq, and show how powerful imaginations are in the nuclear age, driving the production of new infrastructures and with them entirely new forms of danger. These fantasies about dangerous others have much to say about the power of collective fear and militarism in American culture, revealing the role of threat-based reasoning and demonization as core national projects. At the Titan Missile Museum there are only hints of this history and its overdetermined form, like the exhibit on nuclear overkill (see figure 6.8). Overkill is a theory of nuclear targeting that accounts for imagined technical failures in the system by exponentially multiplying the number of nuclear weapons launched. In its ultimate form, this idea produced a U.S. nuclear arsenal of over 36,000 weapons by 1968 and a target list designed to enable a simultaneous global nuclear strike on all communist states regardless of the provocation (Burr 2005). It is difficult today, despite all our current rhetoric of terror and counterterror, to imagine

Figure 6.4. Intercontinental ballistic missile under glass at the Titan Missile Museum.
Figure 6.5. Cables designed to flex during nuclear attack at the Titan Missile Museum.

Figure 6.6. Topside of the Titan Missile Museum.

Figure 6.7. Titan Missile Museum video display showing layout of underground base.

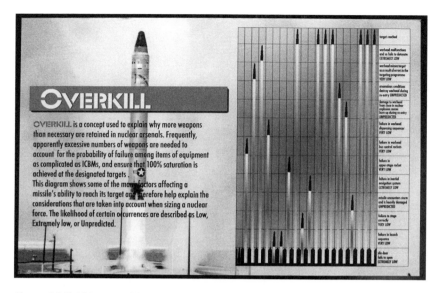

Figure 6.8. Exhibit on overkill, Titan Missile Museum.

the social conditions capable of producing a technological system of such total destruction or a national culture that could accommodate apocalyptic potentials so completely within everyday life that overkill was rendered entirely normative.

The Titan Missile Museum is today largely devoted to veterans, who make up the vast majority of visitors. It is run by veterans, caters to military tourism, and is designed to enable Cold Warriors to have a public site of recognition and remembrance for their service. This call to memory is, however, complicated, supported as much by amnesia and repression as recognition and commemoration. This is because the national security state fundamentally relies on, and strives to produce, an absence of public memory. The ability to shift public fear from one enemy to the next relies on a combination of perception management and state secrecy, enabling, in the case of the U.S., the constant rollout of new threats and new technologies to meet them. Just as declassification can change our understanding of past national security policy and conflicts, public memory is always at odds with a national security apparatus that relies on a highly flexible approach to the production and management of danger.

Put differently, the fears supporting the Cold War balance of terror could so easily morph into those of the War on Terror not because they make any

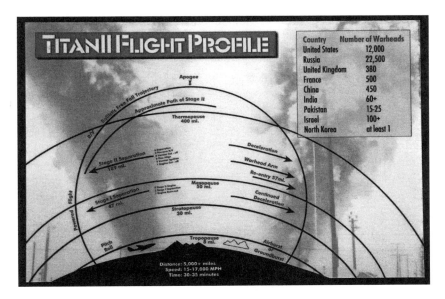

Figure 6.9. Exhibit on Titan II flight profile, Titan Missile Museum.

real sense, but because images of existential threat have been presented to American citizens as both coherent and eternal (see Masco 2014). Efforts to unpack the detailed history of the Cold War, or to address the specific claims of the current counterterror state, inevitably challenge the rationale of the national security state itself. For this very reason, the public history museums and archives that address aspects of American security are both essential and highly politicized. Thus, when Chuck, the narrator of the Titan Missile Museum film, tells us that "peace is never fully won, it is only kept from moment to moment" and thanks the Titan missile crews for a "job well done"— he merely underscores survival and the eternal project of national security. However, the opportunity to walk through the technological infrastructure of the Cold War nuclear complex also enables one to think about the constant nuclear war rehearsal that took place in missile silos and across a wide range of sites (both in the Cold War and to this day). It allows one to consider the production not only of a nuclear deterrent but also of a highly militarized nuclear culture, and the fantasies, fears, and ambitions that get coded into any concept of security (see figure 6.9). Cold War defense, for example, produced a minute-to-minute ability to destroy human civilization at planetary scale and a militarized U.S. national culture that continues to this day to naturalize that possibility as simply an unremarkable aspect of the world system, the minimal form of "defense." The Titan Missile Museum provides access to the origins of this project while occluding the continuing power of these ideas in the United States by presenting them as archaic technology. But as Walter Benjamin argued, one can see in the outmoded the structural terms of the present, the way that capitalist desires and technoscience can promise newness while reinforcing existing power structures (1969; see also Buck-Morss 1991). The Cold War/War on Terror offers one such pairing that reveals a central project of American militarism: the core technology might be more state of the art today, but the current nuclear complex serves a purpose identical to that documented in the museum. The ultimate question provoked by the Titan Missile Museum is, then, what would it take to imagine, let alone engineer and build, a world that does not rely on such mechanized terrors, or a society that will not accept or naturalize such apocalyptic potentials?

7

LIFE UNDERGROUND

What are the long-term psychological consequences of living within a nuclear culture? What can Americans no longer see or think because of their multigenerational investment in the atomic bomb and its accompanying forms of militarization? What fears are now so ingrained in American life that we cannot seem to live without them? How, in other words, has nuclear fear remade everyday American society as permanently insecure, even as the United States has become the most powerful military and economic state on earth?

Of the many astonishing cultural achievements of the atomic revolution in the United States, I want to consider the transformation of the underground, windowless room into a site of both global power and social dreaming. In the nuclear age, the room with no view, often buried and hardened against attack, became a place where futures were both held hostage and reimagined. Here, the critical relationship between citizens and the state was remade, reorganized within a crucible of nuclear fear organized via explicit propaganda campaigns and the very real technical capacities for nuclear war. This turn inward toward built spaces stocked with state-of-the-art technologies and commodities presented a utopian vision of an invulnerable America closed off from the outside world but still functioning perfectly.

One of the first and most powerful effects of the bomb was to transform the U.S. into a special kind of bunker society, fixated on impending nuclear attack while fantasizing about life within both mental and physical fortresses. Positing life in the bunker as livable (even exciting) was a vital mechanism of militarizing American society in the face of an expanding nuclear threat. It also set the terms for a long-running American fantasy about achieving an absolute containment and total form of security. Figures 7.1 and 7.2, for example, are Federal Civil Defense Administration (FCDA) proposals from the mid-twentieth century for the next generation of public schools. The nondescript ground-level building depicted in figure 7.1 pales in comparison to the underground bunker with its carefully diagrammed spaces filled with bunk beds, escape hatches, offices, and infirmary. Similarly, the aboveground swings and slides in figure 7.2 seem no match for the playful imagination of the hidden, windowless spaces below, which promise order, self-sufficiency, and insulation from the universe of danger above. There is no sign here of the reality of nuclear war, of the scorched and barren radioactive landscape, or the extreme trauma of life in a postnuclear environment.[1]

New Fortresses for the Mind and Body

The atomic bomb created fundamental military, social, and psychological contradictions within America society that long-standing concepts of security could not resolve. Instead, federal authorities sought to manage nuclear fear rather than eliminate it, to structure American perceptions of the bomb to enable support for a potentially long Cold War. To this end, the U.S. state sought to normalize a nuclear state of emergency by simply calling it "national security." By the late 1950s, for example, the federal government was not only feverishly building thermonuclear weapons, and the means to deliver them around the world as quickly as possible, it was also considering a massive investment in fallout shelters across the United States, a program promising an entirely new national infrastructure, all underground.

Figure 7.1. FCDA diagram of Group Fallout Shelter for 240 Persons (U.S. National Archives and Records Administration).

Figure 7.2. FCDA diagram of school fallout shelter (U.S. National Archives and Records Administration).

The Rand Corporation, for example, produced a detailed plan to relocate four million New Yorkers deep underneath Manhattan in anticipation of a nuclear attack:

> The shelters were to be excavated 800 feet below the surface, using conventional excavation and mining techniques. They were to be almost completely isolated from the surface, with air purified and enriched with oxygen as in a submarine, with water tapped from the Delaware Aqueduct system of tunnels and treated (or, in emergency, drawn from internal storage), and with power provided from diesel generators vented to the surface but isolated from the shelter proper. Occupants would be assigned berths in a large dormitory, would receive two cold meals and one hot meal per day, and would draw fresh clothing, take showers, and exercise on a rotational basis. Some 91 entrances were planned and distributed according to population, so that every point in Manhattan was within 5 to 10 minutes walking distance of an entrance; elevator design characteristics currently employed in New York should permit about a fourth of the people in the buildings themselves to reach the street every 5 minutes. The entrances were sloped tunnels and had 500-psi blast doors both at the top and at the bottom; provision could be made to collapse any single tunnel if the upper door gave way. (1958, 7–8)

Isolated from the surface as in a submarine. This effort to build in the imagination an underground city, hardened against nuclear attack, would be physically realized in the command and control centers for U.S. nuclear forces. The general public, however, would focus more on constructing psychological defenses in the nuclear age than on actual shelters. Nuclear civil defense was, in this regard, an extraordinarily powerful means of defining the boundaries of both security and threat for the public, while training citizens to think about nuclear war in specific ways.

The civil defense projects of the 1950s formally positioned the bunker as a new American frontier space, populated by a new kind of citizen defined by the constant preparation for nuclear attack. This new Cold War subject was designed to be immune to panic but nonetheless motivated by nuclear fear (Oakes 1994; Masco 2014). Thus, just as Cold War military technologies were being hardened to survive nuclear attack, civil defense efforts sought to engineer a new kind of citizen-soldier, one that was emotionally equipped to support the nuclear state. Hardening both technologies and psychologies against the bomb was a dual project of the early nuclear state—making the nuclear bunker a new site of nation and state building. The embrace of stone and steel and concrete as protective shield transformed the windowless bunker into both a technological challenge and a utopian space. And via the promise of the bunker, the logical outcome of nuclear war—the destruction of the nation-state in a radioactive firestorm—was denied, and a different future horizon opened up.

As Americans contemplated life underground in the early Cold War period, a new kind of social intimacy with mass death was deeply installed in U.S. national security culture. As the military built multiply redundant technological systems for fighting a nuclear war (including always-on-alert bombers, missiles, and submarines), the civil defense program sought to build a society capable of withstanding the internal pressures of living within a constant state of emergency and facing a new kind of totalizing destructive force. Cold War planners explicitly merged nuclear fear with American exceptionalism, hoping to engineer a new kind of militarized society, locking in place ideologies of American power and vulnerability that continue to inform U.S. national security culture to this day. The elevation of the bunker into an icon of state power and social responsibility played a critical role in psychologically preparing and orienting Americans for escalating militarism.[2]

In addition to reconceptualizing schools, government buildings, and mass transit sites as future shelters, the Cold War state constructed a new infrastructure of buried military facilities in support of nuclear weapons systems and for continuity of government operations. Simultaneously, officials recruited private citizens to the shelter project, asking them to build home shelters or risk death or permanent injury in the coming nuclear conflict. In this crosscutting embrace of the bunker as the future of the nation, a new kind of national security culture emerged—one that reorganized everyday life as permanent warfare and mass death as an ever-present potential.

In 1957 the Gaither Committee brought together the leading military-industrial planners in the country to contemplate the benefits of a national fallout shelter program in response to the Soviet nuclear program. In addition to declaring (inventing, it turned out) a terrifying missile gap between the U.S. and USSR (leading to a massive arms buildup in both the late Eisenhower and early Kennedy administrations), the committee recommended a crash shelter program that would cost as much as $55 billion over five years. The committee was explicit about the value of the program: the shelter system was designed not only to save lives as the bombs began to fall but also to communicate to the Soviet leadership an American will to live, and thus win, either a cold or hot war. Civil defense was therefore theatrical as well as practical, a means of sending signals out into the world from underground bunker spaces, both real and imagined. The bunker linked public, private, and military domains in a formal contemplation of nuclear war.

Moving Underground

It is difficult for us to assess today the incredible energy and creativity that went into building American apocalyptic technologies, and the difficult, ongoing social work of normalizing a permanent nuclear war economy in the U.S. Consider the extraordinary national infrastructure built in support of nuclear war. In the first decade of the Cold War, the nuclear state moved underground, supported by a new concept of command and control that focused not on seeing the world directly but rather on approaching the computer screen as world. As missiles, radar systems, and command centers became buried in hardened military facilities across the globe, windowless bunker sites came to link earth, sea, air, and eventually space as data points on technologically mediated screens. The core example of this new system was the North American Aerospace Defense Command (NORAD), located deep within Cheyenne Mountain in Colorado. Authorized in 1958, NORAD tracked all flying objects over North America, a job that became increasingly important as intercontinental missiles and satellites joined bombers as forms of Soviet military power.

The most advanced bunker facility of its time, NORAD perfectly illustrates the passions of the Cold War nuclear project. The central facility is buried 2,400 feet deep inside a mountain of almost solid granite and is supported by 1,319 steel springs (each three feet in diameter and weighing more than one thousand pounds), designed to absorb the shock of nearby nuclear detonations. NORAD was simultaneously the most isolated and the most connected site in the U.S. Secured behind twenty-five-ton blast doors (see figure 7.3), the facility was both locked down and networked to radar systems, computers, and eventually satellite surveillance systems, assembling enormous data sets of moving objects tracked in real time on a giant central screen (see figure 7.4). This central screen was the lens for viewing nuclear threat throughout the Cold War, a powerful tool for orchestrating U.S. military deployments and achieving mutual assured destruction. NORAD was designed as the ultimate panopticon—a form of surveillance enabling crew members, invisible to the world in their hardened underground bunkers, to watch all of North America and provide an early warning of nuclear attack.

Figure 7.3. Twenty-five-ton blast-proof security doors at NORAD, Cheyenne Mountain, Colorado (U.S. National Archives and Records Administration).

Figure 7.4. NORAD command and control center (U.S. National Archives and Records Administration).

The windowless bunker provided a new kind of vision, one that amplified the ability to recognize dots on a giant screen as friend or foe in the minute-to-minute orchestration of the balance of nuclear terror. This representation of the world as data points is among the most profound technological evolutions of the nuclear age. As Paul Edwards (1996) has argued, the Cold War concept of Soviet containment found a perfect technological metaphor in the form of the computer screen, creating a "closed world" system of mutually reinforcing ideologies, metaphors, and technologies.[3] Thus NORAD is both a technological system and a model of an idealized world, one where the points on the global map are preselected for their value and importance and all other forms of information are ignored. Over time the "closed world" vision naturalizes these preselected data points as the world itself, forgetting the messy complexity of cultures, politics, and ecosystems. Like the concept of collateral damage (the unintended violence of warfare), the kinds of information not convertible into dots on a screen (misrecognitions, interpretations, mistakes, malfunctions) were rendered invisible in favor of a machine-to-machine assessment. Nonetheless, the power of NORAD not only was defensive but also lay in its ability to coordinate the use of the 31,000 nuclear weapons in the U.S. arsenal by 1965, demonstrating the extraordinary power of the windowless bunker in the nuclear age.

Life in the hardened bunker quickly became a site of Cold War fantasy for both military leaders and citizens. For the military, it presented a vision of the globe as a totally knowable and controllable space. For citizens, the windowless bunker became a privatized dream space—where time spent waiting for the bombs to fall and the radioactive clouds to clear could be a source of renewal, not ruin. Citizens, however, did not approach the bunker on their own terms or by their own choosing; instead, they were taught how to think about nuclear crisis and their own role in managing it. The project of civil defense in the 1950s was less about the protection of citizens and cities than about the emotional training of the populace and the psychological conversion of U.S. citizens into Cold Warriors in raced, classed, and gendered terms. Developed with the help of advertising experts, psychologists, and military planners, civil defense was primarily a means of instilling nuclear fear, and a coded response to it, within the U.S. population as part of the larger Cold War effort. This took the form of the largest federal media campaign in U.S. history. Relying on newspapers, magazines, radio, television, and film, civil defense was designed to teach U.S. citizens just enough about the dangers of nuclear war to mobilize their support but not enough to produce terror or a public movement to end the Cold War project.

Cold War civil defense was above all an extraordinary national conversation about collective death. The media campaign forced citizens to consider a postnational state of being and eventually, as the power of nuclear arsenals grew, the possible end to life on planet Earth. Civil defense was an unprecedented national project, as federal authorities sought simultaneously to mobilize and naturalize nuclear crisis within the U.S. They did so by teaching citizens to fear an imminent global nuclear attack each minute of the day while also arguing that such a threat could be approached as just another form of potential crisis, alongside floods, fires, and earthquakes. The domestic form of the balance of terror presented a constant problem of emotional and informational calibration to Cold War planners.[4] In one widely distributed civil defense pamphlet from 1959 titled "Ten for Survival: Survive Nuclear Attack," for example, readers learn that "survival" is simply a question of knowing "what to do and how to do it." But this promise that "knowledge is survival power" is paired with a description of nuclear war that overwhelms ducking and covering as a mode of protection:

> Dangers facing you: The bomb produces heat of several million degrees—a good deal hotter than the temperature on the surface of the sun. This heat travels at the speed of light. A megaton explosion could kill an unshielded man 8 miles from ground zero. A 20-megaton explosion could kill an unshielded man 20 miles away. It could blister and cripple the bodies of unsheltered people well beyond that.

At the speed of light. As part of the larger effort to mobilize the public for nuclear war, civil defense authorities increasingly responded to these gruesome facts by seeking first to naturalize, and then to romanticize, shelters. Life in the bunker was depicted as quintessentially American, a new frontier experience where the resilient citizen could outwit a dangerous world with grit, skill, and moral determination.[5]

At the height of the fallout shelter debate, the FCDA produced a photographic exhibit documenting ordinary Americans in their home bunkers. These images represent the fallout shelter as pure dream space, not only privatized but also part of a pastoral landscape. The FCDA presents each shelter in a photographic sequence, beginning with a view from ground level looking at the owners descending into the shelter entrance, followed by a view from the windowless interior. This sequential structure underscores the break between the world above and the bunker below. In each case, the shelter hatch begs to be locked down tight, sealing the inhabitants below in their submarine-like security, locking the inhabitants within a special kind of fantasy space: militarized, privatized, settler colonial, and potentially post-nation-state.

Figure 7.5 presents the arresting image of the suburban home on a seemingly peaceful, sunny day, with a father and daughter slowly descending into a circular hatch cut neatly into the lawn. Framed to enhance the sky and grass, while underscoring the dramatically unhurried nature of the father-daughter descent into the earth, the photograph registers a preternatural calm, belying the context of nuclear war that necessitates this shelter project. Figure 7.6 then shows the neatly ordered family space below, complete with air purifier, stove, and bunk beds, already populated by three generations of happy shelter inhabitants. The father can sleep in this image precisely because he has put forth the labor to build a shelter as a personal response to the international nuclear crisis. The grandparents and daughter simply enjoy the time together in this windowless underground space. The canned goods and medical kits become a register of good parenting in this advertisement, which also suggests that time spent in the bunker can be quality family time.

Figures 7.7 and 7.8 repeat this pictorial structure but with more humor and a repositioning of the shelter as a place to get some peace and quiet, away from the troubles of the world above. In the first image, the smiling male owner pops his head out of the carefully hidden shelter entrance, presenting a covert space surrounded by a thicket of trees and shrubs. On the inside we see him in relaxed pleasure, legs crossed, lying on a bunk bed enjoying a magazine, a slight smile on his face, the very picture of contentment. Here the fallout shelter is presented as a privatized retreat, as much bachelor pad as survival kit. But the hidden entrance to the bunker sends a double message: it is a secret retreat (a place to gather one's thoughts in private) and a regional secret—an implicit recognition of the value of the shelter at a time of nuclear crisis, when less prepared Americans might be scared into violent acts of appropriation. Indeed, one of the immediate concerns of the shelter debate involved how to cope, not with the bomb or a Soviet invasion, but with traumatized neighbors reduced to a violent state of panic.

Figure 7.9 presents the family fallout shelter as pure dream space. As clouds gather on the horizon, a farming family moves into their hidden shelter space, dwarfed by grass and sky. This image magnifies the drama of the world outside the shelter, the enormity of global politics, and replaces it with the cool forward-thinking bunker logics documented in figure 7.10. The mother here sorts her stock of preserved food, revealing months of labor

Figure 7.5. Family Fallout Shelter, residential exterior, FCDA campaign (U.S. National Archives and Records Administration).

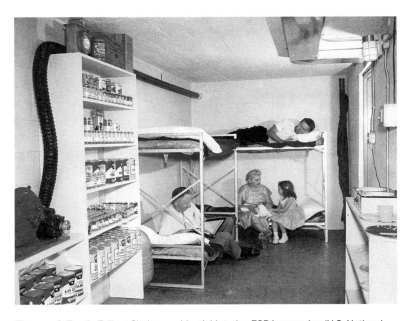

Figure 7.6. Family Fallout Shelter, residential interior, FCDA campaign (U.S. National Archives and Records Administration).

Figure 7.7. Hidden Fallout Shelter, FCDA campaign (U.S. National Archives and Records Administration).

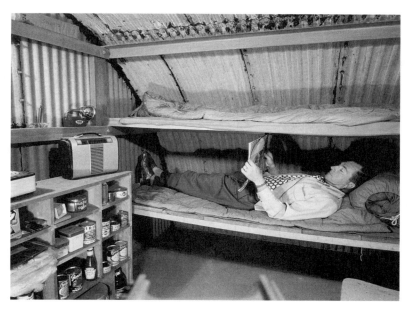

Figure 7.8. Hidden Fallout Shelter interior, FCDA campaign (U.S. National Archives and Records Administration).

Figure 7.9. Rural Family Fallout Shelter exterior, FCDA campaign (U.S. National Archives and Records Administration).

Figure 7.10. Rural Family Fallout Shelter, food storage, FCDA campaign (U.S. National Archives and Records Administration).

already invested in preparing for a postnuclear future. The FCDA sought to divide up shelter responsibilities by gender and age within the family structure, tasking men with shelter construction and organization, women with food and first aid, and children with studying nuclear effects (to keep their parents on track). The family farm could be incorporated into civil defense as well, participating in a larger FCDA campaign for food recovery, including shelters for cattle. These two images merge the survivalist narrative of self-preservation and independence characteristic of Americans' frontier heritage with a pure pastoral image of the farming landscape as cover for the windowless life below. The iconography of a family alone in the wilderness, preparing for the tough winter, is deployed here to make the fallout shelter a uniquely American space, bringing together the rural, the pastoral, and the radioactive in one conceptual drama.

Each of these shelters is also a privatized enterprise, stocked largely with purchased commodities, from generators to radios, bunk beds, and flashlights. The fusion of shelters and consumer capitalism was essential right from the start. President Kennedy asked each American to prepare for nuclear war by finding or building a shelter, and also proposed a $400 million national shelter program one year before the Cuban Missile Crisis, energizing a new industry in store-bought shelters. The FCDA sought to enhance the allure of the shelter by sponsoring a national campaign to design multiuse rooms, good for sitting out a nuclear war or for everyday use before an attack. In the shelter campaign, nuclear families were always depicted together, in good health and happily underground when war broke out. These conceptual designs start to explain why: the FCDA was attempting to relocate this vision of an idealized white American family into the nuclear bunker—to make the bomb the source of family life rather than the destruction of it.

Figures 7.11 and 7.12 document this FCDA effort to normalize the nuclear bunker as a part of everyday life—useful before, during, and after nuclear war. Designed by the Los Angeles firm of Dorothy H. Paul, figure 7.11 is a concept drawing for the Fun Room Fall-Out Shelter—a dual-use playroom and bunker. Instead of windows, the walls of this shelter are painted with a playground scene of children in a park, running and climbing trees— precisely the environment that would likely be scorched or radioactive after a nuclear exchange. Stations are set up for book reading and for viewing films; board games are stacked along the wall. The fun to be had here requires both faith and imagination, transforming the terror of a nuclear war into an opportunity for game playing and other modes of distraction. Figure 7.12 takes this argument about the value of time in the shelter to its logical conclusion.

Figure 7.11. Fun Room Fall-Out Shelter design (U.S. National Archives and Records Administration).

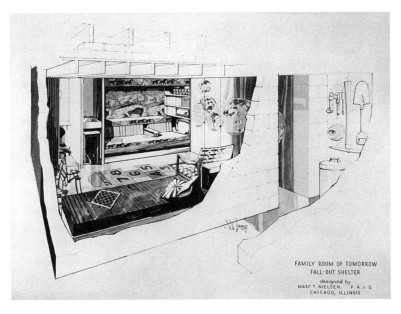

Figure 7.12. Family Room of Tomorrow Fall-Out Shelter design (U.S. National Archives and Records Administration).

Figure 7.13. Duck-and-cover drill (U.S. National Archives and Records Administration).

Designed by Marc T. Nielsen of Chicago, it presents the Family Room of To-morrow Fall-Out Shelter. Also a windowless, cinderblock bunker, the design includes both Stone Age wall paintings and a world map, as if to raise the question of what kind of tomorrow the family will have—the prehistoric or the modern? This design was shown in full-scale mock-up at a Chicago trade show, where it met not with praise and admiration, but with the anger of a crowd sickened by the assumption about what a nuclear tomorrow might look like.

Despite this effort to romanticize the shelter and to construct it as a dual-use room suited for all kinds of catastrophe as well as for entertaining guests, most Americans did not—indeed, could not—build nuclear bunkers. Instead, figure 7.13 depicts the most wide-ranging response to the bomb: the duck-and-cover drill that every American schoolchild practiced for the forty years of official Cold War. Here, face down, internalized in one's own mind, and completely vulnerable to the world around, is the ultimate Cold War posture—a sightless, private bunker of the most pathos-driven kind.

The FCDA campaigns always offered citizens the best-case scenario for nuclear war—in which the bombs explode well over the horizon—allowing

Americans time to get to their shelters and minimize the most destructive effects. The FCDA consequently focused on the middle-class, suburban family living on the periphery of urban centers, creating and reinforcing an image of America as an exclusively white nuclear family. This left unrepresented vast groups of Americans while ignoring the predominantly urban concentration of U.S. populations and those colonized by the nuclear test program or already affected by its fallout. Nonetheless, the FCDA campaign sought to link the shelter to a specific American narrative of frontier survivalism and, in so doing, presented the bunker largely as a commodified dream space rather than a disaster zone. Via civil defense, federal authorities promoted an idea of an invulnerable American—able to exist outside of time and space—located within a new mythology of perfect national security.

Scientists and activists almost immediately challenged this denial of death. They critiqued the factual claims of civil defense, helping to foment peace, civil rights, and environmental movements. Perhaps the most devastating critique of the bunker society came in Stanley Kubrick's 1963 film *Dr. Strangelove, Or: How I Learned to Stop Worrying and Love the Bomb*. At the end of the film, as the president and his war council are gathered in the closed world command center known as the war room, a huge computer screen follows the path of U.S. and Soviet bombers on their final bombing runs, detailing the now unavoidable outbreak of global nuclear war. Rather than producing despair, however, the president's science advisor, Dr. Strangelove, suggests that the U.S. could now move a "nucleus of human specimens" to the deepest mine shafts and prepare them (with nuclear reactors for energy and greenhouses to produce food) to wait out the radioactive fallout for a few hundred years. Suggesting a 10:1 ratio of women to men to repopulate the human species, the erotics of the shelter produce immediate desire among the president and his all-male war council, as well as a renewed state of competition with the Soviets, this time to prevent, over the hundreds of years it would take for surface radiation to decay, the development of a "mine shaft gap!" The nuclear bunker is revealed here as pure masculinist fantasy, participating in an erotics of death that is not subject to self-analysis even as the bombs begin to fall.

From a Secure, Undisclosed Location

What has become of the Cold War bunker society in the twenty-first century? In the days after the terrorist attacks on the World Trade Center and the Pentagon in September 2001, one of the most theatrical people in the country was Vice President Dick Cheney.[6] Having spent much of his career thinking about continuity of government plans for nuclear war (see Graff 2017), Cheney issued his public statements from a "secure, undisclosed location." Almost instantly a joke, it was funny precisely because most Americans could picture the windowless, underground bunker (now outfitted with the internet and video conferencing) that the vice president chose to speak from. Energizing the entire Cold War system for nuclear crisis, Cheney began to orchestrate from his buried control center the start of a global military response that he called the "new normal." The bunker here was not the idyllic space imagined by the FCDA for citizens. Rather, it was the militarized bunker linked to global technologies for war.

One of the Bush administration's first projects in the War on Terror was to once again normalize a state of permanent crisis, using the legal, rhetorical, and emotional structures of the Cold War security state to radically change both foreign and domestic policy (see Masco 2014). By calling what they were doing over the following years—multiple wars, unprecedented domestic surveillance, global renditions, the suspension of the writ of habeas corpus, and torture—national security, the Bush administration was able to suspend law and moral order in the U.S. in the name of defense.

We do not build nuclear shelters anymore. This is not because the bunker society has been outmoded, but because it has been so completely integrated into public life. Early Cold War civil defense was concerned primarily with militarizing the public and mobilizing citizens for a long wartime commitment. The long-term success of that project has created a national security culture that is unprecedented in human history. Today, federal authorities no longer ask citizens to go into underground rooms made of steel and concrete, but into bunkers of the imagination. These conceptual bunkers free the national security state to operate in an uncontested field of global action. No state in history has given as much to security as the United States. Currently the U.S. has less than 5 percent of the world's population but nearly outspends the entire world combined on its military. Yet this extraordinary military expenditure does not produce a sense of security—quite the opposite.

The history of the Cold War bunker tells us why: the focus has never been on stopping violence but on preparing psychologically to endure it, which has created a perverse concept of security. Certain rituals of security today—the airport screenings that do not enhance security, the acquiescence to domestic electronic surveillance, and the extraordinary sums of money spent on defense—work not to protect but to underscore, and even create, a sense of vulnerability and a more violent world. This evocation of risk is then acknowledged by the security state as a call for more security (in the form of preventative wars, covert actions, and greater secrecy), leading to an escalating militarization of national life (in form of more domestic violence, a more militarized police, and a retrenchment of structures of foundational violence within the United States).

The War on Terror promises, in this way, to end the experience of terror, first by saturating national politics with forms of fear, and then by pursuing an ever-greater counterterrorist response to them, ensuring rebounding circuits of violence. The George W. Bush administration promoted the ideology of the bunker crafted during the Cold War into counterterror, once again asking citizens to define security as a state project and to ignore the vast manipulation of public life conducted in the name of defense. Counterterror demands docility from citizens while enabling policies that are in violation of any concept of democratic governance and that are deadly. Just as the fallout shelters would not have saved many Americans during a nuclear war (indeed, they would have suffocated most in spaces that became ovens under the full force of nuclear warfare), this concept of national security has been used to justify unprecedented sacrifice in terms of life, law, and capital since 2001. Perhaps now that the enormous costs and failures of the War on Terror are known, the concept of national security and its nuclear roots can be formally reconsidered. Perhaps it is even time for Americans to get out of the nuclear bunker once and for all, begin demilitarizing, and reenter the world in all its bright and messy insecurity.

8

ATOMIC HEALTH

What happened to health in the nuclear age? It has been a period of seemingly endless breakthroughs in biomedicine but also a period that has simultaneously proliferated modes of injury, some taking literally decades to
manifest. If we consider health as the absence of illness and thus the opposite
of death, the atomic bomb has fundamentally altered the concept. My dictionary defines health as a "condition of being sound in body, mind, or spirit"
involving "freedom from physical disease or pain." I like this idea, even yearn
for the simple purity it assumes about bodies and knowledge. But this concept of health is at best nostalgic, representing a dream image from an age
long surrendered to petrochemical capitalism and nuclear nationalism. The
atomic bomb has not only produced a new social orientation toward death, it
has insinuated itself at the cellular level to challenge the very structure of all

living organisms (plant, animal, human) on planet Earth. In order to assess a transformation of life on a planetary scale, it is important to understand how the atomic bomb has inverted definitions of health and security, remaking them from positive values into an incremental calculus of death.

This form of American necropolitics enables, after 1945, the possibility of instant mass death and radiation-induced disease as normalized conditions, producing a new logic of defense mediated by injuries that work on different time horizons and with varying degrees and intensities across all communities. The inability to think beyond these atomic potentialities—let alone to reduce the technological, political, and environmental conditions that continue to support them—renders these nuclear effects normalized, a routine part of everyday life. In the nuclear age, incipient death has become in this way a strange new form of health, both normalized and rendered as inescapable. Health, in this formulation, is therefore a social construct that regularizes certain potentialities for the human body through an increasingly perverse process of exposure, naturalization, and forgetting. This chapter tracks the profound psychosocial effects of the atomic bomb on American society by exploring how the long-standing state concern with hygiene as a joint project of public health and state security mutated during the Cold War arms race and continues to inform the War on Terror.

After the atomic bombing of Hiroshima and Nagasaki in August 1945, the technological potential for nuclear war expanded exponentially in the United States, quickly producing a world in which life, and just maybe all life, could end within a few short minutes of warfare. Always on alert intercontinental missiles, nuclear submarines, and long-range bombers ensure that nuclear war can begin any second of the day and, in the first minute of conflict, exceed the total destructive power unleashed in all of World War II many times over. The Cold War state installed this new form of total destruction within American everyday life remarkably by calling it national security. The technological capability for a totalizing mass death has not changed since the dissolution of the Soviet Union and the formal end of the Cold War. It remains a brute fact of the life that Americans live, and have for generations, in an everyday space imbued with the potential for an unprecedented form of collective death—an unhealthy situation, to say the very least.

But a radically foreshortened social future is only one possible effect of the nuclear revolution; the other is individualized, covert, unpredictable, and cellular. The atmospheric effects of nuclear weapons development and nuclear power accidents injected radioactive materials into the global biosphere—creating twentieth-century fallout as our current condition. Taken up by global wind currents as well as by plants and animals, these materials were delivered into each and every person on the planet and deposited in varying amounts within their genomes. As a result, all of us carry traces of plutonium, strontium, and cesium from the U.S. nuclear program in our bodies, making life on planet Earth quite literally a postnuclear formation (see Makhijani and Schwartz 1998; Masco 2006).

But who talks about atomic health these days? Since 2001, Americans have largely ignored the domestic costs of the U.S. nuclear project in favor of the more generic discourse of terrorism and wmds. These terms project responsibility for nuclear fear outward onto often nameless and faceless others, often riding on long-standing racist stereotypes (Masco 2014). They deny that the United States has been the global innovator in nuclear weapons, responsible for every significant technological escalation of the form. The United States also remains the only country to have used nuclear weapons in war, and, in terms of its nuclear development program, both maintains the current state-of-the-art nuclear arsenal and remains the most nuclear-bombed country on earth (with 904 detonations at the Nevada Test Site alone). The United States has also created a unique form of nuclear colonialism from the indigenous territories of the U.S. Southwest to Alaska and the Marshall Islands. Indeed, the social process of coming to terms with an imminent fiery death or a slower, cancerous one has now been normalized as a fact of everyday American life. The roots of nuclear anxiety, however, have not dissipated over time but rather have become more deeply woven into American culture and individual psyches (Kaplan 2003). Whether we choose to recognize it or not, every American is now a postnuclear creature, living in a political, biological, and emotional world structured by the cumulative effects of the U.S. commitment to the bomb.

If you don't believe me, if you resist my definition of nuclear health as incipient death as absurd or extreme or simply too depressing, consider the hyperrationalist argument about radioactive life presented by Herman Kahn in his 1960 treatise On Thermonuclear War. Writing as a Rand Corporation strategist, Kahn was influential in conceptualizing U.S. nuclear policy in the early Cold War period. He set out to "think the unthinkable" and work through the details of a nuclear conflict in his book, taking readers from the first salvo of atomic bombs through the collapse of the nation-state and into possible forms of social recovery. Kahn was a central inspiration for the character of Dr. Strangelove in Stanley Kubrick's 1964 film, and like the character in the film, he delighted in the shock effects he produced in his audience by exploring the details of nuclear conflict and the damaged conditions of a postnuclear society (see Ghamari-Tabrizi 2005). On a surface level, On Thermonuclear War is an effort to calculate via cost-benefit analysis the economic, environmental, and health effects of different forms of nuclear war. The text, however, also reveals the absurd biological and social stakes of Cold War national security, calling into question the rationality of the nuclear state. Kahn begins by breaking nuclear war into eight stages. He then assesses the resulting "tragic but distinguishable postwar states" of nuclear conflict depending on the specific war strategy and scale of the conflict (1960, 34). For Kahn, nuclear war is a universe of physical, emotional, and social misery in which decisions still have to be made with stark consequences at each stage of the conflict, from military strategy to medical mobilization and economic recovery. To those who would reject this line of thinking as immoral or perverse, Kahn simply asks: "As a policy maker, would you prefer a postnuclear America with fifty million dead or a hundred million dead, or environmental ruin lasting ten years or fifty?" (1960, 19).

Nuclear conflict is rationalized here as a problem set, as is its vast range of effects, in order to open up a new possibility for postnuclear governance. Kahn ultimately runs the gruesome numbers to assess the degree of suffering Americans should be willing to accept in order to fight a nuclear war. He also attempts to calculate the precise point at which the nuclear destruction would be so great that the "survivors would envy the dead," thus rendering the Cold War null and void as a collective project (1960, 40; and see figure 8.1).

In making these calculations, Kahn provides a new vocabulary of collective risk as well as a variety of new metrics for assessing health in the nuclear age. Consider just the figure titles he uses to illustrate the consequences of different nuclear scenarios: "Acceptability of Risks," "Genetic Assumptions," "The Strontium-90 Problem," "Radioactive Environment 100 Years Later," "Morbidity of Acute Total Body Radiation," "Life Shortening," and "Seven Optimistic Assumptions." While these tables detail a scale of suffering that is unprecedented in human experience, Kahn's ultimate metric is not radiation exposure rates or "life shortening" effects or the economic cost of rebuilding destroyed cities and infrastructure but a rather new kind of social calculus: the "defective child." Acknowledging that the nuclear test programs of the United States and Soviet Union had distributed vast amounts of strontium-90 in the form of fallout into the global biosphere, Kahn assesses the damage to the human genome. Recognizing that the health effects of strontium-90 contamination can be both immediate (cancer) and multigenerational (genetic damage), Kahn calculates how many American children will be born severely disabled because of U.S. investment in the atomic bomb. This is a remarkable moment in American history as it recognizes that national

```
◆◆◆◆◆◆◆◆◆◆◆◆◆◆◆◆◆◆◆◆◆◆◆◆◆◆◆◆◆◆◆◆◆◆◆◆◆◆◆◆◆◆◆◆◆◆◆◆◆◆◆◆◆

                        TABLE 3
        TRAGIC BUT DISTINGUISHABLE POSTWAR STATES
                                        Economic
                    Dead              Recuperation
                  2,000,000             1  year
                  5,000,000             2  years
                 10,000,000             5  years
                 20,000,000            10  years
                 40,000,000            20  years
                 80,000,000            50  years
                160,000,000           100  years

            Will the survivors envy the dead?

◆◆◆◆◆◆◆◆◆◆◆◆◆◆◆◆◆◆◆◆◆◆◆◆◆◆◆◆◆◆◆◆◆◆◆◆◆◆◆◆◆◆◆◆◆◆◆◆◆◆◆◆◆
```

Figure 8.1. Herman Kahn's nuclear war calculations in *On Thermonuclear War.*

security—traditionally defined as a defense of both citizens and the state
from outside dangers—has been fundamentally altered in the nuclear age,
requiring new forms of internal sacrifice. Kahn, however, goes much, much
further in his assessment of the strontium-90 problem, revealing the new
terms of nuclear health in a security state that will consider paying any cost
right up to the edge of total annihilation in order to win the Cold War:

> I could easily imagine a war in which the average survivor received
> about 250 roentgens. . . . This would mean that about 1 percent of the
> children who could have been healthy would be defective; in short, the
> number of children born seriously defective would increase, because of
> war, to about 25 per cent above the current rate. This would be a large
> penalty to pay for a war. More horrible still, we might have to continue
> to pay a similar price for 20 or 30 or 40 generations. But even this is
> a long way from annihilation. It might well turn out, for example, that
> U.S. decision makers would be willing, among other things, to accept
> the high risk of an additional 1 per cent of our children being born de-
> formed if that meant not giving up Europe to Soviet Russia. Or it might
> be that under certain circumstances the Russians would be willing to
> accept even higher risk than this, if by doing so they could eliminate
> the United States. (1960, 46)

It might well turn out . . . In a world where a security state can imagine as a viable calculus exchanging the health of its children in perpetuity for a political victory, the terms of both public health and security have been permanently altered.[1] We have moved from a notion of health as an absence of disease to a graded spectrum of dangerous effects now embedded in everyday life and connected to an equally changed notion of security. Health, as Kahn presents it here, is a statistical calculation rather than a lived experience, and it is precisely by approaching health as a population effect rather than an individual one that he creates the appearance of rationality.[2]

Kahn's interest in thinking through nuclear warfare, however, does force him, in a few rare but telling moments, to confront the raw physical reality of the human body. Food, for example, would be a major concern in a postnuclear world, and Kahn (1960, 66) imagines nuclear war scenarios in which U.S. agriculture could be "suspended" for fifty to a hundred years. Since nuclear war in the era of thermonuclear weapons would spread its effects over the entire continental United States, Kahn focuses on how to manage food produced in a largely contaminated environment. His answer once again points to a new concept of health as incipient death. He proposes to classify food based on the amount of strontium-90 contamination it contains in groups labeled A (little contamination) to E (heavily contaminated), and then to distribute the food based on the following criteria:

> The A food would be restricted to children and to pregnant women. The B food would be a high-priced food available to everybody. The C food would be a low-priced food also available to everybody. Finally, the D food would be restricted to people over age forty or fifty. Even though this food would be unacceptable for children, it probably would be acceptable for those past middle age, partly because their bones are already formed so that they do not pick up anywhere near as much strontium as the young, and partly because at these low levels of contamination it generally takes some decades for cancer to develop. Most of these people would die of other causes before they got cancer. Finally there would be an E food restricted to the feeding of animals whose resulting use (meat, draft animals, leather, wool, and so on) would not cause an increase in the human burden of Sr-90. (1960, 66–67)

Most of these people . . . Thus, while contamination is total, linking all Americans in a postnuclear reality, the role of governance is not to prevent disaster but to distribute its effects through the rational calculation of individual age versus the longevity of radioactive materials in the distribution of food.

Again, there is no concept of health here if by health we mean an absence of disease or risk. There is rather the naturalization of a new baseline reality (in this case a very contaminated North America and a damaged human genome) within which to begin anew the calculations of effective medical governance. Specifically, the length of time it takes for cancer to appear is calculated against the expected longevity of middle-aged Americans in a postnuclear world and thereby minimized as a concern. Under this line of thinking, it is not a sacrifice if you die before the health effects of eating radioactive food give you a fatal cancer.

Kahn recognizes that the psychology of a postnuclear world would also be a major source of conflict. His analysis participates in a long-running state concern about how emotions—fear, panic, and terror—influence mass populations at a time of constant crisis. He asks his readers to consider this:

> Now just imagine yourself in the postwar situation. Everybody will have been subjected to extremes of anxiety, unfamiliar environment, strange foods, minimum toilet facilities, inadequate shelters and the like. Under these conditions some high percentage of the population is going to become nauseated, and nausea is very catching. If one man vomits, everybody vomits. It would not be surprising if almost everybody vomits. Almost everyone is likely to think he has received too much radiation. Morale may be so affected that many survivors may refuse to participate in constructive activities but would content themselves with sitting down and waiting to die—some may even become violent and destructive. (1960, 86)

If one man vomits, everybody vomits. For Kahn, the question here is not how to avoid a world where nuclear war is possible but rather how to help individuals understand the meaning of their own gag reflexes. Thus, he proposes a national program to distribute radiation meters throughout all towns and cities as a means to help survivors determine if their physical responses are acute radiation poisoning, the flu, or merely the correct reaction to a destroyed world. Kahn here moves from nausea to panic as an immediate problem of a postnuclear world. In doing so, he participates in the chief project of civil defense in the early Cold War period—an emotional adjustment of the American public to the reality of nuclear warfare rather than a prevention of conflict. Having provided radiation meters, the state can now say that citizens possess the means of self-regulating their emotions in a postnuclear moment, thus refocusing the issue from one of mass casualties and destruction to the issue of how individuals control themselves.

The crucial point here is that Herman Kahn's examination of the effects of nuclear war, though widely read in government circles, did not produce a retreat from the escalating arms race but rather an ongoing project to normalize nuclear war as simply another element of risk in everyday life. The Geiger counter becomes the perfect emblem of this logic, as it cannot prevent radiation exposure, only measure its immediate scale. Put differently, nuclear terror—with all its stomach-turning, mind-wrenching, multitudinous forms of anxiety—was never the enemy during the Cold War; this terror was a core tool of the U.S. security state. U.S. officials did not define mental and physical health during the height of the Cold War as an absence of anxiety or injury but rather as the correct response to it, an emotional self-discipline grounded in normalization rather than resistance.

What kind of governance is this? And what has happened to the idea of public health as a state project devoted to improving the lives of citizens? While nuclear war has not yet occurred on the scale Kahn imagined, the effects of the nuclear test project distributed fallout and other environmental contamination on a massive scale to U.S. citizens and globally. The combined effects of environmental damage and social anxiety created by the nuclear arms race fundamentally altered—indeed, placed in opposition—the concepts of national security and public health. In other words, the U.S. effort to build an atomic bomb did not just create a new kind of weapon; it both revolutionized American society and accelerated a larger industrial transformation of the biosphere. It is important to remember that the nearly seven thousand nuclear weapons that the United States maintains in its current arsenal are capable of holding the entire planet hostage.[3] Since there is no interior or exterior to this global logic, which makes a claim on every living being on the planet, the bomb does not produce "bare life" (a reduction to a purely biological condition) or a "state of exception" in Giorgio Agamben's (1998) formulation; in its totalizing scope and effects, it is something rather new in human history.

The modern state form is grounded, as Michel Foucault has argued, in the management of internal populations and a constant effort to improve the security of that population from a variety of risks. The state's effort to improve and regulate the lives of citizens in terms of hygiene, disease, mental health, and education not only produced the social sciences but also mobilized state power in ways that touched every citizen from taxes, to inoculations against disease, to the structure of the school system, to the safety of roads, to military service, and to the logics of imprisonment (for crime, insanity, and infectious disease). Modern technology as well as modern social science provided the means for constant social improvement as the nation-state form developed, constructing for citizens an imagined future in which health was to be an endless horizon of better living and part of an increasingly less violent world. More state security was thus coterminous with the promise of more security for the individual; that is, a happier, healthier life. This narrative of an idealized progress was possible until the atomic revolution, which both underscored the reality of radical technological change and invalidated the state's ability to regulate society at the level of health and happiness. Security and health, which were linked for several hundred years in the development of the modern state concept, became contradictory ideas after 1945, transformed by nuclear nationalism and petrochemical pollution.

Foucault (2000, 365) seems to acknowledge this in his lectures on security. He notes that something fundamental about the state changes after 1945, disrupting his theory about the evolution of state power from monarchal authority through the modern nation-state form, which relies on a variety of means of influencing individuals (discipline) and populations (biopower) in constituting its power. In *Society Must Be Defended*, he argues:

> The workings of contemporary political power are such that atomic power represents a paradox that is difficult, if not impossible, to get around. The power to manufacture and use the atom bomb represents the deployment of a sovereign power that kills, but it is also the power to kill life itself. So the power that is being exercised in this atomic power is exercised in such a way that it is capable of suppressing life itself. And, therefore, to suppress itself insofar as it is the power that guarantees life. Either it is sovereign and uses the atom bomb, and therefore cannot be power, biopower, or the power to guarantee life, as it has been ever since the nineteenth century. Or, at the opposite extreme you no longer have a sovereign right that is in excess of biopower, but a biopower that is in excess of sovereign right. (Foucault 2003, 253)

The *excess* biopower produced by the bomb is a topic that bears much scrutiny, for the United States has literally built itself through nuclear weaponry (see Schwartz 1998). After the atomic destruction of Hiroshima and Nagasaki, the relationship between military, governmental, industrial, and academic institutions grew as these institutions supported a U.S. security state that was founded on nuclear weaponry and anticommunism. The Cold War nuclear standoff consequently became the ground for a new articulation of state power as well as a new social contract in the United States, transforming the terms of everyday life as well as the very definition of public health.

The atomic revolution, however, presented immediate contradictions, troubling U.S. policy makers' efforts to define security and health. By the early 1950s, it was clear that the atomic test program in the Pacific was distributing fallout globally even as the expanding arms race with the Soviet Union made possible the extinction of both nation-states and whole ecosystems. Similarly, the decision to open a continental test site in Nevada in 1951 (to lower the costs of nuclear weapons research) enabled the direct exposure of Americans with each and every aboveground detonation, ensuring that the fallout of nuclear nationalism would be experienced at a cellular level and across the generations. The construction of this new national security apparatus, which attacked public health with each detonation, thus required a new kind of collective sacrifice located in the distribution of a range of fallout elements, from iodine to plutonium. Not able both to pursue the atomic bomb and to protect citizens (in the classic sense of not exposing them to damaging health effects), the United States chose instead to normalize the nuclear crisis as a new form of nature. In effect, Cold War officials minimized the health effects of the atomic test program while constantly inflating fears of a Soviet attack in order to create a perception-based form of risk management. It then told citizens that the central problem of the nuclear age was just in their heads. Fallout was officially converted into a question of emotional self-control.

In other words, mental health was increasingly fused with national security after 1945 as the United States mobilized nuclear logics to remake its social institutions and its approach to global affairs. Nuclear fear, a unique physiological and mental state first achieved via the atomic bombing of Hiroshima and Nagasaki, quickly became the basis for a permanent wartime economy in the United States and the total mobilization of American political, scientific, academic, and military institutions. With the first Soviet nuclear detonation in 1949, the United States formally became a paranoid formation, with federal officials seeing communists and proliferating nuclear threats at home and around the world. The nuclear project not only coordinated American institutions in support of a military agenda, it enabled a vision of the entire world as defensible, vulnerable space. "Containing communism" around the world placed U.S. citizens in a new relationship to the security state, which required not only unprecedented financial commitments during supposed peacetime but also a parallel project to transform Americans into Cold Warriors. For U.S. policy makers, an immediate question was how to avoid creating an apathetic public on the one hand or a terrorized one on the other—how to create public support for an unprecedented, and potentially unending, militarism (see Oakes 1994).

At the height of the Cold War emotional management project, a new form of mental health practice materialized. As Jonathan Metzl (2003) has documented, the discovery and first mass marketing of antidepressants in the United States occurred in the midst of widespread anxieties and nuclear fears. Psychopharmacology produced a revolution in the very idea of mental health, as individuals could now regulate their brain chemistry in an effort to achieve a state of internal calm. Metzl shows how the arrival of psychopharmaceuticals immediately began to replace psychotherapy as the dominant paradigm in treating mental illness. Thus, psychotherapy moved away from personal history and trauma as an explanatory mode for mental illness at precisely the moment in which trauma was both nationalized and codified within the Cold War system as essential. By eliminating history and experience as an explanatory mechanism, mental treatment could be reimagined as solely a chemical negotiation, not one involving the social contradictions produced by a nuclear arms race. And by calibrating their emotions to the expectations of Cold War society through drugs, many Americans moved closer to normalizing a state of emergency in everyday life. Mass anxiety, however, was both a resource and a problem for the early Cold War state (see Orr 2006).

For the architects of the Cold War system within the Truman, Eisenhower, and Kennedy administrations, the solution to public mobilization was a new kind of project, one pursued with help from social scientists and the advertising industry, to teach citizens a specific kind of cognitive and emotional attitude toward the bomb. Drawing on the historic concept of defense as a protection of citizens, the federal program for civil defense was actually a quite radical effort to psychologically and emotionally remake Americans as Cold Warriors. It turned the idea of public protection—a classic definition of security—into a mental operation, concerned almost exclusively with perceptions, emotions, and self-discipline. This project took the form of an elaborate propaganda campaign involving films, literature, town meetings, and educational programs designed to teach Americans to fear the bomb; to define and limit that nuclear fear in ways useful to the Cold War project; and to move responsibility for domestic nuclear crisis from the state to citizens, enabling all citizens to have a role in a new collective form of American militarism. Through the 1950s, the FCDA staged yearly simulations of nuclear attacks on the United States in which designated American cities would act out nuclear catastrophe. Local newspapers would run banner headlines such as "Washington DC, Detroit Destroyed by Hydrogen Bombs"—allowing civic leaders and politicians to lead theatrical evacuations of the city for television cameras (see Davis 2007; McEnaney 2000). The formal goal of this state program was to transform nuclear terror, which was interpreted by officials as a paralyzing emotion, into nuclear fear, an affective state that would allow citizens to function in a time of crisis. As Guy Oakes (1994, 47) has documented, civil defense programs of the 1950s and 1960s were designed to do nothing less than "emotionally manage" U.S. citizens through nuclear fear.

Moreover, since the Cold War was conceived as a state of long-term crisis, the concept of "civil defense" was designed to create a new kind of citizen equipped with a psychological and emotional constitution capable of negotiating the day-to-day, minute-to-minute nuclear threat for the long haul. In addition to turning the domestic space of the home into the front line of the Cold War, atomic civil defense argued that citizens should be psychologically prepared every second of the day to deal with a potential nuclear attack. Thus, the Cold War state demanded that citizens accept personal responsibility for surviving nuclear conflict. The key move in this shift from emphasizing protection to vulnerability in public safety was a campaign to make panic—not nuclear war—the official enemy. As Val Peterson, the head of the Federal Civil Defense Administration (FCDA) wrote:

> Ninety per cent of all emergency measures after an atomic blast will depend on the prevention of panic among the survivors in the first 90 seconds. Like the A-bomb, panic is fissionable. It can produce a chain reaction more deeply destructive than any explosive known. If there is an ultimate weapon, it may well be mass panic—not the A-bomb. (1953, 99)

Panic is fissionable. Indeed, Peterson not only argued that Americans were particularly "susceptible to panic" but offered a checklist on how citizens could become "panic stoppers" by training themselves for nuclear attack and becoming like "soldiers" at home (see figure 8.2). Thus, the official message from the early Cold War state was that self-control was the best way for citizens to fight a nuclear war, revealing a national project to both colonize and normalize everyday life with nuclear fear. Panic, as Jackie Orr has so powerfully shown, became more than a means of managing populations in the nuclear age: it remade the individual as a permanently insecure node in the larger Cold War system (Orr 2006, 14). Regulating the psychology of a nation-state at this level, however, demanded that Cold War policy makers understand how to produce panic as well as calm it. Orr has argued this effort produced a collapsing field of mental health, national security, and individualized identity formation across the frontiers of gender, family, expertise, and self-knowledge. The U.S. nuclear project writ large required citizens to

PANIC STOPPERS

How to keep from being a victim of panic

Face the Facts — The more you learn, the safer you are. Insulate yourself against panic by finding out all you can about the enemy's weapons — A-bombs, germ and gas warfare, sabotage and rumor war. Misinformation and lack of information breed panic.

Get Ready at Home — Preparedness is good preventive medicine against panic. Prepare and train your family so that the members can perform their duties like trained soldiers under fire. Here's how:

1. Talk to your family about the dangers you face. Work out practice drills so you all know what to do—at home, at work or at school.

2. Get a civil defense emergency first-aid kit together and learn how to use it.

3. Put away a three-day emergency supply of food and water—enough to take care of the whole family and its special needs.

4. Build a home shelter if you live near a target area. If you can't build one, pick out the safest shelter area in your home. Personal shelter can help save your life.

5. Be sure you have a workable AM Radio, preferably battery-operated, in your shelter area. Remember the Conelrad frequencies—640 and 1240—where in an emergency you can get official news and civil defense instructions.

6. Take a Red Cross first-aid course as soon as possible. In the meantime, study the civil defense booklet, Emergency Action to Save Lives. You can get it at your local defense office or at the Government Printing Office, Washington 25, D.C. It costs five cents.

7. Practice fireproof housekeeping; learn how to fight small fires in your home before they can become big ones. There's a nickel government manual for that, too: Fire-Fighting for House-holders.

8. Learn the simple steps your family should take to protect themselves against germ warfare. That calls for one more government pamphlet: What You Should Know about Biological Warfare. Cost: 10 cents.

Get Leadership Training — Invest a few hours a week in basic training for one of the organized civil defense services so that you will be ready for group action in any emergency.

Make Fear Work For You — Don't be ashamed of being scared. If an attack comes, you will be scared and so will everyone else. It is *what you do* when you are afraid that counts. Fear can be healthy if you know how to use it; it can make you more alert and stronger at a time when you and your neighbors must act to protect yourselves.

Spike That Rumor — Don't swallow everything you hear. Recognize wartime rumor and gossip for what they are—enemy weapons of the most dangerous kind. Don't let the enemy play you for a sucker — don't pass on rumors. Check any story you hear. Make sure that the facts are from official sources before you repeat them.

Figure 8.2. Val Peterson's panic-stopper instructions (Federal Civil Defense Administration).

accept as normal social conditions that were both pathologically insecure and intellectually irreconcilable with either health or security.

The FCDA effort to regulate the national public via images of nuclear conflict took on extraordinary proportions, involving massive public exercises in which citizens acted out their own destruction and where the state set out to show citizens what a postnuclear world might look like (Masco 2008). The Cold War security state ultimately sought to use nuclear fear to promote a new kind of social and psychological hygiene, one uniquely suited for a nuclear age. In the 1954 FCDA film *The House in the Middle*, for example, we see that nuclear fear could be harnessed to any kind of domestic project, including household cleanliness (see figure 8.3). Presented as an atomic experiment, the film documents how nuclear flash, heat, and blast effects engage model houses built at the Nevada Test Site. The three model houses presented in the film are in different stages of cleanliness and repair, placed in a row, and filmed against the stark desert landscape. The narrator offers this description of the project:

> Three identical miniature frame houses, with varying exterior conditions, all the same distance from the point of the explosion. The house on the right: an eyesore. But you've seen these same conditions in your own hometown: old unpainted wood, and look at the paper, leaves and trash in the yard. In a moment, you'll see the results of atomic heat flash on this house, the house on the left. Typical of many homes across the nation: heavily weathered, dry wood, in run-down condition. This house is the product of years of neglect. It has not been painted regularly. It is dry and rotten—a tinderbox ready to turn into a blazing torch. The house in the middle: in good condition, with a clean, unlittered yard. The exterior has been painted with ordinary, good quality house paint. Light painted surfaces reflect heat and the paint also protects the wood from weathering and water damage. Let's see what happens under atomic heat. (FCDA 1954)

Let's see what happens. The moralizing tone of the narration underscores that this film is ultimately an effort to recuperate the classic definition of hygiene as a social responsibility, and in so doing to create an image of a state that treats nuclear emergency as it would an infectious disease or a natural disaster. The centerpiece of the film is the slow-motion footage of the atomic blast wave hitting the model houses. The houses on the right and left ignite and burn to the ground, leaving the house in the middle standing. After contemplating this slow-motion destruction in detail, the narrator reexamines the ashes of the houses on the right and left and asks against somber background music:

Which of these is your house? This one? The house on the right? Dilapidated with paper, dead grass, litter everywhere? The house on the left—unpainted, run-down, neglected? Is this your house?" [Then on an upbeat music cue, the narrator concludes,] "The house in the middle—cleaned up, painted up, and fixed up, exposed to the same searing atomic heat wave—did not catch fire. Close inspection reveals only a slight charring of the painted outer surface. Yes, the white house in the middle survived an atomic heat flash. These civil defense tests prove how important upkeep is to our houses and town. (FCDA 1954)

Only a slight charring. Household cleanliness is directly linked here to the likelihood of winning or losing a nuclear war. Hygiene, as a classic domain of state intervention into public health, is remade as a means of surviving not illness but nuclear attack. Indeed, the film does not mention fallout or radiation effects at all. The implicit message of the film is that each citizen should patrol his or her neighborhood for trash and feel free to discipline neighbors into perfect home performances. *The House in the Middle* argues ultimately that appearances are more important than reality, that a fresh coat of paint is more important than recognizing the city-killing power of nuclear weapons. Indeed, it offers citizens the opportunity to manically tend to their homes in every detail, from paint and yard work to furnishings and foodstuffs, as a means of achieving public health and national security, even as the reality of thermonuclear warfare promises little to no hope of survival.

The House in the Middle demonstrates how the terms of everyday life in the nuclear age became saturated with a new kind of state discourse, one that used nuclear fear to promote its policies at home and abroad. The challenge in such a psychological strategy, of course, is one of modulation—enough fear to produce support for U.S. Cold War policies but not so much that it generates a countermovement. Indeed, the debates about nuclear fallout and the ineffectual nature of the civil defense program in case of actual nuclear war eventually forced the nuclear program into a major reorganization in the early 1960s. Civil defense, at this time, was factually wrong in many of its claims about the ability to survive a nuclear war. Moreover, the effort by Herman Kahn and others to think the unthinkable revealed to many the impossibility of civil defense in the thermonuclear age. U.S. scientists also produced a powerful antinuclear counterdiscourse that emphasized the health effects of nuclear testing, both challenging the false claims of civil defense and demanding that the state return to concepts of security and health committed to improving living conditions rather than normalizing nuclear danger. But the first

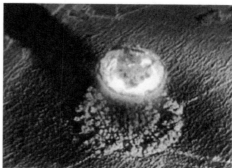

decade of the Cold War witnessed the development of an entirely new form of governance, one in which a very public national security discourse was used strategically by the state to both mask and enable a global vision grounded in the sacrifice of citizens both born and unborn. Public health, in this context, became secondary to a vision of national security that installed new forms of individual death within a larger structure of mass death in the mid-twentieth century. Civil defense amplified the foundational U.S. violences of settler colonial dispossession and antiblackness by conjuring a distorted version of an American public that could be protected because it was white, middle class, and suburban. The social consequences of the nuclear arms race ultimately inverted the concept of health as absence of disease, replacing it with an increasingly naturalized vision of health as incipient death.

The effects of this joint transformation in the logics of health and national security are still with us today and are even ascendant. The reactions to the suicide-hijacker attacks on Washington, DC, and New York City in September 2001 reinvigorated the emotional management strategy and returned Americans to the logics of survival and sacrifice that structured the Cold War period. The threat of terrorism was magnified by the George W. Bush administration, mobilized to shift U.S. global ambitions as well as domestic policy. Just as the first Soviet nuclear test in 1949 was mobilized by the Truman and Eisenhower administrations to construct the Cold War state, so did the Bush administration use nuclear fear to create a new counterterror state (see Masco 2014). The federal appeal to citizens after 2001 was also modeled directly on the early civil defense campaigns as it argued for a normalization rather than an elimination of a totalized threat. Consider, for a moment, the first round of civil defense advertisements produced by the newly formed Department of Homeland Security (DHS) in 2003 (see figure 8.4). One commercial begins with a young girl working her way across the monkey bars at a playground. Halfway though she stops; while hanging on the bars, she looks directly at the camera and recites the following list: "Batteries, a first-aid kit, enough water for three days, a flashlight, transistor radio, a whistle, a dust mask, a plan." As she exits the apparatus, text flows onto the screen, stating:

BE PREPARED

READY.GOV

In a second DHS civil defense commercial, a Little League baseball game is underway, and in mid-pitch the pitcher and batter stop to trade preparedness info (see figure 8.5):

Figure 8.4.
Stills from 2003 "America Prepared" playground commercial (Department of Homeland Security).

Figure 8.5.
Stills from
2003 "America
Prepared"
baseball
commercial
(Department
of Homeland
Security).

PITCHER: My dad's work number: 212-327-1845.

HITTER: My aunt Judy: 281-837-4066.

PITCHER: A meeting place.

HITTER: A plan.

BE PREPARED
READY.GOV

Fifty years after Val Peterson's national campaign to teach citizens to fear panic more than the bomb, the official position is still that every second of your life should be spent rehearsing the possibility of disaster, training yourself as a citizen to take responsibility for events that are by definition out of your control. Repeating the civil defense logics from the first decades of the Cold War, the state is absent here except in its desire to install a specific kind of fear within everyday life through advertising. The first ninety seconds of a crisis are still the most important, requiring that children be prepared to recite emergency information between swings of a Little League bat or while hanging on a playground apparatus. These commercials reiterate the lessons of nuclear civil defense, that everyday life is structured around the possibility of mass injury from one moment to the next and that citizens must take responsibility for their own survival.

One of the most difficult cultural logics to assess is the arrival of a new social relationship to death. The vulnerability of children is one immediate register of American ideas of death, whether revealed in Herman Kahn's meditations on the number of "defective children" it will take to win the Cold War or in these DHS commercials that present children as robots, preprogrammed to respond to emergency, rehearsing their lifeline phone numbers even in the midst of play. Since 1945 the United States has built its national community via contemplation of specific images of mass death while building a defense complex that demands ever more personal sacrifice in the name of security. What is impossible to see today is the counterfactual, the infrastructures that might have been built or a social order not infused with the logics of nuclear nationalism. Health as an absence of disease or anxiety is long gone. What we have instead is a negotiation of degrees of contamination, of degrees of anxious association, of degrees of escalating threat. The initial concept of public health as a rational coordinate of the modern state system has been replaced by a governmental calculus based on individual sacrifice and threat escalation. The War on Terror requires that Americans once again naturalize a notion of health as incipient death, inviting each and every citizen to dust off the familiar logics of Cold War sacrifice and embrace the further collapse of mental health into national security. Demilitarizing the mind by rejecting the counterterror state project thus contains revolutionary potential; it might finally overthrow a national security project that both relies on and installs ever more deeply the possibility of violence and death into everyday life. In the twenty-first century, the last thing we need is more of this kind of health. Demilitarizing the mind, body, and spirit of American citizens by getting rid of the bomb, however, might just open up an entirely new kind of nature—post–national security, post-counterterror, post-panic.

9

THE END OF ENDS

The concept of the extreme is relational, assuming a counterpoint to everyday experience marked regular, unexceptional, banal. Yet American life for decades has been founded on ideas, logics, and machines that are simultaneously infrastructural (and thus part of a normalized everyday) and extreme in the absolute sense of unprecedented and utterly violent. Instrumental rationality has—in the form of the atomic bomb—produced a world that is simultaneously normal and extreme, at once capable of informing everyday life or of ending it in a flash. In the atomic bomb, technological means and ends combine in a new constellation, one that exceeds modernist rationality, creating epistemic problems that remain emblematic of our moment. The kind of technical expertise responsible for producing the atomic bomb has engineered an industrialized, globalized, networked world, one now experiencing the combined pressures of political, military, economic, and environmental disruption. In such a world, which relies on a highly developed social commitment to normalizing extremes in the effort to secure profit and knowledge, reflexive critique becomes both ever more vital, yet also more inherently fraught.

In an extreme age, we might well ask: what are the possibilities for a productive shock, an experience or insight that would allow us to rethink the terms of everyday life? In the discipline of biology, the discovery of microbial extremophiles in deep-sea volcanic vents has challenged long-standing scientific definitions of life (Helmreich 2008). Living under conditions of extreme heat and pressure, these methane-eating beings have redefined the very limits of life on planet Earth and beyond. What could produce a similar effect in the domain of security? Opportunities for such a critique are ever present, an endless stream of moments in fact, yet constantly subsumed by the normalizing effects of a national security culture committed to a constant state of emergency. A return to basic questions of how to define profit, loss, and sustainability is a key concern today in the United States, and this chapter asks, what kind of analysis could begin to redefine the limits of a collective security? What kind of defamiliarization and/or productive shock might allow insight into the cultural terms of expert judgment today in the United States, allowing us to rethink the logics and practices that have simultaneously produced a global war on terror, a global financial meltdown, and a planetary climate emergency in the twenty-first century? How can Americans—extremophiles of the national sort—assess their own history within a national-cultural formation devoted to the normalization of violence (as war, as boom-and-bust capitalism, as environmental ruin) as the basis for everyday life?

This chapter does not provide an answer to these questions but rather seeks to offer a provocation and a meditation on paths constantly not taken in U.S. national security culture. It asks, how can one read against the normalizing processes of the security state to assess alternative futures, alternative visions rendered invisible by the complex logistics of military science, economic rationality, and global governance? To do so is to break from the normalizing force of everyday national-security capitalism and to interrogate the assumed structures of security and risk that support a global American military deployment and permanent war posture. To accomplish this kind of critical maneuver, however, one needs to be able to recognize the alternative futures rendered void by the specific configurations of politics and threat empowering military-industrial action at a given moment. An extreme critique requires the ability to assess the alternative costs and benefits that remain suspended within the spaces of an everyday American life constantly rehearsing (via media, political culture, and military action) terror as normality. What follows then is both an examination and a performance of extremity—pushing a critical history and theory well beyond the usual scholarly comfort level. It seeks less to settle and explain than to agitate and provoke.

To engage an extreme point of view on crisis, let's turn to a spectacular new technology that seemed to offer just such a perspective on U.S. security culture in 1960—that of an exterior gaze on planet Earth. The first satellite imagery was not only a technological revolution of profound importance to the military (and ultimately the earth and information sciences), it also constituted a rare moment of objective critique to American Cold War fantasies at their most virulent and violent. Covert and extremely fragile, the first Corona satellite was secretly launched into outer space in August 1960, offering a new optics on Cold War military technologies and fantasies. Imagine if you will a rocket carrying not a warhead but a giant panoramic camera (see figures 9.1 and 9.2), slung into a low orbit over Europe, running a long reel of 70 mm film, specially designed by Kodak to function in outer space. The satellite makes a series of orbits exposing its film over designated areas via a timer and then ejects a fireproof capsule back into Earth's atmosphere carrying the exposed film (see figure 9.3). As the capsule descends via a series of parachutes, it emits a homing signal, allowing a specially equipped plane to detect the signal and swoop in, capturing the now-charred film canister in midair via a giant hook (see figure 9.4). On August 18, 1960, the Corona project became the first space-based reconnaissance system, providing the U.S. government with the first satellite photographs of Soviet military installations (Day, Logsdon, and Latell 1998; Peeples 1997). Corona provided the most accurate images of Soviet military capabilities to date, offering concrete photographic evidence of Soviet missile capabilities at a time of near-hysterical speculation about imminent Soviet attack. Soon U.S. officials knew via photographic documentation of communist military bases that the Soviets did not have a vast and growing ICBM superiority capable of overwhelming U.S. defenses; in fact, the U.S. had something on the order of a ten-to-one advantage in missiles, and even more in nuclear devices.

At this moment in the Cold War, outer space reconnaissance provided a clear and impartial assessment of nuclear threat. The always strategically valued "view from above" (Haffner 2013) produced photographs that dramatically changed how U.S. officials viewed the immediacy of nuclear war, shifting official affects and imaginaries via a new material infrastructure in orbit (Richelson 2006). Over the next decade, the race to the moon

Figure 9.1. Launch of Corona satellite (National Reconnaissance Office).

Figure 9.2. Diagram of Corona panoramic cameras (National Reconnaissance Office).

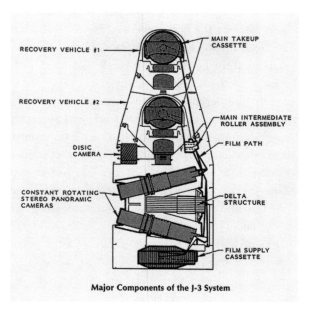

RECOVERY VEHICLE #1

MAIN TAKEUP CASSETTE

RECOVERY VEHICLE #2

MAIN INTERMEDIATE ROLLER ASSEMBLY

DISIC CAMERA

FILM PATH

CONSTANT ROTATING STEREO PANORAMIC CAMERAS

DELTA STRUCTURE

FILM SUPPLY CASSETTE

Major Components of the J-3 System

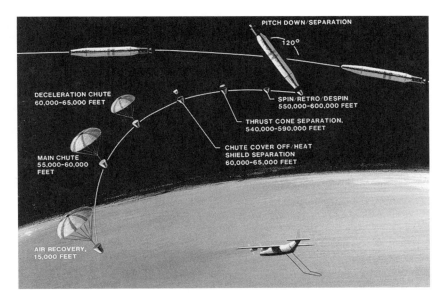

PITCH DOWN/SEPARATION

120°

DECELERATION CHUTE
60,000-65,000 FEET

SPIN/RETRO/DESPIN
550,000-600,000 FEET

THRUST CONE SEPARATION,
540,000-590,000 FEET

CHUTE COVER OFF/HEAT
SHIELD SEPARATION
60,000-65,000 FEET

MAIN CHUTE
55,000-60,000
FEET

AIR RECOVERY,
15,000 FEET

Figure 9.3. Diagram of Corona recovery sequence (National Reconnaissance Office).

Figure 9.4. Catching a Corona film capsule after reentry from space (National Reconnaissance Office).

became the public face of a covert enterprise to extend and expand space surveillance. Plans for manned photographic studios in space with Hubble telescope–sized lenses pointed toward Earth soon were enhanced by digital communications that allowed instant transmission of data (see Willis 2007). The Corona cameras evolved quickly, moving from the forty-foot resolution offered in 1960 to five-foot resolution by 1967, a revolution in optics that was soon followed by digital satellite systems capable of three-inch resolution, infrared imaging, and the near-instantaneous transfer of information. These remote sensing technologies have since revolutionized everything from geography, to earth sciences, to the now ubiquitous GPS systems so crucial to communications and supply chain logistics.[1]

The Central Intelligence Agency (CIA) has long considered the Corona satellite one of its most important achievements, a pure success story. As director of the CIA, Richard Helms held a ceremony in honor of the Corona program on its retirement in 1972 (in favor of the next-generation digital satellite system). He presented a documentary film titled *A Point in Time* to CIA personnel detailing the crucial history of the top-secret program, its technological achievements, and its central role in Cold War geopolitics. A Corona capsule and an extensive photographic display of Corona satellite imagery was then centrally installed at CIA headquarters in Langley to document its success for all future employees. On display through the end of the Cold War, components of this exhibit can now be seen at the National Air and Space Museum. The extensive Corona photographic archive became available for public use at the U.S. National Archives in 1995, declassified by President Bill Clinton via Executive Order 12951. A central player in this declassification effort was Vice President Al Gore, who saw in the Corona image archive the opportunity for new kinds of earth science research, as the satellite imagery surveyed not only military machines but also millions of miles of the earth—including its lakes, oceans, and glaciers—with precise detail (Cloud 2001). The Corona project continues to be a productive information system, informing climate science, archaeological research, and a variety of earth sciences. But while the CIA remembers Corona as a fantastically successful covert spy system, and others today value its photographic record for nonmilitary scientific research, a basic lesson of the Corona achievement remains unrecognized: the first satellite system not only offered a new optic on Soviet technology, it also revealed how fantastical American assessments of Soviet capabilities were in the 1950s. It offered a new remote viewing photography but also new insight into the American national security imaginary and its dangerous countersubversive projections (Rogin 1988). The first

Corona images have much to say about the ferocious U.S. commitment to nuclear weapons and a global nuclear war machine already set on a minute-to-minute trigger by 1960 as about Soviet weapons. The first Corona images foundationally contradicted expert U.S. judgments of Soviet capabilities and desires, providing a powerful counterweight against arguments for a pre-emptive U.S. attack on the Soviet Union (see figures 9.5 and 9.6). The slightly blurry satellite photographs thus hold the potential for a radical critique of American perceptions of the Soviet Union, showing that U.S. officials were as much at war with their own apocalyptic projections in 1960 as with Soviet plans for territorial expansion.

An anthropology of extremes requires a nonnormative reading of culture and history, an effort to push past consensus logics to interrogate what alternative visions, projects, and futures are left unexplored at a given historical moment. The rapidly evolving historical archive provides one opportunity for this kind of critique: our understanding of the twentieth-century American security state is changing with each newly declassified program and document, dramatically reshaping what we know about U.S. policy, military science, and threat assessments since World War II.[2] As the enormous military state apparatus that constitutes the core of the American political and economic machine is grudgingly opened to new kinds of conceptual inter-rogation, Americans should seize the opportunity to learn about their own government's commitments, political processes, and security imaginaries. Indeed, the national security archive is one place where we can formally con-sider how the twentieth-century balance of terror has been remade in the twenty-first century as a war on terror—following the affective politics, tech-nological fetishisms, and geopolitical ambitions that have come to structure U.S. security culture. The declassified Cold War archive allows us to pursue an extreme reading of U.S. security culture, one committed to pushing past official policy logics at moments of heightened emergency to consider how threat, historical contingency, technological revolution, propaganda, and geopolitical ambition combine in a specific moment of extreme risk. The first Corona images, for example, constitute a moment when administrators of the national security state had their own logics and fears negated in the form of direct photographic evidence, opening a potential conceptual space for radical reassessment of their own ambitions, perceptions, and drives, all powerfully revealed in black-and-white photos as a dangerous fantasy. We might well ask why the Corona imagery (and any number of similar moments when existential threat has objectively dissolved into mere projection—most recently, the nonexisting weapons of mass destruction used to justify the

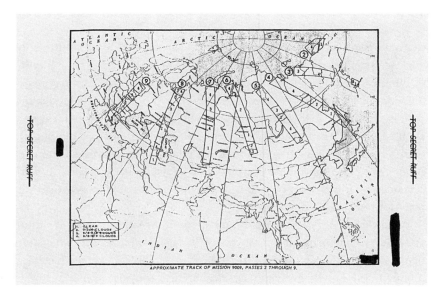

APPROXIMATE TRACK OF MISSION 9009, PASSES 2 THROUGH 9.

Figure 9.5. Photographic path of Corona missions over the Soviet Union (from CIA "Joint Mission Coverage Index, Mission 9009," August 18, 1960).

Figure 9.6. First Corona satellite image, Mys Shmidta airfield, USSR (National Reconnaissance Office).

PARKING APRON

RUNWAY

18 AUGUST 1960 IMAGERY

U.S. invasion of Iraq in 2003) did not produce a radical self-critique in the United States. Put differently, when documented material fact contradicts national security assumptions, why does that not produce a change in strategy or public discourse or accountability?

The Cold War nuclear standoff installed existential threat as a core structure of everyday American life, making nuclear fear the coordinating principle of U.S. geopolitics and a new psychosocial reality for citizens increasingly connected via images of their own imminent death. Indeed, few societies have prepared so meticulously for collective death as did Cold War America while simultaneously denying the possibility of an actual ending. From large-scale civil defense drills in which the destruction of the nation-state became a kind of public theater to the articulation of a Cold War militarism that understood all global political events as potentially conditioning everyday American life, the height of the Cold War worked in novel ways both to enable and deny the possibility of a collective death. The early history of the Corona satellite system offers a compelling story about the technological achievement of a total ending, and the Cold War hysteria of the years 1957–62 in the United States. This is a moment of maximal danger but also of new perspectives—crucially those derived from outer space—that momentarily opened up multiple contingent and radically different security futures. For an anthropology of extremes, this period of Cold War can be approached as an ur-moment, foundational in terms of the technology, politics, affects, and ambitions supporting the American security state. Interrogating this first period of global nuclear danger via recently declassified materials allows us to ask: How does one end the possibility of a total ending? How does a society pursuing war as a normalized condition of everyday life pause and reflect on its own intellectual and psychosocial processes, and even imagine de-escalation or, more radically, peace?

Within modern political theory, the means to an end has been embedded within the very concept of rationality, making ends and means synonymous with progress, a perpetual engine of improving the infrastructures of everyday life as well as the morality of those living within it. Within this modernity—glossed here as the application of reason to nature as progress—we have few efforts to theorize the reality or implications of conceptual blockages or blindnesses within the very notion of security. The assumption that instrumental reason is not only a means to an end but also an essential good structures a Euro-American modernity in which superstition is set against the possibility of an unending technological progress (Horkheimer and Adorno 2002, 1). Benjamin (1969) offers perhaps the most powerful critique of progress by showing how the promise of the new can be the vehicle of social mysti-fication and entrenchment. His call to "brush history against the grain" and establish a critical method that can "seize hold of a memory as it flashes up at a moment of danger" is ultimately a call to resist the normalization (and naturalization) of violence in everyday life. But how, and under what terms, can this be accomplished in a national security state that is premised on the total ending of nuclear war? Having built the war machine as a global system of 24/7 always-on apocalyptic capacity, how can a settler colonial society turn toward an alternative notion of security, one not grounded in the tech-nological possibility of nuclear war or indifferent to climate disruption?

How, indeed, does thinking about an absolute ending work to install a new set of fantasies and short circuits that prevent reflexive critique? How do rational modes of planning work not to eliminate the possibility of col-lective death but rather, through self-mystification, to install its possibility ever deeper into an expert state system? Kant (1986) articulated one central area where reason is installed as a compensation for a lack of understanding in his notion of the sublime. Sublime experience, in his view, overwhelms the human sensorium, providing that strange mix of pleasure and terror involved in surpassing one's cognitive limit. For Kant, the experience of incomprehensibility is then managed by an act of categorizing—by a naming of the event—rather than through understanding. Compensation rather than comprehension is thus achieved, installing at the very center of his notion of reason an irreducible problem about means, ends, and the ability of human beings in extreme moments to comprehend both. Terror has an inherent sublimity, one that has been multiplied across contemporary violent potentials—war, economy, environment—to create a new complex configuration of planetary risk that exceeds the power of the national secu-rity state (Masco 2010). Nuclear terror, as a state system, however, is not a momentary experience (as Kant's sublime requires) but is instead a global infrastructure—one that coordinates American military power as well as its domestic politics. This infrastructure requires constant affective as well as technological support, merging complex social and technological pro-cesses that become fused in perceptions of global risk.

Put differently, instrumental reason (imagine here as free of affect, let alone terror) has enabled a globalized, economized, technologized moder-nity, but it has also installed a set of compensations for those events, desires, and biological facts that disrupt specific calculations of progress/profit. By the mid-twentieth century, the products of instrumental reason—the very means to an end—produced new forms of war that ultimately challenged collective survival and a related set of petrochemical economic commitments that disrupts climate. The atomic bomb stands as both a rational technology—produced via the combined work of physicists, engineers, chemists, industrialists, military planners, defense intellectuals, and civilian policy makers—and as a limit case to that instrumental reason (see Edwards 1996; Oakes 1994). In the early days of the nuclear age, some Manhattan Project scientists hoped this new technology would be so terrible that it would simply end the possibility of war (e.g., FAS 1946). Instead, U.S. war planners built a global system for nuclear war that could end most global life itself within a few hours of actual conflict. Each new nuclear system—bomber, submarine, and missile—was both a technological achievement of the first order and an accelerating progression toward the end of this technomodernity in the form of nuclear conflict.

These experts were attempting to negotiate through engineering a basic relationship to death, committing to a perverse project of building ever more destructive machines in the name of producing security. Indeed, displacing the threat of one machine (the atomic bomb) with another (the hydrogen bomb) became the basis for deterrence theory, a way of organizing and containing the thought of death by expanding technological systems. Freud (1991) saw this contradiction in militarism early on, and in his remarkable 1915 essay "Thoughts for the Times on War and Death," he is definitive that it is impossible to comprehend—to actually believe in—one's own death. Thus, he notes, even as the human organism moves closer to death with each tick of the clock, the ego pursues a program of immortality and works to relocate the onrushing reality of death to exterior locations—to novels, to foreign populations, to distant wars, to a radical outside. Thus, the thought of an ending here literally produces a new set of means—fantasies, projections, displacements, and amnesias all mobilized to suture together an idea of an eternal self. In American national culture, the Cold War performed this task through a series of circuits: the communist threat was simultaneously everywhere and nowhere, and the imminent threat of nuclear war was mitigated by a fetishistic focus on technological detail. Cold War planners managed the threat of nuclear war through constant proliferation—of weapons, delivery systems, images, theories, and calculations. Through this proliferation, Cold War planners pursued a program of intellectual compensation for the confrontation with a new kind of death. They did so by mobilizing expert resources (changing the very temporal horizon of war from days, to hours, to minutes in the process), as well as by pursuing proxy wars and covert actions around the world. In the process, Americans learned how to be committed to total war as a precondition for everyday life while locating death as exterior to the nation, even as the war machine grew ferociously in its technological capacities. This represents a distinctive national-cultural achievement: a notion of security that brings collective death ever closer in an attempt to fix its location with ever more precision. By the time of the first Corona photograph, the U.S. nuclear system was on constant and permanent alert, managing on a minute-by-minute temporal scale a global war machine—one that imagined a Soviet nuclear strike could come with less than seven minutes of warning (Keeney 2011, 186).

U.S. military systems became both the most direct application of technical rationality and the location of deep fantasies about national immortality and the possibility of systems of total control. In the first decade of the Cold War, for example, the lack of detailed intelligence about the Soviet Union enabled an American national security project that was both technologically utopian and driven by increasingly apocalyptic visions of an omnipotent other. A top-secret, blue-ribbon panel studying the possibility of nuclear civil defense in 1957, known as the Gaither Committee, not only recommended a nationwide commitment to building underground bunkers and training citizens to think calmly about experiencing nuclear war, its members also concluded that a "missile gap" with the Soviet Union left the United States increasingly vulnerable to a devastating "first strike" (Security Resources Panel of the Science Advisory Committee 1957). Reinforced by the hysteria over Sputnik later in 1957—the first artificial satellite in space—U.S. national security debates, by the end of the 1950s, were structured by visions of a Soviet sneak attack that would destroy urban America in an instant. The Gaither Committee leaked to the press their conclusion that by 1959 the Soviets would have a decisive advantage in ICBMs (see Roman 1995; Snead 1999). The domestic politics informing the missile gap narrative became part of the battle between military branches for nuclear resources and soon was a key to John F. Kennedy's presidential campaign strategy of positioning his Republican rivals (Eisenhower and then Nixon) as weak on national security. Thus, a threat projection with multiple political uses became codified as a kind of truth in U.S. national security policy, leading to massive increases in defense spending at the end of the Eisenhower administration and then again at the start of the Kennedy administration, as these officials tried to demonstrate their anticommunism and nuclear resolve. The U.S. nuclear triad—of bombers, ICBMs, and submarines—is built at this moment, providing multiply redundant systems for waging nuclear war and giving each branch of the military a nuclear capability.

Today one can see that in addition to the new weapons systems built at the end of the 1950s, there was also an important political discovery crucial to the evolving Cold War: namely, the universal utility of threat proliferation in U.S. security culture. The raw political value of existential threat as a motivating narrative became a well-worn domestic strategy in the United States, one linking the missile gap of the 1950s to the window of vulnerability of the 1970s, to the Strategic Defense Initiative of the 1980s, to the space-based Pearl Harbor narratives of the 1990s, to the terrorist WMD discourses of the 2000s as illustrations of a nuclear culture. In each of these cases, we can see how the bomb (as a consolidated technosocial form of existential threat) has been good for Americans to think with, becoming the basis for building a nuclear state and a global military system but also for transforming raw military ambition into a necessary form of defense. But if the bomb has been crucial to constituting U.S. superpower status, it has also produced a complex new domestic affective political domain, allowing images of, and appeals to, existential threat to become a central means of establishing and expanding a militarized national security culture.

By 1961, U.S. war planners sought to rationalize a vast set of military logics and capabilities into a comprehensive war plan—known as the Single Integrated Operating Plan or SIOP. The first plan, known as SIOP-62, promised to reduce contingency and error during nuclear war—to coordinate a U.S. war machine that included bombers, submarines, and missiles deployed globally, as well as a vast array of frontline nuclear technologies, from nuclear cannons, to backpack bombs, to atomic land mines (see Ball and Toth 1990; Burr 2004; Sagan 1987). The first SIOP had two attack options, each involving a total assault on the communist bloc—preemptive war and retaliation. What is crucial to acknowledge today is that SIOP-62 was not a war plan in any traditional sense; rather, it articulated in technologically feasible terms a total ending (see Burr 2005; Keeny 2002; Rosenberg 1981). The preemptive option could be triggered by signs of an imminent Soviet attack. What constituted a definitive sign of such an attack, however, was left unstated, creating potential slippages between officials in different organizations—the Strategic Air Command, the Navy, and the White House, for example—who might interpret Soviet actions differently. American Cold War state and nation building was also increasingly devoted to rehearsing a surprise attack on the United States and to applying worst-case scenario thinking as normative.

The preemptive option in SIOP-62 committed the full U.S. arsenal in a simultaneous global nuclear strike, involving 3,200 nuclear weapons delivered to 1,060 targets around the world. In short, it was a plan to eliminate communism from the earth with a few hours of nuclear war, involving targets not only in the Soviet Union but also China (not yet a nuclear power) and all of their allied states. Hundreds of cities and more than 500 million people would be destroyed in a few hours of nuclear war, followed by millions more from radiation injuries. Not included in this calculation were nuclear counterstrikes or the environmental or climatic effects of nuclear war, which would have magnified and spread these effects to all corners of the globe.

The scale of destruction detailed in SIOP-62 is a distinctive moment in human history and is, in Kant's strict technical sense of the term, sublime.[3] It is beyond comprehension, which raises a crucial issue about how the nuclear state resolves such terror/complexity. In national security planning, the compensation for this experience of cognitive overload was a fixation on command and control, as well as the articulation of specific war calculations, marking degrees of violence for different nuclear war scenarios (Kahn 1960; see also Eden 2004). What would likely be an unknown chaos of missiles and bombs launched for the first time from a vast range of technologies, located all over the planet under deeply varied conditions, appears on paper as a rational program of cause and effect, threat and preemption, attack and counterattack. This was an apocalyptic vision presented simply as math. From 1962 and continuing until today, the SIOP nuclear war plan has been continually revised and rationalized for different global political contexts but never truly abandoned (McKinzie et al. 2001). The United States maintains the ability to destroy all major population centers outside the continental U.S. within a few minutes of nuclear conflict. It is important to recognize that this technical capacity to deliver overwhelming violence to any part of the world in mere minutes has relied on structures of the imagination as well as on machines, on threat projections, national security affects, and fantasies as well as physics and engineering.

U.S. policy makers have experienced many moments of rupture in their global vision, shocks that might have recalibrated how threat, security, fears, and technology were organized. After U-2 pilot Gary Powers was shot down over the Soviet Union in 1960, covert spy flights over the USSR were stopped, leaving policy makers in the United States with no definitive intelligence on Soviet military activities. It is difficult today to imagine a period more fraught, more susceptible to paranoid fantasy and projection, and more primed for nuclear conflict. U.S. policy makers lacked basic information about Soviet society and military capabilities, creating a huge information gap that invited speculation, fantasy, and paranoia. In a national security culture constantly rehearsing surprise attack, and negotiating increasing political confrontations in Europe, Southeast Asia, Africa, and Latin America, what could provoke a de-escalation in this nuclear system, which by the early 1960s was already primed for nuclear war on a minute-to-minute basis? The Corona system offered a radically new perspective on Cold War realities, but its role was historically and culturally limited to revealing the objective facts of Soviet nuclear capabilities, not the American fantasies that generated the missile gap in the first place.

The Corona system was both cutting-edge technology and a new form of expressive culture, a nascent planetary technology mobilized to combat official panic. The missed opportunity provided by the first Corona photographs was to evaluate the fantasies and paranoia of an American military system that had so thoroughly misjudged the scale of the Soviet technological capabilities that preemptive nuclear war was under consideration. The missile gap narrative was never publicly retracted, and the satellite photographs that disproved this major assumption of the early Cold War were classified top secret until 1995. Classification protected the technology but also the national self-critique Corona photographs might have generated of official U.S. projections. Thus, an opportunity for a public discussion of how national fears are constituted out of a lack of information, fantasy, and political demonology was lost. Instead a new effort to normalize nuclear danger was pursued. The U.S. nuclear stockpile grew to over thirty thousand weapons by the end of the 1960s, and space became an increasingly militarized domain. The SIOP target list would continue to grow through the 1980s, eventually including tens of thousands of global targets and constituting a nuclear war system so complex that it is very likely that no single human being understood its internal logics or its consequences. American ideologies of nuclear fear have consistently threatened to overwhelm the material evidence of danger and have become a core part of a now multigenerational commitment to militarism for its own sake in the United States. The result is that the United States continues to outspend the rest of the world on military matters and has built a global infrastructure of bases and linked technological systems, but has not yet achieved anything like security.

The Corona system offers us, in Benjamin's terms, an important opportunity to "brush history against the grain," as it was both a technological marvel—a demonstration of the power of instrumental rationality—and a stark reality check on U.S. national security culture itself, offering a new optics on what Jackie Orr (2006) would call the "psychopolitics" of the nuclear age. The first photographic survey of the Soviet Union from outer space showed that U.S. policy makers took the world to the brink of nuclear war in response to their fantasies of Soviet power, not the reality of Soviet capabilities. This now well-documented insight might have produced a fundamental rethinking of how threat, security, and nuclear power were organized in the United States, establishing a cautionary tale at the very least. But instead the Corona photographs remained a highly classified set of facts throughout the Cold War. This secrecy enabled a system of nuclear normalization to be reinforced rather than interrogated, securing the project of Cold War nuclear nationalism for the next thirty years. In the end, the new optics offered by Corona (on both Soviet machines and American fantasies) were reduced simply to a push for new space technology—higher-resolution photographs, better real-time transmission of data, and so on. In other words, the structure of the security state did not change even when confronted with evidence of its own fantasy projections and error. The success of Corona ultimately produced an American Cold War project even more focused on technological innovation and the projection of nuclear power rather than one capable of rethinking its own cultural terms, expert logics, or institutional practices.

The constant slippages between crisis, expertise, and failure are now well established in American political culture. The cultural history of Cold War nuclear emergency helps us understand why. Derrida (1984), working with the long-running theoretical discourse on the sublimity of death (which, as I have suggested here, links Kant, Freud, and Benjamin), describes the problem of the nuclear age as the impossibility of contemplating the truly "remainderless event" or the "total end of the archive." For him, to write any form of nuclear criticism is to politically engage in a form of future making that assumes a reader, thus performing a kind of countermilitarization and antinuclear practice. In the early 1960s, the U.S. nuclear war policy was officially known as overkill, referencing the redundant use of hydrogen bombs to destroy targets (Rosenberg 1983; see also Ellsberg 2017). This overkill installs a new kind of biopower, which fuses an obliteration of the other with collective suicide. The means to an end here constitutes an actual and total end, making the most immediate problem of the nuclear age the problem of differentiating comprehension from compensation in the minute-to-minute assessment of danger.

This seems to be a fundamental problem in U.S. national security culture—an inability to differentiate the capacity for war from the act itself, or alternatively to evaluate the logics of war from inside war. Space is now filled with satellites offering near-perfect resolution on the surface of the earth and able to transmit that data with great speed and precision to computers and cell phones, as well as early warning systems and intercontinental missiles. What we cannot seem to find is an exterior viewpoint on war itself—a perspective that would allow an assessment not only of the reality of conflict but also of the motivations, fantasies, and desires that support and enable it. Indeed, expert systems of all sorts—military, economic, political, and industrial— all seem unable to learn from failure and instead in the face of crisis simply retrench and remobilize failed logics. War, for example, is not the exception but the norm in the United States today—which makes peace extreme. So what would it take for Americans not only to consider the means to an end— that is, the tactics, the surges, the counterinsurgencies, the preemptions, the obliterations, and the surgical strikes—but also to reevaluate war itself: what would it take to consider an actual end to such ends?

CELLULOID NIGHTMARES

THE THIRD PART OF *The Future of Fallout, and Other Episodes in Radioactive World-Making* explores the role of film in both constituting and psychosocially managing existential dangers. By "constituting," I mean the ways that apocalyptic forms that have not yet happened come to have a life in public culture, with a defined set of images, affects, and political consequences. I track this across the domains of nuclear culture, climate emergency, and counterterror, asking how it is that cinema works to both install and ideologically contain images of the end. In "Celluloid Nightmares," Hollywood productions meet classified documentary films and public propaganda efforts to convey images of existential danger and the role of the security state in managing violence. Thus, I read these texts as building blocks, affective recruitments that also provide conceptual anchors, to ideas about collective danger. Of key concern is the way that certain forms of violence, colonial and imperial, nuclear danger and climate danger, are staged as distanced, as far away from the viewer, allowing a mode of recognition that is also simultaneously a mode of detachment (and, at times, empowerment). This idea of the distanced viewer, set up to observe but not be touched by the intended and unintended power of technoscientific revolutions across military and petrochemical industries, is a key psychosocial method of normalizing violence in the United States and of denying coexisting alternatives to national security or the possibility of a shared, peaceful world. Ultimately, this section explores how such violence inevitability proliferates and returns, not only producing vast fallout but also multiplying lost opportunities to build alternative security imaginaries and global orders.

10

TARGET AUDIENCE

Few Americans have witnessed firsthand the explosive power of a nuclear weapon. Nonetheless, most have some idea of its existential danger. How is this possible? More directly, how have policy makers come to understand the power of the nuclear arsenal at their disposal and the visceral consequences of nuclear war—especially considering that no U.S. president directly observed any of the 1,054 nuclear detonations of the Cold War U.S. weapons program?[1] The answer is simple: They watched movies.

After World War II, the cinematic atomic bomb became the crucial way in which the government communicated the new weapon's power to soldiers, citizens, and policy makers alike. Film not only documented the effects of the exploding bomb but also shaped and controlled the meaning of the technology for each of these domestic audiences. This makes the visual record of the aboveground test era, which began in 1945 with the Trinity test and ceased in 1963 with the landmark Limited Test Ban Treaty, a curious archive of scientific fact, speculation, and outright propaganda. It constitutes a detailed visual record of U.S. efforts to develop a state-of-the-art nuclear arsenal but also a larger political effort to militarize American society through the crafting and deployment of nuclear fear on film. This record is crucial to assess today. For in an age of terrorism, preemptive war, and renewed political mobilization of nuclear fear at home and abroad, American understandings of nuclear technologies have never been more important or blurred.

It has been many generations since the explosive power of a U.S. nuclear weapon has been visible to the world and thus subject to full critical apprehension, despite the fact that most nuclear weapons on the planet were built after 1963. U.S. nuclear weapons science was conducted underground from 1963 until the current U.S. test moratorium began in 1992. Since then, programmatic efforts within U.S. national laboratories have established a nuclear weapons complex capable of producing new nuclear weapons without conducting nuclear explosions at all—underground or otherwise—and have made continual improvements in the precision and lethality of Cold War–era nuclear designs.[2] As a result, while the weapons themselves have become more sophisticated and more embedded within U.S. geostrategic military policy, they have also become more invisible and easier for the American public to ignore or forget. Consequently, nuclear subjects are increasingly reliant on films, graphics, and computer programs to convey the bomb's destructive power.[3]

Each of the aboveground U.S. nuclear test series was, however, extensively photographed and the footage edited into a variety of films aimed at specific audiences—from classified documentaries shown to policy makers to more general descriptions of test activities delivered to the public.[4] The Air Force relied upon a Hollywood studio, Lookout Mountain Laboratory, to produce classified technical films on weapons science, in addition to overviews of the major test series in the Marshall Islands and Nevada.[5] Alongside the Department of Defense, Lookout Mountain also made films to indoctrinate soldiers to fight on an atomic battlefield, while the Federal Civil Defense Administration (often working with Lookout Mountain Laboratory) produced films to prepare citizens for life in the nuclear age.

Thanks to post–Cold War declassification efforts, citizens have some ability to assess the vast archive of originally classified films that were used to craft the U.S. nuclear narrative across the public/secret divide. In this chapter, I assess three films in particular—*Exercise Desert Rock* (1951), *Operation Cue* (1955), and *Special Weapons Orientation* (1956)—which calculate the nuclear danger differently for specific sectors of U.S. society and thus offer a cross-sectional view in the building out of the nuclear state. One film made for soldiers (*Exercise Desert Rock)* and another made for civilians (*Operation Cue*) helped establish nuclear weapons as a new normative reality, promoting a kind of self-reliance when confronted with the minute-to-minute possibility of nuclear war. These early efforts to mobilize Americans as Cold Warriors focused on emotions rather than intellect, as soldiers and citizens viewing these films were presented with a highly politicized portrait of nuclear war. On the other hand, *Special Weapons Orientation*, aimed exclusively at nuclear policy makers in a highly classified format, offers a different emotional appeal: absolute strength through the possession of an unprecedented destructive power.

In each of these films, a new kind of governance grounded in nuclear fear, and mediated by secrecy, can been seen taking shape. These films attempt to unify all U.S. citizens via a relationship to the bomb by scripting specific roles that soldiers, citizens, and policy makers can play in the new nuclear age. After Hiroshima and Nagasaki, the atomic bomb became first and foremost a powerful psychological weapon in the United States: officials soon discovered that the political uses of nuclear fear worked as well domestically as they did internationally. Existential danger became a coordinating logic of American statecraft. Controlling the image of the bomb—and thus the nuclear danger itself—was important, a multifaceted political tool, fusing geopolitics and domestic politics in a new way. This is important today because U.S. culture still relies on many of the images and political logics of self-discipline and nuclear fear first articulated in the government test films of the early Cold War, which viewers today often read as simple propaganda or atomic kitsch because of the film conventions (disembodied voice-over narrations and displays of outdated consumer items). These films, nonetheless, dare us to interrogate the War on Terror not only for the official portrayal of terrorism, dirty bombs, and WMDS, but also for the concomitant domestic counterterror political strategy, its imagistic registers and affective circuits (Masco 2014). In what follows, I track the early deployment of an idea of nuclear power for American audiences, tracking how degrees of vulnerability and superiority were first imagined. The central point I wish to make is that the bomb was quickly mobilized as a coordinating technology in the United States, a way of organizing geopolitics, technical systems, and compartmentalized knowledge programs but also of bringing disparate publics together at an affective level through nuclear imaginaries.

FILM: *Exercise Desert Rock* (1951)
PRODUCED BY: Department of Defense
RUNNING TIME: 27 minutes
PRIMARY AUDIENCE: Soldiers

From 1951 to 1957, the Defense Department ran Exercise Desert Rock at the Nevada Test Site, a series of military operations designed to psychologically prepare troops for fighting on an atomic battlefield. Each of the exercises consisted of a war game that involved the United States using tactical nuclear weapons against an imaginary invading army, quickly followed by a march on ground zero by U.S. troops. First and foremost, the exercises were experiments, designed to test the psychological responses of soldiers to atomic warfare. Defense officials also studied the effects of the exploding bomb on military equipment and developed nuclear warfighting strategy, normalizing the bomb as a basic tool within the U.S. military arsenal.

Exercise Desert Rock presents an overview of the first Desert Rock experiment in 1951. The black-and-white film provides interviews with soldiers before and after the explosion and tracks their progress to ground zero, assessing their readiness for the atomic battlefield. It was circulated within the military as a training film and became part of the indoctrination of U.S. military personnel for nuclear conflict throughout the Cold War.

Early in the film, the narrator informs viewers that the exercise intends to test the tactical field uses of nuclear weapons. But soon that message is refined, placing the focus on the psychological effects of nuclear fear on soldiers: "An understandable concern is usually expressed by troops about the dangers of entering an atom-blasted zone. In airbursts, like the one the men will see and the type which would normally be used against troop concentrations, no serious amount of radioactivity remains on the ground."

Promising that troops can be kept physically safe on a nuclear battlefield with careful planning, the problem ultimately becomes how to overcome and internally manage nuclear fear: "It is believed they will experience less fear during the blast because they have learned that radioactive elements from airbursts are carried into the stratosphere in a cloud, where they mix rapidly with the upper air currents. The bomb will be detonated only if all predetermined requirements are met, including weather conditions."

The test also exposed a wide array of military equipment (tanks, artillery, bridges, planes, ammunition, communication systems) to the exploding bomb. Foxholes dug at various distances from ground zero were populated with dummies or living soldiers (see figure 10.1). Sheep were also placed in trenches or in aboveground pens at various distances from ground zero. Radiation dosimeter badges were given to soldiers, placed on the dummies, and located throughout the test range. More than five thousand personnel participated in this nuclear war-fighting exercise. Taught that "radiation is the least of one's worries" on an atomic battlefield, the film shows soldiers watching the detonation from seven miles away. They then turn away from the exploding bomb during the flash to protect their vision; seconds later, they experience a shock wave that covers them in dust (see figure 10.2). An interview with one soldier elicits the following discussion about the emotional costs of nuclear war in the film:

> INTERVIEWER: Can you tell us whether you think the orientation you had for this weapon prepared you for what you saw out here?
>
> SOLDIER: Yes sir, it did.
>
> INTERVIEWER: What about the fear that you felt? Did they prepare you against that?
>
> SOLDIER: Yes sir, they did. They told us enough so that our fear was cut so much more than what it was before the orientation that we hardly had any fear at all.
>
> INTERVIEWER: Do you have confidence that you would be able to go right in there now and carry out your tactical mission after the blast?
>
> SOLDIER: Yes sir.
>
> INTERVIEWER: How close, now that you've seen it, would you be willing to be?
>
> SOLDIER: Well sir, I'll tell you that after I see them positions up there.

The staged nature of these interviews is apparent, as each soldier knows exactly what he is supposed to say. The startling confidence in their statements is nevertheless undercut by both nervousness and a controlled hesitation about committing to life on the front line of a nuclear battlefield.

The film then follows the troops as they march on ground zero and encounter a carefully prepared course of objects as well as animals exposed

Figure 10.1. Soldiers entering foxholes on the nuclear battlefield in Exercise Desert Rock (U.S. National Archives and Records Administration).

Figure 10.2. Soldiers observing the mushroom cloud before march toward ground zero (U.S. National Archives and Records Administration).

to the blast at different distances. Two miles from ground zero, little damage is visible, but beyond that, heat and blast have scorched military equipment and dummies. The sheep left in trenches are declared untouched by the bomb, but those situated above ground suffered burns that the troops carefully observe. The official lesson: foxholes and good military planning can protect soldiers on the atomic battlefield, and nuclear fear is a greater danger than the bomb itself. The film ends with a radiation check of soldiers, a quick decontamination sweep with brooms, and a voice-over that declares tactical field weapons can be used safely.

This scripting of danger and stage managing of nuclear effects became increasingly sophisticated at the Nevada Test Site in the 1950s, eventually including parallel civil defense material aimed at civilians. Quite formally, panic, not nuclear destruction, was positioned as the real danger in nuclear warfare. This argument was made via a careful crafting of the images of nuclear warfare, a censoring of nuclear effects such as fire and radiation, and a focus on atomic bombs rather than the much larger thermonuclear weapons already in the U.S. arsenal.

Mobilizing psychological studies of bombed communities during World War II (particularly Irving Janis's 1951, *Air War and Emotional Stress*), defense intellectuals sought to calibrate nuclear fear at a national level, producing a new kind of society for a new kind of cold war (Oakes 1994; Peterson 1953). Within this scheme, terror was imagined as a paralyzing emotion, but fear could be managed, controlled, and directed. Therefore, defense planners sought to instill in soldiers and civilians a specific idea of nuclear war that would harden them to the difficult realties of a postnuclear environment and focus them on emotional self-discipline during the ongoing nuclear crisis (see Masco 2014; Orr 2006).

FILM: *Operation Cue* (1955)

PRODUCED BY: Federal Civil Defense Administration

RUNNING TIME: 16 minutes

PRIMARY AUDIENCE: Civilians

Operation Cue was the largest civil defense exercise conducted at the Nevada Test Site. It involved the construction of a model U.S. city, complete with mannequins representing "Mr. and Mrs. America," which was then incinerated on live television for 100 million viewers. The exercise promised to reveal what a postnuclear U.S. city would look like, and the Federal Civil Defense Administration went to extraordinary lengths to make the test city

Figure 10.3. Overview of civil defense programs in *Operation Cue* (U.S. National Archives and Records Administration).

look real. Declaring "Survival Is Your Business," Operation Cue was part of a larger campaign to make every American responsible for their own safety in nuclear war (see figure 10.3). Contemporary-style homes were stocked with the latest furnishings donated by 150 industry associations. An elaborate food test program placed packaged and frozen food throughout the test site. The food that survived the explosion was later used as the ingredients for dishes served during a postblast feeding exercise.

Following the script developed in *Exercise Desert Rock*, the black-and-white film takes viewers through test preparations, the detonation, and a posttest assessment of the ruins to convey the methodical nature of the proceedings. But in *Operation Cue*, a female narrator introduces viewers to this "program to test the effects of an atomic blast on the things we use in everyday life"—an effort to militarize the domestic space of the home. The mannequin families were posed in moments of domestic normalcy—eating at the kitchen table, napping in bed, or watching television (see figures 10.4–10.7). In other words, viewers were invited to think of themselves as mannequins

Figures 10.4–10.7. Setting up the mannequin families in *Operation Cue* (U.S. National Archives and Records Administration).

Figures 10.8 and 10.9. Civilians in foxholes during the detonation (U.S. National Archives and Records Administration).

Figure 10.10. Apple II detonation at the center of *Operation Cue* (U.S. National Archives and Records Administration).

caught in an unannounced nuclear attack and to watch *Operation Cue* for signs of what their postnuclear environment would be like.

Much as the soldiers did in *Exercise Desert Rock*, a group of civilian volunteers populated a forward trench to test their reactions to the nuclear blast (see figures 10.8 and 10.9). Testing the cognitive effects of a nuclear blast on civilians was part of the psychological experiment of Operation Cue. The film ultimately promised viewers that nuclear war could be incorporated into the known universe of emergencies and treated alongside natural disasters such as hurricanes, earthquakes, and floods. The overt message was that emotional self-discipline and preparation are the key to surviving crisis—whether that crisis is a Soviet nuclear attack, fire, or bad weather.

In *Operation Cue*, there is no discussion about radioactive fallout or the extensive fires that the atomic bombings of Hiroshima and Nagasaki produced (see figure 10.10). Instead, the film provides a detailed portrait of a survivable postnuclear state. Rescue personnel pull damaged mannequins from the rubble, flying several to off-site hospitals; meanwhile, the

Figure 10.11. Households after the blast in *Operation Cue* (U.S. National Archives and Records Administration).

Figure 10.12. Administering first aid on the mannequins after the blast in *Operation Cue* (U.S. National Archives and Records Administration).

mass feeding takes place alongside standing homes and power lines (see figures 10.11 and 10.12). Later, the mannequins scorched by Operation Cue went on a national tour of J. C. Penney department stores, which had provided the clothing used in the test, offering an explicit portrait of nuclear survival to the U.S. public.

But a closer reading of *Operation Cue* reveals a more complicated message: the film is training citizens to accept nuclear war as a normative danger, employing nuclear fear to craft a militarized society organized around preparing for nuclear war every minute of every day. To accomplish this, the portrait of nuclear danger presented in *Operation Cue* is partial, a carefully edited version of nuclear science. Indeed, nuclear experts had already disproved much of the civil defense guidance via the test programs in Nevada and the South Pacific due to the increasing power of nuclear weapons in the thermonuclear age. In actuality, the radioactive fallout produced by nuclear tests such as Operation Cue traversed the continental United States, creating negative health effects for soldiers and civilians alike—a much starker reality than *Operation Cue* promises viewers (see chapter 1; Miller 1986).

FILM: *Special Weapons Orientation: The Thermonuclear Weapon Part VI* (1956)
PRODUCED BY: U.S. Air Force
RUNNING TIME: 29 minutes
PRIMARY AUDIENCE: Policy makers

A classified film made by the Lookout Mountain Laboratory, *Special Weapons Orientation* provides a cumulative overview of the U.S. thermonuclear weapons program from 1950 to 1955. It begins with a discussion of the basic science of atomic (fission) and hydrogen (fusion) weapons, noting the potentially unlimited explosive power of hydrogen bombs. It then explains the results of the Pacific test program, documenting that Ivy Mike, the first thermonuclear event, vaporized the island of Elugelab on November 1, 1952, leaving behind a one-mile crater. The color film informs viewers that because of its size (twenty-one feet tall and eighty tons) and reliance on massive amounts of cryogenically controlled fuel, Mike was not a "deliverable" nuclear device—that is, a transportable weapon.

Technological breakthroughs, however, soon enabled weapons scientists to miniaturize and weaponize hydrogen bombs—moving from the first

41,000-pound weapons in 1953 to easily delivered 3,000-pound devices by the mid-1950s. This remarkable ability to increase the power of thermonuclear explosives while rapidly decreasing their physical size reveals the intensity of nuclear weapons science during this period. These atomic secrets remain powerful today, revealed in odd moments when the declassified soundtrack of *Special Weapons Orientation* drops out as certain issues pertaining to the intricacies of nuclear weapons science arise. The abrupt silences in the film are redactions made during the post–Cold War era declassification, under-scoring the strategic military relevance of nuclear weapons science that are still relevant in the twenty-first century.

Unlike *Exercise Desert Rock* or *Operation Cue*, the effects of atmospheric fallout are a central concern of this film, revealing that there was an interest in the military uses of fallout and fire (see Eden 2004). Noting that "millions of tons of earth" are elevated into a cloud that rises above seventy thousand feet in a high-yield explosion, the film reveals that fallout can traverse an enormous territorial range, delivering deadly levels of contamination for hours and days after detonation (see figure 10.13). The narrator explains that the widespread contamination produced by the first shot of the 1954 Castle Test Series created an opportunity for biological research (see figure 10.14): "Wind factors caused contamination of distant populated atolls, providing a completely new source of study on these effects and showing graphically, the tremendous area contamination from a high-yield surface burst. Two hun-dred and twenty-nine natives and twenty-nine American personnel received doses from 12 to 200 roentgens."

After displaying images of Pacific Islanders with skin bleached white by fallout, the narrator states that none of the exposure rates appear to be of "immediate combat significance," referencing official concern about how such exposures would affect soldiers on the atomic battlefield (not as future sufferers). Next, a graphic illustrating a zone of lethality in the Pacific cover-ing some "seven thousand statute square miles" for high-yield explosions is presented, which changes the concept of nuclear war entirely. To drive the point home, a map of the United States is offered, with three comparable zones of fallout in California, Colorado, and Wisconsin (figure 10.15). Here, emotional management is subverted, and the unprecedented destructive power of the hydrogen bomb is celebrated.

Special Weapons Orientation presents policy makers with a new range of weapons both capable of annihilating another country and offering little hope of a postnuclear society.[6] The film concludes by assessing the effects of

Figure 10.13. Thermonuclear event, still image from *Special Weapons Orientation* (Nevada Nuclear Testing Archive).

Figure 10.14. Castle Romeo, Marshall Islands, fifteen-megaton detonation (U.S. National Archives and Records Administration).

Figure 10.15. Demonstration of radioactive fallout from Pacific nuclear tests superimposed on the continental United States in *Special Weapons Orientation* (Nevada Nuclear Testing Archive).

thermonuclear weapons on exposed troops and cities, using Washington, DC, as a reference point (see figures 10.16 and 10.17):

> The real military importance of high-yield blast effects lies not in their type or quality but in their enormous range compared to kiloton weapons. A 100-kiloton weapon at optimum height will cause severe damage over an area of 5 square miles and moderate damage over 12 square miles. Contrast this—5 and 12—with 80 square miles of severe damage and 240 square miles of moderate damage from a fifteen-megaton surface burst like Castle Shot I. Two hundred and forty square miles, more than twenty Hiroshimas in a group, more than ten Manhattans, in which blast compounded with fire would bring almost total destruction. The big bonus from multimegaton weapons is the longer, positive phase, producing blast damage far beyond that of kiloton weapons.

The big bonus. The hydrogen bomb thus enables a new kind of absolute destruction—offering the capacity to annihilate a whole civilization—even

Figure 10.16. Blast radius of U.S. atomic weapon overlaid on Washington, DC, from *Special Weapons Orientation* (Nevada Nuclear Testing Archive).

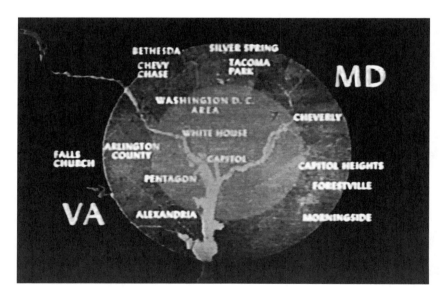

Figure 10.17. Destructive force of a thermonuclear weapon blast overlaid on Washington, DC, from *Special Weapons Orientation* (Nevada Nuclear Testing Archive).

as it installs new possibilities for domestic emotional management at home. *Special Weapons Orientation* thus only hints at the new kind of governance enabled by the hydrogen bomb, as nuclear fear is quickly mobilized across the United States as the basis for a new kind of global order as well as a new kind of American society, one simultaneously militarized, vulnerable, and threatening.

11

THE AGE OF (A) MAN

If there were an emblematic text of the Anthropocene, a cultural statement so singular as to eliminate any doubt about mid-twentieth-century ambitions for the industrial transformation of the natural world, it might well be the 1973 Atomic Energy Commission (AEC) film *Plowshare*. A survey of the previous fifteen years of work on "geographical engineering," the twenty-eight-minute film offers a comprehensive portrait of the fusion of nuclear weapons and industrial capitalism (see figure 11.1). It conjures a world of white masculinity armed with an engineering mindset and a planetary vision. The surface of the earth is presented as an inherently faulty design, one that can now be corrected in the name of both convenience and profit. Or as the invisible, godlike narrator of *Plowshare* intones in a confident mid-twentieth-century baritone:

Figure 11.1. Still image of the narrator of *Plowshare* (Nevada Nuclear Testing Archive).

To bring water and food where there is only parched earth and people where there is desolation; to bring freedom of movement where there are imposing barriers and commerce where nature has decreed there will be isolation; to bring forth a wealth of material where there are vast untapped resources and a wealth of knowledge where there is uncertainty; to perform a multitude of peaceful tasks for the betterment of mankind—man is exploring a source of enormous potentially useful energy: the nuclear explosion. He sees the potentials and he sees the problems. To investigate both, and to develop the technologies that will turn potentials into realities, the United States is conducting for the benefit of all nations a program it calls Plowshare.

Man sees potentials. The film documents the engineering attitude of the mid-twentieth century, at the very start of what is now known as the "great acceleration" of human consumption, that exponential expansion in travel, industrial production, and globalization that generates a compounding problem for earth systems today (see McNeill and Engelke 2014). The invention of new synthetic chemicals and the extensive use of plastics were key parts of an emergent, petrochemical-based American society. Each innovation in this chain of technological relations not only enabled a middle-class consumer lifestyle, it also contributed in some way to the greenhouse gas emissions that have subsequently shifted the chemical composition of the atmosphere with rebounding effects across oceans, ice caps, and climate. We cannot understand the current planetary condition without interrogating this historical fusion of revolutionary industrialism, involving both petrochemical capitalism and nuclear-powered American nationalism.

Plowshare offers a future-perfect version of nuclear science, conjuring the possibility that nuclear explosions could be made safe, that radioactive fallout could be eliminated, and that the serious work of remaking the geology of the earth would be merely the next act in an unfolding technological revolution involving better health, energy, and economy (see Kaufman 2012; Kirsch 2005). The conditional, however, persists through the film—"may," "perhaps," "could," "might"—these are important factual qualifiers, but they are overwhelmed by the narrator's enthusiasm for remaking the surface of the earth and thereby enabling a new kind of species supremacy based in expert knowledge:

> Before each experiment, experts in geology, seismology, hydrology, meteorology, radiobiology, and many other fields bring their specialized knowledge and equipment into the field. Working with public health authorities, they assure that the specific experiment is being conducted within accepted safety standards. This same thorough application will precede the actual applications of nuclear explosions wherever and whenever they may be. What are these actual applications? Some will be dramatic in their effect, as nuclear explosions move huge masses of earth in excavation jobs, reshaping the geography of the land in dimensions never before possible, to meet the needs of man, needs he can see as he struggles against the geography nature has pitted against him.

Within acceptable safety standards. Plowshare offers an emancipatory narrative for a world not perfectly arranged for global capital, a technical means of resolving unruly natural formations through the combined work of earth scientists and nuclear weapons experts. The program ultimately conducted thirty-five nuclear detonations between 1961 and 1973, in addition to a wide range of chemical explosive tests at many sites. These experiments sought to demonstrate the industrial potential of "underground engineering" for extractive industries or "excavation applications" for improved transportation (see figures 11.2 and 11.3). Geographically, the tests ranged from Mississippi

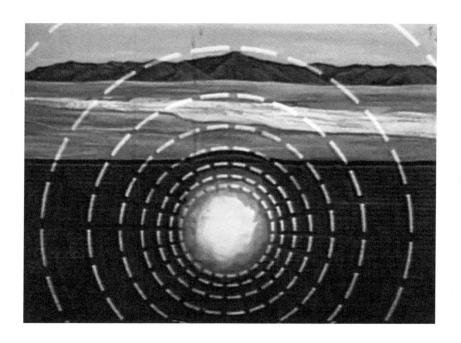

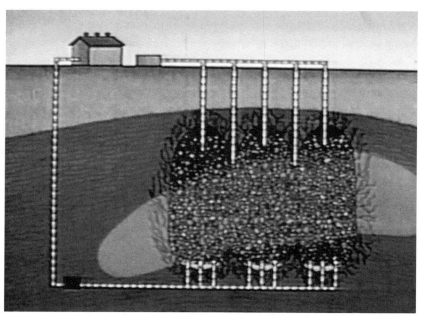

Figures 11.2 and 11.3. Still images from *Plowshare* detailing nuclear excavation techniques for resource extraction (Nevada Nuclear Testing Archive).

to New Mexico to the Rocky Mountain states to Alaska, with a majority taking place at the Nevada Test Site. Improving nature—narrated in the film as a conquest—is cast in *Plowshare* as a peaceful project, a progressive effort to convert a weapon of mass destruction into simply an everyday tool. The atomic bomb is used to mobilize the next stage in an ongoing settler colonial project, one that positions the western frontier as a geological problem, as well as an incomplete territorial pursuit.

If the Plowshare program existed for fifteen years in the conditional mode, it nonetheless made nature a theater for active nuclear science. The detonations were in the world, producing environmental destruction and multiple forms of fallout, contributing to the transformation of the global biosphere in the nuclear age. *Plowshare*, despite its stated commitment to safety and precision, turns such unwanted effects into externalities that, again in the future perfect conditional, would ultimately be eliminated via the next stage of research. Thus, the world is rendered as malleable and nuclear science is rendered as perfectible in the same anticipatory gesture. The future as imagined by Plowshare proponents, however, was not the future that emerged, as industrial effects accumulated across the biosphere to produce not an ever more secure world economy but a planetary distortion in earth systems visible today in rising temperatures, melting ice caps, an acidifying ocean, and accelerating extinction rates.

Plowshare was a promotional film aimed at congressional funders; it sought to recruit viewers to a world that did not yet exist but that seemed already to be in sight. The film conjures up a vision of a nuclear-mediated American economy, but one not ruled by the nuclear fear that dominated the Cold War. Listen to the promissory note offered to energy companies about the benefits of geographical engineering through nuclear detonations:

> Nuclear explosions deep underground break and splinter huge areas of rock. These massive effects may permit highly promising recovery of resources that have been impossible, or economically impractical, to extract from the earth. . . . They can see how nuclear explosions could increase the total recovery and rate of recovery of vast natural gas and oil reserves by effectively breaking the rock so that these valuable resources can flow through. They can see how copper could be extracted from the ground more efficiently, as nuclear explosions shatter the surrounding rock, letting through the solutions that dissolve the copper and carry it to the surface. They can see how the huge area of broken and fractured rock can be used for receiving as well as

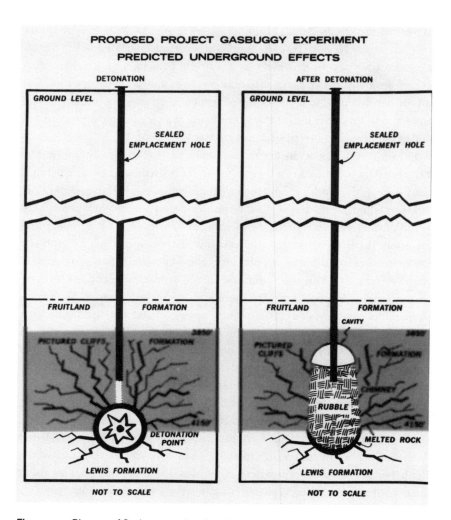

PROPOSED PROJECT GASBUGGY EXPERIMENT

PREDICTED UNDERGROUND EFFECTS

Figure 11.4. Diagram of Gasbuggy nuclear fracking experiment (U.S. Department of Energy).

releasing materials, for storing natural gas near its market areas, for storing rainwater that could seep down underground where it would not evaporate, or even for storing chemical waste materials in underground formations.

Valuable resources can flow. This kind of nuclear fracking did not prove profitable, but the promise of the concept endured (see figures 11.4 and 11.5). Some of the experts on Plowshare continued to pursue technological breakthroughs in nonnuclear hydraulic fracturing, ultimately enabling the

Figure 11.5. Installing the Gasbuggy device, Carson National Forest, northern New Mexico (U.S. Department of Energy).

shale formations from Texas to North Dakota to the Canadian tar sands to be developed by energy companies in the early twenty-first century. Indeed, fracking of the kind proposed in *Plowshare* turned the United States into one of the world's leading energy producers in 2019. Thus, even in failure the Plowshare project contributes to a future of expansive energy exploration and extraction. These innovations, and decades of petrochemical-based consumption and industry, now present a profound challenge as they have destabilized a planetary-scale climate system.

The kind of profit/loss calculation depicted in *Plowshare* assumes a universal value system, one embedded in petrochemical capitalism, and a vision of undeveloped land as waste. This notion of a singular human economy, a singular value system, was challenged by local populations wherever Plowshare experiments were proposed. The first major effort, Project Chariot, was an attempt to build a new channel at Cape Thomson in Alaska. The idea was to detonate five nuclear devices in a row and create both a new harbor and channel connecting the harbor to the ocean. Extensive studies were made of the geology, but local communities, including Inuit populations with long-standing cultural ties to the area, were not consulted. The project conducted multiple tests with high explosives (see figure 11.6), creating lasting environmental problems, but the nuclear component was ultimately defeated by an unusual coalition of indigenous groups, activists, and biologists who challenged the Plowshare safety plan at each step (see O'Neill 2007). Due to this activism, Project Chariot was halted in 1962. However, the vital history of environmental activism against Plowshare is not acknowledged in the 1973 film despite its claimed comprehensive overview of the program. This silence suggests that public protest could be cast by the AEC as another kind of externality, one more thing to be overcome in the perfection of geographical engineering. The failure of Project Chariot was largely due to public concerns about radioactive fallout. By the 1960s activists could draw on an extensive public record of environmental damage from nuclear testing in the U.S. Southwest and Marshall Islands dating back a full generation. And indeed, a number of Plowshare tests produced unexpected outcomes—from elevated fallout levels to local resistance—making the experimental program a key node in the development of a global antinuclear, peace, and environmental justice movement.

As the likelihood of finding a space within American territories for a large-scale demonstration of geographical engineering diminished after the demise of Project Chariot, Plowshare administrators looked internationally (see figure 11.7). As the film's narrator informs viewers:

> But there is no doubt that most applications of nuclear excavation would be not in the United States, but in other countries. The most dramatic example so far is in Central America: the blasting of a sea-level, Atlantic-Pacific interoceanic canal. Studies are being planned for both conventional and nuclear excavations on four possible routes for such a cut across Central America to supplement, and eventually replace,

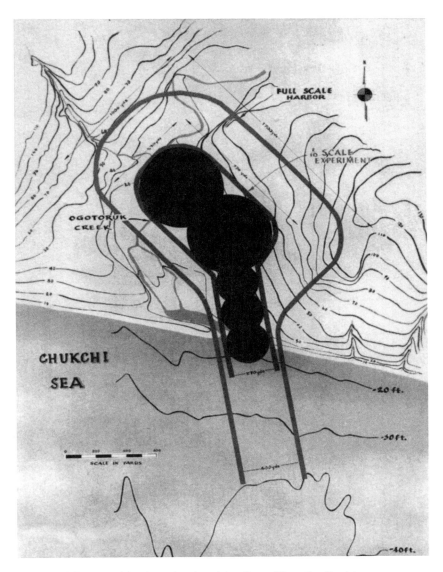

Figure 11.6. Diagram of the planned nuclear detonations of Operation Chariot (U.S. Department of Energy).

Figure 11.7. Plowshare project diagram of possible canal locations in Central America (U.S. Department of Energy).

the Panama Canal, where ships now wait long hours to strain through the narrow, complex lock system and others can't make it through at all. Before long it will be inadequate. Even before it was built half a century ago the complexities and limitations of this lock type were realized. Men dreamed of a sea-level canal but it remained a dream. Plowshare may be able to make that dream a reality. And it is being considered. It is estimated that for certain routes, nuclear explosives could excavate the sea-level canal at one-third the cost of conventional excavation and in considerably less time. The end result would be a much wider and much deeper channel. A nuclear-excavated route across Central America could produce a navigable channel one thousand feet wide and up to two hundred feet deep at midchannel, offering a virtually unlimited capacity. No wonder this enormous project has so stimulated the imagination of the world: for a canal of this immensity, representing years of planning and development, complex engineering, and precise execution would be one of the greatest civil engineering feats of all time.

Men dreamed. The Panama project generated immediate local fears of environmental damage, an index of the growing international antinuclear movement, which linked indigenous groups, citizens, and experts from within the broader earth scientist community (Lindsay-Poland 2003; and see also Carse 2014). This notion of empty land ready for commercial development was thwarted by diverse interests who were already imagining a global ecology in need of protection, and by those with long-standing cultural investments in maintaining nonindustrialized territories (see figures 11.8–11.11). Plowshare, in other words, which had been a zone of pure engineering potential and geopolitical abstraction, became immediately politicized whenever it touched down in a specific place, fomenting environmental justice movements. The AEC argument that geographical engineering through nuclear explosives was faster and cheaper than any other industrial means of earth moving was met by those with increasing experience of nuclear effects in a global biosphere transformed by Cold War military science, and who fought for different understandings of both value and profit.

Plowshare as a historical document reveals, however, the planetary spectacle of the nuclear age itself. It presents the rush for monumental projects and the desire for ever greater evidence of human ability to transform the natural world. *Plowshare* may well be unsurpassed as a cultural expression of hubris, but it also marks an early commitment to what we would now call geoengineering—the effort to consciously transform earth systems to make them more amenable to human needs. Lawrence Livermore National Laboratory remains a pioneer of geoengineering research, linking Plowshare to a vast number of contemporary proposals to cool the planet through direct intervention into the atmosphere (Hamilton 2013; see also Morton 2015). The collective environmental future—with all its radical contingency—continues to produce programs for mechanical correction and even fantasies of planetary-scale control, despite the multiple forms of fallout from industrial practices across radionuclides, synthetic chemical, and greenhouse gas emissions.

Plowshare thus has a once-and-future potential, offering a slippery challenge to the current historical moment. Indeed, perhaps that is its essence: *Plowshare*, we should remember, was produced on 16 mm film stock, a petrochemical medium that is both a form of fossilized time and an outmoded technology in the twenty-first century. The emulsions that allow photochemical filmic vision derive from the deep geological history of the planet. The dead plant and animal life that accumulated in watery sediments and was subject to vast pressures and tectonic shifts in the geological periods we now

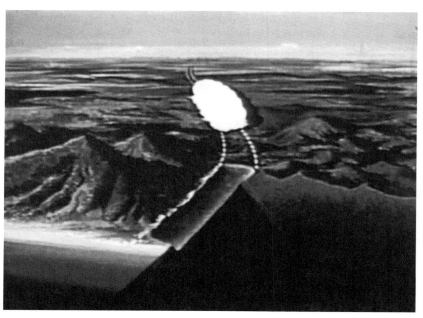

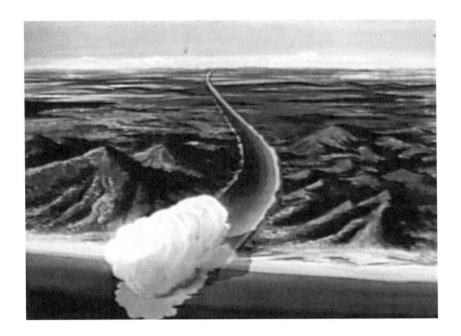

Figures 11.8–11.11. Still images from *Plowshare* sequence of how to use nuclear explosives to build a new Panama Canal (Nevada Nuclear Testing Archive).

call the Carboniferous, Permian, Triassic, and Jurassic become the essential chemicals for analog photography. Thus, a motion-picture film about monumental earth moving offers an enfolding set of temporal registers as the deep geology of the planet produces the very materials that enable the cinematic remaking of mountains and rivers as well as the promise of even more petrochemical discovery in shale. Watching *Plowshare* today offers viewers an opportunity to visit an outmoded future of geoengineering that may also be a portent of what is to come. The film's stylistic anachronism begs the question: What is actually different today in the realm of extractive industries, other than the now odd language of "geographical engineering"? What, if anything, has changed in the ambition of people for extraction regimes and planetary control?

It is important to pause here for a moment to ask, what was that Enlightenment dream again—the one about human mastery of nature, accelerating revolutions in science and technology, and the ultimate perfectibility of Man? In the mid-twentieth century, the splitting of the atom seemed to supercharge this imaginary in the United States, signaling the imminent arrival of superabundance, promising continuing breakthroughs in health, energy, and a consumer economy. After 1945, Americans embraced a dream world based in nuclear nationalism and petrochemical capitalism that, if it did not end in the fiery flash of nuclear war, would push relentlessly and inevitably toward a perfected capitalist society. This was the first "Age of Man"—a nuclear-powered fantasy that miraculously transformed an unprecedented destructive force into the expectation of a world without limits. The new rational order of science and engineering would remake everyday life in all its qualities, generating a series of new frontiers to be sequentially colonized, linking extractive industries to new urban landscapes to global communication and transportation systems to outer space in a spasm of industrial-scale world-making. Pause, just for a moment, to consider the intoxicating rush of this conceptual enterprise, the creative energy of making things that work on this kind of scale, of believing that people could finally shape reality rather than merely submit to it. The nuclear revolution promised to remake war, health, energy, and security, inaugurating a new golden age of human achievement in which long-standing social problems would fall in rapid order to the combined achievements of American technoscience.

The physicist Edward Teller, chief architect and advocate of the Plowshare program, put it succinctly to a broad American readership in *Popular Mechanics* magazine: "We're going to work miracles" (1960, 97). For Teller, weather control is not out of the question in 1960, and the global environment is positioned as an unruly domain that will be sorted out in short order via the explosive power of nuclear science. His vision is galactic and transcendent, identifying an earthly landscape to be remade for human commerce and convenience, as well as a communist foe to be endlessly fought via military nuclear power. As perhaps the most vigorous twentieth-century advocate for nuclear weapons, Teller pushed for hydrogen bomb development in Los Alamos before the first atomic explosion was achieved in July 1945. The United States built Teller his own California research facility in 1952: Lawrence Livermore National Laboratory was designed to be competition for Los Alamos in the field of nuclear weapons science, but also a place for Teller to pursue his vision of the nuclear revolution.

For the next forty years, Teller argued in favor of one high-tech weapons system after another and against every nonproliferation and disarmament effort. Indeed, he promised presidents from Truman to Reagan that weapons science would fix the problem of the nuclear age—the minute-to-minute possibility of global nuclear war—not by eliminating the bomb but by perfecting it. Resistant to test bans and dismissing radioactive fallout concerns, Teller provided a rationale for a vigorous arms race with the Soviet Union while also promising a world remade via the benefits of nuclear science. By the 1980s he convinced President Reagan that the way out of the Cold War's nuclear danger was to embrace yet another technological revolution, a so-called "third wave" of nuclear science after those of the atomic and thermonuclear breakthroughs (Broad 1992). Teller proposed to surround the earth with space-based lasers that could destroy Soviet missiles on launch in midair, a proposal that President Reagan embraced as the Strategic Defense Initiative, nicknamed Star Wars (which in lesser forms continues as a research project to this day without objective success despite hundreds of billions of dollars spent on research). Reagan ultimately chose to pursue the Strategic Defense Initiative over President Gorbachev's proposal that the United States and USSR simply dismantle their nuclear arsenals by the year 2000 (FitzGerald 2000).

In his commitment to remaking the world through nuclear weapons science, Teller approached the earth system as something that was filled with vital resources but deficient in significant ways. In 1958 he proposed the concept of "geographical engineering" to overcome such natural barriers to commerce, launching Operation Plowshare at Lawrence Livermore National Laboratory (Teller et al. 1968). The timing of his proposal was sublime, coming in the midst of worldwide fears about nuclear war as well as amplifying worries about the health and environmental effects of radioactive fallout from atmospheric nuclear detonations, and as the United States and USSR began discussions about a comprehensive test-ban treaty. Thus, Plowshare offered a positive image of nuclear detonations in the midst of intensifying global nuclear fear, offering a vision of a world that—if it could just avoid nuclear war or permanently damaging the biosphere and humanity via radioactive fallout—might be a utopia for industry, commerce, and society. At a historical moment of maximum nuclear terror (with biologists discussing the effects of nuclear testing on the human genome, civil defense asking citizens to regularly rehearse nuclear war, and a geopolitics of nuclear intimidation underpinning Cold War conflicts around the world), Plowshare was offered as a means of recapturing the utopian potential of the bomb. Teller sought to publicly transform the bomb from a global menace to a vital form of capitalist creative destruction.

In the current expert search for the golden spike of the Anthropocene—that indelible marker in the strata of planet Earth that will end the Holocene epoch in favor of a new Age of Man—earth scientists are increasingly focused on the radioactive signature of early Cold War nuclear explosions (see Bonneuil and Fressoz 2016). Earth scientists report that plutonium from atmospheric nuclear explosions will be "identifiable in sediments and ice for the next 100,000 years" and have identified a sharp spike in cesium, strontium, and plutonium beginning in 1952 with the first thermonuclear detonation (see Waters et al. 2016). This Anthropocene—this new Age of Man—by infusing political time with geological time now threatens to swallow whole historical eras like the Cold War, transforming that planetary-scale national competition into a permanent postnatural formation visible in the stratigraphy of the earth.

November 1, 1952, is the date on which the first thermonuclear explosion, known as Ivy Mike, was detonated by the United States at Eniwetok Atoll. Designed by Edward Teller and Stanislaw Ulam, it produced a ten-megaton detonation that created a mushroom cloud twenty-five miles high and one hundred miles wide. The fallout from Ivy Mike circled the globe and remains so comprehensive that it offers today one key marker of planetary-scale industrial effects. This explosion is now part of a nested series of temporalities: it is the start of a thermonuclear age inside an already established atomic age, a key moment in the Cold War, and now one possible anchor for a new geological epoch, the Anthropocene.

Teller's vision of a world transformed by nuclear science has come true but in a highly perverse fashion. For we all now live in a world that is still capable of nuclear war and that is marked by the plutonium, strontium, and cesium of Cold War–era nuclear weapons tests. It is a world still committed to ever more dangerous forms of resource extraction (deep-water drilling and hydraulic fracturing) and is increasingly interested in a geoengineering fix to the resulting damage to the earth system from a petrochemical-based economy. Transformed by the nuclear modernist visions of the mid-twentieth century, earth systems are now influenced in ways subtle and profound by industrial activity. Thus, perhaps our increasingly dangerous era is best thought of as a specific industrial-modernist achievement—the Age of Man as the materialized dreamscape of one radical but highly influential man— a Teller-ocene.

12

CATASTROPHE'S APOCALYPSE

*In our obsession with antagonisms of the moment, we often forget how much unites all
members of humanity. Perhaps we need some outside, universal threat to make us
recognize this common bond. I occasionally think how quickly our differences worldwide
would vanish if we were facing an alien threat from outside of this world.*
—Ronald Reagan, speech to the United Nations, September 21, 1987

*Today at the edge of our hope, at the end of our time, we have chosen to believe in each other.
Today, we face the monsters that are at our door. Today we are canceling the apocalypse.*
—Guillermo del Toro and Travis Beacham, Pacific Rim

In director Guillermo del Toro's (2013) summer sci-fi blockbuster, *Pacific Rim*,
invaders from another dimension open a rift in the floor of the Pacific Ocean,
sending gigantic creatures through the portal hell-bent on destroying humanity. Striding out of the ocean depths as literal leviathans, these monsters
have no language, no culture, no purpose, except that of pure destruction.
Set in the near future, the film imagines an oceanic regional effort to fight
this overpowering otherworldly force, providing the context for righteous
violence, multinational camaraderie, and heroic individual sacrifice. Defense
comes in the form of nuclear-powered humanoid machines, allowing a martial arts contest of giant robots (*mecha*) against giant monsters (*kaiju*), both
of which level city spaces and produce mass casualties without comment or
concern. This is an old story, one that draws on twentieth-century Japanese

Figure 12.1. "Go Big or Go Extinct," promotion for a total species war, *Pacific Rim*.

and American atomic cinema (particularly the giant radioactive creature films *Godzilla* and *Them!*) as well as manga, and its familiarity is precisely the source of its presumed pleasure (see Broderick 1996; Evans 1999; Kalat 2010). The remarkable conceit of *Pacific Rim* is to merge a Japanese popular culture genre of nuclear victimization with an American nuclear triumphalism via the personal charisma of a military leader of uncertain nationality (played by Idris Elba), who quite literally promises to cancel the apocalypse. Viewers learn that the nonhuman invaders tried once before to colonize Earth, in the era of the dinosaurs, but found the climate inhospitable and have been waiting for human industrial activities to warm the atmosphere to a cozy level for their species—making *Pacific Rim* a nuclear narrative as well as a climate narrative, all in one. The suture here is thus not only between national nuclear cultures but also between apocalyptic concepts. The film is an act of catastrophic bricolage, a cutting and pasting of twentieth-century disaster tropes to imagine a humanity unified by environmental destruction, nuclear technologies, and total war (see figure 12.1).[1]

The implicit promise of the film is the delivery of a state-of-the-art technological depiction of a child's universe of superpowered beings and interdimensional conflict, enabling a war that does not need to be ideologically or morally assessed or defended. It relies on a total war as normality frame but locates itself at a moment of maximal precariousness for people. Depicting a world that has largely collapsed, with citizens living in the ruins of Pacific

Coast cities, as well as in the carcasses of the leviathans, *Pacific Rim* serves up for viewer enjoyment a last battle for a world already destroyed. The Japanese filmic genre kaiju (featuring highly imaginative species of monsters) is important in that it frequently offers up allegories of nature's revenge against the industrial world: for more than a half century, incredible creatures (some the imagined product of irradiated ocean ecologies) have made fictional war on Japanese urban life, with special attention to nuclear power plants (eerily prefiguring the tsunami that flooded the Fukushima Daiichi nuclear power plant in 2011 to such tragic effect). Tellingly, one almost always identifies with the monsters in this genre, as the nonhuman becomes a vengeful subject quite justified in attacking urban populations for crimes against nature (articulating long-standing Japanese anxieties about war, the unmemorialized dead, and ecological costs of urban consumption). The kaiju genre depicts a kind of nature outside of human control but directly tied to human actions, constituting a distinctly non-American nuclear culture of ecological disruption, mutation, and revenge. *Pacific Rim* merges this genre with an American technological fetishism and nuclear-powered militarism to create the imaginary grounds for transnational, -ethnic, and -gender belonging. Del Toro's ambitious film is lusciously absurd at every level: it is a form of ideological, historical, and cinematic dada.

The timing of this film about (ending the) apocalypse also is well worth interrogating (see Stewart and Harding 1999). Depicting a world of total war relying on the human/machine interface of new military technologies (including robots and drones) with a plot organized around suicide attacks and demonic, all-but-unknowable others, the film evokes the U.S. War on Terror, which also relies on images of an unstoppable and dehumanized enemy that cannot be reasoned with, who is committed to relentless violence in perpetuity. But if the first decade of counterterror has demonstrated anything, it is the power of this enemy formation combined with a discourse of imminent catastrophic danger (the "terrorist armed with a weapon of mass destruction" in President George W. Bush's memorable configuration) to mislead. The terrorist enemy, in practice, has proven not only to be those who crash planes into buildings but also a vast field of misrecognition and projection, sweeping up fantasized threats with the spectacularly outgunned, the abjectly poor, noncombatants, and children in many parts of the world. Killing, in the second decade of counterterror, has lost its heroic narrative for attentive U.S. citizens, evoking more readily crimes against humanity rather than a national regeneration through righteous violence. The declaration of what White House officials have alternatively called "the War on Terror," "the long war," or simply, "the new normal" committed the United States in 2001 to a permanent war mobilization against the image of an implacable, and all but unlocatable, foe—terror itself. But this concept of war is itself catastrophic, constituting a vastly violent, radically undemocratic, and spectacularly expensive global mobilization that offers up no vision of victory, truce, or a return to peacetime. Instead, the counterterror state now addresses the future itself as a domain of unending existential threat, constituting a permanent field of emergency (see Masco 2014).

The leviathans of *Pacific Rim* are thus offered as an attempt to lure viewers into a universe where nonhumans, spectacularly rendered through computer-generated imagery but lacking motivation or complexity, can be killed without remorse, and the aesthetics of their death can be offered up as a source of both pleasure and social renewal. The commercial tag line of the film, delivered by the charismatic British actor Idris Elba (who also portrayed Nelson Mandela in 2013), is thus a hopeful comment on the contemporary War on Terror moment but also fundamentally a lie: the film cannot cancel the apocalypse because it relies entirely on the promise of total destruction to create its appeal and market. The film, despite its ambition to be something more, is an "us or them" depiction of total war played out at the species level. In the summer of 2013, a time of widespread crises across the domains of war, finance, politics, and the environment, it was impossible to avoid this cinematic promise of an end to the apocalypse, shouted globally via an aggressive advertising campaign, installing all of its infantile desires for righteous killing and total victory into public spaces already saturated by counterterror, collapsing markets, and ecological dislocation. *Pacific Rim*, and the larger apocalyptic cinema genre it engages, offers us insight into the familiarity of the catastrophic as a social text in the early twenty-first century. It invites us to consider how evoking the catastrophic, as well as claiming the ability to control and defer the catastrophic, has become the very basis for the political today, a core feature in American storytelling, politics, and visions of the future.

Del Toro, for example, cinematically enacts President Ronald Reagan's (1987) public fantasy about how Cold War antagonisms could be overcome simply by the arrival of a new existential danger in the form of an extraterrestrial invasion. Competing national subjects would then become unified species subjects in Reagan's vision, ending the Cold War nuclear standoff instantly in favor of planetary defense. What is naturalized and thus unaddressed in both Reagan's and del Toro's visions is the commitment to total war. Both assume that threat constitutes the social and rely on a species-level friend/enemy distinction (Schmitt 2007) to organize human life on a new scale (constituting through war a social revolution without a difference). After the three world wars of the twentieth century, it is a remarkable project to transform total war—an engineered catastrophe—from an exception into the normative basis for society. Rehearsing and fantasizing collective disaster in this way also ultimately works to ward off consideration of actual destruction, as violence is imaginatively transformed from irrevocable loss into the exclusive basis for community and belonging (mirroring the long-standing American ideology of the frontier; see Slotkin 2000).

Spectacles of disaster strive to be mesmerizing and, through constant repetition, have the power to block thought and to colonize ideas about danger with specific images tuned for maximal political effect.[2] Computer-based technologies have opened a universe of potentially limitless storytelling, constituting ever-evolving and advanced technologies of visualization (see Whissel 2014). Hollywood's summer blockbuster concept is indebted to this technology revolution, which has been devoted almost entirely to depictions of war and disaster, worked out in increasing resolution and detail. Thus, a very real question involves how to consider the catastrophic and not be intellectually overwhelmed or neutralized by its spectacle (see Derrida 1984; Freud 1991). American society has rehearsed certain forms of absolute danger now for generations, making them (particularly the mushroom cloud) the very tools of state and nation building, filling the conceptual space of the catastrophic with specific images and fears to the exclusion of other concerns and potentials.

In other words, the catastrophic remains a highly aestheticized and thus a highly politicized conceptual space in the twenty-first-century United States. But the wide-ranging utility of the catastrophic narrative today also reveals its ideological overdetermination, as the truly catastrophic leaves no remainder. Why then is the catastrophic—as the designation of an ultimate violence—so conceptually powerful at this historical moment that it displaces all other modalities of future making in the United States? At what cost comes this historically generated familiarity with the catastrophic, this intimacy, indeed pleasure, in end-time thinking? And what does the catastrophic render invisible in its depiction of both everyday violence and total endings?

Pacific Rim's promise to make the catastrophic fun again by creating a species-level war belies the lived reality of collapsing infrastructures, ecological imbalance, and the cumulative effects of the war machine in the twenty-first century while simultaneously evoking each of these topical concerns to constitute a consumerist relation to the apocalyptic. It assumes that viewers are walking out of the theater into an unbroken world, thus allowing its vision of end times to be experienced through the pleasures of the sublime and the relative security of everyday comfort. The catastrophic here is simulated in order not to provoke thought and action but rather to satiate and dull viewer sensibility—to contain and reduce thought about external threats, environmental disruption, and war.

In terms of domestic box office, *Pacific Rim* was the thirty-fourth most successful film of 2013. Its moderate success (at odds with the popularity of kaiju as filmic genre as well as its $200 million special effects production and the talent of its director), however, might well be considered diagnostic of an overdetermination in the mass media of disaster today. Perhaps a shift is occurring in the very terms of catastrophic reasoning—marking a more general problem in the nature of endangerment in the early twenty-first century. Driven by the proliferation (and repeated political exploitation) of claims on end times, this would mark a social exhaustion in the U.S. with efforts to regenerate the national community through (both real and simulated) violence. Perhaps today we are witnessing nothing less than catastrophe's apocalypse.

What would this mean? A catastrophe is not the same as a crisis or the apocalyptic. Each of these concepts evokes a different degree of violence, operates on a different temporal scale, and offers up a specific perspective on the future. Each also has a different relation to a normative everyday and points to a different course of action. Crisis implies a threat to a system or infrastructure, and precisely because it is not yet catastrophic presents an opportunity for maximal political urgency and utility. One can talk about the political crisis of the federal government today because the gridlock of the two-party system is not yet recognized as a catastrophe; that is, an irrevocable violence. The resolution of a crisis maintains the existing structure of a system, while a catastrophe involves the ruination of that system in some kind of permanent manner. Crisis evokes a dangerous potential, but catastrophe is a lived ending, an actual form of destruction. An apocalypse, however, evokes more than just destruction; it also designates a revelation, an intellectual uncovering of matter as it actually is, an uncovering of some kind of previously inaccessible truth. An apocalypse produces new insight through destruction, a disclosure of hidden knowledge, which is why it is linked so strongly with religiosity—it is a reality hidden behind the social world made visible through ruination.

So, in a contemporary era of counterterror and normalized end-time politics, what would transform the catastrophic into a form of revelation, a mode of social critique that could register more than just damage? What would denaturalize existing catastrophic practices and blunt simple fear-based emotional management campaigns to make contemplating the end an opportunity for critical insight and self-understanding? In North America one would have to recognize that the foundational violences of indigenous dispossession and antiblackness were waged as end-times projects for specific communities while the U.S. consolidated an idea of the national community in the twentieth century via images of nuclear war. In what follows, I explore catastrophe's apocalypse in two major visions of the end: in U.S. nuclear war plans from the height of the Cold War, and in the projections of contemporary climate science, exploring not only the futurities but also the revelatory potentials embedded in assessing life as ongoing catastrophe. In particular, I wish to consider the historical conditions of possibility for assessing catastrophic potentials, as well as to interrogate the slippages or disconnects between agency and imagination for those living in a highly mass mediated, and technologically infused, universe of trouble.

Nuclear End Times

In the United States, nuclear fear colonized the very idea of the catastrophic in the twentieth century. As I have argued throughout this book, nuclear fear was officially deployed to create a new kind of national security state and, with it, a new citizen-state relationship mediated by images of absolute destruction. During the Cold War, the nuclear state not only built a meticulous global machinery for nuclear war, it also taught Americans to think and feel as nuclear subjects, to contemplate a sudden end of the United States and transform that cataclysmic vision into a perverse new form of nation building. The cataclysmic became a formal basis for political life in the early Cold War, making claims on the imminent death of the nation a powerful new form of state and nation building. The nuclear revolution was thus both technological and psychosocial, simultaneously material, cultural, and emotional.

We forget today that the nuclear danger has not always been present, that before 1945 the future had many worries but not one overpowering, totalizing one. In the United States, the atomic bomb has always been a double-edged revolution, simultaneously installing a new domestic vulnerability (in the form of surprise nuclear attack) as well as an absolute offensive power (in the form of the U.S. nuclear arsenal). The bomb becomes the basis for U.S. superpower standing but also reorganizes collective death as imminence, a pure potential loaded into every second of everyday life. Thus, it sutures the ability to destroy and be destroyed in a new machine form, one that folds official terrors and hegemonic desires together in a novel configuration. Beginning in the early 1950s, the public project of civil defense was to teach Americans to respond to nuclear danger productively as Cold Warriors, to train the public to psychologically engage nuclear emergency as the basis of American power and international order (Oakes 1994; Orr 2006). Civil defense constituted (i.e., both invented and installed) a new register of threat in everyday American life, the surprise nuclear attack that would decimate urban America and leave the rest of the country a radioactive ruin in a matter of minutes. Civil defense was rehearsed for generations in public schools and through national mass media campaigns and informs official disaster planning to this day. Its extraordinary achievement was to turn contemplating the end of the nation-state into a form of nation building, constituting an affective relation to destruction as the terms of a new collective beginning (see Masco 2014).

From this point of view, the atomic revolution installs a new kind of catastrophic potential into everyday life (one that is mirrored by the emerging unfolding environmental force of other industrial fallouts—notably petrochemicals, greenhouse gases, and plastics). But this historical fact raises another set of important and even more difficult and subtle questions: How has the nuclear danger—now approaching its eighth decade—shifted the ability to see and consider catastrophe itself, altering American thought and perception across the generations? What discursive forms have evolved to negotiate and/or naturalize the minute-to-minute collective danger of nuclear catastrophe; that is, where can we see nuclear fear publicly articulated, socially managed, and psychologically contained? What can transcend or expose a social world so structured by the possibilities of its own ending that contemplating catastrophe becomes socially normative, or merely a form of entertainment, or even just boring? Above all, how does the cultural preoccupation with a specific vision of catastrophe block perception of other dangers (particularly slower-moving crises, like global warming and toxic contamination) less tuned to our postnuclear sensibilities, encouraging their ultimate expression?

An image of all-encompassing catastrophe constituted the public side of nuclear war planning and was extraordinarily influential in the twentieth-century United States, enabling a multigenerational consensus of anticommunism and consumer capitalism through mass psychosocial domestic regulation. In other words, by deploying an idea of existential danger and using official secrecy to carefully calibrate the depiction of nuclear threat, the Cold War nuclear state transformed catastrophe itself into a politicized and instrumental vision, a core tool of domestic governance and nation building. Evoking the sudden end of American civilization has since become a basic tool in governance, a reliable means of blocking domestic debate as well as taking extraordinary international actions (including a vast range of covert actions as well as invading other states and conducting deadly drone strikes around the world under the logic of counterterror).

But if the public side of Cold War nuclear emergency was civil defense, with its commitment to emotional management via images of the end of the nation-state, what about official logics and registers; that is, what of the actual governance of nuclear war? With that question in mind, consider the U.S. nuclear war plan of the early Cold War, the first formally coded U.S. nuclear war strategy, an official program for planetary destruction (see Ball and Toth 1990; Sagan 1987). Conceived during a period of hyperactive U.S. and Soviet thermonuclear testing, the first official U.S. nuclear war program was breathtakingly simple and unprecedentedly violent in concept (see Keeney 2002, 2011). The U.S. nuclear war plan consisted of two versions of the same option: a preemptory strike against global communism and a retaliatory strike against global communism (Rosenberg 1981, 1983). Both plans involved using the entire U.S. nuclear arsenal to eliminate communism worldwide (from the Soviet Union to North Korea to China) with a few hours of nuclear warfare. Thus, it inscribed as U.S. policy a commitment to maximal violence as minimal defense. This program was depicted in a U.S. Air Force film, *The Power of Decision*, commissioned in 1958 strictly for internal military use. It was declassified and publicized by the openness activists at the National Security Archive via the U.S. National Archives and Records Administration in 2010, likely not having been watched in decades (see Burr 2011). This is a rare record of how those in control of the nuclear arsenal first imagined and internally discussed fighting a global nuclear war. It was made for restricted internal Air Force use only and thus was not trying to minimize the consequences of nuclear war for a public audience along the lines of civil defense films but rather sought to shape ideas about the rationality and reliability of the nuclear system itself for nuclear war fighters. As the American public was practicing duck and cover in the event of nuclear war, the command and control officers were learning how to push the buttons to launch a new kind of world-ending violence.

Walking viewers through the command and control logics of nuclear weapons and war, the film offers a factual, and remarkably affectless, depiction of how the United States and the Soviet Union would consume each other under mushroom clouds. The film constitutes the ability of U.S. command and control to survive a nuclear attack and successfully retaliate as a victory, regardless of the subsequent global nuclear cataclysm. Viewers are told early on that the United States has the power to "strike anywhere in the world" and, in a few hours of nuclear war, deliver "more explosive power than has been used in all the previous wars in human history combined." Thus, this film is also about American self-fashioning as a reluctant but supremely powerful warrior state, articulating the imaginary terms for righteous revenge against a surprise attack. *Power of Decision* depicts a psychosocial field of projection and fantasy, but one mediated by a global technological infrastructure of mass destruction.

Film has always been a key means of establishing—giving both form and image to—the nuclear danger in the United States. Nuclear fear had to be learned before it could be felt. The nuclear security state created films for every audience—military personnel, civilians, scientists, and politicians—each crafted to bring them into a specific relationship to the bomb. The vibrant production of public films for civil defense was exceeded only by the production of classified films for use within the military, in weapons laboratories, and for elected officials. *The Power of Decision* establishes the serious authority and closed world system (Edwards 1996) of early nuclear war plans within the classified networks of the time but also, in detailing how the U.S. would conduct a nuclear war, demonstrates the paradox of that authority. Here security and insecurity meet under the sign of the mushroom cloud, and nuclear governance—despite an all-out effort to make it logical and proportional—is rendered absurd as officers mobilize to generate hundreds of millions of deaths worldwide in a few minutes of nuclear warfare in order to declare victory.

In the opening frame of *The Power of Decision*, viewers meet an Air Force officer who stares directly into the camera and introduces the film. The style of his presentation is that of a military briefing, blunt but with certain flourishes: Declaring that he is standing hundreds of feet underground in a blast- and radiation-proof bunker, our narrator theatrically walks through layer upon layer of internal security to the command center itself, stating, "From this room, the [Air] Force throughout the world is controlled and monitored twenty-four hours a day—in peace as it would be in war." Rendering the distinction between war and peace suddenly murky, our narrator quickly introduces viewers to the Big Board—an analog map of all the various strike routes aimed at the Soviet Union, as well as the exercises that are currently taking place. A tangled web of multicolored lines, the diagram obliterates the USSR under the weight of Air Force bomber vectors, actual planes in the air, potential exercises, feints, and alerts. We are told that attack vectors are being flown every minute of every day and, to keep "the enemy" from being able to predict American routes and strategies, that there are fake exercises mixed into the planned assault strategy. Viewers are introduced to the "red phone," which overrides all other communications in an alert, as well as the multiple systems for gaining information about the global fleet of American planes and the military actions of enemy states. This depiction of a global early warning and command and control system is the formal project of the film, but steely determination to fight a nuclear war is the fetish. Defense and deterrence are collapsed into nuclear war-fighting ability in this presentation, which depicts nuclear war as an affectless circuit of human-machine interfaces and necropolitical expertise. The will to fight is portrayed as equally crucial to the technological infrastructure of nuclear war as the bomb itself.

The film is organized in two parts: the first is a briefing of Air Force nuclear logistics focused on Operation Quickstart (the ongoing training for nuclear attack), while the second, Operation War Dance, offers a live-action illustration of the process of recognizing a Soviet attack, pursuing an American counterstrike, and then conducting a post–nuclear war damage assessment. In the first part, an animation of the globe demonstrates how U.S. and Soviet aircraft can now fly over the polar north to attack one another, underscored by a second animation of a globe covered in mushroom clouds (see figure 12.2). This animation is the precursor to dramatizing the global sequence of nuclear war, this time structured around actual U.S. nuclear test footage of thermonuclear detonations, as well as blast and destruction sequences from the nuclear test program, all intercut with staged command and control decision making. The largely analog universe of American command control and information systems is presented as cutting-edge technology, allowing near-instantaneous global communications, a 24/7 monitoring of Soviet activities, and an always-on-alert nuclear Air Force that has at least 15 percent of its fleet in the air at all times. This is a system claiming the highest level of rationality: technological precision is combined with exacting timetables, sequential assessments, and escalating actions, but inevitably this technoscientific system results in the end of the known world. Thus, the hyperrationality of the nuclear system is mobilized in an attempt to override the inevitable reality of its use, showing how security and defense have paradoxically merged with mass violence on a new kind of planetary scale in Cold War nuclear logics.

As reports come into the command center of a Soviet first use of nuclear weapons in Europe and Japan, a general intones, "By giving up the initiative, the West must expect to take the first blow." This is a coded reference to preemption, as nuclear debates in the Cold War focused on the illogic of allowing a nuclear strike on the United States if it could be preempted by a surprise U.S. nuclear attack on the Soviet Union. The head of the Strategic Air Command, Curtis LeMay, advocated striking the Soviet Union before their nuclear forces reached parity with the United States (Keeney 2011). But a U.S. military culture founded on the Japanese "sneak attack" at Pearl Harbor

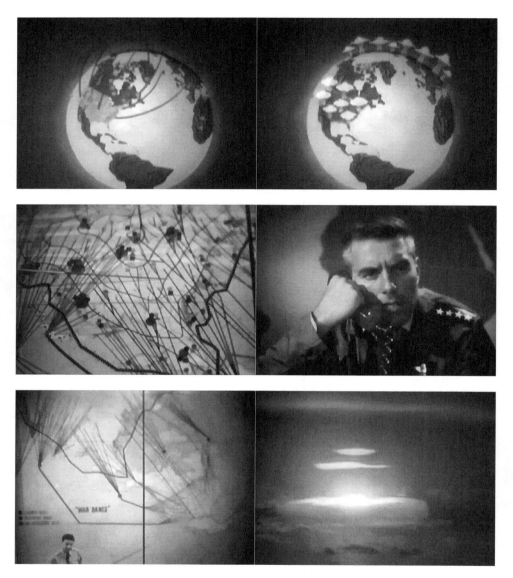

Figure 12.2. Stills from *Power of Decision* (U.S. Air Force, courtesy of the National Security Archive).

resisted the logics of nuclear preemption, arguing that such an assault would be against American values. Moreover, in the age of thermonuclear weapons, a preemptive attack would not eliminate the possibility of a nuclear counterattack (precisely what is documented in *The Power of Decision*). As the film theatrically presents, no matter which party starts a nuclear conflict, massive destruction occurs all around the world: there is no place of safety on planet Earth during a nuclear war. *The Power of Decision* is ultimately a documentary about a defense system that is also a planetary mechanism of collective suicide (see also Hoffman 2010).

The Air Force soon unleashes its nuclear bombers, staging sequential and incremental runs across Soviet territories to close in on Target M, presumably Moscow, which is soon reported destroyed. After less than a day of nuclear warfare, the U.S. has eliminated the Soviet Union; as one U.S. general puts it: "They must quit: we have the air and the power and they know it." But what does such a victory look like? The postwar assessment, also a briefing on the big board, reveals a stark reality: while the U.S. nuclear system worked perfectly in terms of command and control, over sixty million Americans are dead or injured. The industrial core of the United States—Detroit, Chicago, and Pittsburgh, as well as New York—is destroyed. Similarly, major cities in Europe and Japan as well as much of the Soviet Union and China are radioactive ruins. Viewers do not get an assessment of the total global dead. But in addition to the urban destruction, radioactive fallout would travel globally, bringing a second wave of death in the form of radiation injury. In 1958, a nuclear winter—produced by the combined atmospheric effects of the particulate matter elevated into the stratosphere by destroying cities on this scale—was not yet an operative concept (see Eden 2004; Ehrlich et al. 1984). Thus, weather is only discussed as a problem for managing planes in flight and is not yet part of the postnuclear world assessment, which we now know would likely include a massively destabilized climate. But, even on its own terms, *The Power of Decision* documents the nuclear cataclysm as a technorational system, one in which the ability to exert American will on the Soviet Union is constituted as a victory despite the hundreds of millions of deaths worldwide, leaving an image of victory at the end that is apocalyptic at its core. The insight that war is now too deadly to actually fight is a repeated refrain in the film. But this refrain is undermined by the obvious pleasure in detailing exactly how the nuclear war machine would function in a matter of minutes to bring about an unprecedented, and perhaps final, global calamity.

This ever-expanding technical capacity to fight a global nuclear war constitutes the first purposefully engineered planetary crisis. In the first decade of the

Cold War, people faced the possibility of an absolute ending of their own making for the first time, a political deployment of a global infrastructure of mass destruction in which there might not be a human left to tell the story of what happened and why. In this regard, *The Power of Decision* does not contemplate what the world would be like for the nuclear war–fighting team as they leave the bunker, return to the surface, and enter the postnuclear ruins. The newly ascendant American empire would also be highly radioactive, subject to a radically destabilized climate, and structured by unprecedented levels of material damage and psychological trauma. It might be a technical victory for the United States within the logics of the Cold War system, as the film claims, but a planetary cataclysm nonetheless, all achieved in less than a day of warfare. *The Power of Decision* offers no insight into the cause or logic of the Soviet attack, nor does it pause to consider the terms of existence of the nuclear war machine itself, opting instead for a factual treatment of machines, vectors, targets, and casualties. There is no room for diplomacy in this vision, only military action. What is also lost in the description of closed-world machines and nuclear delivery systems is the extraordinary amount of work that it took to build this global doomsday system. With each frame of the film the nuclear fetish is ever more naturalized, making catastrophe the basis for state power rather than a feat of human engineering that could simply be dismantled in the name of collective security. Indeed, after 1958, the U.S. nuclear arsenal only grows in both numbers and explosive power, reaching a peak of over 35,000 nuclear weapons by the end of the 1960s, enough to destroy every major city on the planet many times over. U.S. defense remains to this day founded on the ability to strike anywhere on planet Earth and to destroy all major population centers outside the United States, within a few minutes of nuclear warfare (see Kristensen 2006).

Culturally, this notion of the end—of a nuclear strike that obliterates totally and almost instantaneously—has come to define American notions of the cataclysmic. From nuclear war to the War on Terror, U.S. security logics are structured by fear of the surprise attack that is constituted as both imminent and complete. To a remarkable degree, nuclear fear has been coded into the idea of catastrophe in American culture, only allowing counterformations that attempt to be equally total, equally surprising, equally violent. In this way, building a countercommunist state during the Cold War (and a counterterror state in the twenty-first century) has relied on certain images of the end, promoted and magnified via official state systems as a means of affectively mobilizing diverse publics and experts. With constant technological improvements in missiles and warhead design, speed soon became a particular problem in the nuclear age. By the 1960s, the technological terms of nuclear war had advanced to such an extent that the entire system had to be slowed down to allow human decision making in the midst of emergency. Everything from the telephone hotline between U.S. and Soviet leaders (established after the Cuban Missile Crisis) to nuclear war plans themselves were structured around the realization that a nuclear war could start before there was time for a political debate or alternative action to launching a full counterstrike (Burr 2004, 2005). In other words, by the 1960s, the always-on-alert system of missiles-bombers-submarines armed with thermonuclear weapons made *not* launching a nuclear war a minute-to-minute calculus and then naturalized that restraint as the basis of an ethical and necessary defense.

In psychosocial terms, this means that Americans have lived for more than a half century in the temporal space in which the missiles may have always already been launched—that is, within the fifteen-minute window offered by early warning systems. The nuclear cataclysm thus may have always already happened, with simply the global fallout to be negotiated. Nuclear danger has in this way come to structure the very idea of catastrophe in the United States, where the shock of a total ending becomes the basis for thinking large-scale threat. The slower violences of petrochemical capitalism across energy, health, and the environment (see Nixon 2011) become difficult to see as forms of cataclysmic violence precisely because images of nuclear war continue to overwhelm, offering Americans a perfected and speedy image of the collective end. This concept of cataclysmic danger as totalizing and short is profoundly at odds with those threats that exceed the power of the nation-state itself and that move incrementally but accrue ever greater force over time, achieving the catastrophic through a relentless acceleration.

Atmospheres of Destruction

Warming of the climate system is unequivocal.

Human influence on the climate system is clear.

It is very likely that the Arctic sea ice cover will continue to shrink and thin. . . .

Continued emissions of greenhouse gases will cause further warming
and changes in all components of the climate system.
—IPCC, Climate Change 2013

The ongoing projections of the Intergovernmental Panel on Climate Change (IPCC) are startling, depicting a new kind of collective violence that is escalating and will play out over the coming centuries in every ecosystem on Earth (see figure 12.3). The extraordinary achievement of the IPCC is its radical interdisciplinarity and multinational cooperation, allowing teams of scientists across a vast range of fields to integrate huge data sets and, via computer simulations, to project atmospheric effects out into the coming decades (Edwards 2010). The portrait of the coming century that the IPCC presents, however, is not pretty and asks readers to seriously rethink industrial age understandings of both progress and catastrophe. The predicted elevation of the global temperature by between two and six degrees by midcentury, the IPCC argues, will create increasingly volatile earthly conditions. The reduction in polar ice will lead to rising ocean levels, which will flood islands and coastal cities worldwide. It will also produce a more acidic ocean, leading to vast oceanic dead zones. Similarly, extreme weather patterns (producing regional droughts and flooding) will challenge food production worldwide while changing habitat zones on a massive scale and enabling new emerging diseases. Moreover, the expanding number of people on Earth, potentially rising from seven to nine billion by 2050, will create more petrochemical consumers and only increase pressure on the global environment. The resulting ecological stress could exceed what ecologists calculate is the carrying capacity of the global biosphere, leading to widespread scarcity or even more shocking ecological destabilizations.

Earth scientists state that over 99 percent of the life forms that have ever lived on planet Earth have gone extinct. Extinction is thus not the exception but rather the rule over the long, *longue durée* of planetary life. The best estimates today are that some four billion species have evolved over the past 3.5 billion years. In addition to the process of natural selection in eliminating and promoting particular species, there have been five mass extinction events, periods when, due to asteroid collisions or planetary-scale climatic changes, two thirds or more of all the organisms on Earth have disappeared. In light of the IPCC assessments, there is much discussion of a sixth mass extinction event—an ongoing shift in the terms of living on Earth drawn from the combined impacts of habitat destruction, pollution, overharvesting, invasive species, and human population growth. This sixth mass extinction will be unique, as it does not arrive in the form of an asteroid collision or volcanic eruption but rather through the hyperactive work of one late-blooming species: human beings. More specifically, the industrial age consumer has become an extraordinary planetary force, impacting the atmosphere, oceans, ice flows, and biosphere in ways that promise less and less biodiversity and radical swings in weather (see Kolbert 2014).

Climate disruption thus now posits a vision of end times that rivals that of the nuclear danger, as the incremental and cumulative effects of the petrochemical industry have foundationally shifted the atmospheric chemistry on

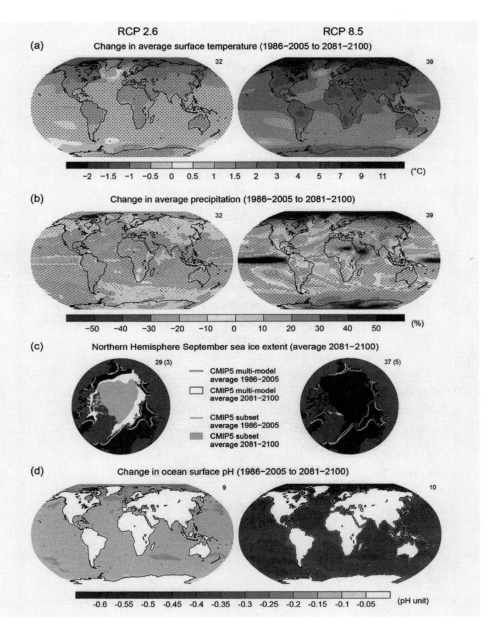

Figure 12.3. IPCC chart on climate change dynamics in the twenty-first century across temperature, precipitation, sea ice loss, and ocean acidification.

Earth, setting off a reverberating chain of effects throughout the biosphere. But if the global nuclear danger is characterized by its shocking immediacy, climate danger works on an opposite temporality, constituting a slower violence that is treacherous precisely because it is so incremental that it is difficult in any given moment to sense a change in the environment or to connect discrete issues (such as sea level or drought or fires or violent weather) to industrially generated greenhouse gas emissions. It is a cumulative and momentum-driven process, operating on so vast a scale that it raises basic questions about human perception, memory, and the terms of visualization appropriate for a planetary-scale problems. In light of such industrial fallout, geologists are now debating how to sequence planetary time to recognize the effects of human industry. As Steffen et al. put it:

> The advent of the Anthropocene, the time interval in which human activities now rival global geophysical processes, suggests that we need to fundamentally alter our relationship with the planet we inhabit. Many approaches could be adopted, ranging from geoengineering solutions that purposefully manipulate parts of the Earth System to becoming active stewards of our own life support system. The Anthropocene is a reminder that the Holocene, during which complex human societies have developed, has been a stable, accommodating environment and is the only state of the Earth System that we know for sure can support contemporary society. The need to achieve effective planetary stewardship is urgent. As we go further into the Anthropocene, we risk driving the Earth System into a trajectory toward more hostile states from which we cannot easily return. (2011: 739)

Life support systems. Geoengineering, planetary stewardship, hostile environmental states—these are the terms of a radically new kind of emergency, one that operates on the global scale of the biosphere. The ten thousand-plus years of the Holocene emerge as a temporary atmospheric condition on planet Earth, one particularly beneficial to humans, who, living in that special air, rose to become the dominant species, inventing agriculture, writing, cars, computers, and atomic bombs in the process. A Euro-American concept of the planet is now fundamentally shifting, from literally stable ground, unchangeable in its nature, to a runaway system: this emerging understanding underscores that the environmental envelope on which all life depends is both fragile and changing under accumulated industrial stresses and a lack of political resolve to do anything substantial about it.

Climate change in its monumentality merges human history with natural history (Chakrabarty 2009), creating a new kind of temporality that radically undercuts long-standing logics of economic progress and development. This collapsing of human time into geological time forces us to think on unfamiliar scales—such as the planet—and to think not of nation-states and groups, but of species-level human impacts (earth systems of air, ice, water, and geology). Thus, climate change as a collective problem challenges existing political, economic, and industrial orders, requiring not only a reverse engineering of global infrastructure to prevent a worsening ecological condition but also new conceptual structures. Here, the built universe of things and the desires that organize Global North consumption patterns are revealed to be literally catastrophic. The petrochemical economy that has revolutionized social order—enabling mass production, urbanization, and global transportation—has unintentionally generated an unprecedented planetary-scale environmental disaster, one that transforms the smallest of everyday activities—driving in a car or eating a hamburger—into a new kind of end times. Hamburgers, the quintessential American fast food, are ruinous for the planet. In fact, earth scientists now use the global proliferation of McDonald's restaurants as an index of anthropogenic environmental change (Steffen et al. 2011, 742). Every aspect of the mass-produced burger—from the territorial management of cattle to the global supply chains of distribution to the plastic containers—is now a planetary force. Here, the catastrophic is revealed to be not just an external threat, an asteroid strike or foreign attack; it is now coded into the everyday tastes, desires, and naturalized modes of consumption for those embedded in petrochemical capitalism and nuclear nationalism. The everyday consumption patterns of such people, unremarkable in their singularity, have become cumulatively destructive in their totality (despite the many different modes and ways of living that continue to exist). This makes the basic requirements of a consumer society (including food, transportation, heating, clothing) fundamentally dangerous to the future stability of the climate, as they are embedded in a petrochemical economy protected by nuclear nationalism. The virtues of modernization, globalization, and technology have thus been turned upside down by climate change: rather than extending equality, security, and comfort, these practices are a negative form of geoengineering, putting ever more pressure on atmospheric conditions. McDonald's Big Mac burger has now perversely joined the atomic bomb as a threat to the collective future in the twenty-first century.

How could such a calamity—with so many vectors of change—appear so suddenly in American life, challenging contemporary social orders to simultaneously reinvent economy, consumption, security, and governance? Global warming has, of course, been a scientific concern for decades, emerging from the data sets and theories of Cold War earth sciences (see Jamison 2014; Masco 2014; Weart 2008). Indeed, one can find speculations about radical climate change from the mid-twentieth century that are eerie from a contemporary point of view (e.g., see Robin, Sorlin, and Warde 2013). Consider Frank Capra's 1958 educational film, *Unchained Goddess*, part of the Bell Laboratory Science Series, a post-Sputnik campaign to interest young Americans in scientific careers hosted by literary professor Frank Baxter. The film, which merges cartoon characters, experts, actors, and documentary footage, presents an overview of meteorology but ends with a disturbing hypothesis about the future (see figure 12.4). After a discussion of the possibility of weather modification and control, Baxter cautions that these are

> extremely dangerous questions, because with our present knowledge we have no idea what would happen. Even now Man may be unwittingly changing the world's climate through the waste products of his civilization. Due to our release through our factories and automobiles every year of more than six billion tons of carbon dioxide, which helps air absorb heat from the sun, our atmosphere seems to be getting warmer.... It's been calculated that a few degrees rise in the earth's temperature would melt the polar ice caps. And if this happens, an inland sea would fill a good portion of the Mississippi Valley. Tourists in glass-bottom boats would be viewing the grand towers of Miami through 150 feet of tropical water. For in weather we are not only dealing with forces of a far greater variety than even the atomic physicists encounter but with life itself. Without air and water, which are weather, Man would never have appeared on this small planet Earth. There would be no sky, no ocean, no fields, no forests, nothing but a barren rock rotating in an airless void.

Tourists in glass-bottom boats over Miami. What was part of a basic public survey of climatology in 1958 for children has thus suddenly become a collective emergency in the twenty-first century. The privileging of economy and nuclear threat over all other concerns in the second half of the twentieth century required a subsuming of climate danger, with mounting consequences. Thus, the environment emerges here as a problem not just of knowledge but also of perception, not just of understanding but also of collective memory. Catastrophe's apocalypse is to recognize the human agency not only in producing anthropogenic changes in the environment but also

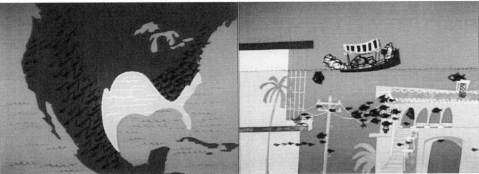

Figure 12.4. Stills from *Unchained Goddess* sequence on the consequences of carbon emissions on ice cap melt and future sea levels over Miami.

to identify the mechanisms of mystification and occlusion supporting such violence while the problem intensifies.

Given the scale of environmental emergency today, one of the immediate problems concerns its visualization and narration—of how to make hypercomplex planetary dangers intelligible to nonexperts. There is not yet a vibrant popular culture of climate danger to match that of the nuclear danger, but it is emerging (see Kaplan 2016; Streeby 2018). J. C. Chandor's 2013 film, *All Is Lost*, offers a disciplined start to such an endeavor. The plot is simple: a seventy-something white American male (played by Robert Redford) is alone, "somewhere in the Indian Ocean," sleeping comfortably in his sailboat when an errant shipping container afloat in the open ocean ruptures the hull. After attempting to patch the hole, he endures a massive storm and is forced onto an inflatable lifeboat when the sailboat sinks. Drifting into shipping lanes, he repeatedly tries to signal gigantic freighters (stacked with the kind of containers that damaged his ship) for help, but they pass him by unnoticed, completely indifferent to his plight. Eight traumatic days later, out of supplies and hope, he sees a light on the nighttime horizon that might be a small boat. He accidentally ignites his lifeboat in hopes of drawing attention to his plight and watches from underneath the water as his sole means of shelter goes up in flames. The last frames of the film show a hand from a small rescue boat reaching down into the ocean, offering our protagonist one last chance for survival, which he swims toward.

A story with one character, known simply as Our Man, and only two real words of dialogue—"help" (thrown in vain at shipping vessels) and a singular "fuck" (when the situation turns irrevocable)—is ultimately about the fragility of all lifeboats.[3] Our Man is the quintessential master of industry. He is likely retired and wealthy enough to own the boat. He is also a man of action, both able and strong. When problems appear, he does not complain or hesitate but responds with a learned confidence (even taking time to shave before the giant storm hits). Our Man does not make any real mistakes. The weather and ocean are simply too strong for his technology, which continually breaks down, but it is more than bad luck. It is as if his vision of danger is out of sync with the universe he now inhabits and despite his best efforts and seriousness, his world falls apart. The story can also be read as an illustration of the indifference of global capital to individual suffering: the shipping container that strikes his boat is carrying children's sneakers, a marker of the global industrial trade and not unlike the shoes Our Man is also wearing. His boat is filled with consumer products promising comfort and safety that ultimately prove insufficient. He is the big man rendered small in the face of linked planetary forces—capitalism and climate.

The film begins almost at the end of his story, with a voice-over reading of a note Our Man puts in a jar and tosses into the ocean, a last message to his family and friends, set adrift in hopes of finding a reader:

> Thirteenth of July, 4:50 p.m. I'm sorry. . . . I know that means little at this point, but I am. I tried. I think you all agree that I tried: to be true, to be strong, to be kind, to love, to be right. But I wasn't. And I know you knew this, in each of your ways. And I am sorry. All is lost here . . . except for soul and body . . . that is, what's left of them . . . and a half-day's ration. It's inexcusable really. I know that now. How it could have taken this long to admit that I'm not sure, but it did. I fought until the end. I'm not sure what that is worth, but know that I did. I have always hoped for more for you all. I will miss you. I'm sorry.

I tried. The embarrassment in the face of calamity here is the high note of the film. A man who is in control—and might well be part of the American elite that built the global infrastructure of neoliberal capitalism, petrochemical industry, and nuclear nationalism—loses that control when his technology fails in the face of global capitalism and planetary environmental forces. He should have known better (given the obvious violence of global capital) but instead trusted his abilities and technology and resourcefulness. The global supply chain is weaponized here in the form of the shipping container and the uncaring transport ships. A powerful storm—presumably amplified by global warming, a side effect of the petrochemical economy—merely finishes the job, leaving Our Man sinking in the open sea to contemplate his decisions and fate. We do not know how far into the future the film is set—or if Our Man's boat is traveling over any flooded cities as predicted in *Unchained Goddess*—but the fragility of the environment that can support human life on planet Earth is underscored in every frame. Our Man's message in a bottle is thus a profound projection of what we all might say in a few decades. It assumes a singular mode of life on Earth embedded in petrochemical capitalism and nuclear nationalism—that might profoundly fail. It is an insufficient if heartfelt apology for embracing an economic form that offered short-term comfort in exchange for amplifying future dangers, and that abandons individuals increasingly to the uncontrollable and violent forces of capital/climate.

When Is the Catastrophic?

Think about the strangeness of today's situation. Thirty, forty years ago, we were still debating about what the future will be: communist, fascist, capitalist, whatever. Today, nobody even debates these issues. We all silently accept global capitalism is here to stay. On the other hand, we are obsessed with cosmic catastrophes: the whole life on earth disintegrating, because of some virus, because of an asteroid hitting the earth, and so on. So the paradox is that it's much easier to imagine the end of all life on earth than a much more modest radical change in capitalism.
—Slavoj Žižek, Zizek! (Astra Taylor, director)

"In relation to the history of organic life on earth," writes a modern biologist, "the paltry fifty millennia of homo sapiens *constitutes something like two seconds at the close of a twenty-four-hour day. On this scale, the history of civilized mankind would fill one fifth of the last second of the last hour." The present, which, as the model of Messianic time comprises the entire history of mankind in an enormous abridgement, coincides exactly with the stature which the history of mankind has in the universe.*
—Walter Benjamin, "Theses on the Philosophy of History"

In the early twenty-first century, narratives of end times proliferate—terrorism, peak oil, emerging disease, boom-and-bust capitalism, and a destabilized biosphere compete with each other for public attention. The difficulty of prioritizing which catastrophe should take precedence over all the others has created a curious new kind of psychosocial fatigue, where claims of imminent destruction are met with a retreat inward or simply a shrug. How is it that Americans, residents of the most powerful country in human history (unchallenged across military, economic, and political domains) have come to feel so precarious and vulnerable? It is important to note that the politics of catastrophe involve cultural formations as well as material assessments; they are historical projections that articulate fear but can also work to block both thought and action. Žižek (building on similar comments by Jameson [1998, 50; 2003, 76] about how, after the Cold War, capitalism seems more permanent than the actual world) helps us see one dimension of this problem by underscoring the current lack of alternative ideologies to constitute the future today. The demise of the large social engineering projects of the twentieth century, and the rise of an unrestrained neoliberalism in their wake, combine to create a vision of a market-driven future that can only produce profit by generating boom-and-bust cycles and extraction regimes that leave ruin in their wake. Disaster has actually become a powerful industry in recent years, revealing an unplanned obsolescence for urban infrastructure that is breaking down under shifting environmental conditions and lack of maintenance. This has enabled radical new kinds of corporate experimentation and profit making, rendering disaster highly lucrative (Funk 2014; Klein 2006). The formal end of the welfare state project (largely coterminous with the end of the Cold War, if not the nuclear danger or voter suppression) has also diminished the public space devoted to positive visions of a collective future in American life. It is difficult to find official commitments to a steady improvement in the qualities of collective life of the kind once used to balance images of nuclear catastrophe. Today Americans are several generations removed from the kind of social contract that engineered most U.S. institutions and are instead increasingly reliant on market logics to design the collective future (Buck-Morss 2000). Thus, Americans have inherited from the twentieth century's contest of utopian visions a world still organized by nuclear weapons and petrochemical industry but are increasingly subject to the radically destabilizing effects of a boom-and-bust global capitalism that operates on ever-shorter windows of profitability and with fewer restraints and responsibilities. The reluctance to imagine different futures, let alone to organize society on behalf of them, leaves crisis—a highly conservative medium—as the predominant mode for political expression, as declarations of imminent danger become the primary motivating force outside of capital.

Consequently, competing domains and scales of endangerment now seem to buffet U.S. citizens without respite, as the bursting of bubble economies resides alongside the minute-to-minute danger of a nuclear blast within the century-long sequence of anthropogenic environmental change.

In a striking passage from his "Theses on the Philosophy of History," Walter Benjamin (1969) evokes geological time as a way to shift the story of human beings on planet Earth. All human history becomes a brief moment of planetary time from this perspective, which raises the important question of how temporality itself informs the cataclysmic and whether human beings have the right senses to understand collective danger at all. Prefiguring the language of the Anthropocene, Benjamin uses geological time to disrupt the time of capital and to reposition humanity as merely one kind of life on planet Earth, a species that may or may not be able to avoid the cataclysmic end most creatures meet. But if danger incubates in the present, revealing itself in the catastrophic act, how can we see through a normative everyday to assess accruing danger operating on all possible temporal scales—particularly the forms that people generate and thus could collectively control? Benjamin suggests that a radical emancipatory insight is also incubating in the present, a messianic potential that could shift perception itself, allowing a different kind of time to emerge, one that is not coded as progress (tied to homogenous empty time) and that is outside of capitalism. For Benjamin, just as the cataclysmic is coded into everyday life, so is the possibility for a radical shift in perception and with it an emancipatory politics. That this potential has not been activated is, for him, the ongoing state of emergency that he critiques so forcefully. In this way, he shifts the emergency from the narratives of violence that can function as heroic vehicles for self-sacrifice and warfare in the moment to a more structural assessment of how social institutions normalize and render invisible the violence of capitalism itself. What Benjamin asks us to consider is how social institutions function as an expression and achievement of human engineering, and thus how the human-made can be remade under different concepts of value and with different futures in mind. Catastrophe's apocalypse would, in this case, be to see the agentive behind the everyday crisis, to see the possibility of a social order not yet conceived as forestalled in the name of history, class, or the status quo; that is, it would be to think beyond nuclear nationalism and petrochemical capitalism. Catastrophe's apocalypse would be to enter into a radically different temporality, a perspectival space for Benjamin in which structural violence is revealed as manufactured (tied to racial formation, property relations, and imperial state competition), enabling the current moment to be opened as a space of revolutionary critical potential. From this perspective, perhaps the proliferation of catastrophic images and narratives today has less to say about new objective degrees of endangerment than a shift in the psychosocial mechanisms of normalization and absorption. And here we might focus on a temporal paradox of our security culture today concerning the relation of nuclear danger to climate disruption.

The nuclear confrontation of the Cold War—the fear of a war that would consume global civilization in an instant—seems distant to many Americans in the twenty-first century, but the technological systems built to enable it are still present and active. The global nuclear infrastructure remains on high alert, and nuclear war could still be launched at a moment's notice and between ever more nuclear powers. The presidents of the United States and of Russia still carry launch codes with them every second of the day, and weapons scientists and defense personnel maintain a state-of-the-art global system for nuclear war fighting. Americans tend to see nuclear danger now as an issue of the past, a matter for the last century (replaced by a wide range of terrorist threats). But today there are many more nuclear weapons on the planet than in 1958 when *The Power of Decision* was made, and the U.S. has committed to maintaining a state-of-the-art arsenal for the indefinite future (see U.S. Department of Energy 2013; Wolfsthal, Lewis, and Quint 2014). Thus, while perceptions of nuclear danger have changed markedly since 1958, the technological possibility of a total ending has only increased in sophistication: Americans live today on the edge of nuclear war and just do not seem to notice it anymore (see McKinzie et al. 2001). What was once a national fixation on nuclear danger no longer mobilizes in the same way, attaining an embeddedness in everyday life that can be ignored by most citizens in favor of other concerns, other dangers, other fears.

Similarly, the climate emergency of the twenty-first century was already present in 1958, when *The Power of Decision* articulated the terms of national nuclear danger and *Unchained Goddess* warned viewers of a destabilized future environment. In the first decade of the Cold War, earth scientists publicized disturbing trends in their data sets, documenting shifts in air, water, and land quality via industrial pollutants. The debates about radioactive fallout from nuclear testing led in 1963 to the Limited Test Ban Treaty, which moved U.S. nuclear testing underground, eliminating the production of new radioactive fallout from the U.S. test program. However, the larger lesson of how industrial activity was harming the biosphere was left unaddressed as a major security problem for decades. Had climate change risen to the level of a collective emergency in the 1950s, the world would have been spared the coming destabilization of ecosystems, species die-offs, flooding, illness, and drought projected in the IPCC reports. Indeed, climate scientists now identify the mid-twentieth century as the beginning of the "great acceleration"—a period of startling changes in human consumption patterns linked to the advance of the middle class and escalating carbon emissions (Steffen et al. 2011; see also McNeill and Engelke 2014).

In other words, the inauguration of the global nuclear danger was also the inflection point for global warming, simultaneously installing two catastrophic potentials into everyday life that operate on vastly different time scales. Americans focused on the immediacy of nuclear war in the twentieth century while ignoring the other incremental but existential danger of their own making, the expansion of a consumer economy that has become a highly destructive force on planet Earth. Thus, nuclear and climate dangers are engineered emergencies decades in the making and are deeply embedded within a petroleum-based capitalist-militarist-industrial system. After World War II, the security state embraced nuclear danger as its coordinating principle while rejecting the environment as a major security concern. Partly this is explained by the radically different temporalities evoked by each kind of danger: nuclear danger playing out in minutes and hours while climate danger plays out over decades and centuries. However, each emergency also evokes a different kind of sovereignty and requires very different kinds of governance. A global denuclearization project could substantially reduce the nuclear danger very quickly, but global warming is a multifaceted planetary phenomenon that requires vast international cooperation across industries and consumer habits—indeed, it now demands a postnational security logic of planetary defense. Perhaps this is also why so many images of climate change in the U.S. rely on tropes developed to communicate the danger of nuclear weapons, a way of acknowledging a collective danger without forcing a change in existing conceptual structures or modes of response.

In U.S. public discourse, nuclear and climate dangers are both grounded in images of a world that is no longer capable of supporting human society. This kind of catastrophic narrative, in its depiction of a perfect and total loss, however, requires an apocalyptic rendering precisely because it is a historical and highly politicized artifact. What is required now is a critical engagement that assesses not only the possibility of total endings but also the instrumentalities, ideologies, and practices that inform them. Perhaps today this could take the form of a reassessment of industrial reasoning itself and an effort to cancel the apocalypse, not by a heroic suicide bombing (as in *Pacific Rim* or *The Power of Decision*) but rather by attending to local infrastructure itself as a social project that needs constant critical reassessment and reinvention to acknowledge radically changing environmental conditions. This would mean embracing both middle and deep futures as a collective security project and thinking through multigenerational toxic legacies as well as threat (see Masco 2014; Murphy 2017a; Orff and Misrach 2012). Above all, it would mean focusing expert and public energies not on rehearsing the perfect catastrophes of total endings, but rather on the qualities, consequences, and insights of living in messy aftermaths.[4]

13

COUNTERINSURGENCY, *THE SPOOK*,
AND BLOWBACK

In the summer of 2003, U.S. special operations officers at the Pentagon—then confronting an amplifying insurgency in post–U.S. invasion Iraq and ongoing conflict in Afghanistan—organized a screening of the classic 1966 Gillo Pontecorvo film, *The Battle of Algiers* (see figures 13.1–13.4). As *Washington Post* reporter David Ignatius (2003) saw it, the screening marked a "hopeful sign that the military is thinking creatively and unconventionally about Iraq," noting that a Pentagon advertising flyer for the event had asked provocatively:

> How to win a battle against terrorism and lose the war of ideas. . . .
> Children shoot soldiers at point blank range. Women plant bombs in
> cafes. Soon the entire Arab population builds to a mad fervor. Sound

familiar? The French have a plan. It succeeds tactically but fails strategically. To understand why, come to a rare showing of the film.

Sound familiar? Looking back on the summer of 2003, this is a striking and perplexing moment of self-reflexivity among U.S. war planners. *The Battle of Algiers* offers a textbook study of both insurgency and counterinsurgency. The film documents not only the various forms of armed resistance to French power but also the counterterror strategy, media manipulation, and torture practices that enabled the French to win the battle but lose the war. Thus, what was presented to U.S. special operations theorists as a study in tactics and countertactics—terror and counterterror—in the decolonization struggle over Algeria was also a pointed lesson about the political limits of counterrevolution. After all, to succeed tactically but fail strategically is hardly an endorsement of the French approach. And yet, in the years to follow, the U.S. military reproduced the full range of counterinsurgency techniques documented in Pontecorvo's film—contributing to the longest war in United States history (followed by the counterinsurgency campaign in Vietnam). Indeed, the film screening was followed not by a fundamental revision in the U.S. global project known as the War on Terror but rather by a profound reinvestment in the conceptual power of counterinsurgency.

Filmed with a beautifully grainy black-and-white cinematography, in a documentary or newsreel style, *The Battle of Algiers* articulates a clear vision of the uses of terror—by both revolutionaries and the colonial state. Cast largely with nonactors (including a few participants in the actual battle of Algiers), the film ultimately presents many of the techniques recently adopted by Al-Qaeda and the broader insurgencies in Iraq and Afghanistan. The revolutionary National Liberation Front (FLN) party organizes itself in cell structures and instructs its members not to talk for twenty-four hours if caught by the French military, to allow comrades to escape; its supporters do not wear uniforms but frequently use the veil as both disguise and cover for smuggling weapons. The escalating campaign of street attacks on French military personnel (by men, women, and children) leads to attacks on civilians, including a bombing campaign involving multiple simultaneous strikes, as well as suicide attacks. In response, the French military moves to identify and decapitate the terrorist cell structures via assassination, raids on homes, and ultimately the destruction of whole neighborhoods (not unlike the U.S. effort to pacify the Iraqi city of Fallujah in 2004). The French also embrace a full spectrum of torture techniques—stress positions, the use of electricity, and (what Americans now call) waterboarding. Colonial Mathieu, the leader of the French forces, when questioned about these techniques by the media, states that the word "torture" is never used—it is simply interrogation designed to break the subject's resistance within the twenty-four-hour window in which information might stop a bombing (thus presenting a version of the ticking time bomb scenario often evoked after 2001 in the U.S. to justify torture).[1] By the end of the film, the French forces have killed or captured the known FLN members but have also fomented a national revolutionary movement that within a few years will force the French to abandon Algeria. Thus, the tactics of counterinsurgency win a reprieve for French colonial interests but ultimately produce a more massive countermovement among the general Algerian population. Pontecorvo's film may be positioned by U.S. military counterterror personnel as a study of the techniques of imperial control; however, it presents an even more powerful argument about the structural contradiction of the colonial project and the political power of decolonization.

Theorists of counterinsurgency have consistently recognized that success depends on perception management—victory is as much grounded in public sentiment as in military action. David Galula, for example, states categorically that the "basic mechanism of counterinsurgency warfare" is to "build (or rebuild) a political machine from the population upward" (2008, 95). Thus, it is as much about constructing a positive view of external governance as eliminating insurgents. Counterinsurgency involves both the destruction and construction of a public; indeed, it is ultimately a fight over the annihilation and production of a nation. Peter Paret, like Galula a theorist of the Algerian insurgency, underscores the French effort to psychologically reprogram Algerian revolutionaries to be colonial subjects:

> The first step in the process was to "disintegrate the individual." The internee was isolated, his fears and guilt feelings were exploited by his monitor, he was made to feel ashamed of his past and induced to acknowledge his errors. The period of brainwashing (*lavage de crane*) was followed by a period of reconstruction or brainfilling (*bourrage de crane*). Lectures and discussion presented the internee with the Army's views on history, current affairs, and the future of North Africa. In the final stage, the individual was brought into a disciplined group of converted fellow prisoners, which acted as an unfriendly collective superego toward recalcitrant inmates and which participated in the psychological campaign against the FLN beyond the barbed wire by writing propaganda letters to relatives and issuing manifestos. (1964, 64)

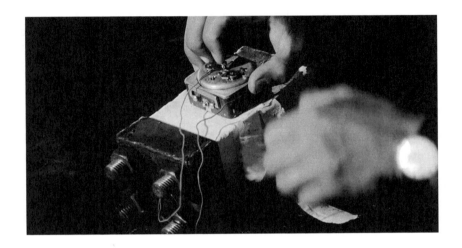

Figures 13.1–13.4. Stills on counterinsurgency techniques from *The Battle of Algiers.*

To disintegrate the individual. The recent French defeat in Indochina provided a specific motivation for this project of remaking an imagined colonial subject in Algeria, as well as for its brutality. However, the effects of counterinsurgency are totalizing: as Paret notes, it is a characteristic of counterrevolution that it transforms revolutionary and counterrevolutionary alike (in terms of both national and moral identities). This raises important questions today about not only how to translate the almost exclusively colonial context of counterinsurgency theory into the current American global military project but also about the long-term effects of the War on Terror on U.S. national culture.

The Battle of Algiers, from this point of view, raises the vital, but underanalyzed, issue of the temporality of counterinsurgency—for what does it really mean to say that a counterinsurgency campaign can ever be successful? What are the secondary effects of such targeted violence now and into a deep future? And finally, what are the domestic costs of counterterror as U.S. national policy? For U.S. officials did not take the lesson of the film to be the impossibility of delivering democracy to Iraq via invasion and counterinsurgency. Rather, they seem to have accepted the value of torture, media manipulation, and covert action in extending American power throughout the region. Indeed, the failures of U.S. operations in the region have been positioned within U.S. security debates as a failure of expertise or knowledge rather than as an illustration of a lack of popular support for the U.S. military presence in Iraq, or for the fundamental ideological weakness of the War on Terror as a concept.

Thus, as the failure to achieve stability in both Afghanistan and Iraq has become more obvious, one key move of U.S. military planners has been to assume that more expertise will solve the problem of counterrevolution, resulting now in the widely publicized "cultural turn" at the Pentagon. These efforts include deploying social scientists on the front lines in Human Terrain Teams, as well as recruiting academics to help on key military problems via targeted funding.[2] This effort to finally get it right has also produced the first new *U.S. Army/Marine Corps Counterinsurgency Field Manual* in a generation, updating the lessons learned from Korea and Vietnam, as well as the covert campaigns in Central America during the 1980s, for the current wars in Afghanistan and Iraq (see Nagl 2002). However, the record of previous U.S. counterinsurgency engagements, like the screening of Pontecorvo's film, present a continuing lost opportunity to recognize the limits of military action designed to produce or destroy a new national consciousness, or to acknowledge the long-term global effects of deploying U.S. military power in this manner. As a result, counterinsurgency theory today says much more about the fantasy of U.S. military power, and official desires to realize U.S. hegemony in the twenty-first century, than it does about expert knowledge of politics on the ground.

This remains a vital problem because the George W. Bush administration's inauguration of the War on Terror in 2001 committed the United States to nothing less than a planetary program of counterinsurgency. President Bush declared war not simply on the perpetrators of the attacks on Washington, DC, and New York in 2001 but on terror itself, promising to cleanse the world of both the act and the emotion via an elimination of Al-Qaeda and related networks. The radical nature of this concept of war is hard to overstate. It was, and is, (1) an overt assertion of American global hegemony, as the Bush administration declared a right to wage preventative and preemptive war against any state or entity, as well as to deploy military forces covertly into any nation-state in pursuit of terror; (2) a de facto declaration of a permanent state of war (for when can terror ever be finally and absolutely purged from individual minds or collective experience?); (3) a deployment of terror to create a state of emergency that allows suspension of law—constituting a rather fundamental revision of the social contract within the United States and a direct challenge to the idea of international law; and (4) a radical experiment in U.S. military power, linking new technologies of direct and covert action within a novel concept of global war. This War on Terror was imagined from the start as a multigenerational project that would link foreign and domestic policy under a new kind of permanent war footing. In this regard, terror has been deployed in a revolutionary way within the United States, enabling an official break with collective expectations of governmental process, legality, and the limits on both militarization and violence. Declaring so formal a "war" on terror, in short, constituted the United States as a counterterror state, a transformation that profoundly changes the citizen-state relationship as well as the U.S. position within international order going forward (see Masco 2014).

Secretary of Defense Donald Rumsfeld's dream of a "revolution in military affairs" was well underway before 2001; but after the attacks, this project was fused with the concept of a "war on terror" to create a new global laboratory for war (e.g., see Rumsfeld 2002). His commitment to a smaller military armed with high technology, a reliance on expeditionary forces, and a broad spectrum of covert actions was ultimately designed not just to pursue Al-Qaeda into Afghanistan and then topple Saddam Hussein's government in Iraq. It also was meant to send a signal to world leaders. The invasions of Afghanistan in 2001 and Iraq in 2003 were designed to demonstrate overwhelming American military power and the will to use it, and thereby communicate to all political leaders not aligned with U.S. interests that after the fall of Saddam Hussein's regime, they could be next. Thus, the invasion of Iraq (politically justified by a fabricated linkage of Saddam Hussein to Al-Qaeda leader Osama bin Laden, and by exaggerated fears of nuclear, biological, and chemical weapons attacks on the U.S.) provided a global theater for demonstrating U.S. power. Indeed, each stage of the invasion—from the shock-and-awe bombing campaign to the quick military victory and occupation of Iraq through the current counterinsurgency operations—was not only massively violent but also a theatrical effort to both establish and make visible the U.S. as the sole global military superpower.

In doing so, the Bush administration mobilized the Cold War model of global engagement for a new century by replacing nuclear deterrence with counterterror as the central motivating logic. The achievement of the early Cold War was the establishment of a mode of governing that was extraordinarily stable and violent, involving a Cold War consensus that linked policy makers, military leaders, journalists, and academics to an unprecedented degree through anticommunist militarization and covert action. After the September 2001 attacks, the Bush administration sought to articulate a state structure that could orchestrate American domestic and foreign policy on a similar scale while locking into place a more aggressive military-industrial agenda for the twenty-first century. Many of the domestic logics and cultural assumptions of the Cold War state have been simply reworked to enable the War on Terror. The mobilization of U.S. citizens through nuclear fear, the protection of U.S. policy through expanding state secrecy, and the reliance on covert action are all techniques developed in the U.S. during the Cold War to produce militarized consent on state-articulated terms. To a large extent, the Bush administration's media strategy for the War on Terror has been reliant on the cultural tropes of the Cold War—in particular the idea of an imminent nuclear threat—to enable a global counterinsurgency campaign. The terrorist armed with a WMD has been the linking image between past and future, suturing together the collective understandings about global threat developed during the Cold War but redirecting them against a global Al-Qaeda conspiracy. But if the tools for mobilizing the American public as a nation under imminent threat are grounded in Cold War logics, the waging of preventative war in Iraq represents a profound new stage in U.S. militarism.

What kind of national security is the U.S. pursuing in the twenty-first century? And how does it differ from its Cold War predecessor? It is easy to find a precise vision of U.S. power in its military policy. In a U.S. Joint Chiefs of Staff report on the status and future orientation of the combined U.S. military, known as *Joint Vision 2020*, U.S. military leaders asserted their goal as "full spectrum dominance," defined as the ability to

> defeat any adversary and control any situation across the full range of military operations. . . . U.S. forces are able to conduct prompt, sustained, and synchronized operations with combinations of forces tailored to specific situations and with access to and freedom to operate in all domains—space, sea, land, air, and information. (U.S. Joint Chiefs of Staff 2000, 6)

The freedom to operate in all domains. As part of this mission, the U.S. is now spending almost as much money on defense as the rest of the world combined.[3] Much of this amount is black budgeted, meaning there is no possibility for either government accountants or the public to discover how it is being spent.[4] The United States is also the world's largest arms dealer (Grimmett 2007, 4). While maintaining more than 761 military bases in 132 countries, as well as a triad of bombers, submarines, and missiles that could obliterate any city on the planet in thirty minutes or less.[5] The militarization of space and cyberspace also proceeded through incremental expansions in U.S. missile defense and satellite systems. Throughout this expansion, the Bush administration has systematically resisted international institutions, treaties, and logics that could infringe on the idea of full-spectrum dominance across military, political, and economic domains. To this end, President Bush relied on the emergency powers granted to the commander in chief to an unprecedented degree, avoiding the usual legislative process in the United States by evoking imminent threat as a basic matter of course and thus rather fundamentally changing the American political process. These emergency powers have been maintained by the Obama and Trump administrations, normalizing counterterror as a means of expanding presidential authority (see also Wills 2010).

To get at how nuanced and imaginative this view of American power is, consider how the Project for the New American Century, the conservative think tank that provided much of the geopolitical vision and military policy for the George W. Bush administration, imagined the foot soldier of the near future:

> Future soldiers may operate in encapsulated, climate-controlled, powered fighting suits, laced with sensors, and boasting chameleon-like "active" camouflage. "Skin-patch" pharmaceuticals help regulate fears, focus concentration and enhance endurance and strength. A display mounted on the soldier's helmet permits a comprehensive view of the battlefield—in effect to look around corners and over hills—and allows

the soldier to access the entire combat information and intelligence system while filtering incoming data to prevent overload. Individual weapons are more lethal, and a soldier's ability to call for highly precise and reliable indirect fires—not only from Army systems but those of other services—allows each individual to have great influence over huge spaces. Under the "Land Warrior" program some Army experts envision a "squad" of seven soldiers able to dominate an area the size of the Gettysburg battlefield, where in 1863, some 165,000 men fought. (Project for the New American Century 2000, 62)

Future soldiers. This science fiction seeks to enable the kind of quantum leap in military power that the Cold War state was able to produce with some regularity in nuclear technologies; it also assumes a permanent revolution in military affairs and an unending U.S. war posture. Arguing explicitly that the project of Cold War containment should be replaced with a new global Pax Americana in the twenty-first century, the writers of this 2000 report were already calling for a massive expansion of the security state, as well as for immediate military action in Iraq, well before the 2001 terrorist attacks on the United States.[6] The War on Terror provided a new overarching logic—as well as a new marketing strategy—for this idea of total dominance, an idea of American power promulgated largely by politicians and advisors without any firsthand military experience. In this vision, a handful of future supersoldiers, linked to the combined U.S. military forces on land, sea, air, space, and cyberspace, could call in nuclear strikes, direct space-based weaponry, and through near-instant global engagement maintain a terrifying technological edge over all potential adversaries. The dream image of the supersoldier here is an index of the Bush administration's concept of American superpoweredness, which extends across the full spectrum of military, economic, and political affairs.[7] This is the long-standing fantasy of the über-soldier, who embodies the full strength of the U.S. military on the front line as global counterinsurgent. The military rebranding of the War on Terror as global, or GWOT, was designed precisely to underscore the totalizing reach of the conflict and, with it, of American power. In light of the failure to stabilize Afghanistan and Iraq, the GWOT has been downgraded in military discourse to simply the "long war"—a telling conceptual reduction in the definition of the war from a named enemy to simply one of temporal duration.[8]

Nevertheless, the global infrastructure of U.S. counterterror has been partially exposed: in addition to a retaliatory war in Afghanistan and a preventative war in Iraq, the counterterror state has pursued a rendition program of kidnapping, one that does not recognize state borders or international law. The CIA and other U.S. agencies have established a global gulag stretching from Guantanamo Bay, Cuba, to sites in Eastern Europe, Thailand, and the Middle East to hold these detainees and others picked up on the global battlefield (see Mayer 2007). These prisons, as well as the concepts of the detainee and torture that support them, have been defined by the Justice Department to be outside of international law and U.S. law, and not even subject to the humanitarian review of the International Red Cross. Thus, rather than reindoctrinating prisoners on the brutal French Algerian model of counterinsurgency, the Bush administration sought to establish a system for permanent imprisonment for subjects who are not protected by the Geneva Conventions or endowed with habeas corpus rights. The War on Terror was thus designed to be a pure statement of U.S. hegemonic power—with individuals taken at will globally and installed in sites that were not subject to legal review, where prisoners could be interrogated with techniques known for generations to be the definition of torture.

Domestically, the counterterror state set up a system outside of the law for wiretapping and electronic surveillance, in addition to expanding the uses of state secrecy to foreclose legal challenges and to protect even the most basic rationales for counterterror policy. President Bush declared his authority to designate citizens as enemy combatants and thereby revoke U.S. citizenship—and with it, the right to contest one's imprisonment. The U.S. Supreme Court has challenged a number of these propositions, creating a state of limbo in the U.S. between the national security rulings of the judicial branch, the national security legislation passed by Congress, and the actions of an executive branch that has evoked state-of-emergency war powers to avoid both legal and congressional review. The Obama administration sought to regularize and legalize many Bush-era counterterror policies (for example, disavowing waterboarding) but remained deeply invested in counterterror itself (for example, using drones for an expanded global assassination program). Thus, the ambiguity at the international level over the terms of the War on Terror has been matched by the ambiguity at the domestic level over the power of the executive branch and the status of basic civil liberties. It is important to recognize twenty-first-century counterterror as a transformative U.S. state project: the declaration of a global counterinsurgency has fundamentally changed the terms of American democracy at home and abroad.

Former national security advisor Zbigniew Brzezinski has argued that the fundamental problem with U.S. foreign policy in Iraq is that "America is acting like a colonial power in Iraq. But the age of colonialism is over.

Waging a colonial war in the post-colonial age is self-defeating" (2007, A19). Thus, Brzezinski reiterates the ultimate lesson posed by *The Battle of Algiers*; namely, that counterinsurgency is simply violence when it is not supported by a widely shared political worldview and, in this case, by an ethical and legal commitment to democratic process, human rights, and legality. David Kilcullen, a key theorist of the Iraq counterinsurgency and a contributor to the new counterinsurgency field manual, has been even more blunt, stating in 2008, "The biggest stupid idea was to invade Iraq in the first place" (Ackerman 2008). However, for Kilcullen, the problem remains one ultimately of expertise, reportedly leading him to write a second manual, *U.S. Government Counterinsurgency Guide*, for elected officials (U.S. Department of State 2009). Thus, while there seems to be a rather remarkable failure rate in U.S. counterinsurgency campaigns, there remains a deep and abiding commitment to the idea of counterinsurgency itself. Put more directly, the view of freedom and democracy that the Bush Administration promulgated through the War on Terror has not only failed to be achieved in Afghanistan and Iraq, it has—through torture, media manipulation, financial corruption, and an overwhelming reliance on military force—substantially undermined the conceptual power of those terms. The resulting global resistance to the United States is not simply a problem of U.S. military expertise or of not understanding regional cultures; it is an inevitable reaction to pursuing U.S. national interests through counterterror. Historically, counterinsurgency has been, in its most favorable light, a short-term military technique to buy time for a political process to generate mass support; it is not and cannot be a system of planetary rule as imagined by its current proponents. The global reaction to the War on Terror is increasingly less likely to depend on the exceptional power of the U.S. military and more likely to turn on the antidemocratic and often illegal actions taken in the name of counterterror. The effort to fuse counterterror with the rhetoric of democracy not only is oxymoronic, it massively undermines any claim to moral or intellectual coherence. Moreover, the day-to-day practices of contemporary U.S. counterterror—kidnapping, torture, secret prisons, rejection of the Geneva Convention and habeas corpus rights, psyops campaigns at home and abroad, and preventative war—all produce profound effects, regardless of the notion of American power supporting them. The War on Terror thus needs to be assessed not only for its lack of internal coherence as policy but also for the world it actually is creating, to reactions and retaliations, now and into a deep future.

In this regard, a striking omission from U.S. counterinsurgency theory is a discussion of what the CIA calls "blowback" (see Johnson 2000). Blowback commonly refers to foreign retaliation for U.S. covert actions. However, the concept has a secondary aspect of equal importance to the first: because covert actions are invisible to U.S. domestic audiences, U.S. citizens have no way of understanding the rationale or history behind such retaliatory acts. Thus, what is in local terms a reaction to U.S.-sponsored violence becomes for U.S. citizens literally unrecognizable. This has a perverse effect that is amplified by the concept of waging a war on terror. Since U.S. citizens have no insight into the terms of U.S. covert warfare around the world, retaliatory acts against U.S. interests appear to the American public to be without cause or context, and thus irrational. Since the premise of the War on Terror is that the terrorist is an irrational and violent being dedicated to destroying the United States, blowback empowers yet another level of American fantasy: namely, that the U.S. is not a global military actor until provoked by irrational violence, terrorist acts, or imminent threat. Thus, the War on Terror as a form of domestic U.S. strategy promotes a self-fulfilling prophecy of global chaos, which works to justify both extraordinary military expenditures at home and global military engagements abroad. Thus, the Bush administration's initial argument for a counterinsurgency campaign in Iraq—captured by the slogan "We need to fight them there, so we don't have to fight them here"—is wrong on two scores, because (1) the terrorist "them" in this formulation is in reality a vast set of interests responding to a vast array of global conditions rather than a singular political subject, and (2) war always comes home in some fashion.[9] In addition to creating new subjects around the world angered by U.S. invasions, drone strikes, and counterinsurgency violences, counterterror always has a domestic counterpart to the geopolitical.

In this regard, the Pentagon might also have screened for its counterinsurgency theorists back in the summer of 2003 another classic film devoted to counterinsurgency and decolonization: *The Spook Who Sat by the Door* (1973, directed by Ivan Dixon).[10] Based on the novel of the same name by Sam Greenlee ([1969] 1989), *The Spook* tells the fictional story of the first African American CIA agent, Dan Freeman (played by Lawrence Cook), who, after spending five years learning spy tradecraft at Langley, returns to Chicago to mobilize citizens and gang members in a national resistance campaign of black liberation (see figures 13.5–13.8). The film is both a brutal critique of Cold War militarism and a race fantasy, as the white/black divide in the United States is presented as intractable and in a state of unacknowledged war. The decision to racially integrate the CIA, for example, is driven by the crass political calculus of a congressional reelection campaign, not by a commitment to racial equality. After the first class of one hundred African Americans

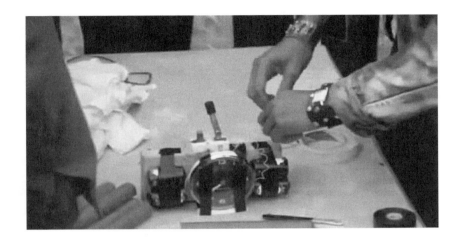

Figures 13.5–13.8. Stills on revolutionary war techniques from *The Spook Who Sat by the Door.*

is reduced to just one viable candidate, Freeman is welcomed into the "finest intelligence and espionage agency in the world" as the "best of [his] race." Assigned to a new position as Reproduction Section Chief, Freeman spends the next five years running the photocopy machine in the basement of the CIA and serving as a token African American CIA agent to be displayed for visiting officials. Unknown to his superiors, however, Freeman's ingratiating manner is in fact a strategy designed to unlock the secrets of insurgency and espionage training. In addition to becoming an expert in martial arts, guns, explosives, and espionage techniques, Freeman spends his nights studying in the CIA library and reads the classified materials he is asked to photocopy during the day, thus gaining an insider's view on U.S. Cold War policy as well as on CIA counterinsurgency tactics. On leaving the CIA, Freeman moves to Chicago to assume a cover identity as a social worker. But his true mission, as he tells the clueless head of the CIA, is "to teach my people some of what I learned here," by which he means not white supremacy but rather the techniques of terror and armed resistance.

Freeman then organizes the African American gangs on the south side of Chicago, telling them, "If you really want to mess with Whitey, I can show you how," before recommending that they look into the histories of "Algeria, Kenya, Korea, and 'Nam" for examples of what he has in mind. Presented as a filmic mirror image of his CIA training, Freeman then teaches recruits firearms, explosives, and hit-and-run military techniques while organizing them into cells with a military command and control structure. He also uses white prejudice as a weapon, stating that "a black man with a broom is invisible in this country." To prove his point, he assigns one of his subordinates disguised as a janitor to rob the mayor's office while the mayor is sitting in it. As his revolutionary struggle takes off, Freeman also correctly judges that the leadership of the CIA and FBI will blame the Soviet Union for the violence in Chicago rather than acknowledge any inherent military prowess coming out of the ghetto.

Freeman transforms Chicago gang members into soldiers of a new revolutionary army and prepares them for a national campaign. Telling his cell, "What we have now is a colony and what we want to create is a new nation," he recruits gang members in major American cities to the cause. He also targets African American soldiers coming back from Vietnam, sees prisons as indoctrination centers, and imagines turning African American workers in police departments, businesses, and city jobs into double agents. After a police shooting starts a riot in Chicago, the Black Freedom Fighters begin formal guerilla operations, shooting police, then fighting the National Guard, and eventually waging war against the Army's Eighty-Second Airborne Division. As the violence escalates, the head of the CIA contemplates establishing concentration camps for the black residents of Chicago, but then realizes that the city is too dependent on African American labor to do so and therefore launches a "decapitation" project to get the leadership of the insurgency. The south side of Chicago thus becomes the site of a terror and counterterror campaign, mirroring many of the logics portrayed in *The Battle of Algiers* and on display through the War on Terror in Afghanistan, Pakistan, Iraq, Yemen, and Somalia.

Freeman articulates the geopolitics of the film when a lieutenant asks if the freedom fighters can win:

FREEMAN: In guerilla warfare winning is not losing. When you sleep on the floor you can't fall out of bed.

LIEUTENANT: Then what are we trying to do, man?

FREEMAN: Fight Whitey to a standstill. Force him to make a choice between the two things he seems to dig most of all. There is no way the United States can police the world and keep us on our ass too—unless we cooperate. When we revolt, we reduce it to a simple choice: Whitey finds out he can't make either.

LIEUTENANT: What about the other brothers and sisters on the street?

FREEMAN: Their choice is when we start. If they don't follow our program and turn us in to the cops, we lose in a week. But if they support us, then it's hit and run, harass and hound, and we can paralyze this country.

Harass and Hound. Seeking to "turn the American Dream into a nightmare," Freeman uses the terror tactics he learned in the CIA—including sabotage, assassination, and radio propaganda—to promote black liberation. His guerilla war brings down the full weight of the U.S. military on Chicago but also ignites a revolutionary movement that sweeps across the country ghetto by ghetto, leaving the United States in the last frame of the film in a full state of civil war.

The Spook Who Sat by the Door explores an essentialized race fantasy within the structure of terror and counterterror. Not unlike the Bush administration's framing of the War on Terror as a "with us or against us" global realignment, *The Spook* engages revolutionary violence through a set of binary racial oppositions within the United States. In doing so, it powerfully acknowledges the domestic costs of Cold War covert actions by playing out the logic of revolutionary violence at home. It also anticipates the revelations of the Church and Pike committees on domestic CIA and FBI activities made public three years after the release of the film. These commissions documented the surveillance and harassment of civil rights leaders and the infiltration of activist groups over several decades of the Cold War.[11] Thus, the film plays out a version of what the CIA and FBI actually feared: that the civil rights movement within the United States could embrace revolutionary violence and promote an Algeria-like uprising within the United States. It is important to remember the lessons learned about the security state at this Cold War moment: namely, that U.S. covert actions were never limited only to foreign territories but also (1) included the infiltration, surveillance, and subversion of domestic groups, including the anti–Vietnam War movement, the Black Panthers, and the American Indian Movement; and (2) sought to undermine the political power of civil rights leaders from Malcolm X to Martin Luther King Jr. (see Cunningham 2004). As a result of these post-Watergate revelations, new laws were written to limit the domestic scope of U.S. intelligence agencies. These new domestic security laws were either eliminated by the passage of the USA Patriot Act a few weeks after the 2001 attacks or, in the case of domestic wiretapping laws, simply ignored by the Bush administration in the name of counterterror and then retroactively authorized by Congress. Thus, among the first acts of the new counterterrorist state in the fall of 2001 was an expansion of covert actions within the United States and a figuration of all citizens as potential terrorists. Thus, if the message of *The Battle of Algiers* concerns the failure of counterinsurgency when confronted with the political power of decolonization, *The Spook* reminds us of the domestic side of global militarism and the multigenerational consequences of legitimizing the techniques of terror as simply another form of state politics. Kathleen Belew (2018), for example, tracks an explicit post-Vietnam project among white power activists to "bring the war home" and to use the paramilitary techniques learned in the U.S. military to foment a race war in the United States. The War on Terror has also enabled a white nationalist project that informs the heightened xenophobia and anti-immigrant politics of the Trump administration and threatens the very idea of a multiracial, multiethnic society.

The Bush administration's declaration of the War on Terror in 2001 reinstalled terror as the operating logic of the security state after decades of Cold War nuclear terror, reanimating the foundational terrorist violences informing antiblackness, settler colonial dispossession, and the decades of covert dirty wars (see Singh 2017). The War on Terror eliminates the (always somewhat illusionary) distinction between the foreign and the domestic by constituting the entire globe as a battlefield and commits to producing terror in the name of ending it. Importantly, counterterror is not the elimination of terror but rather the apotheosis of it; this fact is visible in the U.S. tactics of preventative war, rendition, torture, and extrajudicial imprisonment. By constituting the terrorist threat as a singular global problem, the Bush administration sought to open a literally unrestricted field for planetary military action and to establish the terms of a new kind of American global hegemony. Instead, it undermined the very concepts it has used to justify the War on Terror—national security, democracy, human rights, and individual freedom. The War on Terror has also set the terms for generations of blowback against the United States around the world and has rather fundamentally altered the terms of the social contract within the United States. Dismantling counterterror thus requires a vision even more revolutionary than the neoconservative project that launched it, because it must confront the very idea of American power and consider a postnational form of security. In addition to disavowing covert action abroad, the immediate challenge of a post-counterterror state is to recognize and constitute a nonmilitarized form of politics. Indeed, after nearly seven decades of a nuclear balance of terror and two decades of a war on terror, the most difficult and necessary project of all is now to find ways of thinking outside the terror and counterterror dialectic—to even imagine a radically demilitarized, actually democratic, society.

IV

AFTER COUNTERREVOLUTION

THIS FINAL PART OF *The Future of Fallout, and Other Episodes in Radioactive World-Making* examines the conditions of possibility for nonviolence, or even thinking about peace and justice, from within a counterterror state embedded in nuclear nationalism and petrochemical capitalism. I begin by considering the ferocious social energies that constituted the Cold War—comparing the technoscientific commitments to the bomb to social movements devoted to disarmament and peace. I then examine a recalibration of these histories in the early 2000s, assessing the terms by which the Cold War confrontation with the Soviet Union was repositioned in relation to the War on Terror by retired intelligence professionals and a KGB spymaster, consolidating, rather than complicating, a history of that multigenerational conflict. I follow by examining the political effects of the social media revolution and the linked domestic surveillance by the counterterror state. Considering the demise of privacy in digital worlds as well as the challenges to political activism under the terms of counterterror, chapter 16 theorizes a world where the citizen is endlessly open to both corporations and intelligence agencies, while the security state itself recedes almost entirely from view in the name of national security. Chapter 17 then interrogates how the language of crisis across nuclear danger and climate danger now functions as a counterrevolutionary form, a way to try to stabilize the very structures that are infrastructural to violence today. The "Crisis in Crisis" considers the contemporary terms for responding to the existential dangers—nuclear weapons and climate disruption—that people have built through decades of military industrial agency. The book then concludes with an epilogue that reconsiders the relationship between technological revolution, militarism, and democratic political imaginations, interrogating the lessons of the Cold War and the War on Terror and exploring how the ability to invent new technical capacities might be refocused in the name of a peaceful collective future.

14

SHAKING, TREMBLING, SHOUTING

Vibration is a basic form of energy; it can be both destructive and sympathetic, the oscillating source of destruction, or sound, or social effervescence (see figure 14.1). In this chapter I consider how the atomic bomb has functioned over the past half century as a vibrational force, one that has not only unlocked and transformed matter into energy, remaking the material world and international order, but has also become a vehicle for lively social engineering in both negative and positive keys. For how a technoscientific revolution plays out in the *longue durée* of history in the process of remaking world, society, and consciousness is a matter of institutions and logics as well as affects and atmospheres.

In the early days of the Manhattan Project, Los Alamos theoretical physicists postulated, dreamed of really, a massively slowed-down nuclear event,

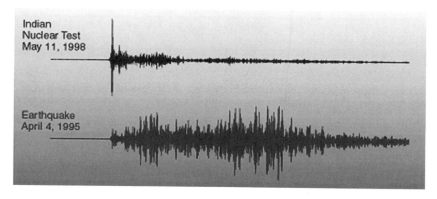

Figure 14.1. Seismograph comparison of an underground nuclear detonation shock wave versus an earthquake (from Heller 1999).

attempting to visualize fission one atom at a time. The idea was to chart atomic fission from the first splitting of a nucleus through each subsequent generation, tracking at the subatomic level the development of a chain reaction leading to a massive release of energy in the form of an explosion. They invented an informal unit of measure to describe the time they theorized it took one atom of uranium to fission—a 100 millionth of a second (.01 microsecond). They called it a "shake," slang for a "shake of a lamb's tail" (see Glasstone and Dolan 1977, 17; McPhee 1973, 115). A nuclear explosion, perhaps the single most destructive human-engineered event, occurs in less than one hundred shakes. This means that all the nuclear detonations in human history—the 2,100 or so nuclear events that constitute an unprecedented human intervention into the biosphere, remaking both geological and human time—do not collectively add up to a single second of linear time. Each of these detonations was also a planetary seismic event, producing the sharp spike of a shock wave watched by geoscientists and security states of all kinds. Indeed, the Cold War, from one key perspective, was fought on a shake-by-shake basis, not only in laboratories and testing sites but also seismically. In the 1950s, a global network of geological sensors was built to record the distinctive wave of a nuclear detonation, becoming a surveillance tool, a scientific research platform for geologists, and a new planetary mode of communication (see figure 14.2). Nuclear states, in other words, used their research and development programs not only to create nuclear arsenals but also to communicate with each other via nuclear testing itself. They used the vibrational force of each nuclear detonation, transmitted by the global

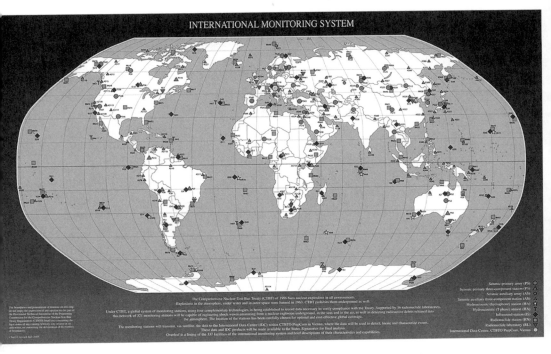

Figure 14.2. International monitoring system for nuclear detonations (courtesy of Comprehensive Test Ban Treaty Organization).

seismic sensor array to all interested parties, as an illustration of their technological capability and political resolve.

Researching the shake, and studying the resulting seismic quakes, became a total project in the U.S. nuclear complex, one that evolved across radically shifting experimental regimes: aboveground testing (1945–62), underground testing (1962–92), and computer simulations (1993 to today). Understanding the bomb in a shake-by-shake manner energized a phenomenal expenditure of money, energy, and technoscientific and military-industrial power in the United States—just under a $6 trillion investment in the twentieth century alone (Schwartz 1998). Indeed, the technoscientific challenge of the shake has only recently moved from a concept to a capacity, as the cumulative knowledge of the U.S. nuclear program can now be projected into virtual-reality spaces, allowing weapons scientists to interact with the exploding bomb one simulated shake at a time (see figure 14.3). Moreover, there is increasing enthusiasm in the U.S. for completing the Manhattan Project, not by getting rid of the bomb, but rather by rejuvenating and rebuilding the U.S. nuclear complex,

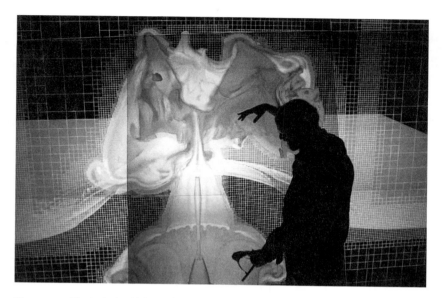

Figure 14.3. Manipulating high-resolution data in virtual cave simulation at Los Alamos National Laboratory (Los Alamos National Laboratory).

producing twenty-first-century nuclear weapons that could sit on the shelf for decades without degradation and still be used militarily at a moment's notice (U.S. Department of Energy 2013).

Still shaking, after all these years. These post–Cold War, War on Terror efforts to reconstitute the bomb should place the recent U.S. wars over weapons of mass destruction—both real and imagined—in a new light while underscoring the continuing conceptual hold the bomb has on American society. For across seemingly opposed political regimes in the twenty-first century, three U.S. presidents (Bush, Obama, and Trump) have worked to build new and improved nuclear weapons, reenergizing the U.S. nuclear production complex and, with it, a serious affective, technoscientific, and political commitment to the shake.

A nuclear nationalist project running parallel to the shake as a measure of atomic time has been the long-term engineering focus on overcoming vibration and shock in military equipment. For more than a half century the test regimes from New Mexico to Nevada to Alaska and the Marshall Islands were orchestrated to a large extent around the physical power of vibration and shock as a destructive force. Each experimental detonation was used to simultaneously explore how blast, heat, and radiation would affect machines,

Figure 14.4. Springs supporting the NORAD facility in Colorado (U.S. National Archives and Records Administration).

structures, and biological specimens of all kinds—staged for both nuclear war fighting and civil defense purposes. Here vibration and shock were carefully engineered, studied, and managed by developing high-speed test cables capable of moving experimental information from the explosion itself to distant computers just slightly ahead of the destructive force itself. Moreover, diagnostic equipment was installed on giant springs throughout the test site, allowing sensor arrays and equipment rooms to literally absorb the shock of the blast by bouncing high in the air and riding the shifting land mass underneath, thereby gaining the precious milliseconds needed to transmit more data off site. Indeed, the entire nuclear Cold War system could be read as a multigenerational project to predict and counter shock through engineering hardened but flexible structures. From nuclear test facilities to nuclear bunkers to ICBM silos scattered across the United States—all were built to roll and bounce and absorb a high degree of physical shock during a nuclear attack. The most fortified structures ever engineered were thus also designed to be highly flexible, as steel and concrete were built not only to protect but also to rock and roll. The North American Aerospace Defense Command (NORAD), for example, not only required twenty-five-ton nuclear blast-proof doors for the underground command and control facility in Colorado, the entire structure was built on springs and could shift and sway to the tune of a nuclear attack (see figure 14.4).

The experimental politics of the shake produced a national infrastructure designed literally for shaking—with machines, springs, and vibrational force the organizing principles of the nuclear state.

It is hard to describe the extraordinary conceptual, financial, and industrial energy empowering this system. Literally millions of experts, designers, engineers, military personnel, and politicians were coordinated through nuclear logics, need-to-know command and control systems, and the politics of shock. The nervous system of the nuclear state has also always been actually nervous—a quivering universe of experts building systems for, and imaginatively rehearsing over and over again, apocalyptic scenarios. The study of shakes and shaking also has meant quivering and worrying, threatening and bullying on a global scale. A total social formation, the U.S. nuclear project remade American politics, science, environment, and emotions, informing today how business, defense, education, geopolitics, and danger itself are now understood (see Masco 2014).

The affective universe produced by the nuclear revolution has always been one of its most powerful achievements. In 1945, the future became radically split for Americans between apocalyptic visions of nuclear war and utopian hopes for advanced technology and a world without war. Key moments of global nuclear terror—1955, 1962, 1983, to locate a few famous geopolitical emergency moments—turned international order into a quivering system, beset by worst-case scenarios and nightmare visions of the end. However, we tend to forget today how energizing the bomb was for activists of all political agendas. From the late 1950s on, the fight to denuclearize the world empowered and linked social movements devoted to peace, the environment, and human rights. Nuclear fear and the critique of Cold War militarism enabled vast networks of actors to see each other as allies, mobilizing alternative notions of society and the future in ways that have also foundationally remade American society across race, gender, justice, and the environment (see Zaretsky 2018).

Activists marched by the millions from the late 1950s through the end of the Cold War, sympathetically linked by national security affect and the desire for a different and better world (see Wittner 2009). Some of these protests started small, as when a few women took their children to the park in New York in the late 1950s instead of practicing the end of the world in civil defense drills. The Mothers against the Bomb movement brought gender into antinuclear activism immediately, as did protests from inner-city groups noticing that atomic civil defense was focused almost exclusively on white suburban families rather than on a multiracial, urban, and rural America. Indigenous and colonial subjects organized globally as their homelands were threatened by nuclear tests, uranium mining, and military expansion. Sexuality was always central to the Cold War system, as officials prosecuted homosexuality as a national security threat and weaponized sex. The politics of radioactive fallout generated similarly foundational concerns about the stability and toxicity of the global environment, energizing activists to protect not only Americans from total nuclear war but also living beings from the cumulative biological effects of the nuclear test programs themselves.

The nightmarish world of nuclear danger—which promised to end everything in a radioactive flash—invited everyone to think about the qualities of life and the nature of politics and power, and to articulate their commitments to one another and the future. The bomb became both a symbol of American military power and a direct challenge to a democratic system increasingly organized through the official secrecy, covert actions, and the end-time visions of the Cold War. People from all walks of life sought to articulate the terms of a better way of living in the face of the Cold War system, a state-based emotional management project seeking to ground Americanness in a specific kind of naturalized militarism, technological determinism, and apocalpyticism. Camping out in front of nuclear production sites and military bases, some activists devoted their lives to visibly opposing the nuclear state on precisely these terms; others sought to build alliances capable of supporting alternative visions of everyday life not based on managing apocalyptic potentials as a standard mode of politics—opting out, tuning in, mobilizing, critiquing.

In addition to the protests and marches (and arrests and acts of sabotage), there were explicit opportunities to shake it up. Consider the Give Peace a Dance project, an annual twenty-four-hour dance marathon organized in Seattle in the mid-1980s to raise money for local antinuclear groups as part of the larger Nuclear Freeze campaign seeking a halt to the nuclear arms race. It was formally a "legs against arms" campaign, fighting Cold War doom and gloom with activism, social energy, and humor. Participants organized into costumed teams, collected sponsors, and danced through the night, trading turns on the dance floor to keep their team (and, one could say, antinuclear activism itself) alive. The project soon went global with dance-a-thons for a nuclear-free world occurring on multiple continents. Instead of offering end-of-the-world images, Give Peace a Dance promoted the idea of a denuclearized planet, one that could be free of the minute-to-minute danger of nuclear war.

Art Chantry's posters for the event immediately became iconic Cold War political statements and constitute perhaps the happiest antinuclear art ever produced. For the 1986 event (see figure 14.5), Chantry created a montage

Figure 14.5. Art Chantry's 1986 *Give Peace a Dance* nuclear disarmament poster (courtesy of Art Chantry).

of dance step diagrams (the fox trot, monkey, twist, polka) overlaid against an atomic bomb (marked "the big reason"). Playing off John Lennon's anti-war song "Give Peace a Chance" (introduced during his famous Bed-Ins for Peace protests with Yoko Ono in 1969), the dance marathon suggested that more collective agency is needed to remake the world, inviting participants to dance their way to a better geopolitics. For the following year's dance marathon, Chantry famously offered a waltzing, cross-dressing Reagan and Gorbachev, presenting them as couples in a spectacular (anti)nuclear dance (see figures 14.6 and 14.7). These posters play on the October 1986 summit in Reykjavik, Iceland, in which, as leaders of the United States and Soviet Union, Reagan and Gorbachev discussed a radical end to the Cold War arms race—namely, the complete elimination of nuclear weapons. Reagan's commitment to the idea of a space-based laser shield against intercontinental ballistic missiles (known as the Strategic Defense Initiative, or Star Wars) killed the possibility not only of an end to the arms race but also of an affirmative global project of immediate denuclearization. The U.S. has spent hundreds of billions of dollars on space-based missile defense over the past three decades but has not yet produced a viable technology, leaving the world with around fourteen thousand nuclear weapons in 2019.[1] Chantry's posters are subversive not only for imagining Reagan and Gorbachev in drag but also for suggesting that an arms race requires a partner, just as peace requires a dance team.

For his 1988 poster, Chantry literally changed the frame on everyday reality. A jitterbugging couple, ecstatic in their physical and musical connection, literally kick the bomb out of the frame, creating a disjointed view that points to a new world almost in sight (see figure 14.8). Rejecting the rectangular format of the standard poster, Chantry here demands that we change our perception, break with convention, and ignore the rules of the Cold War system. Inviting viewers to "Kick the habit!" and "Vote with your feet!," the poster promises not just a less violent world but also a happier one without nuclear weapons. The kinetic energy of dancing and denuclearizing at the same time is beautifully illustrated as a worldview-altering process, one in which participants are not isolated in the despair of Cold War apocalypticism but rather energized by social action and an elimination of collective dangers. Here the good vibrations involve the coming together of people across class, race, gender, and sexuality to confront military states and argue for a better social contract and an alternative notion of security. The Give Peace a Dance project is the flipside of the international seismic signaling of nuclear tests, a world of technologies, bodies, and affects remade by both fear and promise,

DRUM) / PURE JOY / SANDY BRADLEY & THE SMALL WONDERS / RED DRESS / CRAZY 8's / TOTAL EXPERIENCE CHOIR / MAIN ATTRACTION / TIM
NOAH / PEGGY PLATT / DAVID KOCH / REBECCA STOCKLEY / MATT SMITH / PAUL KILLAM / VIDEOS / SPECIAL GUESTS / PRIZES / AND MUCH MORE! / BEST EVER / NEW LOCATION
DUFFY BISHOP & THE RHYTHM DOGS / JE KA JO (WITH DUMI) / RUMOURS OF THE BIG WAVE / JR CADILLAC / ANNIE ROSE & THE THRILLERS / BOCHINCHE / BAKATARA (STEEL
FIFTH ANNUAL
Lead a team raise $$$ for peace!*
Call 441-6544 for more information!
* Brochures at Budget Tapes & Records, Tower Records, and at your local businesses.
LEGS AGAINST ARMS, SANE AND UNIVERSITY SANE PRESENT
GIVE PEACE A DANCE
a 24-hour dance marathon
JUNE 20, 21 1987 SATURDAY 2 PM TO SUNDAY 2 PM
U. OF W. HUB BALLROOM

Figures 14.6 and 14.7. Art Chantry's 1987 *Give Peace a Dance* posters with Reagan and Gorbachev dancing nuclear weapons away (courtesy of Art Chantry).

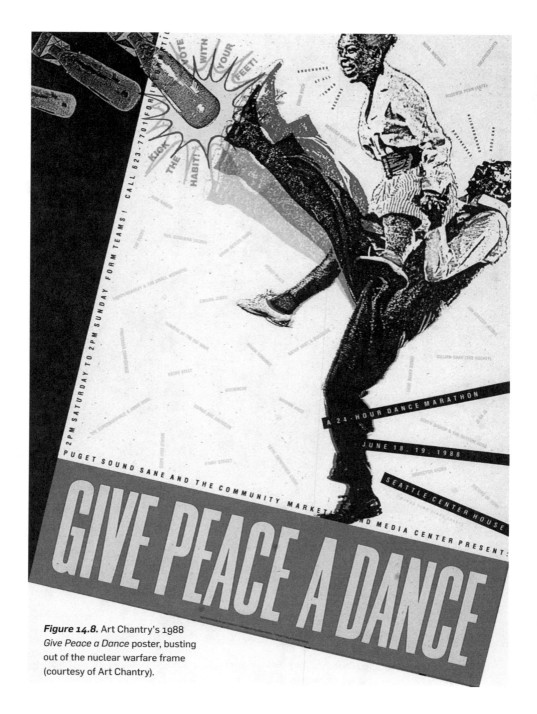

Figure 14.8. Art Chantry's 1988 *Give Peace a Dance* poster, busting out of the nuclear warfare frame (courtesy of Art Chantry).

sympathetically organizing on behalf of specific futurities. The excitability of the national subject in the nuclear age—under forms of terror, outrage, and hope—has been as powerful as the technology itself in reshaping American society.

Well into the second decade of the twenty-first century's War on Terror, we might well ask about the state of our national security excitations. A vast new national security apparatus has been built over the past decade in the name of ending terror. The investment in counterterror has not only created multiple war fronts and a high body count but also entirely new departments and disciplines (homeland security, cybersecurity, biosecurity, etc.). Indeed, the counterterror state has expanded its reach on a scale only matched by that of the early Cold War nuclear state. But what now of the activisms? In February 2003, a synchronized global march to protest the imminent U.S. invasion of Iraq showed that the political energy is still there, as is the capacity of people to unify across social and national divisions, and to do so on record terms. However, while linking a vast set of organizations, this antiwar march produced a profound moment but not a lasting political movement. But then, the massive protests of the Cold War system only really emerged about fifteen years into the U.S.-Soviet nuclear confrontation. So perhaps it takes a new generation of people raised under the radical conditions of a new kind of war to see the emerging future and decide they want a different one. If the twentieth century offers any guide, we know that these kinds of social vibrations can start small and amplify to become a serious political force (of the kind that drove Reagan, the ultimate Cold Warrior, to meet with Gorbachev in Iceland in the first place to consider global denuclearization; see FitzGerald 2000). Perhaps then, just around the corner, the negative affects of counterterror will be matched by a renewed commitment to social organizing and peaceful future building, to shaking it in a positive key for a less violent world—now, wouldn't that be a good vibration?

15

"ACTIVE MEASURES"

In August 2003, a rather extraordinary event went largely unnoticed by an American news media transfixed by escalating violence in Iraq and the domestic terrorist warnings issued by the new Department of Homeland Security. Oleg Kalugin, the former head of KGB operations in the United States, an acknowledged handler of Cold War spies, and a key player in the four-decades-long covert war between the CIA and KGB, was granted U.S. citizenship (Stout 2003). Unlike most immigrants to America, Kalugin's newly professed love of America came at the end of a career explicitly devoted to overthrowing the government of the United States. His 1994 autobiography details an energetic career of recruiting U.S. spies, directing espionage activities against the U.S., managing anti-American propaganda campaigns around the world, and participating in at least one political assassination involving a poison-tipped umbrella (Kalugin 1994). Given the number of high-profile cases in which the mere appearance of espionage accelerated the classification of government information and the lockdown of U.S. facilities, Kalugin's new legal status was a provocative post–Cold War development. Similarly, the lack of widespread media coverage of his story is remarkable in a country fascinated with espionage that is also pursuing counterterror globally.

What intrigues me most about Citizen Kalugin's career, however, is what it reveals about the ongoing transformation of the U.S. from a countercommunist to a counterterrorist state. Kalugin's shift from anti-American KGB agent to pro-American celebrity spy participates, I believe, in a larger domestic project to recalibrate historical memory of the Cold War in order to enable a specific vision of American power in the twenty-first century. Specifically, the Cold War is no longer an episode in U.S. history from which we all narrowly escaped, but rather provides the structural model for how to wage an unending global war founded in secrecy and covert action.

From Russia, with . . .

I first encountered Oleg Kalugin on a bus tour of Washington, DC, in 2003 (figure 15.1), during the expansive U.S. counterterror campaigns in Afghanistan and Iraq and as a revolution in social media technologies was enabling an entirely new scale of covert surveillance. Teamed with Connie Allen, a former U.S. Army counterintelligence special agent, Kalugin was on board the bus to provide tourists, ex-military personnel, former members of the security state, and at least one anthropologist with a tour of how he tried to crack the U.S. capital. The presence of retired (counter)intelligence agents from both the U.S. and USSR promised a firsthand look at the covert terms of the Cold War as fought in Washington, DC.

The Centre for Counterintelligence and Security Studies (CI Centre), founded in 1997 by two former FBI counterintelligence agents, was responsible for organizing the tour. The CI Centre is part of an evolving set of private institutions created by former Cold Warriors to capitalize on their expertise, to tell their story, and to advocate a specific role for spies and counterintelligence in the post–Cold War world of counterterror. Allen and Kalugin are both listed as professors at the CI Centre, which has amassed an impressive array of security experts drawn from the CIA, FBI, U.S. Air Force, U.S. Navy, the Canadian RCMP, and the KGB. The CI Centre provides training to government agencies and corporations about counterintelligence techniques and

Figure 15.1. Oleg Kalugin giving a bus tour of KGB espionage sites in Washington, DC.

offers a variety of "espionage-themed travel excursions," including SpyDrives of Washington and Moscow, a luxury SpyCruise, and a four-star SpyRetreat.

Part autobiography, part historical analysis, part propaganda, the bus tour was designed not only to entertain and educate but, more importantly, to expose a field of invisible but constant threat and subversion. Kalugin, for instance, who was presented as the proverbial "man behind the curtain" in advertisements for the tour, was on the bus to share with us some of the covert methods and practices used by Soviet intelligence operations in the United States during the Cold War. Allen, by contrast, offered a historical counternarrative that focused on how U.S. intelligence agents caught spies in America, detailing the damage done by, as she put it, the "traitor bastards" (e.g., John Walker, Aldrich Ames, and Robert Hanssen) who helped the Soviets. Taken together, Allen and Kalugin presented an image of a nation-state that is under unending assault from spies, saboteurs, and enemy agents.[1] Moreover, in their respective narratives it has always been, and always will be, this way. The Cold War was not an exception—a mutation in global affairs caused in large part by the development of nuclear weapons—but rather part of a seamless history of intelligence gathering, espionage, and the counterpursuit of traitors and spies. The specificity of the Cold War in fact dissolves under the weight of their narrative, becoming simply a distinct configuration of an ongoing battle against the combined assault of subversive agents, foreign and domestic. Counterintelligence and espionage are, for these professionals, a forever project.

The bus tour begins in downtown Washington, DC, and soon we are driving by the offices of the FBI and the State Department while hearing tantalizing tales about compromises and listening devices, packet exchanges, and successful recruitments. Allen points out the Mayflower Hotel where Aldrich Ames received his first payment for spying. Kalugin then shows us his old spy haunts: the Occidental Club on Pennsylvania Avenue and the National Press Building at the corner of Fourteenth and F Streets. He tells us a story about electronically intercepting a phone call between then Secretary of State Henry Kissinger and his wife in which Kissinger repeatedly asks his wife for reassurance about how good he looks on television. Kalugin tells us that the information, though strategically useless, was nonetheless sent right to the top of the KGB to demonstrate the degree to which Soviet spies had penetrated U.S. institutions. The intimacy of the Cold War struggle is revealed here in the everyday details of surveillance, recruitments, and counterespionage.

Moving into Georgetown, we stop in front of seemingly innocent restaurants, homes, and side streets. We hear about covert meetings between "handlers" (managers) and their "assets" (spies) while looking for "dead drops" (information drops) and "signal sites" (covert messages). At Chadwick's pub on K Street, we learn that Aldrich Ames sold the names of scores of CIA and FBI assets over a meal (leading to the prompt execution of several individuals within the USSR). We stop in front of Au Pied de Cochon, the French bistro where KGB defector Vitaly Yurchenko gave his CIA handlers the slip in 1985. We drive by Alger Hiss's house and then stop at Thirty-Seventh and R Street in front of a blue U.S. Postal Service mailbox (see figure 15.2) used by Aldrich Ames as a signal site for communication with his Soviet handler. We learn that the mailbox is a new one, the original now housed in the International Spy Museum, a hugely popular institution that opened in downtown DC in 2002 with Kalugin sitting on the board of directors.

Despite its appeals to contemporary cloak-and-dagger intrigue, much of the tour focuses on the trade in secrets during World War II, a time when the United States and Soviet Union were actually allies. This is because it is the most publicly documented era of spying, thanks in part to the declassification of the Venona transcripts in 1995 (see Haynes and Klehr 1999). This means that much of the content of our tour took place decades before our tour

Figure 15.2. Site of the U.S. Postal Service mailbox used by Aldrich Ames to send signals to his Soviet handlers in Georgetown.

Figure 15.3. Park bench in Washington, DC, presented as a key espionage site.

Figure 15.4. The former Soviet embassy in Washington, DC.

guides entered the (counter)intelligence game. The slippages that begin to emerge in their presentation over expertise, historical context, and firsthand knowledge are, however, irrelevant to the larger mission of the tour—that of documenting threat and vulnerability on an invisible but totalizing scale. Given this ideological project, much of the tour is, nonetheless, anticlimactic: after all, the stuff of spying is rooted not in architecture but information, and the act of spying is ultimately not something that you can document for a tourist audience from the comfort of an air-conditioned bus. We stop, for example, in front of public parks in Washington and are informed about the various covert conversations, exchanges, and recruitments that took place in their open spaces. The empty park bench (see figure 15.3), in fact, becomes the prime site of espionage in the tour, making a claim that spying can take place anywhere and proliferating the point to a humorous degree.

Allen and Kalugin's narrative of constant vulnerability and threat falters most when we arrive at the Soviet embassy (figure 15.4). Built in the 1980s on one of the highest peaks in the district, the embassy we learn was a perfect site for Soviet electronic surveillance of the nation's capital. The U.S. embassy in Moscow, built at the same time, was famously compromised by KGB electronic devices; as Kalugin put it, "the entire building was a transmitter," leading to one of the most contentious international incidents of the late Cold War. We learn, however, that the U.S. was not so naive. Allen informs us that superspy Robert Hanssen told the Russians about one of the most secretive projects of the Cold War: the construction of a tunnel underneath the Soviet embassy in Washington allowing U.S. agents to place taps on all the phone lines and install other information-gathering technologies. Within the intelligence community, rumor has it that privileged members of Congress would be offered tours of this several-hundred-million-dollar covert operation to eavesdrop on Soviet conversations and witness America's Cold War tax dollars at work.

This was the first moment in the tour where the U.S. was presented not as a victim of espionage but as one of its many practitioners. But it was also the last. The role of espionage, misinformation, and spying in U.S. foreign and domestic policy was not mentioned again on the SpyDrive. The covert U.S. actions in Iran, Afghanistan, Guatemala, Chile, and Congo, for example, go unmentioned. Similarly, there is no mention of the revelations in the Church hearings of the mid-1970s, which led to new laws regulating the domestic power of the CIA and FBI.[2] We hear nothing about the scale of U.S. intelligence gathering on U.S. citizens, the secret program to read citizens' mail, the FBI harassment of civil rights leaders like Martin Luther King Jr., or the infiltration of activist groups like the Black Panthers and the American Indian Movement by covert U.S. agents (see Churchill and Vander Wall 2002; Moynihan 1998; Olmsted 1996).

Similarly, the McCarthy era is not mentioned until the end of the bus ride, when I (JM) have the following exchange with Allen (CA) and Kalugin (OK):

JM: I have to ask: how do you both now see the McCarthy period—looking at it from a contemporary perspective with the end of the Cold War?

CA: We always say that McCarthy was right for the wrong reasons. We certainly had the penetration [by a foreign intelligence service]. He just didn't know why we had the penetration. It was an unfortunate time, where people got wrapped up in something that was sometimes beyond their control. There were a lot of allegations made that were never proven, and a lot of people suffered. But at the same time, there were people denounced as communists who were communists and were also spies and got away with it as well. It was just a very difficult period of time for us. We hope we have learned as a society, at many levels, about that kind of thing. Oleg would you like to respond?

OK: It is not an easy question to answer. From the standpoint of America's democracy it was an anomaly. It was a distortion of American values. That's what McCarthy means to me, absolutely nothing other than a distortion. On the other hand, it alerted the United States, and particularly the government of the United States, to some of the dangers that they either ignored or did not understand. So there was a value: as a result of McCarthy's attacks on America's democracy, the U.S. had to take measures to purge its institutions from potential risks. And in that sense, well, there was some progress made. So it was not just one line—either very good or very bad. It was both. Well, the Cold War is over and hopefully we will never experience McCarthy or anything of that kind again in our lives.

In her account, Allen presents the McCarthy period as ultimately a problem of professional expertise. The senator had identified the problem correctly but simply did not know the counterintelligence trade. The unresolved aspect of her narrative is drawn not only from the damage done to innocents but also to the spies that got away with it. But the lack of commentary here on abuses of power within the U.S. (counter)intelligence community is telling, especially in our contemporary moment in which the USA Patriot Act reactivated most of the concerns of the McCarthy period about civil rights within a national security state and as the National Security Agency was covertly attempting to gather all U.S. digital communication. The call by these counterintelligence experts to learn from the past is, thus, made impossible by their near-complete avoidance of it. But then again, to acknowledge the U.S. security scandals of the 1950s, 1960s, 1970s, 1980s, 1990s, or 2000s would also be to invite questions about the status of intelligence operations under the War on Terror, which might undermine the value of the renewed counterintelligence project stressed so explicitly at each step in the tour.

Kalugin's narrative is even more surprising in that he does not gloat over the fear of the communist in 1950s America or tell stories about how McCarthy's theatrics played in the Kremlin—no, he speaks as an American. This might be simply amusing if Kalugin's role in contemporary American political culture were more neutral. But Kalugin's immediate value in the U.S. rests in his ability to leverage his résumé as a KGB spymaster in order to validate a specific narrative of the Cold War for an American security audience. His version of the Cold War confirms, rather than complicates, American perceptions of the Soviet Union, thus enabling a purification of history in the midst of the call for a resurgent U.S. counterintelligence mission in the twenty-first century. The SpyDrive tour, while entertaining and led by highly charming and polished professionals, is in this regard not history at all; it is public relations. More precisely, it is what Kalugin calls "active measures."

KGB 101

My second encounter with Oleg Kalugin came at the International Spy Museum, which opened in July 2002 just a few blocks from the Mall. The museum has become one of the most popular tourist venues in Washington, smashing all box office expectations during its first year of operation. Founded by former members of the intelligence community, the International Spy Museum is an innovative answer to the problem of commemorating a covert war. Unlike previous generations of soldiers, who could expect national recognition on Veterans Day, as well as monuments to their bravery installed in public spaces across the country, Cold Warriors were left in the dark in the 1990s. Deprived of a victory parade—a moment of national celebration and recognition for winning the longest war in U.S. history— Cold Warriors similarly are not likely to receive a memorial on the Mall in Washington commemorating their service and sacrifice to the nation. Indeed, because the vast Cold War security apparatus remains intact and still grounded in secrecy, the contribution of America's spymasters is likely never to be officially acknowledged or publicly remembered. At the International Spy Museum, the intelligence community gets its space near the Mall, but it does so on completely privatized terms. The purpose of the museum is simple: to communicate the huge contributions that covert operatives have made to the United States. In doing so, the International Spy Museum capitalizes on the popular fascination with spies both for profit and for the good of the security state. It is history museum, war memorial, and recruiting center all in one, not only an effort to tell the covert story of the nation but also an explicit attempt to reproduce a new generation of intelligence specialists (see figure 15.5).

On entering the exhibit space, for example, one is asked immediately to select a new identity and cover story, allowing visitors to enter the exhibits literally as undercover agents. A melodramatic film presentation then lays out the risks of spying and asks each audience member directly, "Do you have what it takes to be a spy?" The subsequent exhibits present the history of spy culture through a complex blurring of historical fact and popular fantasy— James Bond's Aston Martin (complete with machine-gun headlights) is on display, as are images of television spies like Mrs. Peel from *The Avengers* and

Figure 15.5. School for Spies exhibit (courtesy of International Spy Museum).

Maxwell Smart from *Get Smart*. These fictional icons are blended with arti-facts and stories from World War II and the Cold War espionage trade: visi-tors can inspect listening devices used by both the CIA and KGB, Minox spy cameras, and weapons disguised as ordinary household items (e.g., a lipstick gun; see figure 15.6), as well as viewing exhibits on covert communications, code breaking, and surveillance techniques. The museum is designed like a maze, forcing visitors through a historical survey of spying dating back to biblical times before providing access to exhibits on the Cold War. A small exhibit on the McCarthy period acknowledges that innocent people were accused of being spies, but the intelligence reforms of the 1970s, and the decision-making processes behind these reforms, are not mentioned in any of the museum's exhibit texts. The final exhibit spaces then become deadly serious, detailing the crimes and captures of Aldrich Ames and Robert Hans-sen, before ending with a chilling film that argues that future terrorist at-tacks, like those on September 11, 2001, can only be prevented with a reju-venated and globally aggressive covert intelligence campaign. The museum that begins with spying presented as a game, supported by nostalgic images

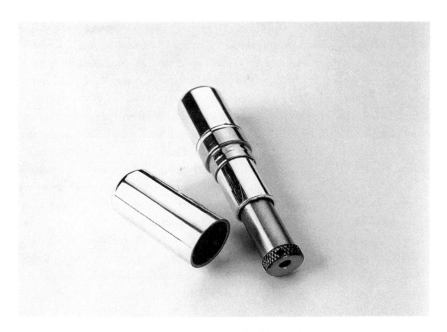

Figure 15.6. Lipstick gun (courtesy of International Spy Museum).

from Cold War popular culture, ends with a ruthless contemporary pitch for expanding intelligence budgets to meet an expanding global mission. When the lights come up, visitors are then delivered directly into a large, and extremely well-stocked, espionage-themed gift shop.

On this particular July night, however, I am at the International Spy Museum not to see the exhibits, but to hear a two-part lecture by Kalugin on the Soviet security state titled, simply, "KGB 101." Speaking to a packed house, Kalugin is introduced by the director of the museum (a thirty-five-year CIA veteran) as well as by the president of the CI Centre (a twenty-five-year FBI counterintelligence man), which cosponsored the talk. Kalugin's impressive résumé is the immediate focus of the presentation. We learn via a Power-Point presentation, choreographed to Stalin's national anthem, that Kalugin was the youngest officer in KGB history to attain the rank of general. His successful career of espionage in the United States included recruiting John Walker, the U.S. Navy intelligence officer who is alleged to have given the Soviets the codes for all Pacific communications, including the nuclear launch commands for U.S. submarines. We learn that Kalugin first arrived in the U.S. in 1959 as a twenty-four-year-old KGB officer and Fulbright exchange student. His success in recruiting spies, as well as his skill in spreading Soviet misinformation and propaganda, took him from undercover journalist to acting chief of the Soviet embassy in Washington, DC, and eventually back to the Soviet Union in the 1970s to head the KGB's foreign counterintelligence operation. In his autobiography, *The First Directorate*, Kalugin (1994) identifies his return to the Soviet Union as politically transformative. Having spent much of his adult life in the United States, Kalugin describes seeing the Soviet system really for the first time as the head of the KGB counterintelligence project and being shocked by its corruption, cruelty, and inefficiency. By 1990, he had denounced the KGB leadership and was officially stripped of his rank. He was then elected to the Soviet Parliament before watching the USSR come apart and immigrating to the United States in 1995. In 2002, Russian President Vladimir Putin ("my former KGB subordinate," as Kalugin puts it) convicted Kalugin of treason in absentia, citing evidence from Kalugin's 1994 autobiography. If Kalugin were to return to Russia, he would likely face immediate arrest and possibly a long prison sentence.

Kalugin begins his "KGB 101" lecture by describing himself as a true believer in the Soviet system, a person who genuinely believed that communism would deliver "paradise on earth in our lifetime." He underscores that he has never been a defector, presenting himself more as a disillusioned believer living on the other side of history. Indeed, his narrative of professional accomplishment and moral conviction within the KGB, followed by resistance to the Soviet system, is an impeccable résumé for one wishing to be embraced by the U.S. intelligence community. At each step, Kalugin counterbalances historical evidence of his professional duplicity with overtures to his authentic patriotism and personal character. His charm is in precisely the ability to be pitch perfect in his delivery, with just the right touches of humor and gravitas to deflect attention away from the sordid business of professional lying and espionage.

The most interesting aspect of Kalugin's talk is his discussion of the KGB's training program for its intelligence agents. Years of language training in local dialects and a focus on the philosophy and literature of target countries were at the center of the program. It was training designed to enable small talk, allowing the recruitment of potential assets to be on casual and local terms. The United States, in this regard, was not just Kalugin's assignment; it was always a serious object of study, one that he embraced with obvious enthusiasm. He notes that as a young KGB trainee he had access to the world's news media and literature, texts that were denied to citizens of the USSR. It is here that one can sense the slow seduction the U.S. held for Kalugin. In his autobiography, he describes arriving in Manhattan and being shocked by the size and texture of the city (its architecture, arts, and the freedom of movement of its citizens) as well as by the extreme poverty that seemed unaddressed by the state.

Kalugin follows these personal epiphanies with a detailed description of the organization of the Soviet security state, emphasizing the infiltration of the KGB into every institution of Soviet society. He states that at the height of the Cold War there were nearly 500,000 KGB agents in Russia, in stark contrast to the tens of thousands of FBI and CIA agents in the United States. A discussion of the purges within Soviet society, the mass murders, leads into a discussion of KGB techniques for dealing with internal dissent. Kalugin describes several episodes in which the KGB detonated a bomb in the name of a dissent group to enable violent regional reprisals by the state. He describes the eighty-six fake CIA groups the KGB formed in Afghanistan in the 1980s to draw out mujahideen fighters for execution. The foreign and domestic duplicity of the KGB within Soviet society was matched by KGB propaganda efforts against the United States. Kalugin describes organizing mass protests of U.S. policies overseas—stating that for a mere $5,000 one could manufacture tens of thousands of protestors in front the U.S. embassy in India, for example—demonstrating how easily one could create an international anti-American incident during the Cold War. Here, Kalugin describes the "active measures" taken to defeat the West:

> At the heart and soul of Soviet intelligence operations were active measures aimed at, well, the eventual destruction of the Western societies—through disinformation, through subversive actions, through guerilla warfare, through terrorism, through civil war, whatever. That was part of the program. Let me give us some innocuous figures from the Russian KGB top-secret report for 1981. In that year alone, the KGB reported to the Party Central Committee, to Mr. Brezhnev, that it financed, produced, or in one way or another, was involved in the publication of seventy books and brochures worldwide, sixty-six documentary and feature films worldwide, 4,800 articles published in various newspapers worldwide, 3,000 conferences and exhibitions worldwide, 1,500 radio and television programs, and finally, 170,000 lectures—like the one I am delivering tonight—across the country, across the world. That was the total of KGB active measures that year.

A week earlier, on the SpyDrive, Kalugin had made a similar point directed specifically at the United States:

We launched a major liberal magazine in New York City. Two Nobel laureates were on our editorial board—Linus Pauling and Bertrand Russell. None of them knew that the magazine was funded by the KGB, that the editor was a KGB guy. And then one day you open the *New York Times* and find an advertisement saying, "Down with the United States' involvement in Vietnam. It is high time to withdraw U.S. troops—it is a shame and a disgrace"—signed by hundreds of luminaries in science and the arts. They did not know that I paid $10,000 for that advertisement, and that they were dupes in a sense.

Like the lecture I am delivering tonight. As tantalizing as these personal stories are, they come mixed with wild pronouncements unsupported by any firsthand evidence. Kalugin tells us, for example, that J. Robert Oppenheimer and Enrico Fermi were Soviet agents and that they provided secrets to the USSR about how to build an atomic bomb. We hear that it was the KGB that started the rumors that the CIA was involved in the assassination of John F. Kennedy, and it was the KGB that was responsible for spreading the idea that J. Edgar Hoover was a closeted transvestite. We are told that, indeed, it was Ronald Reagan's Strategic Defense Initiative that broke the will of the Soviet state and precipitated the end of the Cold War. In short, we learn from Kalugin that the KGB was as precisely as monstrous as the U.S. always said it was, that internal critique of the U.S. intelligence service during the Cold War was largely the product of the KGB's active measures, and that it was only the confrontational toughness of the U.S. military state that defeated the Soviet Union.

Thus, Kalugin confirms exactly—without deviation—the narrative U.S. Cold Warriors produced about the Soviet Union during the Cold War. He does not challenge their assumptions; instead, he reinforces them. And in so doing, he provides the rationale for dismissing (post–)Cold War critiques in the U.S. as simply a product of KGB machinations. We hear nothing, for example, about how U.S. espionage campaigns were interpreted by the KGB, or about the errors made by the CIA in its estimates of Soviet capabilities, from the famous bomber and missile gaps of the early Cold War to the agency's inability even to imagine the end of the USSR in the 1980s. Indeed, the heroes of the story are implicitly the U.S. intelligence officers who, outnumbered and outmanned, were able to beat the KGB at its own global game. Kalugin concludes by stating that if the U.S. had installed human agents in Saddam Hussein's Iraq, President George W. Bush would not have gone to war with Iraq, arguing that a single bullet could have prevented the U.S. invasion in 2003.

Thus, Kalugin ends his talk with an explicit call for U.S.-sponsored espionage and assassination. In this way, Kalugin's "KGB 101" lecture offers a narrative useful primarily to past and present U.S. intelligence officers. It purifies the past by documenting the brutality and active measures of the Soviet regime and dismisses many of the internal criticisms of the FBI and CIA as Soviet propaganda. It also argues for the centrality of spies in the modern world, making members of the intelligence community the true brokers of both history and security. Kalugin's ideological makeover, therefore, enables a more profound ideological makeover of the U.S. security state as covert agent.

The success of this ideological program was brought home to me later in the year, when I was conducting archival research on the U.S. nuclear program at several government institutions near the West Coast. In Las Vegas, I spoke to a career Nuclear Test Site (NTS) worker who brought up the large-scale antinuclear protests that were staged at the site through the 1980s. These protests, which involved a vast range of groups from the environmental, peace, antinuclear, and Native American activist communities, were part of a global effort to confront the terms of the escalating Cold War arms race and to recognize its foreign and domestic costs.[3] Stating baldly that the protests were funded by the Soviets, this NTS worker dismissed the activists' political critique of environmental contamination and militarism within the U.S. nuclear program. He then asked if I had ever heard of a KGB spymaster named Oleg Kalugin. Kalugin, the lifelong student of America, identified and understood his audience all too well and delivered precisely the narrative they needed at this historical moment.

The intelligence community has always argued that only its failures become part of the public record: the Iran-Contra Affair, Soviet spies Walker, Ames, and Hanssen, or the successful terrorist attacks on Washington, DC, and New York in 2001. However, now that same professional community has some very public, and in some cases very profitable, institutions to spread the good word about U.S. (counter)intelligence. They have their own privately held museum near the Mall (the International Spy Museum); they have a new pedagogical and lobbying institution (the CI Centre); and they have their man from Moscow in America to confirm their version of history. Untouched by historical review or political critique, Kalugin and the institutions that engage him are busily reconfiguring the story of the Cold War in order to reinvent the national security state for the twenty-first century on covert, and thus explicitly antidemocratic, terms.

What's New about the New Normal?

In the immediate aftermath of the suicide-hijacker strikes on New York and Washington, DC, in 2001, political commentators in the United States eagerly identified the attacks as the start of a new American epoch. Rejecting the inherited logics about security and global order gained from the forty-plus years of the Cold War, they called for entirely new understandings of American vulnerability and power. But even as policy changes—from the USA Patriot Act to the execution of preemptive war in Iraq—seem to support the claim that the U.S. has made a radical break with its past, the terms and logics of the War on Terror remain understandable precisely because they are so familiar. Within weeks of the attacks, Vice Present Dick Cheney, for example, declared the new security measures (already codified in the USA Patriot Act) as the "new normal," mobilizing to solidify the terms of the counterterrorist state for the foreseeable future. But what is actually new about the new normal? When were Americans not presented with a global U.S. military campaign—fought largely on covert terms—that did not merge an apocalyptic notion of everyday domestic threat with an expansive use of government secrecy and a demand for ever-increasing military budgets? The structural logic of total war that defined the Cold War remains the defining principle of American security policy, linking the foreign and domestic under a highly reproducible and flexible logic of imminent threat. From this perspective the War on Terror is a global project that seeks to rebrand and perfect, rather than invalidate, the structural logics of the Cold War.

This regeneration of the covert security state was well underway before the attacks of September 11, 2001. Here, we might follow Kalugin's lead and interrogate the active measures of the U.S. security state. Within weeks of the 2001 suicide-hijacker attacks, President Bush sent advisor Karl Rove out to meet with Hollywood executives and producers to discuss the production of patriotic entertainment, vehicles that would educate as well as promote and amplify the dangers of terrorism for the American public (Lyman 2001). But the intelligence community was already way ahead of him, having sent representatives out to Hollywood since the mid-1990s to provide "technical advice." The results were spectacular: already in production as the 2001 attacks occurred were three television shows about terrorism and the heroic exploits of the CIA/FBI: CBS had *The Agency*; ABC had *Alias*; and FOX had *24*. The CI Centre, also an energetic consultant to the entertainment industry, soon participated in a British television production called *MI6* and a television miniseries about the Robert Hanssen spy case. The newly constituted Department of Homeland Security (the second U.S. defense department) soon had its moment as well with the network television arrival of D.H.S.: The Series— an action drama about homeland security. On the series webpage one finds a sepia-toned image of President Bush, Secretary of State Powell, and Secretary of Defense Rumsfeld, heads bowed in prayer, with "How do we know that we are truly safe?" superimposed over their image. Cabinet members and Homeland Security personnel were promised cameos in the television series, yet again blurring the distinction between fiction and reality that was evidenced at the International Spy Museum. What links these productions is not only their constant recitation of vulnerability and threat, but also the assumption that the only way of producing security in such a climate is through state-sponsored covert action, counterterror, and nuclear nationalism.

The inauguration of the counterterror state in 2001 involved not only a regeneration of a security state founded in secrecy and covert action, but also a rescripting of history to enable that mission. The newness of the War on Terror was primarily a public relations move, a means of separating current state activities ideologically from the past, and thus from the known costs and consequences of dirty wars and nuclear confrontation. The goal of this strategy was twofold: (1) to enable a national regeneration through violence (Slotkin 2000), allowing the War on Terror to become an ideological construct based on, but publicly disconnected from, past U.S. policy; and (2) to make it all but impossible for citizens to argue for less militarism or to demand from officials a definition for the concept of security that empowers their radical actions domestically and around the world. Linked to this rejuvenation of the covert security state was, thus, an implicit understanding among counterterror officials that democratic process and security are ultimately incompatible. This is a Cold War line of reasoning, used for generations to validate both an expansion of the military state and an increasing manipulation of public media to produce consent.[4] One way to resist the curtailing of civil liberties, the aggressive global military campaign and its high body count, and the ever-expanding use of state secrecy to prevent debate and avoid international law, is to historicize these very logics as long-standing American Cold War strategies. In order to understand the new normal, it may well be that we need to shed more light on the historical terms, costs, and failures of the security state itself. Actively engaging the historical archive may well be one of the best tools for showing the consequences of unrestrained American power and the ideological power of nuclear nationalism, and for demonstrating the high foreign and domestic costs of accepting a portrayal of the United States as a reluctant, but globally mobilized, counterterrorist state.

16

BOUNDLESS INFORMANT

During the escalating counterterror panic in the fall of 2002, just two weeks after I published an essay on politics inside Los Alamos National Laboratory, an ethnographic account of spy allegations, missing computer hard drives containing nuclear weapons design codes, and the politics of government secrecy inside the U.S. nuclear complex (see Masco 2002), my apartment was burglarized. While a theft of this kind is not an uncommon experience where I live, the details remain interesting. Exactly two items were taken, one of them a laptop computer. The Chicago police took the case seriously and mounted a quick and professional response. But as I sat in my walk-up apartment conversing with fingerprint experts who were explaining to me how the powder they were laying carefully along the door frames would not stick to the highly varnished dark wood finish, preventing them from pulling a viable print, the lead detective arrived. He took one step into my apartment and, without further inquiry, looked directly at me and said, "A missing laptop—I hope there weren't any nuclear secrets on it," and then laughed. *I hope there weren't any nuclear secrets on it.* What is one to do with this statement, let alone the laughter? Of course, at that very moment I was wondering, panicking more honestly, about what loose information was on the laptop, which bits of research data, personal communications, and financial records were now out of my control and circulating in the world. He may even have been referring to the very case I had written about in Los Alamos, which was a national news story. But in the charged political atmosphere of post-2001 nuclear fears, his comment also raised a crypto-possibility—could it possibly be that the security state was somehow involved in the theft and just went out of its way to let me know it (as a few colleagues speculated at the time)? Or was I just being paranoid, making the detective's comments simply an example of the overdetermined national security culture of our times in the United States, in which a random joke concerning weapons of mass destruction could trigger an avalanche of unanticipated associations and meanings?

The computer was lost, but the other item, unbelievably, was quickly returned via the good work of the police. Thus, the question of the laptop computer remains lively to this day: it appears in retrospect as if the computer containing my draft manuscript on nuclear weapons science and culture in the United States was the specific target of the burglary. Paranoia is a necessary effect of engaging the security state, a structuring principle for those inhabiting the expert worlds and spaces of compartmentalized secrecy as well as for members of the public who pause to consider this vast set of American institutions and practices. But at the same time, Americans identify with the covert state in complex ways, assuming a kind of intimacy with covert governance that is directly at odds with democratic principles. For example, a common retort from new acquaintances learning about my longtime ethnographic research on national security sciences and culture in the U.S. is to inquire about "the file"—that is, the modes of surveillance devoted to anyone seeking to understand anything about the secret state. I have always found this a telling moment—a revelation of American sensibilities—as it registers a widespread understanding of state surveillance *inside* the United States but also suggests those activities are addressed only to those who provoke it somehow. It creates a knowing subject position that is untouched by the security state while imaginatively directing those energies only at suspicious others. The evocation of the security file in this manner often reveals belief in a global U.S. security apparatus capable of sublime forms of access, intuition, and action but one that is also directly linked to a public state that is more often actually experienced as deeply unengaged, frequently gridlocked, and incompetent. Such folk beliefs suggest that Americans know their government has plenty of agency but increasingly can only imagine that agency deployed on covert terms, a fantastic distortion of a democratic public sphere.

In antinuclear and peace activist worlds it is not uncommon for individuals considering national security programs to conjure an invisible mode of state attention to their individual movements. Some speak directly to the state when on the telephone, imagining an official eavesdropper carefully taking notes; others assume their everyday activities are being minutely tracked and monitored, developing elaborate rituals of evasion or theatrical modes of self-presentation for an assumed state security viewer. A longtime peace activist once invited me to listen to the clicks on the telephone line in his office and then showed me the electrical grid in his office compound—a giant snarl of multicolored wires, far too complicated and improvised to troubleshoot—to show me how a wiretap could be hidden in plain sight. Others have calculated how they could be hurt by the covert state, reviewing their financial, employment, and everyday activities for weaknesses that could be exploited, thereby conjuring and producing a specific vision of state power. I know more than a few people today who have created email signatures directed at an unknown security state reader, and some who now stack key words—"WMD," "terrorist," "jihadist," and such—in their sign-offs as a general mode of protest of the counterterror state. This attitude toward the security state reveals a real assessment of power (for example, Americans know today that their government assassinates people with and without drones, imprisons others with and without trial, and places activists as well as specific racial and ethnic populations under both overt and covert forms of surveillance). But national security paranoias can also foment a special kind of narcissism, suggesting that simply by recognizing the existence of the military state with its vast range of covert activities, one becomes of interest to that state apparatus. It is very hard to not engage in this mode of thinking at times or to fully resist the conspiratorial impulse in the age of counterterror, where fundamental aspects of the democratic social contract have been suspended. The prevalence of these assumptions, however, is also diagnostic of a larger psychosocial process in the United States, one that assumes a radical break between state activities and public accountability even as forms of ubiquitous surveillance are increasingly positioned as the foundational basis for collective defense. The counterterror state relies on this combination of affective, imaginative, and material infrastructures to produce a vision of global space as both American and increasingly at risk.

The USA Patriot Act, signed into law with little congressional debate a few weeks after the suicide-hijacker attacks on New York and Washington, DC, in September 2001, fundamentally rewrote domestic surveillance laws—and with them, the American social contract. Matched by a series of secret executive orders, a wide-ranging overhaul of intelligence agencies and covert action programs was conducted by the George W. Bush administration to increase the global power of the American security state. These changes were designed to break down the barriers between intelligence and law enforcement agencies constructed in the 1970s after revelations of widespread surveillance of citizens and domestic covert actions (including official programs to read mail and telegrams and to infiltrate and disrupt activist organizations; see Parenti 2003; Prados 2013). After 2001, security agencies were once again authorized to conduct "sneak and peak" operations inside the homes and intimate spaces of citizens (what were once known as "black bag jobs" in the FBI; see Donner 1981), to covertly infiltrate activist, political, and religious groups, and to conduct unprecedented forms of domestic surveillance on raced and classed subjects (see Browne 2015). The first decade of the twenty-first century would soon be universally recognized as a new golden age for state surveillance within the U.S. intelligence community, with a vast array of new laws, technologies, and ambitions restructuring the everyday spaces of an American form of life increasingly embedded in counterterror logics and policies. In an era of preemption, counterterror makes everyone a potential suspect, and the search for clues to the next attack energizes a vast array of government agencies, contractors, and police departments to scrutinize the lives of citizens and try to predict their ambitions, capabilities, and future actions. Surveillance in the era of counterterror both assumes a continual technological revolution in capacities and recognizes no borders, striving to achieve a system of informational collection and social control that can function on a planetary scale (see Masco 2014).

A few years after the break-in I filed a series of Freedom of Information Act (FOIA) requests with the FBI about the incident in my apartment as well as my own standing as a writer on American national security science and culture, an effort to finally see if "the file" actually existed. In sequence, each FOIA request produced a response of "no records were found."[1] While this would seem to settle the matter, this kind of notification often means simply that the request was not specific enough in its language to direct FOIA agents to the precise location a file might be stored (thus triggering a legal responsibility to consider its release), or it could mean a file is protected for national security or for a variety of other reasons. Thus, it can register an actual absence or represent another state of affairs entirely. In the hard recession years following the dot.com crash of 2000 and the September 11 attacks of 2001, I assumed my experience was an unexceptional theft in a neighborhood feeling the bust of boom-and-bust capital. But then I remember the detective's laughter, and his comment "I hope there weren't any nuclear secrets on it," which continues to undermine my confidence, offering me an invitation to think otherwise. The crucial point here is that connecting the dots one way leads to an irritating but common nonpolitical event, while connecting them another way raises questions about how one is positioned in relation to the security state and to the forms of recognition and control that structure the counterterror apparatus inside the United States.

This essay considers the revolution in domestic surveillance after 2001, assessing the modes by which the intelligence agencies constitute their activities as opaque while seeking to render the lives of citizens transparent. Data is now considered a military object, approached by a vast range of state institutions as a space subject to dominance, vulnerability, and covert process. Digital data also rides on a vulnerable material infrastructure, one that enables global communications across military affairs, news, commerce, and social media, forming an increasingly networked globe (see Starosielski 2015). This essay is also, then, an effort to interrogate the implicit social contract emerging in the United States around digital security and to assess the implications of technological revolution for citizen-state relations as digital time and space are recoded for a counterterror world. For what does it mean today, in light of recent revelations about the extensive domestic surveillance activities of intelligence community, that citizens no longer need to fantasize their relation to the security state—they now know everyone is under expansive new forms of scrutiny? In other words, this essay is an effort to consider "the file"—long an object of concern for those writers working in police states (see Ash 1997; Verdery 2014; see also Hull 2012; Riles 2006)—in the American context, and to interrogate the fears and ambitions that have rendered privacy increasingly moot in the name of both profit and security (see Rainie and Anderson 2014).

The All-Seeing Eye

In 2003, the Defense Advanced Research Projects Agency (DARPA) made headlines for announcing an ambitious project called Total Information Awareness (TIA)—a commitment to collecting and analyzing all digital communication to create a prediction capability for counterterror, transforming

Figure 16.1. Logo of the Total Information Awareness project, Defense Advanced Research Projects Agency.

bits of data from email, purchases, web searches, and phone calls into a new kind of predictive policing. The man behind TIA was John Poindexter (who was a key player in the Iran-Contra scandal of the Reagan administration). Poindexter proposed the TIA after the September 2001 terrorist attacks as a Manhattan Project for data collection and management, a way to claim the total information domain for U.S. interests. The project recognized the emerging revolutions in digital communication as a powerful new kind of surveillance resource and sought to build a national security infrastructure devoted to exploiting its future potential. Poindexter was forced to resign when the project, and particularly the logo he personally designed, became public (see figure 16.1), as images of a new kind of Orwellian Big Brother—an all-seeing eye—brought nearly universal condemnation.[2]

But the TIA project recognized a fundamental change in global communication.[3] With proliferating modes of information delivery and reception in a World Wide Web of communications, the TIA can be seen as a key moment in the development of big-data security (data sets so massive you need a set of computer tools to capture, store, visualize, and analyze their content; see Lyon 2014; as well as Mayer-Schonberger and Cukier 2014). The TIA concept, while publicly condemned and formally abandoned, morphed quickly into an official countercampaign for cybersecurity in the United States, a

Figure 16.2. Logo of the new U.S. Cybercommand.

public relations strategy transforming the offensive surveillance of the TIA into a critical infrastructural vulnerability, requiring anticipatory defense. In 2009, the United States created a new military organization to recognize the importance of cyberspace, placing it alongside traditional spaces of military interest in air, sea, land, and outer space—a new terrain to be controlled and exploited (see Clark and Knake 2010; see figure 16.2). The U.S. Cybercommand is responsible for securing all DoD information infrastructures as well as fighting cyber-warfare (and was probably involved in the 2010 cyberattack on Iran's nuclear research facilities, which involved releasing a software worm program known as Stuxnet onto the World Wide Web, specifically targeting Iranian centrifuges; see Harris 2014b, 11). The most vocal public face for the Cybercommand has been its first director, General Keith Alexander, who until October 2013 was also the head of the National Security Agency (NSA), the organization charged with intercepting, decrypting, and assessing global communications. An unprecedented dual directorship, this made the head of signals intelligence gathering also the top cyber-warrior in the United States.

The surprise of the 2001 terrorist attacks was immediately constituted by national security professionals as a problem of information management, of connecting the dots of international terrorist networks, of distilling out of a global sea of data individual pieces of information critical to preempting attacks. This led to a significant expansion in all aspects of intelligence gathering and, via the USA Patriot Act, a massive new investment in both domestic and global surveillance. The NSA operated under an immediate new presidential mandate after the September 2001 attacks, one that overturned the long-standing legal requirement to restrict their intelligence gathering to foreign sources. The NSA operated for years in clear violation of federal law, leading to retroactive legislation by the U.S. Congress in 2007 to protect both the NSA and the telecommunication companies that gave NSA access to their networks. It is also clear that various intelligence agencies—NSA, CIA, FBI—had information on the 9/11 suicide hijackers but did not share—they would say, were legally prohibited from sharing—those pieces of information with each other (see U.S. Senate Select Committee on Intelligence and U.S. House Permanent Select Committee on Intelligence 2002). Consequently, one of the most profound counterterror projects has been a reorganization of the intelligence services (famously competitive with each other) under a new overarching position, the director of national intelligence, created in 2005 to simply coordinate the information gathered by the sixteen intelligence agencies.

The answer to counterterror in the information age has been a commitment, led by the NSA, to expanding surveillance infrastructure and to empowering the world's largest collection of mathematicians, linguists, and computer scientists to own digital communications at a global scale. By focusing on the nodes of global communication traffic—for example, at the AT&T switching facility in San Francisco and perhaps thirty similar sites—the NSA has sought to build a data-capturing capability into the physical infrastructure of the World Wide Web. This example also shows how producing a digital security infrastructure at a global scale also entails highly localized interventions (at switching facilities and data centers) grounded in particular regional economies and technology centers, like that of the Bay Area. These taps can in principle capture and copy all digital traffic flowing through those nodes. Thus, if the TIA project, with its promise of predictive policing through a comprehensive digital dragnet, is disavowed, the NSA has nonetheless long passed a threshold moment in terms of how it conceives of controlling digital data on a global scale. Listen to the public statements of NSA officials for the distinction between collecting and reading: reading U.S. citizen email is frequently disavowed, while collection is not even discussed. The key here is a shift in the definitional meaning of these terms. The U.S. Defense Intelligence Agency's *Intelligence Law Handbook*, for example, begins its entry on "collection" this way:

To begin this journey, it is necessary to stop first and adjust your vocabulary. The terms and words used in DoD 5240.1-R have very specific meanings, and it is often the case that one can be led astray by relying on the generic or commonly understood definition of a particular word. For example, "collection of information" is defined in the Dictionary of the United States Army Terms (AR 310–25) as: "The process of gathering information for all available sources and agencies." But, for the purposes of DoD 5240.1-R, information is "collected" . . . only when it has been received for use by an employee of a DoD intelligence component in the course of his official duties . . . (and) an employee takes some affirmative action that demonstrates an intent to use or retain the information. . . .

So, we see that "collection" of information for DoD 5240.1-R purposes is more than "gathering"—it could be described as "gather, plus . . ." For example, information received from a cooperating source (e.g., the FBI) about a terrorist group is not "collected" unless and until that information is included in a report, entered into a data base, or used in some other manner which constitutes an affirmative intent to use or retain that information. (2004: 3–5)[4]

To begin this journey. The rhetoric deployed here is more than simply that of an expert community (Cohn 1987); it is designed to deceive the non-expert public. Similarly, "reading" conventionally suggests a direct human mediation, an eye on the page, but in the world of big-data analytics such work is conducted by computer algorithms, keyword searches, and sophisticated forms of pattern recognition. The Obama administration issued new guidelines allowing the intelligence community to keep information on U.S. citizens investigated in relation to terrorism for five years (previously such information would have to be destroyed after 180 days unless a crime were discovered): this is one of many markers that big data is gaining historical depth as well as global reach. Now NSA employees talk about decades' worth of data, creating a fundamentally different relationship to the future, as data collected today could be mobilized deep into the future. To deal with this flood of digital data, the NSA expanded its geographic footprint with a massive new data storage facility in Utah (Bamford 2012). The size of the facility has drawn much public attention for a would-be secret agency, provoking a Greenpeace action over the facility using a blimp carrying a sign "NSA illegal spying below" to draw attention to the site—which suggests that spying is beginning to be a two-way street (see figure 16.3). A new supercomputing

Figure 16.3. Greenpeace protest of National Security Agency data facility in Utah (courtesy of Greenpeace).

facility is also being built in Oak Ridge, Tennessee, in addition to existing facilities in Georgia, Texas, Hawaii, and Colorado. This represents multiple Manhattan Projects across the spectrum of data collecting, storage, super-computing, code breaking, and data mining. The global flow of digital data is both spatialized and localized in these particular sites—a reminder that the production of a seemingly immaterial global data surveillance infrastructure has material force in particular locales and is often tied to previous technologies and/or security regimes in the U.S. across settler colonial, imperial, and Cold War formations (see Hu 2015).

In other words, the War on Terror has ridden on top of and even accelerated a technological revolution, one in which the increasingly connected modes of digital communication are remaking sociability, commerce, law, and security in rather fundamental ways. Consider, for example, this statement by David Petraeus, who moved from running the U.S. counterinsurgency programs in Iraq and Afghanistan to become CIA director (until his abrupt resignation in November 2012 for sexual infidelities revealed, ironically, by his use of insecure email). In one of his last official speeches as CIA director to an audience of security contractors, he speculated on the implications of the "smart home" for global spying. He noted that humanity is on the verge of an "internet of things" and predicted that by 2020 as many as 100 billion devices of all kinds could be connected via Wi-Fi. This internet of things, he noted, will enable nothing less than a new era of surveillance in which:

> Items of interest will be located, identified, monitored, and remotely controlled through technologies such as radio-frequency identification, sensor networks, tiny embedded servers, and energy harvesters—all connected to the next-generation Internet using abundant, low cost, and high-power computing—the latter now going to cloud computing, in many areas greater and greater supercomputing, and ultimately, heading to quantum computing. In practice, these technologies could lead to rapid integration of data from closed societies and provide near-continuous, persistent monitoring of virtually anywhere we choose. "Transformational" is an overused word, but I do believe it properly applies to these technologies, particularly to their effect on clandestine tradecraft. Taken together, these developments change our notions of secrecy and create innumerable challenges—as well as opportunities. The CIA and our Intelligence Community partners must be able to swim in the ocean of "Big Data." Indeed, we must be world class swimmers—the best, in fact. (Petraeus 2012)

Providing near-continuous, persistent monitoring of anywhere we choose. Thus, in addition to phone, email, texting, credit card records, and internet searches, toasters, refrigerators, cars, and small electrical appliances of all kinds are imagined here to be emerging new sources of surveillance. Since these technologies are still largely projections—anticipated forms, currently under construction—it is important to underscore that this future imaginary is in fact the huge domestic achievement of the War on Terror: a new federal commitment to engineering the future by continually installing emerging new capacities within it (Masco 2014). This is a new kind of governance, focused on capacities, infrastructural revolution, and deep futures. Biosecurity, cybersecurity, Homeland Security—counterterrorism in all its proliferating forms—are constantly reterritorializing U.S. ambitions and objects of concern. The era of big data is also rendering privacy an increasingly outmoded concept, as both the security state and corporations store increasingly high-resolution information on individuals, allowing pattern recognition and giant data sets to constitute the grounds for new politics of recognition, isolation, criminality, and marketing.[5] The material and imaginary infrastructure of the security state thus spans spatial scales: from the body and the home, to local and regional nodes in digital data flows, to national and hemispheric forms of information gathering.

As Petraeus's career ironically demonstrates, digital surveillance is also a double-edged sword, one that can target official secrets and policy makers as much as citizens (see Coleman 2014). Indeed, the U.S. National Security Agency (2010) offers radical guidance to its employees on how to secure their own personal computers: in addition to a long list of specific user guidelines, the NSA recommends disabling Bluetooth and Wi-Fi and physically removing any camera or microphone capability from the computer. The pursuit of computer security now requires employees to dismantle both hardware and software, and maintain heightened vigilance both online and off, disciplining security operatives against an unknown interested party. But this accelerating technological revolution—despite its multifaceted secrecy and new forms of vulnerability—is also producing new forms of social commentary on the shifting values supporting everyday American life.

Here, for example, we might pause to consider why the TIA project merely at the proposal phase was an immediate scandal in 2003, capable of producing widespread social condemnation, while the revelations about actual ongoing NSA surveillance of Americans since 2013 have yet to produce a substantial change in U.S. policy (see U.S. Privacy and Civil Liberties Oversight Board 2015). Let us turn to one of the most insightful U.S. media sources for clarification; namely, the parodic Onion News Network. In early 2011, the Onion News Network ran an exposé titled "CIA's Facebook Program Dramatically Cut Agency Costs." The fake newscaster reported:

> Congress today reauthorized the funding for Facebook, the online surveillance program run by the CIA. According to Homeland Security reports, Facebook has replaced almost every other information-gathering program since it was launched in 2004. [Cutting to fake congressional testimony by a fake deputy CIA director, who reports,] "After years of secretly monitoring the public, we were astounded that so many people would willingly publish where they live, their religious and political views, an alphabetized list of all their friends, personal email addresses, phone numbers, hundreds of photos of themselves, and even status updates of what they are doing moment to moment. It is truly a dream come true for the CIA." [Cutting back to the fake news announcer, who concludes,] Much of the credit belongs to Mark Zuckerberg, who runs the program for the Agency. The agent code-named "The Overlord" was recently awarded the prestigious medal of

intelligence for his work on Facebook Program. He has called it "the single most powerful tool for population control ever created."[6]

Facebook—the most powerful tool for population control ever created. The Onion here attributes to the CIA the now widely documented surveillance work of the NSA, a joke that those at the NSA home office in Maryland would surely appreciate. But the Onion also correctly recognizes that the digital revolution in surveillance has accompanied the digital revolution in social media, interrogating both the coincidence and the implications. The use of Facebook and related forms of social media—the self-aware constitution of a digital self for known and unknown viewers—marks a fundamental shift in how privacy, publicity, and visibility are configured. The self-construction of a digital self via proliferating modes of social media can also absorb and preempt the surveillance of the security state, constituting a new sociability based on digital transparency. Shoshana Zuboff (2019) calls this revolution "surveillance capitalism" and argues that it represents as significant a challenge to humanity in the twenty-first century as petrochemical capitalism has been to the global environment in the twentieth century.

While the Onion sees the logistical advantage for the state of accessing the photos, schedules, thoughts, and relationships being digitized by the one billion people now using Facebook, it also assumes an endless state capability to collect and interpret such big data. Since 2004, both public and secret digital revolutions are remaking how selves are constituted. Key elements of the American social contract—the rules against search and seizure, and a presumption of privacy—are now increasingly jettisoned concepts, sacrificed to new social public desires, new technology, counterterror anticipation, and the pursuit of both corporate and state power.[7] The citizen-subject is thus the nexus of new modes of self-fashioning through overt (social media), corporate (online purchases), and covert (surveillance) technologies, crafting an emerging subject position that is conditioned by the dual revolutions of the counterterror state and the digital age but also seeking to escape them not through resistance, but rather by moving through them.[8] The security state, in response, is building a deep storage capacity for digital data, creating a new world in which forgetting, anonymity, and privacy are being remade by archives that store digital communication and commerce in perpetuity, allowing future governments and corporations to use the data collected today to recast individual lives (see Mayer-Schonberger 2009). In a world where four out of six people have cell phones, enabling less than five degrees of separation between digital individuals, there is an endless opportunity here for the security state to link individuals through their digital traces and anticipate and/or preempt their future actions (see, Rosenbach, Poitras, and Stark 2013). The counterterror dream of perfect planetary surveillance may still be science fiction, but that does not mean the counterterror state is not reinventing the (affective, imaginative, and material) terms of everyday life by extending its reach ever deeper into both individual lives and collective futures (see Masco 2014)—it just signals that other forces are now at work as well.[9]

Truth Telling in the Age of Ubiquitous Surveillance

I responded in the most truthful, or least untruthful manner, by saying "no."
—James Clapper, Director of National Intelligence

In a March 12, 2013, congressional hearing, Senator Ron Wyden asked Director of National Intelligence James Clapper if the NSA "gathers any type of data at all on millions of Americans." In the hearing, Clapper replied, "No sir. Not wittingly. There are cases where they could inadvertently perhaps collect, but not wittingly." But then in June 2013, the *Guardian* and the *Washington Post* started to publish one blockbuster story after another detailing the specific programs run out of the NSA to collect not just information about American citizens but its efforts to "own the internet," that is, to capture and store all digital communications globally. Based on documents leaked from Edward Snowden, who worked for NSA contractor Booz Allen Hamilton in Hawaii, the ever-emerging story of the scope of NSA surveillance caught Clapper in a classic Washington bind.[10] He is the director of sixteen intelligence agencies involved in a wide range of covert activities but on occasion needs to report to Congress in public hearings. When confronted over his March claim that the NSA did not collect information on American citizens, he made a significant contribution to American politics by saying, "I responded in the most truthful, or least untruthful manner, by saying no." He then sought to define the technical logics of "collection." He noted that the NSA, for example, captures as much digital traffic as possible not to scrutinize Americans but rather to look for "terrorist connections." However, this is a distinction without a difference at the level of practice, as the agency is now deeply invested in storing decades of information and creating ever more sophisticated data mining tools for activating those records via automated processes. Clapper's duplicitous statement illustrates that the intelligence agencies have developed an expert language that deploys common language in novel ways, creating a mode of speaking that is not accountable to democratic process while seeming to be transparent and responsible. Put differently, the "least untruthful" answer that can be spoken in a public setting to a Senate over-sight question about what might be considered the de facto elimination of American privacy and a violation of long-standing federal law is to deny that there is any such capability, or interest in such a capability, at all.

The NSA revelations of Edward Snowden, however, depict an agency that is aggressively exploiting new technologies across digital platforms and building an ever-emerging infrastructure for storing and analyzing digital traffic, as well as fighting new forms of cyber-war (see Appelbaum et al. 2015). Since the central corporate infrastructure of the internet resides in the United States—Google, Yahoo, Amazon, Facebook, Microsoft, Apple, Verizon, and AT&T, to name but a few—the boundaries established in the 1970s to try to distinguish foreign from domestic surveillance have been overturned by technological innovation (see Zuboff 2019). The NSA is now working to break all forms of commercial encryption and also to manipulate encryption standards to enable easier access to corporate platforms (see Appelbaum et al. 2014). Allied heads of state as well as U.S. citizens are finding themselves at the center of the NSA project: German chancellor Angela Merkel was revealed to be a specific target of NSA activities, leading some German officials to suggest returning to typewriters for official business to regain national security in the digital era (Poitras, Rosenbach, and Stark 2014). In light of the Snowden revelations, no less than Russian president Vladimir Putin has declared the internet "a CIA creation" (unintentionally echoing the Onion) and suggested that national security around the world now requires many separate internets, not one World Wide Web. Similarly, the collaboration between major U.S. information technology companies and the counterterror state has produced a global reappraisal of American technology, leading to efforts in Brazil to build new undersea fiber optic cable to avoid routing through U.S. infrastructures, as well as a widespread reduction in the uses of cloud computing (because its digital storage is located within the U.S. and thus subject to NSA programs under U.S. law). At the scale of everyday consumer devices, Apple, along with a host of social media companies, has responded to the Snowden revelations by updating its smartphone to new levels of encryption, promising digital security to consumers as a new marketing strategy.

The breadth and specificity of the Snowden leaks to the *Washington Post*, the *Guardian*, and the *Intercept* newspapers is to date a singular revelation in national security reporting in the United States. Since the first June 6, 2013, article in the *Washington Post*, attentive readers have learned of programs code-named PRISM (which captures information by working directly with information tech companies), Upstream (which captures data by tapping directly into fiber optic cables, digital hubs, and routers), XKEYSCORE (a program for capturing email), COTRAVELER (a program to mine the XKEYSCORE archive and find associations between specific people), BOUNDLESS INFORMANT (which captures global metadata on communications of all kinds), MYSTIC (a system to capture 100 percent of the telephone calls in a country for a thirty-day period and store them for later analysis), DISHFIRE (a program that collects 200 million text messages per day), TURBINE (a program to covertly install software on computers allowing access to video chats), and OPTIC NERVE (which captured Yahoo webcam footage to the tune of 1.8 million user accounts in a one-month period) (see figures 16.4–16.7). Other unnamed programs capture email contacts and buddy lists (over 500,000 per day), have developed tools for hacking gaming platforms (from X-Box to the popular Angry Birds program on cell phones), and designed specific programs to gain access to the major smartphones. *Der Spiegel* has also reported on an NSA program located in Texas that captures computer purchases at the shipping stage, installs software and technology allowing the NSA covert access to the machine, and then repackages the altered machine with original wrapping for normal delivery (Applebaum et al. 2013).

While the Snowden files promise future revelations about NSA activities, the trend is clear: there is a U.S. counterterror state commitment to building access into, or finding a way to exploit, the global information technology infrastructure. If you use a computer, phone, or credit card, you are likely interacting with the security state, and your records are likely to be stored for many years. The NSA, of course, is also just one of sixteen intelligence agencies, and much of what they are doing is also being done by corporations and contractors who are using metadata, consumer analytics, and data mining to create ever more specific portraits of consumers. The internet age has thus not set information free in the sense of fomenting a radically democratic public sphere as much as transformed the citizen-consumer into a radically open-ended interface for intelligence gathering across security state and corporate interests. The smartphone, in particular, is an unprecedented node for commercial and security state surveillance of individuals, creating the possibility of instant communication and commerce alongside multiple competing modes of metadata and informational capture. The platforms are also open to propaganda, strategic capture, misinformation campaigns, and active measures—key forces in the 2016 U.S. election cycle.

Before the transformation of the security state into a counterterror forma-tion in 2001, the kind of surveillance devoted to those interested in the ac-tivities of the nuclear state now seems somewhat comical. Through the post–Cold War period (1991–2001), I attended meetings across the United States on nuclear weapons issues sponsored by the Department of Energy as well as nongovernmental organizations and activist groups. It was not uncommon to have multiple screeners at the entrance, sign-in sheets asking for detailed personal information (name, residence, phone, email, sometimes citizenship, Social Security number, driver's license number). For meetings organized around dissent or to protest specific nuclear complex activities, one could expect to have plainclothes security operatives in the crowd, and others with cameras videotaping the event. I made it a practice to find the fellow with the clipboard recording the license plate of each car in attendance and also tried to track down after many meetings the voluminous handwritten notes the-atrically taken as an official register of public concern (I once found a year's worth of public comments stuffed in a closet in Los Alamos, never to be read again). The linking thread here is the theatricality of the surveillance state itself, and the highly limited space for the public to conceptually engage this state apparatus via a face-to-face encounter. But this post–Cold War world of the 1990s now seems ancient, an analog universe hopelessly outdated in the world of smartphones, Facebook, Google, and an unrestrained counterter-ror apparatus. Indeed, today there would be no need to stage a break-in to capture a laptop computer of a writer working on national security sciences and culture. That machine would already likely be a node in both corporate and security state surveillance systems, rendering one's thoughts, actions, purchases, and entertainments as data for future analysis. The state might own the internet company one uses through various techniques or hack the router in one's home directly, or it might have installed software to track keystrokes and record contacts, video-conferencing sessions, and email (see Gallagher and Greenwald 2014). Or perhaps operatives would simply remotely turn on the computer and download its contents or fly a drone overhead to hack one's network or mimic a major information company to retrieve information (see Angwin and Larson 2014). Or alternatively, opera-tives might just remotely engage the camera and microphone on the laptop and just take live notes—perhaps watching with you as you pursue your daily activities or your latest online entertainments or your work life (Greenwald 2013). This does not, of course, mean that global surveillance is perfected, or

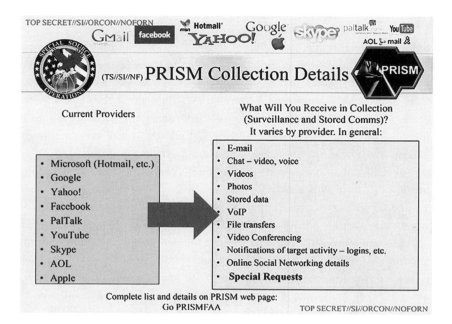

(TS//SI//NF) PRISM Collection Details

Current Providers

What Will You Receive in Collection (Surveillance and Stored Comms)?
It varies by provider. In general:

- Microsoft (Hotmail, etc.)
- Google
- Yahoo!
- Facebook
- PalTalk
- YouTube
- Skype
- AOL
- Apple

- E-mail
- Chat – video, voice
- Videos
- Photos
- Stored data
- VoIP
- File transfers
- Video Conferencing
- Notifications of target activity – logins, etc.
- Online Social Networking details
- **Special Requests**

Complete list and details on PRISM web page:
Go PRISMFAA

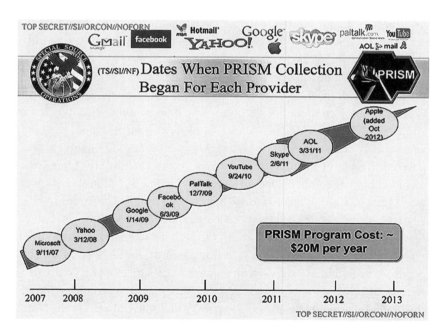

(TS//SI//NF) Dates When PRISM Collection Began For Each Provider

Microsoft 9/11/07 · Yahoo 3/12/08 · Google 1/14/09 · Facebook 6/3/09 · PalTalk 12/7/09 · YouTube 9/24/10 · Skype 2/6/11 · AOL 3/31/11 · Apple (added Oct 2012)

PRISM Program Cost: ~ $20M per year

2007 2008 2009 2010 2011 2012 2013

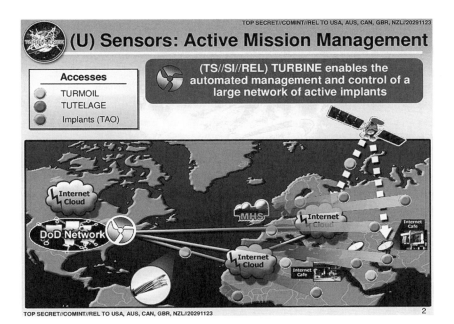

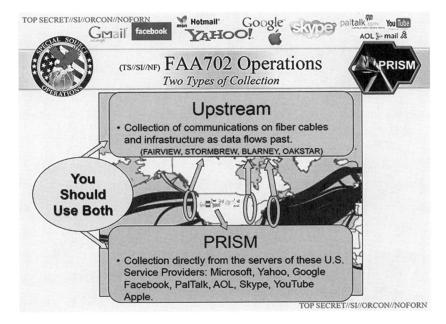

Figures 16.4–16.7. National Security Agency data collection program slides leaked by Edward Snowden.

fully automated, but it does underscore the ambitions and anticipations of an emergent counterterror state apparatus committed to preempting certain futures in a world without borders.

Thus, in this moment of counterterror and surveillance capitalism there is no longer one "file" to fetishize as the emblem of national security attention but rather an unfolding set of automated relations within a multiscalar and global archive of digital data, stored for increasing lengths of time, involving anyone that uses information technology. This set of institutions, capabilities, and attitudes is different from the Cold War–era surveillance work of agencies like the East German Stasi (who sought to intimidate populations through analog surveillance techniques; see Bruce 2010; Verdery 2014) or even the FBI (who sought to disrupt Cold War activist groups from within via embedding double agents; Weiner 2012). The NSA now desires both complete anonymity and a free hand in its total digital surveillance, striving for a full integration into global-scale communications systems and ever-evolving capacities. With an emergent internet of things and the surveillance of one's most intimate spaces, habits, and activities, the security state is transforming the spaces of everyday life within its reordering of global security space. Big data surveillance is not only longitudinally powerful in grasping a current moment of collective activity but also is stored in ever-deeper orders of time, reordering the past, present, and future in accelerating new ways. The immediate social project is not then to recover an archaic notion of privacy increasingly jettisoned by consumers, corporations, and national security agents alike. It is to see the ownership and control of data as delineating the very terms of citizenship, commerce, and insecurity in the twenty-first century.

17

THE CRISIS IN CRISIS

If you tune in to the mass-mediated frequency of crisis today, it quickly becomes overwhelming. News of infectious disease outbreaks (Ebola, antibiotic-resistant illnesses, disease outbreaks among purposefully unvaccinated children), wars in the Middle East, Africa, and Eastern Europe, new stages in the multigenerational U.S. campaigns against drugs and terror, talk of a new Cold War between the U.S. and Russia, or maybe one with China, the elimination of privacy by surveillance programs (run by both corporations and the security state), financial contagions, fears of economic collapse, new extremes in global inequality, species die-offs on an unprecedented scale, megadrought, megasnow, megacold, megaheat, proliferating toxicities and corruptions, racialized violence (state driven, terroristic, individual), stand your ground laws, ocean acidification, the near-eternal longevity of plastics, peak oil, peak water, smogocalypse in China, arms races (nuclear, biological, cyber)—the everyday reporting of crisis proliferates across subjects, spaces, and temporalities today and is an ever-amplifying media refrain.

This raises an important historical question about how and why crisis has come to be so dominant in our media cultures. On any given issue—disease, finance, war, or the environment—there are specific historical moments more violent than today. Yet the configuration of the future as an unraveling, a slide into greater and greater degrees of structural chaos across finance, war, and the environment, prevails in our mass media. In the United States, a 24/7 media universe offers up endangerment on a vast range of scales, making it so ever present as to dull consumer senses. The power of crisis to shock, and thus mobilize, has diminished due to narrative saturation, overuse, and a lack of well-articulated positive futurities to balance stories of end times. Put differently, if we were to remove crisis talk from our public speech today, what would remain? And if crisis is now an ever-present, near permanent negative "surround," as Fred Turner (2013) might put it, what has happened to a normative, non-crisis-riven everyday life, not to mention the conditions of possibility for positive futurities?

In short, there is a crisis *in* crisis today, one that I think is diagnostic of twenty-first-century American military industrial capitalism. The United States exists in a structural contradiction, one drawn from being both a democracy and an imperially inclined superpower: since the 1980s, the federal government has increasingly exchanged domestic welfare programs for mass incarceration and permanent war, rewriting the social contract in foundationally undemocratic ways.[1] The infrastructures of everyday security—employment, environmental safety, justice—are no longer the primary goals of a state that relies on warfare and markets to engineer the future. The resulting uncertainty, as well as endangerment of existing infrastructures across health, welfare, and economy, creates new forms of emerging and predictable violence that crisis talk attempts to manage.

This chapter examines American sensibilities about crisis, seeking to historicize and critique the collapsing of a more robust political sphere into the singular language of crisis. Crisis is, in the first instance, an affect-generating idiom, one that seeks to mobilize radical endangerment to foment collective attention and action. As Janet Roitman (2014, 82) writes in her extended study of the term, crisis is "an observation that produces meaning" by initiating critique within a given condition. It is thus a predominantly conservative modality, seeking to stabilize an existing structure within a radically contingent world. As social theorists as diverse as Reinhart Koselleck (1988), Susan Buck-

Morss (2000), and David Scott (2014) have also noted, crisis and utopia have structured the modernist Euro-American project of social engineering, constituting a future caught between a narrative of collapse and one of constant improvement (see also Benhabib 1986). The language of collective social improvement has all but disappeared from political debates in the U.S. over the last generation, a victim of a post–welfare state mentality and neoliberal economics. Progress is no longer tied to collective social conditions (for example, the elimination of poverty) but increasingly restricted to the boom and bust of markets and changes in consumer technology product cycles. Jonathan Crary (2013, 9) attributes the current "suspension of living" to a 24/7, always-on, media and work environment, one that foments a new kind of temporality that increasingly disallows fantasies about improved collective conditions while recruiting increasing indifference to the structural violence supporting this economy.

In the twenty-first century, information technologies offer perhaps the most immediate and available sense of radical change, a sign of how far the social engineering through state planning of the twentieth century has contracted into the market engineering of consumer desires. Technological revolution in consumer electronics is now constant, creating a new kind of psychopolitical space marked by consumer anticipations of ever-improving informational capacities and a continual transformation in the commodity form. Consider the social effects of the major communication revolutions of the past twenty years in the U.S.—the internet, social media, and the smartphone—each of which has been integrated into everyday American life with astonishing speed and ubiquity. This experience of revolution in the marketplace is, however, matched by a formal political culture that is theatrically gridlocked at the national level, unable to constitute significant policy on issues of collective endangerment across the domains of finance, war, and the environment. Moreover, policy failure in each of these domains over the past generation has not produced a radical reassessment of supporting assumptions or institutions. Even as shifting information technologies secure an experience of radical structural change in every life today, formal political processes perform being unable to imagine even minor shifts in existing logics or practices, despite financial collapse, military failure, and environmental disaster. Thus, while communication has never been easier, and information about matters of collective concern never more abundant, the media spaces crafted for always-on information systems deliver largely negative portraits of the present and future.

There is, in other words, a steady invitation in American media worlds to fear the future and to reject the power of collective agency to modulate even those systems explicitly designed by industry, finance, or the security state. This marks the arrival of a new kind of governance, one based not on eliminating fears through the protective actions of the security apparatus, but rather on the amplification of public dangers through inaction. It also produces a suicidal form of governance, one that cannot respond to long-standing collective dangers (for example, climate change) while generating new ones (such as the poisoning of the public water system in Flint, Michigan, in 2014 by emergency managers seeking cost savings). The affective circuit of the counterterror state privileges images of catastrophic future events over such everyday violences, multiplying fears of the future while allowing everyday structural insecurities to remain unaddressed (Masco 2014). Sloterdijk has suggested that the resulting psychic agitation is one important effect of a globalized economy:

> This has progressed to such an extent that those who do not make themselves continuously available for synchronous stress seem asocial. Excitability is now the foremost duty of all citizens. This is why we no longer need military service. What is required is the general theme of duty, that is to say, a readiness to play your role as a conductor of excitation for collective, opportunist psychoses. (Sloterdijk and Henrichs 2011, 82)

Excitability is a duty. This is to say that crisis talk serves a wide range of psychosocial purposes, creating across the domains of finance, war, and the environment an ever-expanding invitation to engage the future through negative affects. Thus, the American public can simultaneously know the U.S. to be an unrivaled military-economic-scientific superpower, a state with unprecedented capacities, agencies, and resources, and yet feel powerless in the face of failed U.S. military, financial, and environmental commitments. The lack of investment in infrastructure (across health, welfare, and the environment) means that everyday conditions are actually deteriorating, despite American wealth, military power, and scientific expertise. Instead of the crisis/utopia circuit that empowered the high modernist culture of the mid-twentieth century, we now have a crisis/paralysis circuit, a marker of a greatly reduced political horizon in the United States.

I am interested in this lack of political agency for those living within a hyperpower state and wish to interrogate it via a conceptual and historical assessment of the two linked existential dangers of our time: nuclear crisis and climate crisis. Existential danger makes a claim on being the ultimate form of crisis—a mode of collective endangerment that has historically worked in the era of nation-states to define the boundaries of the community and focus the responsibilities of government. To evoke an existential danger is to call on the full powers of the state and society in the name of self-preservation. In the current moment of counterterror, financial instability, and climate change, the call to existential danger no longer functions exclusively in this way. Indeed, existential dangers are now being crafted and enhanced by both state action and inaction. After nearly two decades of counterterror and hyperviolent geopolitical misrecognitions over weapons of mass destruction, the U.S. nuclear complex is committed to rebuilding the entire U.S. nuclear triad of bombers, missiles, and submarines and arming them with new nuclear weapons designs. Similarly, through new drilling technologies and a suspension of regulatory oversight, the U.S. is the world's largest energy producer— the world's number one petrochemical state—even as earth scientists detail the catastrophic planetary effects of releasing all that carbon from the ground. Thus, the existential security challenges of our time are not being met with programmatic efforts to move out of nuclear nationalism or petrochemical capitalism in the name of collective security. Rather than committing to new security and energy infrastructures, and with them generating a new kind of geopolitics (see Clark 2014), the U.S. is committing ever more deeply to the most well-known and collectively dangerous industrial activities.

In what follows, I interrogate the media politics around the signing of the 1963 Limited Test Ban Treaty (LTBT)—the first arms control agreement as well as the first environmental treaty—to consider an alternate era of crisis management. I then turn to contemporary climate science, interrogating the terms of America's current petro-state strategy. In each case, I consider how existential danger is mobilized via mass media as a collective crisis and consider the conditions of possibility for a radical reconsideration of the terms of everyday life. Put differently, the crisis *in* crisis today marks a new political modality that can experience repeated failure as well as totalizing external danger without generating the need for any structural change. Crisis, in other words, has become a counterrevolutionary force in the twenty-first century, a call to confront collective endangerment that instead increasingly articulates the very limits of the political.

The Nuclear Danger

The period between the Soviet launch of the first artificial earth satellite on October 4, 1957, and the signing of the LTBT on August 5, 1963, witnessed geopolitical and environmental crises of an astonishing range, scale, and scope: In addition to the building of the Berlin Wall, the Bay of Pigs invasion, and the Cuban Missile Crisis, the U.S. and USSR waged fierce proxy wars in Latin

America, Africa, the Middle East, and Southeast Asia. A voluntary nuclear test moratorium between the two powers in the years 1959–60 ended suddenly in 1961 with fifty-nine Soviet nuclear tests. The following year, the Soviets detonated an additional seventy-nine nuclear devices while the U.S. exploded ninety-six. Between the two weapons programs, this amounts to a nuclear detonation every other day for the calendar year of 1962 (see figure 17.1). The speed and ferocity of nuclear detonations in 1962 belies a scientific research program, becoming instead a global theater of nuclear messaging, establishing a U.S. and Soviet commitment to nuclear war. Most of these explosions were conducted in the atmosphere. After the atomic bombing of Hiroshima and Nagasaki in 1945, this makes 1962 probably the most dangerous year in the first two decades of the nuclear age. In addition to narrowly avoiding a nuclear war that would have destroyed North America, Europe, and much of Asia within a few minutes of conflict (see Rosenberg 1981; Sagan 1987), the nuclear testing programs were a substantial disaster for the global environment. Each of these nuclear tests was a planetary ecological event, one that destroyed local ecosystems and sent radioactive fallout high into the stratosphere, where it circled Earth. Aboveground nuclear explosions distributed contamination to every living being on the planet in the mid-twentieth century to a degree that is still measurable today.

The year 1962 thus stands as a superlative year of crisis in the nuclear age, involving a war fought via test programs and covert actions around the world that nearly became a planetary inferno. By 1962, it was well understood that aboveground nuclear explosions were a major environmental and public health risk. Beginning a decade earlier with the first hydrogen bomb tests in the Pacific, earth scientists began tracking radioactive fallout as a means of understanding ecological transport across atmosphere, biosphere, geology, and oceans. In 1952, the Ivy Mike detonation produced a mushroom cloud that rose to over 120,000 feet and was twenty-five miles wide (figure 17.2). U.S. earth scientists used this radioactive cloud as an experimental lens, tracking the global dispersal of strontium-90 as a means of understanding stratospheric flows, showing with a new specificity how earth, ocean, ecologies, and atmosphere interact.

The fallout produced by the Ivy Mike detonation was tracked globally by Machta, List, and Hubert (1956), one of a series of studies that followed the stratospheric transport of nuclear materials produced by atmospheric testing, offering increasingly high-resolution portraits of atmospheric contamination within an integrated biosphere. These wide-ranging studies directly challenged a national security concept that was no longer able to protect

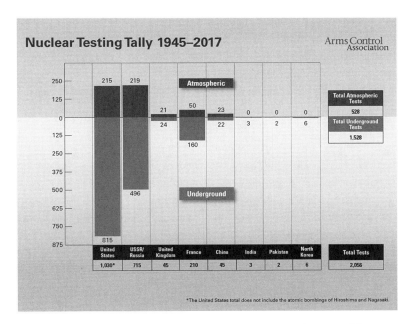

Figure 17.1. Acknowledged nuclear tests by country, 1945–2017 (courtesy of Arms Control Association, https://armscontrol.org).

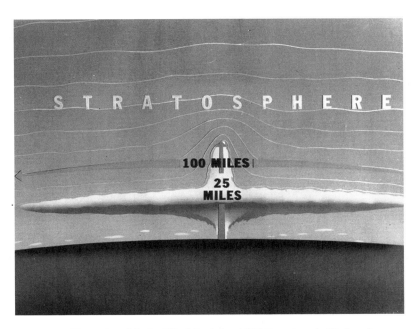

Figure 17.2. Illustration of the Ivy Mike fallout cloud (U.S. Department of Defense).

discrete territories but was instead generating, in Ulrich Beck's (2007) terms, new "risk societies" united not by location, national identity, or language, but rather by airborne environmental and health risks increasingly shown to be global flows (see Fowler 1960a).

Radioactive fallout studies demonstrated that a new kind of species-level injury was emerging on top of the imminent threat of nuclear war; namely, that of an industrially transformed environment. Tracking the radioactive signatures of nuclear tests allowed scientists to map the biosphere as an integrated ecological space, one in which toxicity became a flow that connected geologies, oceans, organisms, and atmospheres in specific ways. Fallout studies required many new surveillance systems and generated major data sets for the emerging earth sciences, now formally pursued with the dual goal of understanding nuclear environmental effects and tracking Soviet nuclear progress. The early Cold War produced a massive investment in air, ocean, geology, the ice caps, and, increasingly, outer space research. The U.S. nuclear project sought to militarize nature for national advantage (see Fleming 2010; Hamblin 2013) but also to understand planetary space in a new way. The resulting data sets established, as Paul Edwards (2010) has shown in detail, a new kind of global information infrastructure, allowing constantly improving portraits of earth systems to be possible. Contemporary understandings of climate change are based on the foundational scientific and big-data work of this early Cold War period. In this way, the nuclear state participated in a larger militarization of the environment in the twentieth century (see Sloterdijk 2009), one that enabled new forms of ecological thinking, including a scalar multidisciplinary commitment to connecting locality with regional and global technological infrastructures and ultimately planetary-scale processes.

By 1960 earth scientists could already document the stratospheric height of fallout, connect it to specific nuclear detonations, and show how U.S. and Soviet nuclear detonations were merging the Global North and Global South as irradiated space (see figure 17.3). The development of U.S. national security in the form of the hydrogen bomb was thus linked to the production of (1) an entirely new global ecological danger, and (2) a new technoscientific and environmental investment in understanding ecological transport in an integrated environmental space, leading to revolutions in biomedicine, computing, geology, oceanography, and atmospheric sciences.[2] The nuclear danger created research programs that continue to this day, including biomedical studies of exposed populations, from Hiroshima and Nagasaki to the Marshall Islands to the vast population of workers within the nuclear complex itself.[3] These forms of internal and external sacrifice—operating

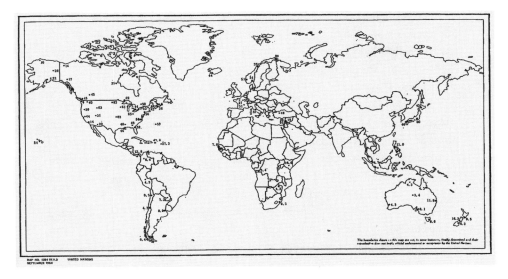

Figure 17.3. Global strontium-90 distribution from atmospheric nuclear fallout as measured in soil samples in 1963 (United Nations Scientific Committee on the Effects of Atomic Radiation).

on both fast and slow scales of violence (Nixon 2011)—became embedded within Cold War national security practices, raising basic questions about what kind of a human population was being created via nuclear detonations.[4]

By 1962 the U.S. media space was filled with contradictory visions of the nuclear present and future, offering up a world of imminent danger across territories and ecologies in manner that is difficult to appreciate today. As the Cold War civil defense programs asked Americans to practice the destruction of the nation-state in regular drills, earth scientists detailed the dangers to the human genetic pool posed by atmospheric nuclear explosions. Visions of an end of the nation-state in the flash of nuclear war were thus matched in newspaper, radio, and television accounts by portraits of a human species being transformed by the long-term genetic damage of fallout from the test programs. Consider for a moment the *New York Times* for November 25, 1961: alongside a front-page obituary for one of the world's richest men, Axel Wenner-Gren, the philanthropist that created the Viking Fund (the future Wenner-Gren Foundation for Anthropological Research), and an article on a United Nations vote to ban the use of nuclear weapons and to make Africa a nuclear-free zone, was a detailed report on the Kennedy administration's plan to "dissolve the crisis atmosphere" over atomic civil defense in the U.S. by committing to a large-scale program to build community fallout shelters across the country. This discussion of the national panic over nuclear civil defense was followed on page A-2 by "Babies Surveyed for Strontium 90," an account of a St. Louis–based research program to collect baby teeth to measure the effects of fallout on the human body (Sullivan 1961). Publicized by ecologist Barry Commoner (see Egan 2007), this study of strontium-90 in baby teeth continued through 1970. It projected every American family as potential casualties of nuclear testing, even as the fallout shelter program sought to protect the population at large by moving it underground. Alongside other fallout studies, the baby teeth program documented accumulating strontium-90 in American infants, a startling new metric of industrial contamination. Indeed, it is difficult to imagine today in our so-called age of terror the nuclear crises of this early Cold War moment, which asked Americans to move their lives underground while also testing their children's bodies for new forms of injury created by the U.S. national security apparatus in the name of collective defense. As a result, many new forms of activism arose at this moment, linking issues of war and peace and environmental protection. Nuclear fear realigned race, class, and gender politics in the United States to foment a large-scale social justice movement.

The fraught discussions of this doubled planetary danger—nuclear war and radioactive fallout—in the public sphere enabled an unprecedented treaty between the United States, United Kingdom, and Soviet Union. The LTBT eliminated nuclear testing in the atmosphere, outer space, and under water between those nuclear powers. It was the first act in a forty-year sequence of efforts to manage the global nuclear danger via diplomacy and treaties. It also stands as the first global environmental protection treaty. In his radio address to the nation announcing the treaty, President John F. Kennedy (1963) spelled out the stakes of the moment:

> A war today or tomorrow, if it led to nuclear war, would not be like any war in history. A full-scale nuclear exchange, lasting less than 60 minutes, with the weapons now in existence, could wipe out more than 300 million Americans, Europeans, and Russians, as well as untold numbers elsewhere. And the survivors, as Chairman Khrushchev warned the Communist Chinese, "the survivors would envy the dead." For they would inherit a world so devastated by explosions and poison and fire that today we cannot even conceive of its horrors. So let us try to turn the world away from war. Let us make the most of this opportunity, and every opportunity, to reduce tension, to slow down the perilous nuclear arms race, and to check the world's slide toward final annihilation.

Second, this treaty can be a step towards freeing the world from the fears and dangers of radioactive fallout. Our own atmospheric tests last year were conducted under conditions which restricted such fallout to an absolute minimum. But over the years the number and the yield of weapons tested have rapidly increased and so have the radioactive hazards from such testing. Continued unrestricted testing by the nuclear powers, joined in time by other nations which may be less adept in limiting pollution, will increasingly contaminate the air that all of us must breathe.

Even then, the number of children and grandchildren with cancer in their bones, with leukemia in their blood, or with poison in their lungs might seem statistically small to some, in comparison with natural health hazards. But this is not a natural health hazard—and it is not a statistical issue. The loss of even one human life, or the malformation of even one baby—who may be born long after we are gone—should be of concern to us all. Our children and grandchildren are not merely statistics toward which we can be indifferent.

The air that all of us must breathe. The crisis evoked here is both of the minute and also cast into untold future generations, linking the project of nuclear deterrence to multigenerational health matters in a new way. For Kennedy, the LTBT was primarily an environmental treaty. It also was a public relations project in light of the Cuban Missile Crisis and the well-publicized scientific and environmental activist campaigns against atmospheric nuclear testing. But even with this highly detailed rendering of the violence of nuclear war, and a scientific consensus about the cumulative danger to the human genome and global environment from radioactive fallout, the LTBT did not stop the arms race or eliminate the capacity for nuclear war. Indeed, the move to underground testing consolidated the experimental regimes in the U.S. and Soviet Union, allowing another forty years of active testing. While the atmospheric fallout danger was largely eliminated from the U.S.-USSR arms race, the vast majority of nuclear weapons on planet Earth were built after the LTBT. So in this Cold War moment of existential crisis, the nuclear danger was managed rather than removed, stabilized rather than resolved, allowing the global infrastructure of nuclear war to remain firmly in place to this day. Nonetheless, the LTBT importantly made both public health and the environment national security matters. By twenty-first-century standards, the scope of the LTBT, and its important role in establishing a role for treaties and international law in managing insecurity in the global environment, remains a vital achievement, one that informs every hope and ambition for an international agreement on climate change today.

Climate Danger

In October 2018, the Intergovernmental Panel on Climate Change issued the latest in its startling series of reports on how the cumulative force of industrially generated greenhouse gases are changing planetary conditions, creating an entirely new scale of anticipated environmental crisis (IPCC 2018). Responding to the request of island nations fearing ocean rise from melting ice caps, the IPCC studied the effect of merely a 1.5°C rise in global temperatures above preindustrial levels. Previous studies assumed a 2°C baseline for preventing radical environmental consequences and sought to build a global commitment to staying below that threshold. The 2018 IPCC report was shocking in its portrayal of a world at only 1.5°C temperature rise. Atoll island nations become uninhabitable due to rising oceans, heavy waves, and increasing aridity. The Arctic Ocean has ice-free summers, while heavy rains pound much of the Global North as extreme heat waves roast much of the Global South. The IPCC anticipates increasing food and water scarcity, concentrated particularly in the poorest regions of the world, as well as more disease, malnutrition, and stress levels everywhere. Escalating species loss due to global warming includes the near-elimination of coral reefs and systemic reduction in the amount of life in the oceans. Intensifying poverty, punctuated by extreme weather events (storms, drought, heat waves, and flooding) punctuates life on a planet that is producing less food and has decreasing biodiversity across all ecosystems. Multimeter sea level rise will submerge coastal cities on all continents by the end of the century, creating huge populations of displaced people and vast strains on all existing infrastructures. The IPCC argues that the quality of life at 1.5°C versus 2°C is much, much better but still a galactic set of fast and slow violences playing out in multiple registers simultaneously, with different intensities, literally everywhere.

More than that, these effects are not in a distant future but start to arrive in full force in 2030, a radical shift in the timing of climate disruption. The IPCC concludes that massive shifts are needed in both industrial production and global consumption to slow or reduce these outcomes. The end of coal consumption and radical increases in renewable energy are a start. But even with all existing climate change mitigation ideas implemented on a global scale, staying under a 1.5°C level would also involve physically removing carbon from the atmosphere. Thus, the report suggests that a massive refor-

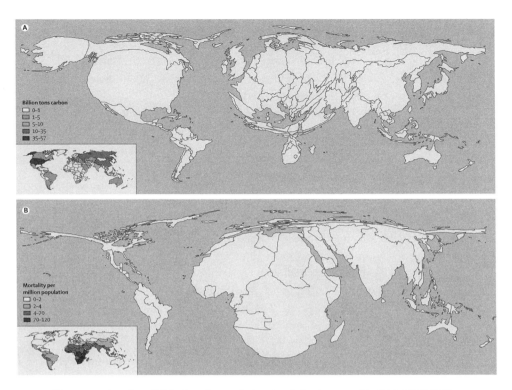

Figure 17.4. Location of historic carbon emissions in relation to proportional negative health consequences of global warming (reprinted from Costello et al. 2009; with permission of Elsevier).

estation project combined with the implication of not-yet-existing carbon capture and storage technologies is needed to keep the world in its already violent condition. The most profound aspect of the report, however, is the way that global warming amplifies all existing inequalities on planet Earth.

In short, global warming reveals and requires a fundamentally new kind of geopolitics, one that can operate both in and above the nation-state level. Consider figure 17.4, an illustration from *The Lancet* documenting the proportion of carbon emissions by country in the top frame in relation to the related health effects from climate change in the bottom frame (Costello et al. 2009). This chart documents an emerging relationship between the Global North and Global South, one played out in the conversion of carbon emissions from the North into new levels of illness in the South. This global circulation requires that one think on a planetary scale while also keeping in focus the differential effects of anthropogenic practices across nation-states and regions. While the Global North was first to industrialize and thus has put in motion the current climatic changes, the race to create consumer middle classes in the Global South promises to amplify these forms of violence for all organisms on Earth (see Parenti 2011).

Anthropogenic climate disruption undoes many of the key logics of modernization as well as assumptions about technoscientific progress. Consider the everydayness of the metrics earth scientists use to document a startling shift in consumption patterns after World War II. Steffen et al. (2011, 742) have graphed human population growth in relation to global GDP, the damming of rivers, water use, fertilizer consumption, urbanization, paper consumption, cars, telephones, tourism, and McDonald's restaurants and found a shocking parallel process: starting around 1950, each of these metrics rise exponentially, mirroring one another in an explosive rate of growth that matches fundamental changes in earth systems, including rising carbon dioxide levels, flooding, temperature change, reduction in fish stocks, forest loss, and species extinctions, among other factors. These metrics confirm a major inflection point beginning around 1950 across consumption patterns, atmospheric chemistry, temperature, and biodiversity loss. Everyday consumption patterns unremarkable in their individual singularity are revealed here to be cumulatively destructive in their collective totality. This makes the basic requirements for a middle-class consumer life (including food, transportation, heating, clothing, tourism) fundamentally dangerous to the future stability of the climate if they remain embedded in the current petrochemical-based global economy. The virtues of modernization, globalization, and technological revolution have thus been turned upside down by global warming: rather than extending equality, security, and comfort, the petrochemical economy has become a slow-moving and highly negative form of geoengineering.

The conceptual implications as well as material consequences of this great acceleration are profound. First, it means that everyday American consumption has been a planetary force since the mid-twentieth century, indexing the U.S. position as top historical contributor to carbon emissions. Second, it makes the American middle-class consumer economy an unprecedented force of violence in the world, one in which planned obsolescence, plastics, and petrochemical innovation have raised standards of living in North America at the expense of the collective environment as well as public health in the Global South. Third, it makes climate crisis and nuclear crisis largely coterminous periods, raising important questions about perceptions of danger, the temporality of crisis itself, and the proper definition of "security."

Today, the mid-twentieth century stands as the period in which people become an existential threat to themselves in two technologically mediated fashions: first via the atomic bomb, and second via the cumulative force of a petrochemical-based consumer economy. These dual problems are embedded within a unique military-industrial economy in the United States and operate on different temporal scales: since 1950, there has literally been a crisis *inside* crisis structuring American modernity, one that is only beginning to be acknowledged in mass media.

As a response to the oil crisis of the mid-1970s, President Jimmy Carter ordered the U.S. national laboratories historically devoted to national security science and the development of nuclear weapons to convert to renewable energy research. By the end of his presidency in 1980, the U.S. national laboratory system was spending over 50 percent of its funds on alternative energy research, promising Manhattan Projects across the renewable energy sector in the coming years. Carter also symbolically installed solar panels on the White House to demonstrate his commitment to finding a way out of a petrochemical-based energy economy. On arriving in the White House in 1981, President Ronald Reagan ordered the solar panels to be removed immediately and then pursued one of the largest military buildups in American history, redirecting the national laboratories to resume the nuclear arms race as their primary concern. The environment and public health were explicitly delinked from national security policy in the Reagan era, allowing both unrestrained militarism and petrochemical extraction to structure American life well into the War on Terror.

Reagan was the first fully committed neoliberal, the first president to break the Cold War logic of balancing large defense budgets with welfare state programs, the first to entrust the market with social engineering. He entertained the thought of winnable nuclear wars and sought ultimately to end the arms race, not through disarmament, but rather by installing a space-based shield against ballistic missiles. Known as the Strategic Defense Initiative, variants of this program remain active to this day, although it has not produced a reliable defense technology despite hundreds of billions in investment since 1983 (Schwartz 2012). Thus, at a key structural moment in negotiating the dual nuclear and energy emergencies, the U.S. moved from a Manhattan Project–type commitment to renewable energy research to a still fantastical quest for missile defense (one that sought to keep U.S. nuclear weapons in place while eliminating the nuclear danger posed by Soviets arsenals). Imagine what an extra thirty years of dedicated research on renewable energy through the extensive national laboratory system, or a redirecting of military budgets to domestic infrastructures during these decades, might have contributed to mitigating the current climate crisis. Here, our contemporary crisis is revealed to be the outcome of explicit policies and economic priorities, not an infrastructure in collapse, but a set of values and choices that have produced multigenerational negative outcomes. The neoliberal experiment in the privatization of infrastructures and the embrace of market-based futures here makes planning for deep-time horizons increasingly impossible at precisely the moment when existential dangers require long-term plans of collective action.

This raises the difficult question of how ideological commitments inform understandings in the United States and the way that crisis talk can work to maintain a status quo. Naomi Oreskes and Erik M. Conway (2010) have examined the techniques certain industries have used to prevent action on environmental and health matters, documenting a variety of media tactics designed to confuse the public over the scientific standing of a collective problem (see also Farrell 2016). The use of deception to defer regulation and maximize profits is often supported by more official acts as well. In 2014, the IPCC (2014) as well as the U.S. Climate Assessment (Melillo, Richmond, and Yohe 2014) released major reports detailing a future of unprecedented ecological instability. In response, the U.S. House of Representatives passed a bill prohibiting the Department of Defense from using any funds to respond to the wide range of security programs detailed in the reports (Koronowski 2014). What is at stake here is nothing less than the definition of security and the role of government in addressing the vulnerabilities, forms of violence, and uncertainties of a radically changing climate. One legacy of seventy-five years of nuclear nationalism in the U.S. is the American tendency to believe that existential dangers can be deterred endlessly. But there are important material and temporal differences informing state-to-state confrontations mediated by nuclear weapons and the cumulative force of industrial carbon emissions across earth systems. Competing nation-states can achieve stability under a logic of mutual assured destruction, while global warming is a set of physical processes only gaining momentum across decades and centuries and that work on a planetary scale. The immediacy of the global nuclear emergency and the longevity of the climate disruption are thus nested within one another (and have been since the mid-twentieth century), making the project of security at once one of protection, perception, and action—all terms that are in question in our current crisis in crisis moment.

Conclusion

The link between nuclear crisis and climate crisis is industrial agency: both of these existential dangers have been incrementally built over generations of labor in the pursuit of security. The nuclear complex is explicit in its goals, mobilizing the fear of mass destruction as the basis for U.S. security in a world of competing nation-states. A changing climate is the collective effect of human industrial activity, an accumulation of a vast set of petrochemical practices dispersed across regions that have made the global economy over time. These emergencies are thus infrastructural achievements of an American modernity, modes of endangerment that are the unwanted effects of modern military and industrial systems. Following Roitman's (2014, 94) suggestion that crisis constitutes a "blind spot" that restricts narrative explanations as well as limiting the kind of actions that can be taken, we could interrogate here how crisis states have become lived infrastructures, linking imaginations, affects, and institutions in a kind of total social formation. The crisis in crisis from this point of view is the radical presentism of crisis talk, the focus on stabilizing a present condition rather than engaging the multiple temporalities at stake in a world of interlocking technological, financial, military, and ecological systems. As Jean-Luc Nancy argues in *After Fukushima*: "Fukushima is a powerfully exemplary event because it shows the close and brutal connections between a seismic quake, a dense population, and a nuclear installation (under inadequate management). It is also exemplary of a node of complex relationships between public power and private management of the installation, not to mention all the other chains of correlation that extend out from that starting point" (2015, 30). Put differently, there are no natural disasters any more, as the imbrication of technology, economy, and nature creates ever-emerging conditions for catastrophe, making crisis seem a permanent condition when it is in fact the effect of financial, technological, militaristic, and political processes interacting with earth systems.

Crisis talk today seeks to stabilize an institution, practice, or reality rather than interrogating the historical conditions of possibility for that endangerment to occur. In our moment, crisis blocks thought by evoking the need for an emergency response to the potential loss of a status quo, emphasizing urgency and restoration over a review of first principles and historical ontologies. In an era of complex interlocking systems of finance, technology, militarism, and ecology, unanticipated effects are inevitable and often cascading processes. In light of a post–welfare state attitude of crisis management, one that does not protect citizens but rather seeks to restore the conditions from which crisis emerged, there is much attention today to precarity as the very condition for living. Precarity and resilience are the twin logics of a neoliberal order that abandons populations in pursuit of profit and then seeks to naturalize those abandonments as the only possible course of action (see Evans and Reid 2014). Put directly, crisis talk without a commitment to revolution becomes counterrevolutionary.

With this in mind, how can we interrogate the blind spots informing nuclear crisis and climate crisis today? Despite the end of the Cold War, and the widespread politicization of weapons of mass destruction under the terms of the War on Terror (Masco 2014), the U.S. Department of Energy (2018) is currently planning to rebuild the U.S. nuclear complex over the next thirty years under the banner of modernization. This plan involves the first entirely new weapons designs since the 1980s, part of a strategic effort to create a nuclear arsenal and production complex that can last through the twenty-first century. These weapon systems will be less complicated mechanically and more robust than the Cold War designs in the current arsenal (which have been painstaking maintained part by part now for over two decades). They will also employ a new generation of weapons scientists through midcentury. These new warheads will not have to be detonated, as did all prior weapons systems, before being deployed into U.S. military arsenals thanks to the last twenty years of nuclear weapons research involving component testing, supercomputing, and simulations (see Masco 2006). The promise of the virtual weapons laboratory now points to a permanent nuclear production capacity in the U.S., one that can maintain a nuclear test ban while also introducing new and improved nuclear weapons. As a DOE programmatic report to Congress declares, "By 2038, a new generation of weapons designers, code developers, experimentalists, and design and production engineers must demonstrate an understanding of nuclear weapons functionality using more predictive and more precisely calibrated computer-aided design and assessment tools than are possible today. High-fidelity experimental capabilities will produce quantitative data that preclude resumption of underground nuclear testing" (2013, 1–6). This commitment to building new nuclear weapons should place the recent U.S. wars over weapons of mass destruction—both real and imagined—in a new light.

In the twenty-first century, the role of treaties in managing nuclear proliferation is also breaking down, an intentional dismantling of one of the key peaceful mechanisms for defusing global conflict. Both the George W. Bush and Donald J. Trump administrations have committed to undoing decades of international nuclear policy by removing the United States from nuclear treaties, including the 1972 Anti-Ballistic Missile Treaty (withdrawn in 2002)

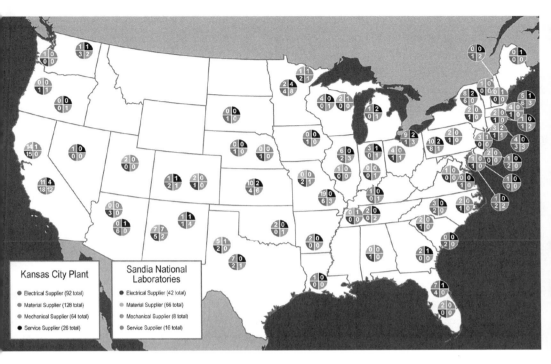

Figure 17.5. Map of current U.S. nuclear weapons production infrastructure (from U.S. Department of Energy 2013).

and the 1987 Intermediate-Range Nuclear Forces Treaty (withdrawn in 2019), while allowing the 2010 Strategic Arms Reduction Treaty to lapse in 2021.

Indeed, even Obama-administration calls for a nuclear-free world were also linked to a multitrillion-dollar commitment over the coming decades in a new U.S. nuclear complex (Wolfsthal, Lewis, and Quint 2014). The nuclear arsenal is being redesigned for a deep future and is gaining new capacities for nuclear war fighting (including warheads, missiles, and lower-yield weapons that are designed for field use, not deterrence; see U.S. Department of Energy 2018). This makes U.S. policy, after seventy-five years of nuclear nationalism and existential danger, a paradoxical program of promising global nuclear disarmament through rebuilding a state-of-the-art U.S. nuclear production complex (see figure 17.5), including the production of entirely new classes of nuclear weapons (see figure 17.6). The crisis in crisis here is the automated renewal of an infrastructure that will necessarily encourage current and future nuclear powers to pursue their own nuclear programs and undercut the collective goal of creating a world incapable of nuclear war. This program also reinvigorates nuclear fear as the coordinating logic of American geopolitics. The DOE National Nuclear Security Administration (NNSA) has turned aging nuclear weapons and experts into a crisis requiring immediate action rather than interrogating and building a new collective security for a post–Cold War, post–War on Terror world. Alongside a new generation of nuclear experts and weapons, future nuclear emergencies are being built into these programs. The U.S. nuclear production complex is approaching a moment unconstrained by arms control treaties for the first time in a half century with a vast agenda for new technologies, creating the terms of an entirely new kind of arms race in the twenty-first century.[5]

The governance of a warming planet has also been thoroughly politicized in the United States, a victim of national security politics (see Masco 2010) and petrochemical industry propaganda (see Oreskes and Conway 2010). Not coincidentally, the George W. Bush administration loosened regulatory rules for domestic shale oil and gas extraction in 2005 (exempting it from the Clean Air Act, the Clean Water Act, and the Safe Drinking Water Act), which, in combination with technological breakthroughs in drilling technology, opened up several large domestic shale formations for immediate exploitation. The Deepwater Horizon oil spill (2010) in the Gulf—alongside Hurricane Katrina (2005), the Fukushima Daiichi nuclear meltdown (2011), and superstorm Sandy (2012)—demonstrated the vulnerability of complex natural-technological-social systems and the near impossibility of environmental remediation. The boom in hydraulic fracturing has allowed the United States to increase its oil production massively even as climate scientists describe in ever-greater detail the collective environmental costs of such extraction for ice caps, atmospheric chemistry, climate, and public health. In its article "The Economics of Shale Oil," the *Economist* (2014) reveals that the U.S. moved from producing 600,000 barrels a day in 2008 to 3.5 million a day in 2014 because of shale oil extraction (see figure 17.7). The *Economist* focuses on the shifting geopolitics of renewed American oil power but does not mention the consequences for the global environment of abundant, inexpensive oil. As of 2020, the U.S. became the world's leading oil producer—the number one petro-state—at precisely the moment when the damage of such an achievement has been scientifically documented across the earth sciences.

Since 2005, a vast new infrastructure of wells, pipes, and ponds, as well as truck and train lines carrying oil and natural gas has been built to exploit shale formations from Texas to North Dakota to Pennsylvania. In addition to greenhouse gas emissions, these infrastructures require vast amounts of water, create waste ponds, and also leak, raising important questions about the environmental safety of these areas over the projected life of each well and into the future. New York State banned hydraulic fracturing because of the long list of unknown effects on water, air, and public health (New York Department of Health 2014), while in Texas and North Dakota there are boom-and-bust towns devoted entirely to the enterprise, and vast land-scapes now covered with industrial infrastructures that produce both energy and radically uncertain environmental futures.[6]

The deregulation of hydraulic fracturing has made petrochemical energy inexpensive and abundant by historical standards at precisely the moment when it would be most socially and environmentally sound to make it ever more expensive. If the neoliberal logics of market determinism were good at engineering a sustainable collective future, the U.S. would not be embracing shale with such unrestrained enthusiasm. The ever-shorter profit cycle of corporate review, in other words, is diametrically opposed to the long-term investments in renewable energy, installing the perfect terms for ongoing environmental and health crises as far into the future as anyone can imagine. Thus, one aspect of the crisis in crisis today is a notion of profit that has been so narrowly defined that a loss of the collective environment is easier to imagine than a shift in the nature of petrochemical capitalism.

Instead of reenergizing a collective imaginary that can engage alternative modes of living and apply resources and agency to collective problems, governance today recommits to exactly those existentially dangerous projects that should be formally disavowed for the public good: nuclear weapons and oil. This creates a public feeling of permanent crisis as well as increasing vulnerabilities across a range of domestic and global issues. One perverse effect of this twenty-first-century circuit is that it encourages social theorists to focus narrowly on the endless modes of precarity that are emerging rather than articulating the alternative futures that are needed, reinforcing a generational gestalt of political gridlock and decline in the United States. It is vitally important to understand how cumulative and asymmetrically distributed industrial toxins (from carbon to plastic to nuclear materials) affect communities and individual bodies, and to articulate the ways that planetary-scale fallouts are now differentially remaking local conditions. The age of neoliberal calculation is one that naturalizes the abandonment of populations that are not immediately useful to the quarterly bottom line and renders invisible those many others affected remotely by financial, military, or industrial policies (see Lorey 2015). It is also important to interrogate the affective recruitments to existential crisis and the political work such recruitments do in

Figure 17.6. Chart of U.S. nuclear weapons production to 2045 including nuclear cruise missiles, low-yield submarine launch missiles, and the first entirely new warheads since the 1980s.

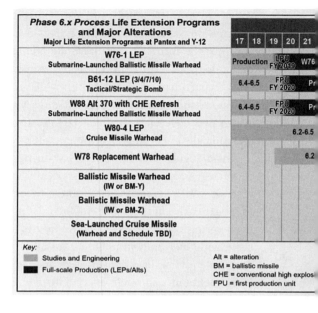

Phase 6.x Process Life Extension Programs and Major Alterations					
Major Life Extension Programs at Pantex and Y-12	17	18	19	20	21
W76-1 LEP Submarine-Launched Ballistic Missile Warhead	Production		LPU FY 2019		W76
B61-12 LEP (3/4/7/10) Tactical/Strategic Bomb	6.4-6.5		FPU FY 2020		Pr
W88 Alt 370 with CHE Refresh Submarine-Launched Ballistic Missile Warhead	6.4-6.5		FPU FY 2020		Pr
W80-4 LEP Cruise Missile Warhead					6.2-6.5
W78 Replacement Warhead					6.2
Ballistic Missile Warhead (IW or BM-Y)					
Ballistic Missile Warhead (IW or BM-Z)					
Sea-Launched Cruise Missile (Warhead and Schedule TBD)					

Key:

Studies and Engineering   Alt = alteration

Full-scale Production (LEPs/Alts)   BM = ballistic missile

CHE = conventional high explosi

FPU = first production unit

Figure 17.7. Location of U.S. shale fields and extraction rates (from *Economist* 2014).

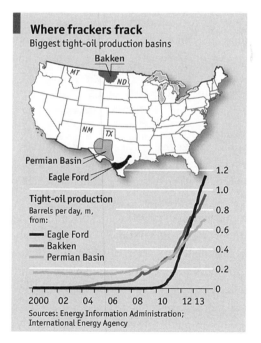

Where frackers frack

Biggest tight-oil production basins

Bakken

Permian Basin

Eagle Ford

Tight-oil production

Barrels per day, m, from:

— Eagle Ford
— Bakken
— Permian Basin

Sources: Energy Information Administration; International Energy Agency

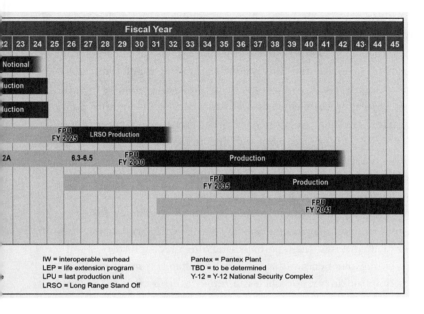

Fiscal Year																								
22	23	24	25	26	27	28	29	30	31	32	33	34	35	36	37	38	39	40	41	42	43	44	45

Notional

luction

luction

FPU FY 2025   LRSO Production

2A   6.3-6.5   FPU FY 2030   Production

FPU FY 2035   Production

FPU FY 2041

IW = interoperable warhead
LEP = life extension program
LPU = last production unit
LRSO = Long Range Stand Off

Pantex = Pantex Plant
TBD = to be determined
Y-12 = Y-12 National Security Complex

supporting existing political structures (Masco 2014). However, it is equally important to recover the capacity to generate positive futurities—what, following Lauren Berlant (2011) we might call the not-yet-cruel optimisms—that can affectively charge collective action, particularly on those issues (like nuclear danger and climate danger) that have been constructed by generations of human agency, and thus are immediately available to reform.

At the end of World War II, the U.S. embraced a new kind of technological utopianism, believing that science would solve the problems of health, welfare, and security. Designing the future for both security and prosperity was the role of the state, allowing significant investments in education, welfare state systems, and the establishment of a variety of environmental protection laws. Indeed, this mid-twentieth-century period of crisis is the moment when many of the key infrastructures and generational investments in education and environmental protections were established that inform the world today. Thus, the most dangerous moment in American history was from this point of view also one of the most productive, creating important commitments to civil rights, education, and the environment while establishing the precedents for international law and treaties to manage existential dangers.

Since the 1980s neoliberal turn in the United States, militarism has remained the project of the state, but the collective future has been assigned to the marketplace, which elevates short-term profitability above all other concerns. What happened to the once-vibrant social debate about alternative futures and the commitment to making long-term investments in improving the terms of collective life? The force of global capital has absorbed the power of crisis talk to shock, and thus mobilize, requiring a different call to action. The crisis in crisis today is the inability for American subjects to both witness the accumulating damage of this system and imagine another politics. A fundamental challenge today is that the key existential dangers of the twenty-first century—nuclear weapons and climate disruption—operate on different scales, creating friction between the global and the planetary while demanding different kinds of governance to deal with accruing fallout. Since we do not yet have planetary-scale institutions that can govern these collective problems, it is easy to focus on the emerging and amplifying forms of precarity. Instead of a more aggressive media space devoted to detailing the current and projected crises, then, perhaps what our specific historical moment requires is an explicit commitment—a critical theory commitment—to generating the nonutopian but nonetheless positive futurities that can reactivate the world-making powers of society.

In July 1945, just as Manhattan Project scientists were completing a proof-of-concept test of the atomic bomb in the New Mexican desert, and as U.S. military leaders projected the imminent conclusion of World War II across multiple front lines of the conflict, Vannevar Bush (1945) asked in a provocative article in *The Atlantic*, "What are the scientists to do next?" Bush was a former dean of engineering at MIT, an acting administrator of the twin wartime revolutions of radar and the atomic bomb, a founder of Raytheon (the future Cold War military industrial powerhouse), and was soon to be the lead advocate for a national research foundation to support basic research in the United States, what became the National Science Foundation (see Nyce and Kahn 1991). Acknowledging that "it has been a war in which all have had a part," Bush contemplates what should come after a total mobilization of society (involving military, industry, science, journalism, politics, and civilians) against a global enemy, wondering aloud: what happens to all that expertise, all that social energy, once the war is over? His radical answer, of course, was to suggest that U.S. institutions simply stay mobilized, permanently. Bush argued that the U.S. could shift from winning a war to winning the future by embracing technological engineering for the good of both commerce and security. Thus, before the atomic bombings of Hiroshima and Nagasaki pushed the Japanese leadership toward surrender, Bush was already thinking of the next act for the fledgling U.S. military-industrial economy, of how the extraordinary productivity of a new kind of technoscientific war machine could be extended into a postwar future.

In a fascinating move, Bush focuses his "As We May Think" article on information technologies, and specifically on the problems of archiving and retrieving knowledge as it proliferates across scientific fields. He focuses on emerging new modes of image making (television, photography, film) and imagines future calculating machines that are eerily prescient of the coming world of personal computers, hypertext communications, and digitization. Bush considers information overload as a barrier to social progress and contemplates how to actualize the full potential of knowledge production across the sciences and professions in real time, in perpetuity. Widely remembered today as a premonition of the coming information economy, his essay could also be read as a road map for a permanent military-scientific mobilization as a basic means of engineering the American future. For example, it is crucial to know that much of the technological innovation in photography during the 1950s would come from military-scientific efforts to photograph the exploding atomic bomb, a process that revolutionized high-speed photography and color and specialty film stocks, and ultimately pioneered high-definition digital imaging. Similarly, our contemporary world of information technologies was founded on the Cold War investment in digital computing by the Defense Department, which invented networked digital communication—the foundation for today's internet—as a means of solving the problem of maintaining command and control during nuclear war. Moreover, work on the atomic bomb continues to push the frontier of supercomputing to this day—with many of the fastest computers in the world residing at U.S. national weapons laboratories, which today model both nuclear weapons and the planetary climate. Thus, while Bush speculates about the potential revolutions for law, medicine, chemistry, and history of instantly available archives of expert knowledge—as he puts it, "science may implement the ways in which man produces, stores, and consults the record of the race"—he also approaches science itself as an instrumental state project, a necessary means of crafting the future through achieving ever-greater technical capacities across the range of expert practices. In this way, science as instrumental reason is implicitly nationalized in Bush's presentation, a game played for American advantage in the dangerous world of competing corporations and nation-states.

Thus, in addition to the specific revolutions in information technologies he forecasts in the summer of 1945, Bush offers a more structural—and profound—articulation of the emerging U.S. social relationship to knowledge production itself. Knowledge has meaning in the first instance in his account as a form of military power, making war the ideal form, as well as the unending motivator, for science and technology. We can imagine that his managerial overview of spectacular wartime achievements—radar and the atomic bomb—cemented this concept of a permanent technological revolution, of continual Manhattan Projects. For Bush anticipated here the language of the Department of Defense at the end of the Cold War (which declared a "revolution in military affairs" to prevent any future rivals from arising) or the George W. Bush administration's War on Terror, which formally cast the future itself as object of anticipatory defense through unending technological revolution and military action. Vannevar Bush concludes his famous essay by stating:

> The applications of science have built man a well-supplied house and are teaching him to live healthily therein. They have enabled him to throw masses of people against one another with cruel weapons. They may yet allow him truly to encompass the great record and to grow in the wisdom of race experience. He may perish in conflict before he learns to wield that record for his true good. Yet, in the application of science to the needs and desires of man, it would seem to be a singularly unfortunate state at which to terminate the process, or to lose hope as to the outcome.

Science is a race to the future. But what are these needs and desires "of the race" in a world of real and imaginary existential threats? Who decides which dangers are important in an economic order structured by settler colonial violence, racial division, poverty, and environmental destruction? When can one know that the future, singular, has been secured and wisdom achieved? At what point might the accruing fallout of this program— toxic environments, boom-and-bust capital, constant conflict (at home and internationally)—create a moment of collective critique?

As Bush predicted, U.S. science has been one of the extraordinary achievements of post–World War II American society, leading to continuing revolutions across health, industry, technology, and communication. But this massive investment in science and engineering was achieved not as a structure of peace, but rather via a permanent militarization of American society (branded first as Cold War and now as the War on Terror). Americans have not thought enough about what it means to give up so completely on the idea of peace or considered how deeply U.S. institutions are imbricated today with militarism. I would suggest this is because permanent mobilization is so materially productive and psychologically seductive, and because the decades of Cold War turned militarism itself into a form of American normality.

In a project of total social mobilization, the boundary of war itself is expanded to all parties. Thus, a civilian National Science Foundation (as advocated by Bush) was conceived also as a supplement to ongoing military research expenditures (that is, unending classified Manhattan Projects)—which in the 1950s accounted for roughly two-thirds of all U.S. spending on science. Similarly, a revolutionary investment in the social sciences under the rubric of area studies focused scholarly energies on those areas of the world of interest to the emerging U.S. Cold War geopolitical strategy. Corporate alliances involved not only military-industrial companies like Raytheon and Boeing, but also Kodak, IBM, Bell, and GM. The ever-deeper imbrication of militarization within American institutions after World War II makes peace a structural problem for American society rather than the goal. Indeed, a recurring problem for this military-industrial-academic establishment is that of endings, of how to reorient from a permanent mobilization in the name of combating imagined existential dangers to address an everyday filled with fallout, especially the slower forms of violence (environmental contamination, multigenerational poverty, and life in a world so intertwined with technologies that there are no more purely natural disasters), while also recognizing the deep challenges to infrastructure as well as sustainability of a growing global population.

In the immediate post–Cold War moment, I began research in New Mexico imagining I would write a book about the end of a multigenerational conflict, hoping to have a discussion with nuclear weapons scientists about winning a war and retooling their scientific capacities for peace. Instead, I encountered an expert community readying both politically and conceptually for a future of unknown but still proliferating existential dangers. At that moment, Los Alamos was a scientific community deeply unsettled by the demise of the Soviet Union and unsure about the future or where existential threat might emerge. But many experts were also convinced of the existence of such a danger, shifting from fears of asteroid strikes against the planet to a resurgent Russia in efforts to articulate a future mission for a nuclear weapons laboratory. Nuclear fear was simultaneously reduced with the fall of the great Cold War enemy and converted into a proliferating affective terrain in the immediate post–Cold War moment, as experts realized it was difficult to imagine the future of a nuclear weapons laboratory without an existential danger to deter and fight. Indeed, one of my first conversations with a weapons scientist focused on the emerging figure of the terrorist—identified already in the early 1990s as a religious zealot committed to hyperviolence that could not be reasoned with (and thus deterred via Cold War nuclear logics). Despite a brief period in which different missions for the national laboratory were formally proposed, permanent mobilization remained the program because no other answer seemed politically possible—a drastic foreshortening of the future in favor of continual threat proliferation. Just as Americans confronted the problem of winning a world war in 1945 by simply redefining war as defense, in this immediate post–Cold War moment, U.S. society did not demobilize but rather began constituting the future itself as negative, its unknowability the grounds for proliferating fears. Unlike war, defense is an unending commitment that can never be won, as there is no specific enemy to defeat but rather the challenge of a proliferating universe of potential dangers to be defeated, not only today but into a distant future (Masco 2014).

When we think about the costs and accomplishments of the U.S. commitment to militarism—which is unique in human history in both its scale and planetary reach—perhaps the most difficult aspect to consider is the counterfactual, to imagine an American society that is interested in and capable of demobilizing, of redirecting its remarkable creative and financial commitments to the war machine to nonmilitarized projects. If war has become infrastructural to American society since the mid-twentieth century, it is also because conflict itself has been crafted to be largely invisible at home, allowing those with no self-conscious warlike commitments to nonetheless participate in the industries, institutions, academies, and electoral processes that are deeply imbricated in maintaining the structural reality of a permanent U.S. global mobilization and a settler colonial society. The Watson Institute's Costs of War project, an unprecedented effort to account for U.S. militarism in real time, has concluded that the War on Terror from 2001 to 2019 has cost $5.8 trillion and documented ongoing U.S. counterterror activities in some seventy-six countries in 2015–17 (see figure E.1; Savell 2019). How many Americans can explain these activities or why they are necessary? How many U.S. citizens understand the global costs (deaths, injuries, blowbacks) of counterterror?

At the start of the third decade of the War on Terror, if we were to revisit Vannevar Bush's question today—What should the scientists now do?—we would have to ask it of a much broader section of American society: to taxpayers as well as experts, to politicians as well as soldiers, to corporations as well as religious figures. The two U.S. defense departments—the Department of Defense and Department of Homeland Security—are key parts of the $1 trillion per year the United States spends (across all agencies) on defense. And yet insecurity is still the dominant theme in American life and is increasing across many registers of health, welfare, environment, and civic life. We might now ask: How is peace thinkable after war itself has been naturalized as the basis for American power? What can come after a multigenerational commitment to a project called defense, one privileged to such an extent

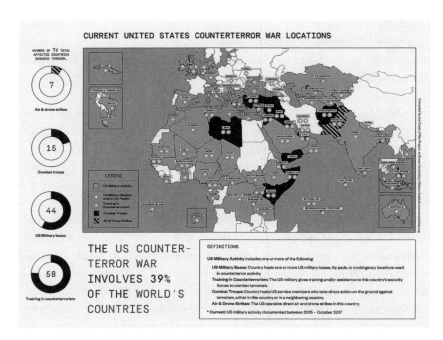

Figure E.1. Map of U.S. counterterror activities between 2015 and 2017 (courtesy of http://watson.brown.edu/costsofwar).

that domestic infrastructures have become both outdated and frayed and that even losing major conflicts (Vietnam, Afghanistan, Iraq, etc.) does not recalibrate official ambitions or national logics? The answer is not at all obvious, and one form that is already emergent is the rise of authoritarianism, as citizens activate their electoral power to disrupt Washington politics rather than to create a coherent collective future. The Donald J. Trump administration was elected under these terms, taking advantage of a wide range of democracy reduction techniques (see MacLean 2017), from voter suppression to the Electoral College to propagandistic uses of social media to anti-immigrant fearmongering in the name of protecting the idea of the United States as a white nation. Trump's accomplishments in office are few but diagnostic—including withdrawing from international agreements on nuclear weapons to embrace a new arms race, rejecting environmental science as well as international action on global warming, offering tax cuts for the hyperwealthy, and ever-increasing military budgets, including support for a new generation of nuclear weapons. The seventy-five-year anniversary of the Trinity test and the atomic bombings of Hiroshima and Nagasaki in

2020 may well prove to be the first year in a half century in which there are no existing international treaty restraints on U.S. nuclear weapons production, and will begin the decade when climate scientists predict radical environmental disruptions to arrive via global warming (IPCC 2018). Under these likely scenarios, the War on Terror will have a set of new and old terrors to confront, creating proliferating opportunities for crises and ever-expanding opportunities for a deeper militarization of American life.

The problem of violence today involves the combined impact, and imbrication, of capitalism, militarism, and environmental change at a scale that exceeds the control of any nation-state. The two existential dangers of nuclear war and global warming are deeply imbricated within industrial capitalism and cannot be solved without both techno-scientific expertise and alternative world building. What might a world look like that did not anchor its science infrastructure in militarism, or assume that technological innovation was simply a code for national advantage? More essentially, if the logics of American modernity are deeply connected to infrastructures (the technoscience, the affective structures, and imaginaries) supporting nuclear weapons, what might a denuclearized American society look like, and how would it engage collective problems linking global warming to racism to poverty?

Partly because of the revolution in information technologies Bush saw coming in 1945, we now know that permanent militarization has a high social cost: the diversion of funds, expertise, and energy to war extracts those resources from domestic life while also chilling the political potential of a democracy and keeping the world on the edge of a nuclear cataclysm.[1] With the annihilation of the Al-Qaeda leadership behind the September 2001 attacks, including its director, Osama bin Laden, the U.S. has had the ability to declare an end to the War on Terror at any time. Similarly, the U.S. could adopt the findings of its own climate scientists and mobilize a significant new collective response to global warming, taking on toxicity as an existential problem for all life on the planet, finally identifying petrochemical capitalism as a force of unprecedented, ongoing violence. Doing so would signal a long overdue recalibration of American society, allowing its extraordinary resources to be directed at nonmilitarizable dangers—climate, energy, and health—which all require technoscientific innovation and have not been part of national security since 1945 (see Masco 2014). Vannevar Bush seems to suggest just such a possibility, hoping that investments in technoscience would create a new American society—that is, once the U.S., or maybe the world, overcame the immediate danger of nuclear war. But in July 1945, war was still war, peace was still thinkable, and American institutions were not yet captured by either the Cold War balance of terror or the U.S. War on Terror. In the twenty-first century, U.S. society has naturalized technological revolution as a form of endless progress—living in an age of constantly changing technical capacities (a register of the incredible vitality and creativity of contemporary science and engineering)—but it has also naturalized permanent war as the basis for American power—restricting its infrastructures, imaginaries, and affective circuits to negative futurities. Perhaps now with nearly perfect digital archives and instant systems of information retrieval and global communication, Americans could focus on remembering a time, actually not so long ago, before war became defense and when peace could be evoked as a collective good.

ACKNOWLEDGMENTS

It is an amazing and deeply humbling project to reflect on all the conversations and individuals that have influenced the chapters in this book. Over the past twenty-odd years, I have had the enormous good fortune to be involved in a wide range of collective conversations, special issues of journals, edited collections, seminars, and public events. The pleasures of academic life, particularly when working on the difficult issues discussed in this book, are located in the incredible scholars and beautiful people that one encounters along the way. My thanks to one and all for all those acts of serious intellectual engagement, and for the conversations and comradery.

For invitations and editorial care with various chapters in this book I would like to thank: Marco Armiero, Debbora Battaglia, Carlo Caduff, Anthony Carrigan, Patricia Clough, Elizabeth DeLoughrey, Jill Didur, Christopher Dole, Raymond Duval, Robert Emmett, Susan Harding, Charles Hirschkind, Beatrice Jauregui, Maria Jose de Abreu, Ivan Karp, John Kelly, Anna Kirkland, Corinne A. Kratz, Mark Laffey, Setha Low, Emily Martin, Katherine McCaffrey, Jonathan Metzl, Sean Mitchell, Gregg Mitman, Valerie Olson, Kavita Philip, Andrew Poe, Beth Povinelli, Eliza Jane Reilly, Daniel Rosenberg, Austin Sarat, Joan Wallach Scott, David Serlin, Ida Susser, Casper Sylvest, Lynn Szwaja, Sandra Trappen, David Valentine, Rens van Munster, Jeremy Walton, Jutta Weldes, Stephanie White, Boris Wolfson, and Tomas Ybarra-Frausto. Special thanks to Cameron Hu for help assembling this volume.

I would like to thank the American Council of Learned Societies, the School for Advanced Research, the John D. and Catherine T. MacArthur Foundation, and the Institute for Advanced Study for support, as well as the

Neubauer Collegium for Culture and Society, the Marion R. and Adolph J. Lichtstern Fund, and the Division of the Social Sciences at the University of Chicago for research support.

A truly wonderful thing happened to me when Lochlann Jain and Jake Kosek invited me to join a new writing group—infinite thanks to Lochlann and Jake and to Joe Dumit, Cori Hayden, Jonathan Metzl, Michelle Murphy, Diane Nelson, Jackie Orr, Elizabeth Roberts, and Miriam Tictin for years of joyful conspiring.

My thinking on environmental conditions is indebted to the Engineered Worlds working group—Tim Choy, Jake Kosek, and Michelle Murphy—as well as to all the participants in the EW seminars and conferences.

I would like to thank my colleagues in the Department of Anthropology, the Committee on Conceptual and Historical Studies of Science, and the Chicago Center for Contemporary Theory at the University of Chicago. Special thanks to all the participants in the U.S. Locations workshop.

For their personal and intellectual support over the years, endless thanks to Nadia Abu El-Haj, Kennette Benedict, Jean Comaroff, Peter Galison, Cathy Lutz, Gregg Mitman, Rosalind Morris, Beth Povinelli, Danilyn Rutherford, Deborah Thomas, Lisa Wedeen, and Ken Wissoker.

And for their incredible scholarship and friendship, my thanks to: Andrea Ballestero, Lauren Berlant, Alex Blanchette, David Bond, John Borneman, Ella Butler, Summerson Carr, Molly Cunningham, Paul Edwards, Didier Fassin, Cassie Fennell, Elaine Gan, Stefanie Graeter, Hugh Gusterson, Orit Halprin, Isao Hashimoto, Gabrielle Hecht, Stefan Helmreich, John Jackson, Cory Kratz, Max Liboiron, Mark Maguire, Kai Mah, Kate Mariner, Andrew Mathews, Amy McLachlan, Greg Mello, Ned O'Gorman, Trevor Paglen, Juno Parrenas, Columba Peoples, Kareem Rabie, Laurence Ralph, Patrick Rivers, Michael Rossi, Nick Shapiro, Audra Simpson, Sverker Sorlin, Christian Tompkins, Anna Weichselbraun, Kaya Williams, and Jessica Winegar.

Finally, I am beyond grateful to Shawn Michelle Smith for always, without question, offering a better world.

NOTES

PROLOGUE

1 For a detailed assessment of the violence (over 800,000 killed), global disloca-
tions (21 million displaced persons), and financial cost ($6.4 trillion) of the
U.S. War on Terror from 2001 to 2019, see the ongoing Costs of War project at
Brown University's Watson Institute: https://watson.brown.edu/costsofwar/.

2 The concept of fallout here addresses modes of exposure and delayed perceptions, as well as the shifting affects and materialities of a lag in understanding. See Thomas (2019) for a vital study of historical aftermaths and political
consciousness in Jamaica, and Sharpe (2016) for an important theorization of
antiblackness and historical consciousness in the United States. See Povinelli
(2016) for a study of life and nonlife in "settler late liberalism," and de la
Cadena (2015) on incommensurable understandings of ecological relationality.

3 On the concept of slow violence, see Nixon (2011). For assessments of the
health and environmental legacies of nuclear production, see Brown (2013),
Johnston and Barker (2008), Makhijani and Schwartz (1998), Makhijani, Hu,
and Yih (1995), and Masco (2004).

4 On industrial aftermaths and the long-term transformation of ecologies, see
Fortun (2012), Liboiron (2020), Mitman, Murphy, and Seller (2004), and Murphy (2017a).

5 For discussion of environmental damage from Cold War nuclear projects,
see Brown (2013, 2019), Cram (2016), and Gallagher (1993). For discussion of
technoscientific nuclear cultures and related forms of radioactive colonization,
see Gusterson (1996, 2004), Johnston and Barker (2008), Kuletz (1998), Masco
(2006, 2014), and Titus (1986).

6 The redefinition of the future as a domain of endless turbulence and proliferating threat now informs a great range of domains, linking militarism to finance
capital, to climate change, to public health. See Caduff (2015) on the anticipatory politics of public health, and see Collier and Lakoff (2015) for an important theorization of governance under conditions of permanent vulnerability.

7 See Paglen (2009) on the geography of state secrecy and how to fill in those blank spots on the map.

8 As of this writing, the Treaty on the Prohibition of Nuclear Weapons has been ratified by eighty-seven countries and is not yet in force. See the United Nations Office for Disarmament Affairs website at http://disarmament.un.org /treaties/t/tpnw.

9 By radioactive world-making I mean a process that combines the material reality of nuclear effects, and the installed global dangers of nuclear war and climate disruption, with the multiple affective orientations and ontological re- alities that support and inform the diversity of ways of living and being. Thus, the concept navigates a shared set of existential problems, but it does not assume a universal or singular understanding of how petrochemical capitalism or nuclear nationalism shapes and informs individual psyches or communities. As a form of world-making, however, it does underscore the processual nature of these engineered dangers, as they continue to remake ideas about place, health, and futurity.

1. THE AGE OF FALLOUT

This chapter first appeared in *History of the Present: A Journal of Critical His- tory* in 2015 and has been revised for this volume.

1 On the question of the planetary, see Cosgrove (2001) and Heise (2008). On the contribution of Cold War sciences to an understanding of the earth system, see Cloud (2001), Doel (2003), Edwards (2010), Farish (2010), Hamblin (2013), Masco (2010), McNeill and Unger (2010), and Oreskes and Krige (2014).

2 See Winiarek et al. (2014) for a thirty-day simulation of the global cesium fallout from the Fukushima Daiichi nuclear accident as it traversed the Pacific Ocean.

3 See Choy and Zee (2015) on the politics of atmospheric suspension; Simmons (2017) on "settler atmospherics"; Mitman (2007) on air quality and allergies; Sloterdijk (2009) on the relationship between environmental thinking, air, and terrorism; and Russell (2001) on the industrial logics and multispecies politics of chemical warfare. See Lindqvist (2001) for a highly innovative reading of bombing from the colonial era through the nuclear age.

4 For innovative studies of toxic legacies and unequally embodied conse- quences, see Agard-Jones (2013), Cram (2016), Graeter (2017), Murphy (2008), and Shapiro (2015).

5 See, for example, Gallagher (1993) for fallout effects in Utah; Johnston and Barker (2008) on the Marshall Islands; and Makhijani, Hu, and Yih (1995) for fallout as a global condition.

6 See Poole (2008) for a historical assessment of the first photographs of Earth; Gabrys (2016) on the evolution of sensing and earth systems science; and Kurgan (2013) on techniques of data visualization.

7 For assessments of the global health effects of Cold War–era nuclear pro- grams, see Lindee (1997), Makhijani, Hu, and Yih (1995), and Makhijani and

Schwartz (1998). For detailed community studies, see Brown (2013), Cram (2015), and Johnston and Barker (2008).

8 See Bonneuil and Fressoz (2016) for a detailed discussion of the wide-ranging debates around the concept of the Anthropocene. See Tsing et al. (2017) on ways of living in radically transformed environments.

9 For proposals, and critical assessments, of geoengineering, see Caldeira, Govindasamy, and Cao (2013), Hamilton (2013), Keith (2013), and Morton (2015).

10 For a technical assessment of the Chernobyl nuclear plant and its management, see Schmid (2015); on the regional environmental and health impacts of the disaster, see Brown (2019), Kuchinskaya (2014), and Petryna (2002).

11 For detailed information about Science on a Sphere visualizations and NOAA's larger public education project, see the Science on a Sphere website: https://sos.noaa.gov/What_is_SOS/index.html.

12 See Hohler (2015) for a history of spaceship earth and the rise of environmental consciousness, Halpern (2014) for an examination of how cybernetics affects concepts of design and environmental thinking, and Jasanoff and Martell (2004) on the emergence of environmental governance.

13 See, for example, Amazon CEO Jeff Bezos's vision of going to the moon, and then Mars, as a way of continuing capitalist expansion (Blue Origin 2019).

2. 5:29:45 A.M.

This chapter first appeared in *Museum Frictions: Public Cultures/Global Transformations*, edited by Ivan Karp, Corinne A. Kratz, Lynn Szwaja, and Tomas Ybarra-Frausto (Durham, NC: Duke University Press, 2006), and has been revised for this volume.

1 Patrick Nagatani is a member of the Atomic Photographers Guild, a project started in 1987 by Robert Del Tredici, Carol Gallagher, and Harris Fogel to photographically document effects of the atomic bomb on bodies and landscapes. The guild has worked methodically to make visible the lasting impacts of the bomb and has been a significant activist organization (see https://atomicphotographers.com).

3. STATES OF INSECURITY

This chapter appeared originally in *Cultures of Insecurity: States, Communities, and the Production of Danger*, edited by Jutta Weldes, Mark Laffey, Hugh Gusterson, and Raymond Duvall (Minneapolis: University of Minnesota Press, 1999). It has been revised and expanded for this volume.

1 For an analysis of the dual-structured, oppositional nation building in the Cold War Berlins, see Borneman (1992), and on oppositional counterstructures in the U.S., see Rogin (1988).

2 See Wolfe (2006) for a discussion of settler colonialism, Tuck and Yang (2012) on the fundamental challenges of decolonization, and Murphy (2008, 2017)

and Agard-Jones (2013) on the complexity of living well in chemically saturated settler colonial worlds.

3 "From time immemorial" is a legal phrase used in land and water rights cases in the U.S. to designate that Native American claims are prior to any other (see Cohn 1941). See also Tallbear (2013) for a discussion of how genetic politics frames indigenous identity with implications for tribal sovereignties and new technologies for exclusion, and Simpson (2014) for a powerful assessment of the problem of moving across incommensurable regimes of sovereignty and the necessary politics of refusal in ethnographic writing from an indigenous perspective.

4 On the history of conflict surrounding Spanish and Mexican land grants in New Mexico, see Briggs and Van Ness (1987), Ebright (1994), Gardner (1970), Nostrand (1992), Ortiz (1980), Pulido (1996), and Rosenbaum (1981).

5 On the concept of New Mexico as a Hispano Homeland, see Nostrand (1992). On "Aztlan" see Anaya, Lomeli, and Lamadrid (1989), Barrera (1988), and Chavez (1984). This split within the Spanish-speaking community in New Mexico over whether to forward Spanish or Native American ancestry in terms of contemporary identity politics is demonstrated in the conflict over naming in northern New Mexico. In the Spanish-speaking villages of northern New Mexico, residents are likely to refer to each other as "Mexicano," but probably use "Hispano" or "Chicano" when speaking in English or to outsiders. "Chicano" is more commonly used by Spanish speakers in the larger urban areas, but current usage varies considerably and is politicized. Thus, I use the collective term "Nuevomexicano" to refer to all Spanish-speaking people in northern New Mexico; I use "Hispano" or "Chicano" only when people self-identified to me that way in conversation.

6 For example, see Acuña (1988), Chavez (1984), Churchill (1993), Jaimes (1992), Ortiz (1980), and Pulido (1996). For detailed studies of the relationship of U.S. nation building to race and territory in the nineteenth and early twentieth centuries, see Drinnon (1990) and Horsman (1981).

7 In fact, the state of New Mexico is only eclipsed by Maryland and Virginia in per capita federal dollars, and the DOE is directly responsible for 13 percent of the total economy of the state (see Lansford et al. 1995).

8 I expand on this exploration of New Mexico's plutonium economy in Masco (2006). For detailed studies of the environmental effects of nuclear production, see Brown (2013), Johnston and Barker (2008), and Kuletz (1998).

9 See Rhodes (1986, 1995) for a detailed history of the first decades of U.S. nuclear nationalism, and see Brown (2013) for a comparison of plutonium production in the United States and the Soviet Union during the Cold War.

10 See Feiveson et al. (2014) for a detailed program about how to "unbuild the bomb" via collecting and managing all fissile material globally.

11 For a discussion of the "social life of things," see Appadurai (1986). For a discussion of how risk structures social relations in an era of industrial toxicity, see Beck (1992).

12 I am speaking here specifically about plutonium-239, which was developed for use in nuclear weapons. See IPPNW and IEER (1992) on the physics and health risks of plutonium, and IPPNW and IEER (1991) on the cumulative health and environmental effects of nuclear weapons tests.

13 With the exception of Hiroshima and Nagasaki, the majority of nuclear weapons tests by the U.S., Britain, France, China, and the former Soviet Union (not including India, Pakistan, and North Korea) have taken place on contested indigenous lands (see Nietschman and Le Bon 1987; see also Hanson 2001; Kuletz 1998; LaDuke and Churchill 1985).

14 For more detail about the post–Cold War mission of LANL and shifts in the experimental regimes surrounding nuclear weapons science, see Masco (2006, 43–96).

15 The Pueblo nations surrounding Los Alamos explicitly articulate their security concerns within a discourse of territorial sovereignty. The difficulty many U.S. officials and security scholars have in accepting this discourse as presented, or in translating the ambiguities around Native American sovereignty into a more familiar discourse of national security, is precisely one of the problems facing indigenous communities in New Mexico and throughout the Americas.

16 I do not mean to suggest that having the vote would have affected the Manhattan Project in any way, as it was a top-secret project that even Vice President Harry Truman was not briefed on until after he had been sworn in as president (Rhodes 1986, 617). I am simply pointing out the legal disparities at work in New Mexico that were instrumental in the development of Los Alamos.

17 On the importance of shrines and pilgrimage sites in Tewa cosmology, see Ortiz (1969).

18 Pueblo governments do have the option of trying to mobilize international opinion and law on their behalf, as several tribes in the Southwest have, in fact, attempted to do. However, there are inherent difficulties in finding international allies that are willing to challenge the U.S. over internal nuclear weapons policy. Since the U.S. can evoke the "supreme national interest" clause in any international treaty or agreement to protect the nuclear weapons complex from lawsuits, local Pueblo nations face an uphill battle simply locating an international forum willing to consider their case.

19 Pojoaque Pueblo did, in fact, shut down U.S. Highway 84/285, just north of Santa Fe, on March 21, 1996, to protest the lack of progress on gaming issues in the state.

20 See Randy Hanson's (2001) analysis of the economics and geopolitical forces informing Native American plans to initiate a nuclear waste storage project. On nuclear politics and environmental justice, see Eichstaedt (1994), Grinde and Johansen (1995), Kuletz (1998), LaDuke and Churchill (1985), and Stoffle and Evans (1988). On concepts of environmental justice, see Bullard (1993) and Pulido (1996).

21 These figures are all drawn from the 1990 U.S. Census.

22 For example, the DARHT lawsuit was ultimately settled in favor of the DOE/LANL only after the DOE provided a classified supplement to the federal judge adjudicating the case. Then NGOs argued that they should be able to find a representative with a security clearance to review the classified documentation in order to mount an adequate rebuttal but were denied that option. Ultimately, NGOs in Santa Fe succeeded in delaying the DARHT project for sixteen months.

23 In 1996, the World Court in The Hague did rule that using nuclear weapons in a first-strike capacity was against international law; however, judges left room in their decision for a defensive use of nuclear weapons. A continuing effort by peace activists resulted in the 2017 Treaty on the Prohibition of Nuclear Weapons at the United Nations, which prohibits the possession, development, or threat to use nuclear weapons. As of 2019, it has been passed by 122 nations and is in the ratification stage of the United Nations process.

24 My intent here is only to point out the structural role the Cold War played in shaping the development of area studies; it is not to make any claim on what individual scholars did within those area studies categories (see Lewontin et al. 1997; Rafael 1994).

4. DESERT MODERNISM

This chapter was originally published in *Histories of the Future*, edited by Daniel Rosenburg and Susan Harding (Durham, NC: Duke University Press, 2005), and has been revised for this volume. *Histories of the Future* began as a seminar at the Humanities Research Institute at the University of California, Irvine, and included a collaborative research project in the greater Las Vegas area.

1 For a remarkable introduction to the environmental politics of the Nevada Test Site, see Coolidge (1996), as well as Stewart (1994). For a historical analysis of the era of aboveground nuclear testing at the test site, see Fradkin (1989), Hacker (1994), and Miller (1986).

2 The Nevada Test Site was renamed the Nevada National Security Site in 2010.

3 For studies of communities suffering the most severe health effects from work at the NTS, see Gallagher (1993) and Kuletz (1998). For an assessment of Cold War human radiation experiments in the U.S., see Advisory Committee on Human Radiation Experiments (1996), and Cram (2015, 2016) for an assessment of radiation exposure standards for U.S. nuclear workers. For a ten-thousand-page, county-by-county dose reconstruction of radioactive fallout from nuclear testing, and its impact on national thyroid cancer rates, see National Cancer Institute (1997). For a global assessment of the environmental impact of military nuclear technology, see IPPNW and IEER (1991).

4 Congress selected the Yucca Mountain site as the permanent repository for U.S. military and civilian nuclear waste in 1987, beginning a long technical evaluation and official licensing process. President George W. Bush approved Yucca Mountain as the primary commercial nuclear waste repository in the

United States in 2002. However, numerous lawsuits, public protests, and continued scientific controversy over the technical viability of the site led the DOE to withdraw from the licensing process in 2010, effectively killing the project after more than three decades, and $15 billion, of work. In 2018, the Trump administration sought once again to reopen the site. See Kuletz (1998) for a reading of the cross-cultural politics of the Yucca Mountain Project, MacFarlane and Ewing (2006) on the technoscientific controversies informing the site, and Jaczko (2019) for a discussion of the Obama-era politics surrounding Yucca Mountain.

5 See Taussig (1999), who defines a public secret as "that which is generally known but cannot be spoken"; and for a sharp analysis of regional monumentalism, see Rosenberg (2001).

6 See Lepselter (2005, 2016) for highly sensitive ethnographic readings of Rachel and the larger UFO community of belief in the United States. See Darlington (1997) on Area 51 beliefs, Stewart and Harding (1999) on American apocalypticism, and Fenster (1999) on conspiracy theory in the United States. See Welsome (1999) for a discussion of covert human experimentation during the Cold War, Weart (1988) for a cultural history of nuclear anxiety in the U.S., and Moynihan (1998) for an analysis of U.S. secrecy since World War II. See Masco (2002, 2014) for discussions of post–Cold War secrecy and security concerns within the U.S. nuclear complex.

7 See the Federation of American Scientists study of satellite imagery of Area 51 (FAS 2000). In September 2001, President George W. Bush renewed a Clinton administration executive order exempting an "unnamed" Groom Lake Air Force facility from environmental laws. This rule has been justified under national security protocols as a way to keep state secrets, but it also has the effect of suppressing the lawsuits filed by former Area 51 workers over toxic exposures. In other words, the state can now argue that since the base does not formally exist, how could anybody have worked there, let alone been poisoned on the job? See Paglen (2009) for a discussion of black sites and how to find them. Byrne and Mehrotra (2018) found that Google Earth stopped updating its satellite photographs of the Groom Lake area from 2008 to 2016 and offer an interesting reading of the politics of satellite images of the military base.

8 In 2013, the CIA acknowledged the existence of a military base at Groom Lake as part of a Freedom of Information Act declassification of two Cold War–era reports on the U-2 and OXCART surveillance programs.

9 Biographical information on Liberace in this section is based on the presentation at the Liberace Museum (Las Vegas), as well as Liberace (1973) and Thomas (1987). For an analysis of gender roles during the height of the Cold War, see Nadel (1995). For a policy assessment of U.S. security clearances and sexual orientation, see U.S. General Accounting Office (1995b). For more on Las Vegas and the culture of aboveground nuclear testing at the NTS, see Titus (1986).

10 The Liberace Museum closed at this location in 2010.

5. THE BILLBOARD CAMPAIGN

This chapter originally appeared in *Public Culture* 17 (3) in 2005 and has been revised for this volume. All photographs are by the author.

1 For the text of the Nuclear Nonproliferation Treaty, see United Nations (1968); and see United Nations (2017) for the Treaty on the Prohibition of Nuclear Weapons, which (as of this writing) has been ratified but is not yet in force.

6. REHEARSING THE END

This chapter originally appeared in a special issue of *On Site Review* on archives and museums in 2008. It has been revised for this volume. All photographs are by the author.

7. LIFE UNDERGROUND

This chapter first appeared in *Anthropology Now* 1 (2) in 2009 and has been revised for this volume.

1 For key texts on the Cold War policy debates over fallout shelters, see Rand Corporation (1958) and Security Resources Panel of the Science Advisory Committee (1957; known as the Gaither Report), and for a detailed history of the commission, see Kahn (1960), Robin (2016), and Snead (1999).

2 For a photographic history of Cold War bunkers, see Ross (2004). For an excellent cultural history of the fallout shelter movement in the U.S., see Rose (2001). See Monteyne (2011) for discussion of how civil defense changed urban planning in the U.S., as well as Galison (2001). For visual analysis of the cultural work of atomic ruins in the U.S., see Masco (2008) and Vanderbilt (2002).

3 For analysis of the Cold War technological system as ideology, see Edwards (1996). For a discussion of how gender roles were positioned in early Cold War civil defense, see McEnaney (2000) and Zaretsky (2018), and for a vital analysis of gendered discourse in Cold War strategic thinking, see Cohn (1987).

4 For a discussion of the politics of fear, terror, and panic in the early Cold War, see Oakes (1994), Orr (2006), and Masco (2014). For a stimulating discussion of the role of psychology in early Cold War planning and its larger effects on American society, see Lutz (1997); and for a critical assessment of civil defense as performance, see Davis (2007).

5 It is important to recognize that American society did not merely commit to building and maintaining a state-of-the-art nuclear arsenal after destroying Hiroshima and Nagasaki in August 1945. The U.S. increasingly built itself through and around the bomb (see Masco 2006; Schwartz 1998; see also Higgs 2007). For a chart of global military expenditures, see GlobalSecurity.Org (n.d.).

6 For crucial filmic insights into the psychology of the Cold War nuclear system, see *Dr. Strangelove, Or: How I Learned to Stop Worrying and Love the Bomb* (Kubrick 1964) and *Fail Safe* (Lumet 1964). For an example of bunker discourse within the War on Terror, see Vice President Cheney (2001).

8. ATOMIC HEALTH

This chapter first appeared in *Against Health: How Health Became the New Morality*, edited by Jonathan M. Metzl and Anna Kirkland (New York: New York University Press, 2010), and has been revised for this volume.

1 See Zaretsky (2018) for an important discussion of how nuclear contamination has challenged ideas about reproductive futurity in the United States and focused American political cultures during the Cold War on the problem of the unborn.

2 See Murphy (2017b) for a critical assessment of how population figures in the governance debates of the twentieth century. See Nelson (2015) for an ethnographic study of diverse modes of accounting and alternate future making in postgenocide Guatemala.

3 For an assessment of global nuclear arsenals as of 2020, see Kristensen and Korda (2020).

9. THE END OF ENDS

This chapter was first published in *Anthropological Quarterly* 85 (4) in 2012, part of the special issue "Extreme: Humans at Home in the Cosmos," edited by Debbora Battaglia, Valerie Olson, and David Valentine. It has been revised for this volume.

1 On the wide-ranging use of satellite surveillance for both security and environmental studies, see Turchetti and Roberts (2014). For a discussion of the "spaceship earth" concept that emerges in the 1970s and influences environmental design, see Hohler (2015), and also Turner (2006). For an overview of environmental sensing and the production of big data earth sciences, see Gabrys (2016).

2 See, for example, the digital "nuclear vault" project at the National Security Archive and the important ongoing Cold War declassification work of historian William Burr: https://nsarchive.gwu.edu/project/nuclear-vault.

3 See Ellsberg (2017) for a recent autobiographical account of a U.S. nuclear war planner, which explores the contradictions within the logics of the SIOP and in the concept of national security at this time.

10. TARGET AUDIENCE

This chapter first appeared in *Bulletin of the Atomic Scientists* 64 (3) in 2008 and has been revised for this volume.

1 The U.S. test program involved 1,149 detonations, including a joint test with Britain and not including the military uses of atomic weapons at Hiroshima and Nagasaki in August 1945. The United States conducted 210 atmospheric tests, 5 underwater tests, and 839 underground tests between 1945 and 1992 (see U.S. Department of Energy 2000).

2 See, for example, Kristensen, McKinzie, and Postol (2017); see Masco (2006) for discussion of weapons science in a post-underground testing era.

3 Lynn Eden (2004) has shown that the extensive effects of fire after a nuclear detonation in an urban area were eliminated from nuclear war planning calculations in the United States during the Cold War, leaving policy makers today with models and targeting plans that can radically underestimate the destruction caused by nuclear warfare.

4 See Virilio (1989) for the classic study of the relationship between militarism and photographic vision, and Weart (1988) for a study of images of nuclear fear.

5 See Kuran (2003, 2007) for a photographic overview of Lookout Mountain Laboratory, and see Hamilton and O'Gorman (2018) for an extensive appraisal of its film work, as well as its design concepts and contribution to building out the aesthetic culture of the Cold War state.

6 See Galison (2001) for an important discussion of how nuclear targeting both worked psychosocially in the United States and affected urban design. See also Alex Wellerstein's *Restricted Data: Nuclear Secrecy Blog* (http://blog .nuclearsecrecy.com), which has extensive discussions of nuclear imaging, public communication strategies, and government secrecy.

11. THE AGE OF (A) MAN

This chapter originally appeared in *Future Remains: A Cabinet of Curiosities for the Anthropocene*, edited by Gregg Mitman, Marco Armiero, and Robert S. Emmett (Chicago: University of Chicago Press, 2018), and has been revised for this volume.

12. CATASTROPHE'S APOCALYPSE

This chapter first appeared in *The Time of Catastrophe: Multidisciplinary Approaches to the Age of Catastrophe*, edited by Christopher Dole, Robert Hayashi, Andrew Poe, Austin Sarat, and Boris Wolfson (Farnham, UK: Ashgate, 2015), and has been revised for this volume.

1 Can the catastrophic structure the very nature of the contemporary world, referencing forms of violence that are difficult to locate precisely because they are so deeply embedded in modern institutions and modes of living that they appear both natural and unending? In his "Commandments in the Atomic Age," the German philosopher Günther Anders was definitive on the subject: "Your first thought upon awaking be: 'Atom.' For you should not begin your day with the illusion that what surrounds you is a stable world" (1961, 11). For Anders, the central conundrum of modernity is how technological capabilities have come to exceed human perception and understanding. This enables wide-ranging forms of violence to proceed as constantly moving instrumental developments operating without a collective critical assessment or social recognition of the new forms, velocities, or scales of violence being unleashed.

The atomic bomb is for him emblematic of this process as in the name of security it installs a new possibility for collective death, making the nuclear age the ultimate example of self-alienation through technological revolution.

2 As Anders, thinking about the long-term effect of the bomb on consciousness, puts it:

> Your second thought after awaking should run: "The possibility of the Apocalypse is our work. But we know not what we are doing." . . . [This is an] effect of the daily growing gap between our two faculties: between our *action* and our *imagination*; of the fact that we are unable to conceive what we can construct; to mentally reproduce what we can produce; to realize the reality which we can bring into being. For in the course of the technical age the classical relation between imagination and action has reversed itself. . . . We humans are smaller than ourselves. (1961, 11)

Here, the incommensurability between the ability to engineer a technologically mediated universe while simultaneously expanding human perception to recognize all the new potentials put in motion within that emerging universe is stark. Catastrophe becomes, for Anders, a potential that is embedded within a modern mode of living that is no longer able to evaluate or register alternative futures or assess the social, material, or moral effects of ongoing technological revolution. Thus, in the nuclear age, an unreflexive allegiance to technological progress installs an escalating minute-to-minute possibility of collective death, challenging the terms of modernist rationality itself (see Erickson et al. 2013).

3 The figure of the lifeboat is often used in neo-Malthusian arguments about environmental futurity. Garrett Hardin (1974) published a highly cited essay piece, "Lifeboat Ethics: The Case against Helping the Poor," that picked up on the limits-of-growth argument and population explosion fears to ask who needs to be left out of the lifeboat so others can survive, offering it as a metaphor for global capitalism. Kyle Whyte (2019) has revisited this lifeboat allegory from an indigenous studies perspective to point out that whatever the allegorized vessel is, it is not already shared—that some live in smaller boats negotiating the turbulence of other ships (militarized, corporate, etc.).

4 For literature that explicitly theorizes life in transformed ecologies, see Murphy (2017a), Tsing et al. (2017), Weston (2012), and Wylie (2018).

13. COUNTERINSURGENCY, *THE SPOOK*, AND BLOWBACK

This chapter appeared in *Anthropology and Global Counterinsurgency*, edited by John D. Kelly, Beatrice Jauregui, Sean Mitchell, and Jeremy Walton (Chicago: University of Chicago Press, 2010), and has been revised for this volume.

1 For the history and critical analysis of the ticking time bomb scenario, see APT (2007) and Luban (2005).

2 For a military overview of the Human Terrain Team concept, see Kipp et al. (2006). For a military overview of the Minerva Project, see "The Minerva Initiative," https://web.archive.org/web/20110722185234/http://minerva.dtic.mil /overview.html; and for critical analysis of these programs, see Commission on the Engagement of Anthropology with the US Security and Intelligence Communities (2009), and Social Science Research Council, "The Minerva Controversy," http://essays.ssrc.org/minerva/.

3 For a discussion and breakdown of U.S. military spending, see Higgs (2007), and for a ranking of world military spending, see GlobalSecurity.org (2019).

4 For analysis of the $34 billion in military research and development black budgets, see CSBA (2009). To this formal military estimate, one must add the black budgets located in the intelligence agencies, the Department of Homeland Security, and the Department of Energy (which includes the nuclear weapons laboratories) for which there is no current public accounting.

5 See Johnson (2004, 2008), Lutz (2009), and Vine (2015).

6 For example, founding members of the project who later joined the Bush administration include Dick Cheney (vice president), Donald Rumsfeld (secretary of defense), Paul Wolfowitz (deputy secretary of defense), and Scooter Libby (Vice President Cheney's chief of staff); see Project for the New American Century (1997).

7 For example, the Air Force Space Command stated in 2005 that the U.S. military is committed to a "global strike" force capable of nuclear and nonnuclear strikes on any target in the world "executed within compressed timelines (from seconds to days) . . . exerting persistent effects at potentially great distances from the continental United States"; see Kristensen (2006) for a detailed discussion of the global strike program.

8 For example, see White and Tyson (2006). For a history of the concept and its media deployment, see Sourcewatch (n.d.).

9 For example, in a speech to the Ohio Highway Patrol on June 9, 2005, President Bush stated, "This is a long war, and we have a comprehensive strategy to win it. We're taking the fight to the terrorists abroad, so we don't have to face them here at home. We're denying our enemies sanctuary, by making it clear that America will not tolerate regimes that harbor or support terrorists. We're stopping the terrorists from achieving the ideological victories they seek by spreading hope and freedom and reform across the broader Middle East. By advancing the cause of liberty, we'll lay the foundations for peace for generations to come." For a full transcript, see White House (2005).

10 I would like to thank Ryan Holland for alerting me to this film, and also for his trenchant analysis of the relationship between policing, militarism, and gang life in Chicago from the Cold War through the War on Terror (Holland 2004).

11 See the Church Committee (AARC 1975–76). See also the National Security Archive for various declassification projects on Cold War activities, including the "CIA's Family Jewels" report—a long-delayed history of illegal activities by

the CIA created after the Church Committee hearing in 1975 but only made available to the public in 2007 (Blanton 2007).

14. SHAKING, TREMBLING, SHOUTING

This chapter was originally written for the "Good Vibrations, Bad Vibrations" panel at the 2013 Society for Social Studies of Science annual meeting in San Diego and has been revised for this volume. Special thanks to Art Chantry for permission to reproduce his *Give Peace a Dance* posters, and to Maire Masco, who helped organize the Give Peace a Dance campaigns, for both historical context and perspective.

1 For a country-by-country breakdown of estimated nuclear arsenals, see Arms Control Association (n.d.).

15. "ACTIVE MEASURES"

This chapter first appeared in *Radical History Review* 93: 285–300, in a special issue, "Homeland Securities," edited by Eliza Reilly, David Serlin, and Kavita Phillip in 2005. It has been revised for this volume.

1 For a history of counterformations and demonization in the U.S., see Rogin (1988) and Siegel (1998). For important conceptual and ethnographic accounts of terrorism that focus on the ideological and psychosocial uses of the term, see Aretxaga (2005), Zulaika (2009), and Zuilaka and Douglass (1996).

2 The fourteen volumes of the Church Committee's 1970s investigation into the CIA and FBI are available on the World Wide Web (AARC 1975–76). See also the final report on the 1980s-era Iran-Contra scandal (Walsh 1993).

3 For a detailed analysis of the complexity and history of the antinuclear movement, see Zaretsky (2018), as well as Lawrence S. Wittner's three-volume history (Wittner 1993, 1997, 2003).

4 See, for example, the arguments about the problem of public dissent raised in "NSC 68: United States Objective and Programs for National Security (April 14, 1950)," a core-planning document of the Cold War (U.S. National Security Council 1993); see also Olmsted (1996) on U.S. media coverage of intelligence activities during the Cold War.

16. BOUNDLESS INFORMANT

This chapter first appeared in *Anthropological Theory*, in a special issue, "Producing States of Security," edited by Setha Low and Zoltan Gluck in 2017. It has been revised for this volume.

1 The FOIA has many built-in exemptions, including classified information for national defense or foreign policy; internal personnel rules and practices, information that is exempt under other laws; trade secrets; interagency or

intra-agency memoranda; personnel and medical files; law enforcement records of information; information concerning bank supervision; and geological and geophysical information. In one of the first acts of the War on Terror, Attorney General John Ashcroft issued a memorandum to all federal agencies in October 2001 requiring a strict interpretation of FOIA exemptions and a general federal reduction in FOIA participation. For examples of FOIA files on civil rights activists, see FBI Records: The Vault (http://vault.fbi.gov/civil -rights). For broader discussion and historical documents related to official secrecy, see Steven Aftergood's *SecrecyNews* blog (http://fas.org/blogs/secrecy/), and also the National Security Archive (http://www2.gwu.edu/~nsarchiv/).

2 The TIA program was broken into several projects after 2003 and formally abandoned. However, similar projects proceeded without public discussion within the classified spaces of the National Security Agency. The TIA proposal continues to have influence internationally, becoming, for example, a concept adopted by the government of Singapore, which has embraced big-data analytics as the paradigm for twenty-first-century security (see Harris 2014a).

3 As the executive chairman of Google puts it in the second edition of his book, trying to keep up with the exponential expansion in capacities and users:

In the first decade of the twenty-first century the number of people connected to the Internet worldwide increased from 350 million to more than 2 billion (it is now over 2.4 billion). In the same period, the number of mobile-phone subscribers rose from 750 million to well over 5 billion (it is now over 6 billion). Adoption of these technologies is spreading to the farthest reaches of the planet and, in some parts of the world, at an accelerating rate. By 2025, the majority of the world's population will, in one generation, have gone from having virtually no access to unfiltered information to accessing all of the world's information through a device that fits in the palm of the hand. If the current pace of technological innovation is maintained, most of the projected eight billion people on Earth will be online. (Schmidt and Cohen 2014, 4)

4 The handbook (U.S. Defense Intelligence Agency 2004, 3–1) also specifies that "collecting" must not "infringe on the constitutional rights" or "privacy rights" of individuals, must be based on a "lawfully assigned function," and must employ the "least intrusive technique" and comply with all "regulatory requirements." In my discussions with NSA personnel, they underscore these requirements as a check on institutional power. However, some of the post-2001 counterterror programs were highly controversial within the NSA, leading to several whistleblower attempts and an unknown number of early retirements. See the *Democracy Now* interview with William Binney (2012). See Bamford (2008) and Aid (2009) for assessments of NSA domestic surveillance activities dating back to the mid-twentieth century.

5 Indeed, big-data analytics are transforming American industry as well as national security logics. For an assessment of the ubiquity of surveillance across the corporate landscape, see Angwin (2014) and Assange (2014). For

a technical assessment of contemporary data security and cryptology, see Schneier (2015), as well as the blog *Schneier on Security* (https://www.schneier .com).

6 See "CIA's 'Facebook' Program Dramatically Cut Agency Costs," Onion News Network, March 21, 2011, https://www.theonion.com/cias-facebook-program -dramatically-cut-agencys-costs-1819594988.

7 For an assessment of how mass surveillance is affecting public speech and writers around the world, see PEN American Center (2014). The Obama administration pursued an unprecedented number of Espionage Act cases against national security reporters in the United States.

8 For a study of how difficult it is to opt out of online corporate surveillance, see Angwin (2014), as well as Mayer-Schonberger (2009). For a consideration of the new nexus of social media, corporate data mining, and government surveillance, see Boghosian (2013).

9 For discussion of online activisms, see Greenberg (2012), as well as Coleman (2014).

10 See Greenwald (2014) for a detailed history of whistleblower Edward Snowden and the negotiations with the *Guardian* and the *Washington Post.* For a catalog of the leaked NSA documents, see "Snowden Revelations," *Lawfare,* https://www.lawfareblog.com/snowden-revelations.

17. THE CRISIS IN CRISIS

This chapter first appeared in *Current Anthropology* in a special issue, "New Media, New Publics," edited by Charles Hirschkind, Maria Jose A. de Abreu, and Carlo Caduff in 2017, and has been revised for this volume.

1 On the lived implications of the demise of the welfare state, see Fennell (2015) for an ethnographic study of the effects on public housing, and see Ralph (2014) on how intensified policing and NGOs replaced public services on Chicago's South Side. Both of these studies detail the material and psychosocial consequences of multigenerational poverty and the loss of a broader social contract in a postwelfare United States.

2 For the linkage been Cold War militarism and environmental science, see Doel (2003), Edwards (2010), Farish (2010), Hamblin (2013), and Masco (2010).

3 For detailed studies of radiation injuries from nuclear detonations, see Johnston and Barker (2008), Lindee (1997), and Makhijani and Schwartz (2008).

4 For studies of fallout and continuing uncertainties around large-scale nuclear events, see Brown (2013, 2019), Kuletz (1998), and Petryna (2002).

5 See International Campaign to Abolish Nuclear Weapons (2020) for an assessment of increased global spending on nuclear weapons in 2019, led by the United States.

6 See Wylie (2018) for a detailed study of citizen science and activism surrounding the new fracking economies.

This chapter first appeared in *Social Text: Periscope*, part of an edited collection, "Always at War," by Sandra Trappen and Patricia Clough in 2013, and has been revised for this volume.

1 For an unprecedented and wide-ranging effort to audit the War on Terror since 2001, see the Watson Institute's Costs of War Project at Brown University: http://watson.brown.edu/costsofwar.

REFERENCES

AARC. 1975–76. *Church Committee Reports*. United States Senate Select Committee to Study Governmental Operations with Respect to Intelligence Activities. http://www.aarclibrary.org/publib/church/reports/contents.htm.

Ackerman, Spencer. 2008. "A Counterinsurgency Guide for Politicos." *Washington Independent*, July 28.

Acuña, Rodolfo. 1998. *Occupied America: A History of Chicanos*. 3rd ed. New York: HarperCollins.

Advisory Committee on Human Radiation Experiments. 1996. *The Human Radiation Experiments: Final Report of the President's Advisory Committee*. New York: Oxford University Press.

Agamben, Giorgio. 1998. *Homo Sacer: Sovereign Power and Bare Life*. Stanford, CA: Stanford University Press.

Agard-Jones, Vanessa. 2013. "Bodies in the System." *Small Axe* 17 (3): 182–92.

Aid, Matthew. 2009. *The Secret Sentry: The Untold History of the National Security Agency*. New York: Bloomsbury.

Anaya, Rudolfo, Francisco Lomeli, and Enrique R. Lamadrid, eds. 1989. *Aztlán: Essays on the Chicano Homeland*. Albuquerque, NM: Academia/El Norte.

Anders, Günther. 1961. "Commandments in the Atomic Age." In *Burning Conscience: The Case of the Hiroshima Pilot Claude Eatherly, Told in His Letters to Günther Anders*, 11–20. New York: Monthly Review Press.

Anderson, Benedict. 1991. *Imagined Communities: Reflections on the Origins and Spread of Nationalism*. Rev. ed. London: Verso.

Angwin, Julia. 2014. *Dragnet Nation*. New York: Times Books.

Angwin, Julia, and Jeff Larson. 2014. "The NSA Revelations All in One Chart." *ProPublica*, June 30.

Appadurai, Arjun. 1986. "Introduction." In *The Social Life of Things: Commodities in Cultural Perspective*, edited by Arjun Appadurai, 3–63. New York: Cambridge University Press.

Appadurai, Arjun. 1991. "Global Ethnoscapes: Notes and Queries for a Transnational Anthropology." In *Recapturing Anthropology*, edited by R. J. Fox, 191–210. Santa Fe, NM: School of American Research.

Appelbaum, Jacob, Aaron Gibson, Christian Grothoff, Andy Müller-Maguhn, Laura Poitras, Michael Sontheimer and Christian Stöcker. 2014. "Prying Eyes: Inside the NSA's War on Internet Security." *Spiegel Online International*, December 28. https://www.spiegel.de/international/germany/inside-the-nsa-s-war -on-internet-security-a-1010361.html.

Appelbaum, Jacob, Aaron Gibson, Claudio Guarnieri, Andy Müller-Maguhn, Laura Poitras, Marcel Rosenbach, Leif Ryge, Hilmar Schmundt, and Michael Sontheimer. 2015. "The Digital Arms Race: NSA Preps America for Future Battle." *Spiegel Online International*, January 17. https://www.spiegel.de /international/world/new-snowden-docs-indicate-scope-of-nsa-preparations -for-cyber-battle-a-1013409.html.

Appelbaum, Jacob, Laura Poitras, Marcel Rosenbach, Christian Stöcker, Jörg Schindler, and Holger Stark. 2013. "Inside TAO: Documents Reveal Top NSA Hacking Unit." *Spiegel Online International*, December 29. https://www.spiegel .de/international/world/the-nsa-uses-powerful-toolbox-in-effort-to-spy-on -global-networks-a-940969.html.

APT. 2007. "Defusing the Ticking Bomb Scenario: Why We Must Say No to Torture, Always." Association for the Prevention of Torture. https://www.apt .ch//content/files_res/tickingbombscenario.pdf.

Aretxaga, Begona. 2005. *States of Terror: Begona Aretxaga's Essays.* Edited by Joseba Zulaika. Reno: University of Nevada Press.

Arms Control Association. n.d. "Nuclear Weapons: Who Has What at a Glance." https://www.armscontrol.org/factsheets/Nuclearweaponswhohaswhat.

Ash, Timothy Garton. 1997. *The File: A Personal History.* New York: Vintage.

Assange, Julian. 2014. *When Google Met Wikileaks.* New York: OR Books.

Atomic Energy Commission. 1968. *Excavating with Nuclear Explosives: Technology Status Report, Plowshare Program.* Documentary. https://archive.org/details /NuclearExcavationExcavatingWithNuclearExplosivesAndPlowshare.

Atomic Energy Commission. 1973. *Plowshare.* Documentary. https://archive.org /details/0418_Plowshare_09_00_47_00.

Baker, Peter, and Choe Sang-Hun. 2017. "Trump Threats 'Fire and Fury' against North Korea If It Endangers U.S." *New York Times*, August 8. https://www .nytimes.com/2017/08/08/world/asia/north-korea-un-sanctions-nuclear-missile -united-nations.html.

Ball, Desmond, and Robert C. Toth. 1990. "Revising the SIOP: Taking War-Fighting to Dangerous Extremes." *International Security* 14 (4): 65–92.

Bamford, James. 1983. *The Puzzle Palace: A Report on America's Most Secret Agency.* NewYork: Penguin.

Bamford, James. 2002. *Body of Secrets: Anatomy of the Ultra-secret National Security Agency.* New York: Anchor.

Bamford, James. 2008. *The Shadow Factory: The Ultra-secret NSA from 9/11 to the Eavesdropping on America.* New York: Anchor.

Bamford, James. 2012. "The NSA Is Building the Country's Biggest Spy Center (Watch What You Say)." *Wired*, March 15.

Barrera, Mario. 1988. *Beyond Azatlan: Ethnic Autonomy in Comparative Perspective*. New York: Praeger.

Beck, Harold L., and Burton G. Bennett. 2002. "Historical Overview of Atmospheric Nuclear Weapons Testing and Estimate of Fallout in the Continental United States." *Health Physics* 82 (5): 591–608.

Beck, Ulrich. 1992. *Risk Society: Toward a New Modernity*. London: Sage.

Beck, Ulrich. 2007. *World at Risk*. Cambridge: Polity.

Belew, Kathleen. 2018. *Bring the War Home: The White Power Movement and Paramilitary America*. Cambridge, MA: Harvard University Press.

Benhabib, Seyla. 1986. *Critique, Norm and Utopia: A Study of the Foundation of Critical Theory*. New York: Columbia University Press.

Benjamin, Walter. 1969. "Theses on the Philosophy of History." In *Illuminations*, 255–67. New York: Harcourt, Brace, and World.

Bennett, Burton G. 2002. "Worldwide Dispersion and Deposition of Radionuclides Produced in Atmospheric Tests." *Health Physics* 82 (5): 644–55.

Berlant, Lauren. 2007. "Slow Death (Sovereignty, Obesity, Lateral Agency)." *Critical Inquiry* 33 (4): 754–80.

Berlant, Lauren. 2011. *Cruel Optimism*. Durham, NC: Duke University Press.

Binney, William. 2012. "Exclusive: National Security Agency Whistleblower William Binney on Growing State Surveillance." *Democracy Now*, April 20. http://www.democracynow.org/2012/4/20/exclusive_national_security_agency _whistleblower_william.

Blanton, Thomas, ed. 2007. "The CIA's Family Jewels." National Security Archive, George Washington University. https://nsarchive2.gwu.edu//NSAEBB /NSAEBB222/index.htm.

Blue Origin. 2019. "Going to Space to Benefit Earth (Full Event Replay)." *YouTube*, May 9. https://www.youtube.com/watch?v=GQ98hGUe6FM.

Bodine, John. 1968. "A Tri-ethnic Trap: The Spanish Americans in Taos." In *Spanish Speaking People in the United States (Proceedings of the 1968 American Ethnological Society)*, edited by June Helm. Seattle: American Ethnological Society.

Boghosian, Heidi. 2013. *Spying on Democracy: Government Surveillance, Corporate Power, and Public Resistance*. San Francisco: City Lights.

Bonneuil, Christophe, and Jean-Baptiste Fressoz. 2016. *The Shock of Anthropocene: The Earth, History and Us*. London: Verso.

Borneman, John. 1992. *Belonging in the Two Berlins: Kin, State, Nation*. Cambridge: Cambridge University Press.

Borneman, John. 1995. "American Anthropology as Foreign Policy." *American Anthropologist* 97 (4): 663–72.

Boyer, Paul. 1998. *Fallout: A Historian Reflects on America's Half-Century Encounter with Nuclear Weapons*. Columbus: Ohio State University Press.

Briggs, Charles L., and John R. Van Ness, eds. 1987. *Land, Water, and Culture: New Perspectives on Hispanic Land Grants*. Albuquerque: University of New Mexico Press.

Broad, William. 1992. *Teller's War: The Top-Secret Story behind the Star Wars Deception*. New York: Simon and Schuster.

Broderick, Mick, ed. 1996. *Hibakusha Cinema: Hiroshima, Nagasaki, and the Nuclear Image in Japanese Film*. New York: Kegan Paul.

Brown, Kate. 2013. *Plutopia: Nuclear Families, Atomic Cities, and the Great Soviet and American Plutonium Disasters*. Oxford: Oxford University Press.

Brown, Kate. 2019. *Manual for Survival: A Chernobyl Guide to the Future*. New York: W. W. Norton.

Browne, Simone. 2015. *Dark Matters: On the Surveillance of Blackness*. Durham, NC: Duke University Press.

Bruce, Gary. 2010. *The Firm: The Inside Story of the Stasi*. Oxford: Oxford University Press.

Brzezinski, Zbigniew. 2007. "Five Flaws in the President's Plan." *Washington Post*, January 12. https://www.washingtonpost.com/archive/opinions/2007/01/12/five-flaws-in-the-presidents-plan/0f0de268-ab71-4b6d-9cb2-aed4ec872b01/.

Buck-Morss, Susan. 1991. *Dialectics of Seeing: Walter Benjamin and the Arcades Project*. Cambridge: MIT Press.

Buck-Morss, Susan. 2000. *Dreamworld and Catastrophe: The Passing of Mass Utopia in East and West*. Cambridge, MA: MIT Press.

Bullard, R. D., ed. 1993. *Environmental Justice: Issues, Policies, and Solutions*. Washington, DC: Island Press.

Burr, William, ed. 2004. "The Creation of SIOP-62: More Evidence on the Origins of Overkill." In *National Security Archive Electronic Briefing Book No. 130*. National Security Archive, George Washington University. https://nsarchive2.gwu.edu//NSAEBB/NSAEBB130/index.htm.

Burr, William, ed. 2005. "To Have the Only Option That of Killing 80 Million People Is the Height of Immorality: The Nixon Administration, the SIOP, and the Search for Limited Nuclear Options, 1969–1974." In *National Security Archive Electronic Briefing Book No. 173*. National Security Archive, George Washington University. https://nsarchive2.gwu.edu//NSAEBB/NSAEBB173/index.htm.

Burr, William, ed. 2011. "'Nobody Wins a Nuclear War' but 'Success' Is Possible." In *National Security Archive Electronic Briefing Book No. 336*. National Security Archive, George Washington University. https://nsarchive2.gwu.edu//nukevault/ebb336/index.htm.

Bush, Vannevar. 1945. "As We May Think." *Atlantic*, July. https://www.theatlantic.com/magazine/archive/1945/07/as-we-may-think/303881/.

Byrne, Brendan, and Dhruv Mehrotra. 2018. "The One Place in the US Google Earth Stopped Mapping." *Motherboard*, October 24.

Caduff, Carlo. 2015. *The Pandemic Perhaps: Dramatic Events in a Public Culture of Danger*. Berkeley: University of California Press.

Caldeira, Ken, Bala Govindasamy, and Long Cao. 2013. "The Science of Geoengineering." *Annual Review of Earth and Planetary Sciences* 41: 231–56.

Campbell, David. 1992. *Writing Security: United States Foreign Policy and the Politics of Identity*. Minneapolis: University of Minnesota Press.

Capra, Frank. 1958. *Unchained Goddess*. Bell System Science Series. 57-minute film.

Carse, Ashley. 2014. *Beyond the Big Ditch: Politics, Ecology, and Infrastructure at the Panama Canal.* Cambridge, MA: MIT Press.

Cattelino, Jessica. 2008. *High Stakes: Florida Seminole Gaming and Sovereignty.* Durham, NC: Duke University Press.

CBS News. 2018. "Hawaii Missile Alert: False Alarm Warns Residents of 'Ballistic Missile Threat.'" cbsnews.com, January 13. https://www.cbsnews.com/news /hawaii-missile-alert-emergency-management-system-false-ballistic-missile -warning-2018-1-13/.

Chakrabarty, Dipesh. 2009. "The Climate of History: Four Theses." *Critical Inquiry* 35: 197–222.

Chakrabarty, Dipesh. 2012. "Postcolonial Studies and the Challenge of Climate Change." *New Literary History* 43 (1): 1–18.

Chandor, J. C., dir. 2013. *All Is Lost.* Lionsgate.

Chavez, John R. 1984. *The Lost Land: The Chicano Image of the Southwest.* Albuquerque: University of New Mexico Press.

Cheney, Richard. 2001. "Remarks to the Republican Governors Association." Presented at the Republican Governors Association, Washington, DC, October 25. http://georgewbush-whitehouse.archives.gov/vicepresident/news-speeches /speeches/vp20011025.html.

Choy, Tim. 2011. *Ecologies of Comparison: An Ethnography of Endangerment in Hong Kong.* Durham, NC: Duke University Press.

Choy, Tim, and Jerry Zee. 2015. "Condition—Suspension." *Cultural Anthropology* 30 (2): 210–23.

Churchill, Ward. 1993. *Struggle for the Land: Indigenous Resistance to Genocide, Ecocide, and Expropriation in Contemporary North America.* Monroe, ME: Common Courage.

Churchill, Ward, and Jim Vander Wall. 2002. *The COINTELPRO Papers.* Cambridge, MA: South End.

Clark, Nigel. 2014. "Geo-politics and the Disaster of the Anthropocene." *Sociological Review* 62 (S1): 19–37.

Clarke, Richard, and Robert K. Knake. 2010. *Cyber War: The Next Threat to National Security and What to Do about It.* New York: HarperCollins.

Cloud, John. 2001. "Imaging the World in a Barrel: CORONA and the Clandestine Convergence of the Earth Sciences." *Social Studies of Science* 31 (2): 231–51.

Cohen, Felix. 1941. *Handbook of Federal Indian Law.* Washington, DC: Government Printing Office.

Cohn, Carol. 1987. "Sex and Death in the Rational World of Defense Intellectuals." *Signs* 12 (4): 687–718.

Coleman, Gabrielle. 2013. *Coding Freedom: The Ethics and Aesthetics of Hacking.* Princeton, NJ: Princeton University Press.

Coleman, Gabrielle. 2014. *Hacker, Hoaxer, Whistleblower, Spy: The Many Faces of Anonymous.* New York: Verso.

Collier, Stephen J., and Andrew Lakoff. 2015. "Vital Systems Security: Reflexive Biopolitics and the Government of Emergency." *Theory, Culture and Society* 32 (2): 19–51.

Commission on the Engagement of Anthropology with the US Security and Intelligence Communities (CEAUSSIC). 2009. *Final Report on the Army's Human Terrain System Proof of Concept Program*. American Anthropological Association, October 14. https://www.americananthro.org/issues/policy-advocacy/statement-on-HTS.cfm.

Commoner, Barry. 1958. "The Fallout Problem." *Science* 127 (3305): 1023–26.

Coolidge, Matthew. 1996. *The Nevada Test Site: A Guide to America's Nuclear Proving Ground*. Los Angeles: Center for Land Use Interpretation.

Cosgrove, Denis. 2001. *Apollo's Eye: A Cartographic Genealogy of the Earth in the Western Imagination*. Baltimore, MD: Johns Hopkins University Press.

Costello, Anthony, Mustafa Abbas, Adriana Allen, Sarah Ball, Sarah Bell, Richard Bellamy, Sharon Friel, et al. 2009. "Managing the Health Effects of Climate Change." *Lancet* 373 (9676): 1693–1733.

Cram, Shannon. 2015. "Becoming Jane: The Making and Unmaking of Hanford's Nuclear Body." *Environment and Planning D: Society and Space* 33 (5): 796–812.

Cram, Shannon. 2016. "Living in Dose: Nuclear Work and the Politics of Permissible Exposure." *Public Culture* 28 (3): 519–39.

Crary, Jonathan. 2013. *24/7: Late Capitalism and the Ends of Sleep*. New York: Verso.

Crow, James. 1960. "Radiation and Future Generations." In *Fallout: A Study of Super Bombs*, edited by John M. Fowler, 92–105. New York: Basic Books.

Crutzen, P. J. 2002. "The Anthropocene." *Journal de Physique IV* 12 (10): 1–6.

CSBA. 2009. "Classified Funding in the FY 2010 Defense Budget Request." Center for Strategic and Budgetary Assessments. https://csbaonline.org/research/publications/classified-funding-in-the-fy-2010-defense-budget-request.

Cunningham, David. 2004. *There's Something Happening Here: The New Left, the Klan, and FBI Counterintelligence*. Berkeley: University of California Press.

Darlington, David. 1997. *Area 51: The Dreamland Chronicles*. New York: Henry Holt.

Daston, Lorraine J., and Galison, Peter. 2010. *Objectivity*. Cambridge, MA: MIT Press.

Davis, Tracy C. 2007. *Stages of Emergency: Cold War Nuclear Civil Defense*. Durham, NC: Duke University Press.

Day, Dwayne A., John M. Logsdon, and Brian Latell, eds. 1998. *Eye in the Sky: The Story of the Corona Spy Satellites*. Washington, DC: Smithsonian Institution Press.

de la Cadena, Marisol. 2015. *Earth Beings: Ecologies of Practice across Andean Worlds*. Durham, NC: Duke University Press.

DeLoughrey, Elizabeth. 2014. "Satellite Planetarity and the Ends of the Earth." *Public Culture* 26 (2): 257–80.

del Toro, Guillermo, dir. 2013. *Pacific Rim*. Warner Brothers and Legendary Pictures.

Derrida, Jacques. 1984. "No Apocalypse, Not Now (Full Speed Ahead, Seven Missiles, Seven Missives)." *Diacritics* 20: 20–31.

Dixon, Ivan, dir. 1973. *The Spook Who Sat by the Door*. Obsidian.

Doel, Ronald. 2003. "Constituting the Postwar Earth Sciences: The Military's Influence on the Environmental Sciences in the USA after 1945." *Social Studies of Science* 33 (5): 635–66.

Donner, Frank. 1981. *The Age of Surveillance: The Aims and Methods of America's Political Intelligence System.* New York: Vintage.

Dower, John W. 2010. *Cultures of War: Pearl Harbor/Hiroshima/9–11/Iraq.* New York: W. W. Norton.

Dower, John W. 2017. *The Violent American Century: War and Terror since World War II.* Chicago: Haymarket.

Drinnon, Richard. 1990. *The Metaphysics of Indian Hating and Empire Building.* New York: Schocken.

Ebright, Malcolm. 1994. *Land Grants and Lawsuits in Northern New Mexico.* Albuquerque: University of New Mexico Press.

Economist. 2014. "The Economics of Shale Oil: Saudi America." February 15.

Eden, Lynn. 2004. *Whole World on Fire: Organizations, Knowledge, and Nuclear Weapons Devastation.* Ithaca, NY: Cornell University Press.

Edwards, Paul. 1996. *The Closed World: Computers and the Politics of Discourse in Cold War America.* Cambridge, MA: MIT Press.

Edwards, Paul. 2010. *A Vast Machine: Computer Models, Climate Data, and the Politics of Global Warming.* Cambridge, MA: MIT Press.

Egan, Michael. 2007. *Barry Commoner and the Science of Survival: The Remaking of American Environmentalism.* Cambridge, MA: MIT Press.

Ehrlich, Paul R., Carl Sagan, Douglas Kennedy, and Walter Orr Roberts, eds. 1984. *The Cold and the Dark: The World after Nuclear War.* New York: W. W. Norton.

Eichstaedt, Peter H. 1994. *If You Poison Us: Uranium and Native Americans.* Santa Fe, NM: Red Crane.

Ellsberg, Daniel. 2017. *The Doomsday Machine: Confessions of a Nuclear War Planner.* New York: Bloomsbury.

Erickson, Paul, Judy Klein, Lorraine Daston, Rebecca Lemov, Thomas Sturm, and Michael Gordin, eds. 2013. *How Reason Almost Lost Its Mind: The Strange Career of War Rationality.* Chicago: University of Chicago Press.

Evans, Brad, and Julian Reid. 2014. *Resilient Life: The Art of Living Dangerously.* Cambridge: Polity.

Evans, Joyce. 1999. *Celluloid Mushroom Clouds: Hollywood and the Atomic.* Boulder, CO: Westview.

Farish, Matthew. 2010. *The Contours of America's Cold War.* Minneapolis: University of Minnesota Press.

Farrell, Justin. 2016. "Corporate Funding and Ideological Polarization about Climate Change." *Proceedings of the National Academy of Sciences of the United States of America* 113 (1): 92–97.

FAS. 1946. *One World or None: A Report to the Public on the Full Meaning of the Atomic Bomb.* Washington, DC: Federation of American Scientists.

FAS. 2000. "Area 41-Groom Lake, NV." Federation of American Scientists, April 2. http://fas.org/irp/overhead/ikonos_040400_overview_02-f.htm.

FCC. *Report and Recommendations: Hawaii Emergency Management Agency January 13, 2018 False Alert.* Washington, DC: Federal Communications Commission.

FCDA. 1954. *The House in the Middle*. Washington, DC: Federal Civil Defense Administration.

Feiveson, Harold, Alexander Glaser, Zia Mian, and Frank N. Von Hippel. 2014. *Unmaking the Bomb*. Cambridge, MA: MIT Press.

Fennell, Catherine. 2015. *Last Project Standing: Civics and Sympathy in Post-welfare Chicago*. Minneapolis: University of Minnesota Press.

Fenster, Mark. 1999. *Conspiracy Theory: Secrecy and Power in American Culture*. Minneapolis: University of Minnesota Press.

FitzGerald, Frances. 2000. *Way Out There in Blue: Reagan, Star Wars, and the End of the Cold War*. New York: Touchstone.

Fleming, Roger. 2010. *Fixing the Sky: The Checkered History of Weather and Climate Control*. New York: Columbia University Press.

Forrest, Suzanne. 1989. *The Preservation of the Village: New Mexico's Hispanics and the New Deal*. Albuquerque: University of New Mexico Press.

Fortun, Kim. 2012. "Ethnography in Late Industrialism." *Cultural Anthropology* 27 (3): 446–64.

Foucault, Michel. 2000. "The Risks of Security." In *Power: The Essential Works of Foucault, 1954–1984*, vol. 3, edited by James Faubion. New York: New Press.

Foucault, Michel. 2003. *Society Must Be Defended: Lectures at the College de France, 1975–76*. Edited by Mauro Bertani and Alessandro Fontana. New York: Picador.

Fowler, John M., ed. 1960a. *Fallout: A Study of Superbombs, Strontium 90, and Survival*. New York: Basic Books.

Fowler, John M. 1960b. "The Rising Level of Fallout." In *Fallout: A Study of Superbombs, Strontium 90, and Survival*, edited by John M. Fowler, 51–67. New York: Basic Books.

Fradkin, Philip L. 1989. *Fallout: An American Nuclear Tragedy*. Tucson: University of Arizona Press.

Freud, Sigmund. 1991. "Thoughts for the Times on War and Death." In *Civilization, Society, and Religion*, 12:57–89. Penguin Freud Library. London: Penguin.

Friedman, Jonathan. 1994. *Cultural Identity and Global Process*. London: Sage.

Funk, McKenzie. 2014. *Windfall: The Booming Business of Global Warming*. New York: Penguin.

Gabrys, Jennifer. 2016. *Program Earth: Environmental Sensing Technology and the Making of a Computational Planet*. Minneapolis: University of Minnesota Press.

Galison, Peter. 2001. "War against the Center." *Grey Room*, summer, 5–33.

Gallagher, Carole. 1993. *American Ground Zero: The Secret Nuclear War*. Cambridge, MA: MIT Press.

Gallagher, Ryan, and Glenn Greenwald. 2014. "How the NSA Plans to Infect 'Millions' of Computers with Malware." *The Intercept*, March 12. https://firstlook.org/theintercept/2014/03/12/nsa-plans-infect-millions-computers-malware/.

Galula, David. 2008. *Counterinsurgency Warfare: Theory and Practice*. Westport, CT: Praeger Security International.

Garcia, Angela. 2010. *The Pastoral Clinic: Addiction and Dispossession along the Rio Grande*. Berkeley: University of California Press.

Gardner, Richard. 1970. *Grito! Reies Tijerina and the New Mexico Land Grant War of 1967*. New York: Harper Colophon.

Gellman, Barton. 2013. "NSA Broke Privacy Rules Thousands of Times per Year, Audit Finds." *Washington Post*, August 15. http://www.washingtonpost.com /world/national-security/nsa-broke-privacy-rules-thousands-of-times-per-year -audit-finds/2013/08/15/3310e554-05ca-11e3-a07f-49ddc7417125_story.html.

Ghamari-Tabrizi, Sharon. 2005. *The Worlds of Herman Kahn: The Intuitive Sense of Thermonuclear War*. Cambridge, MA: Harvard University Press.

Glasstone, Samuel, and Philip J. Dolan, eds. 1977. *The Effects of Nuclear Weapons*. 3rd ed. Washington, DC: Government Printing Office.

GlobalSecurity.org. 2019. "World Wide Military Expenditures, 2019." https://www .globalsecurity.org/military/world/spending.htm.

GlobalSecurity.org. n.d. *World Military Guide*. http://www.globalsecurity.org /military/world/.

Graeter, Stefanie. 2017. "To Revive an Abundant Life: Catholic Science and Neoextractivist Politics in Peru's Mantaro Valley." *Cultural Anthropology* 32 (1): 117–48.

Graff, Garret M. 2017. *Raven Rock: The Story of the U.S. Government's Secret Plan to Save Itself—While the Rest of Us Die*. New York: Simon and Schuster.

Greenberg, Andy. 2012. *This Machine Kills Secrets: How WikiLeaks, Cypherpunks and Hacktivists Aim to Free the World's Information*. New York: Dutton.

Greenlee, Sam. (1969) 1989. *The Spook Who Sat by the Door*. Detroit: Wayne State University Press.

Greenwald, Glenn. 2013. "XKeyscore: NSA Tool Collects 'Nearly Everything a User Does on the Internet.'" *Guardian*, July 31. http://www.theguardian.com/world /2013/jul/31/nsa-top-secret-program-online-data.

Greenwald, Glenn. 2014. *No Place to Hide: Edward Snowden, the NSA, and the U.S. Surveillance State*. New York: Metropolitan.

Grimmett, Richard F. 2007. *Conventional Arms Transfers to Developing Nations, 1999–2006*. Washington, DC: Congressional Research Service.

Grinde, Donald, and Bruce Johansen. 1995. *Ecocide of Native America: Environmental Destruction of Indian Lands and Peoples*. Santa Fe, NM: Clear Light.

Griswold del Castillo, Richard. 1990. *The Treaty of Guadalupe Hidalgo: A Legacy of Conflict*. Norman: University of Oklahoma Press.

Gusterson, Hugh. 1995. "NIF-Ty Exercise Machine." *Bulletin of Atomic Scientists*, October, 22–26.

Gusterson, Hugh. 1996. *Nuclear Rites: A Nuclear Weapons Laboratory at the End of the Cold War*. Berkeley: University of California Press.

Gusterson, Hugh. 2004. *People of the Bomb: Portraits of America's Nuclear Complex*. Minneapolis: University of Minnesota Press.

Hacker, Barton C. 1994. *Elements of Controversy: The Atomic Energy Commission and Radiation Safety in Nuclear Weapons, 1947–1974*. Berkeley: University of California Press.

Haffner, Jeanne. 2013. *The View from Above: The Science of Social Space*. Cambridge, MA: MIT Press.

Hagen, Joel. 1992. *An Entangled Bank: The Origins of Ecosystem Ecology*. New Brunswick, NJ: Rutgers University Press.

Halpern, Orit. 2014. *Beautiful Data: A History of Vision and Reason since 1945*. Durham, NC: Duke University Press.

Hamblin, Jacob Darwin. 2013. *Arming Mother Nature: The Birth of Catastrophic Environmentalism*. New York: Oxford University Press.

Hamilton, Clive. 2013. *Earthmasters: The Dawn of Climate Engineering*. New Haven, CT: Yale University Press.

Hamilton, Kevin, and Ned O'Gorman. 2018. *Lookout America! The Secret Hollywood Studio at the Heart of the Cold War*. Lebanon, NH: Dartmouth College Press.

Hanson. Randel D. 2001. "An Experiment in (Toxic) Indian Capitalism? The Skull Valley Goshutes, New Capitalism, and Nuclear Waste." *PoLAR: Political and Legal Anthropology Review* 24 (2): 25–38.

Hardin, Garret. 1974. "Lifeboat Ethics: The Case against Helping the Poor." *Psychology Today*, September. https://www.garretthardinsociety.org/articles/art _lifeboat_ethics_case_against_helping_poor.html.

Harley, Naomi. 2002. "Laboratory Analyses: Environmental and Biological Measurements." *Health Physics* 82 (5): 626–34.

Harris, Shane. 2014a. "The Social Laboratory." *Foreign Policy*, July 29. http:// foreignpolicy.com/2014/07/29/the-social-laboratory/.

Harris, Shane. 2014b. *@War: The Rise of the Military-Internet Complex*. New York: Houghton Mifflin Harcourt.

Hashimoto, Isao. 2003. *1945–1998*. CTBTO Preparatory Commission. https://www .ctbto.org/specials/1945-1998-by-isao-hashimoto.

Haynes, John Earl, and Harvey Klehr. 1999. *Venona: Decoding Soviet Espionage in America*. New Haven, CT: Yale University Press.

Hecht, Gabrielle. 2012. *Being Nuclear: Africans and the Global Uranium Trade*. Cambridge, MA: MIT Press.

Heise, Ursula. 2008. *Sense of Place and Sense of Planet*. Oxford: Oxford University Press.

Heller, Arnie. 1999. "Seismic Monitoring Techniques Put to a Test." *Science and Technology Review*, April, 18–20.

Helmreich, Stefan. 2008. *Alien Ocean: Anthropological Voyages in Microbial Seas*. Berkeley: University of California Press.

Higgs, Robert. 2007. "The Trillion-Dollar Defense Budget Is Already Here." *Independent*, March 15. http://www.independent.org/newsroom/article.asp?id=1941.

Hoffman, David. 2010. *The Dead Hand: The Untold Story of the Cold War Arms Race and Its Dangerous Legacy*. New York: Anchor.

Hohler, Sabine. 2015. *Spaceship Earth in the Environmental Age, 1960–1990*. London: Pickering and Chatto.

Holland, Ryan. 2004. "Securing Dystopia: Gangs and Terror in Chicago's Urban Imaginaries." Bachelor of Arts thesis, Department of Anthropology, University of Chicago.

Horkheimer, Max, and Theodor Adorno. 2002. *The Dialectic of Enlightenment*. Stanford, CA: Stanford University Press.

Horsman, Reginald. 1981. *Race and Manifest Destiny: The Origins of American Racial Anglo-Saxonism*. Cambridge, MA: Harvard University Press.

Hu, Tung-Hui. 2015. *A Prehistory of the Cloud*. Cambridge: MIT Press.

Hull, Matthew. 2012. *Government of Paper: The Materiality of Bureaucracy in Urban Pakistan*. Berkeley: University of California Press.

Ignatius, David. 2003. "Think Strategy, Not Numbers." *Washington Post*, August 26. https://www.washingtonpost.com/archive/opinions/2003/08/26/think-strategy-not-numbers/f3215739-15bf-4a2e-8504-bfccf74dd323/.

International Campaign to Abolish Nuclear Weapons (ICAN). 2020. *Enough Is Enough: 2019 Global Nuclear Weapons Spending*. https://www.icanw.org/ican_releases_2019_nuclear_weapons_spending_research.

IPCC. 2013. "Summary for Policymakers." In *Climate Change 2013: The Physical Science Basis*. Intergovernmental Panel on Climate Change. http://www.ipcc.ch/report/ar5/wg1/.

IPCC. 2014. *Climate Change 2014: Impacts, Adaptation, and Vulnerability*. Intergovernmental Panel on Climate Change. http://www.ipcc.ch/report/ar5/wg2/.

IPCC. 2018. *Global Warming of 1.5°C*. Intergovernmental Panel on Climate Change. https://www.ipcc.ch/sr15/.

IPPNW and IEER. 1991. *Radioactive Heaven and Earth: The Health and Environmental Effects of Nuclear Weapons Testing in, on, and above the Earth*. New York: Apex.

IPPNW and IEER. 1992. *Plutonium: Deadly Gold of the Nuclear Age*. Cambridge, MA: International Physicians Press.

Jaczko, Gregory B. 2019. *Confessions of a Rogue Nuclear Regulator*. New York: Simon and Schuster.

Jaimes, M. Annette, ed. 1992. *The State of Native America: Genocide, Colonization, and Resistance*. Boston: South End.

Jain, S. Lochlann. 2013. *Malignant: How Cancer Becomes Us*. Berkeley: University of California Press.

Jameson, Fredric. 1998. "The Antinomies of Postmodernity." In *Selected Writings on the Postmodern, 1983–1998*, 50–72. New York: Verso.

Jameson, Fredric. 2003. "Future City." *New Left Review* 21: 65–79.

Jamison, Dale. 2014. *Reason in a Dark Time: Why the Struggle against Climate Change Failed and What It Means for Our Future*. New York: Oxford University Press.

Janis, Irving. 1951. *Air War and Emotional Stress*. New York: McGraw Hill.

Jasanoff, Sheila, and Marybeth Martell, eds. 2004. *Earthly Politics: Local and Global Environmental Governance*. Cambridge, MA: MIT Press.

Johnson, Chalmers. 2000. *Blowback: The Costs and Consequences of American Empire*. New York: Henry Holt.

Johnson, Chalmers. 2004. *The Sorrows of Empire: Militarism, Secrecy, and the End of the Republic*. New York: Henry Holt.

Johnson, Chalmers. 2008. "Mission Creep: America's Unwelcome Advances." *Mother Jones*, August 22.

Johnston, Barbara Rose, and Holly M. Barker. 2008. *The Consequential Damages of Nuclear War: The Rongelap Report*. Walnut Creek, CA: Left Coast Press.

Kahn, Herman. 1960. *On Thermonuclear War*. Princeton, NJ: Princeton University Press.

Kalat, David. 2010. *A Critical History and Filmography of Toho's Godzilla Series*. Jefferson, NC: McFarland.

Kalugin, Oleg. 1994. *The First Directorate: My 32 Years of Intelligence and Espionage against the West*. New York: St. Martin's.

Kant, Immanuel. 1986. "Analytic of the Sublime." In *Philosophical Writings*, edited by Ernst Behler, 201–23. New York: Continuum.

Kaplan, Amy. 2003. "Homeland Insecurities: Some Reflections on Language and Space." *Radical History Review* 85: 82–93.

Kaplan, E. Ann. 2016. *Climate Trauma: Foreseeing the Future in Dystopian Film and Fiction*. New Bruswick, NJ: Rutgers University Press.

Kaufman, Scott. 2012. *Project Plowshare: The Peaceful Use of Nuclear Explosives in Cold War America*. Ithaca, NY: Cornell University Press.

Keeney, L. Douglas. 2002. *The Doomsday Scenario*. St. Paul, MN: MBI.

Keeney, L. Douglas. 2011. *15 Minutes: General Curtis LeMay and the Countdown to Nuclear Annihilation*. New York: St. Martin's.

Keith, David. 2013. *A Case for Climate Engineering*. Cambridge, MA: MIT Press.

Kelty, Christopher. 2008. *Two Bits: The Cultural Significance of Free Software*. Durham, NC: Duke University Press.

Kennedy, John F. 1963. "Address to the Nation on the Nuclear Test Ban Treaty, 26 July 1963." John F. Kennedy Presidential Library and Museum. https://www.jfklibrary.org/learn/about-jfk/historic-speeches/televised-address-on-nuclear-test-ban-treaty.

Kipp, Jacob, Lester Grau, Karl Pinslow, and Don Smith. 2006. "The Human Terrain System: A CORDS for the 21st Century." *Military Review*, September–October, 8–15.

Kirsch, Scott. 2005. *Proving Grounds: Project Plowshare and the Unrealized Dream of Nuclear Earth Moving*. New Brunswick, NJ: Rutgers University Press.

Klare, Michael. 1995. *Rogue States and Nuclear Outlaws: America's Search for a New Foreign Policy*. New York: Hill and Wang.

Klein, Naomi. 2006. *The Shock Doctrine: The Rise of Disaster Capitalism*. New York: Metropolitan.

Kolbert, Elizabeth. 2014. *The Sixth Extinction: An Unnatural History*. New York: Henry Holt.

Koronowski, Ryan. 2014. "House Votes to Deny Climate Science and Ties Pentagon's Hands on Climate Change." *Think Progress*, May 22. https://archive.thinkprogress.org/house-votes-to-deny-climate-science-and-ties-pentagons-hands-on-climate-change-6fb577189fb0/.

Kosek, Jake. 2006. *Understories: The Political Life of Forests in Northern New Mexico*. Durham, NC: Duke University Press.

Kosek, Jake. 2010. "Ecologies of Empire: On the New Uses of the Honeybee." *Cultural Anthropology* 25 (4): 650–78.

Koselleck, Reinhart. 1988. *Critique and Crisis: Enlightenment and the Pathogenesis of Modern Society*. Cambridge, MA: MIT Press.

Kristensen, Hans M. 2006. *Global Strike: A Chronology of the Pentagon's New Offensive Strike Plan*. Washington, DC: Federation of American Scientists. March. http://www.nukestrat.com/.

Kristensen, Hans M., and Matt Korda. 2020. "Status of World Nuclear Forces." Federation of American Scientists, May. https://fas.org/issues/nuclear-weapons/status-world-nuclear-forces/.

Kristensen, Hans M., Matthew McKinzie, and Theodore A. Postol. 2017. "How US Nuclear Force Modernization Is Undermining Strategic Stability: The Burst-Height Compensating Super-Fuze." *Bulletin of the Atomic Scientists*, March 1. https://thebulletin.org/2017/03/how-us-nuclear-force-modernization-is-undermining-strategic-stability-the-burst-height-compensating-super-fuze/.

Kubrick, Stanley, dir. 1964. *Dr. Strangelove, Or: How I Learned to Stop Worrying and Love the Bomb*. Columbia Pictures.

Kuchinskaya, Olga. 2014. *The Politics of Invisibility: Public Knowledge about Radiation Health Effects after Chernobyl*. Cambridge, MA: MIT Press.

Kuletz, Valerie. 1998. *The Tainted Desert: Environmental Ruin in the American West*. New York: Routledge.

Kuran, Peter, dir. 2003. *Atomic Filmmakers: Hollywood's Secret Film Studio*. Visual Concept Entertainment.

Kuran, Peter, dir. 2007. *How to Photograph an Atomic Bomb*. Visual Concept Entertainment.

Kurgan, Laura. 2013. *Close Up at a Distance: Mapping, Technology, and Politics*. Cambridge, MA: MIT Press.

LaDuke, Winona, and Ward Churchill. 1985. "Native America: The Political Economy of Radioactive Colonialism." *Journal of Ethnic Studies* 13 (3): 107–32.

Lansford, Robert R., Larry D. Adcock, Lucille M. Gentry, and Shaul Ben David. 1995. *The Economic Impact of the Department of Energy on the State of New Mexico Fiscal Year 1994*. Albuquerque: DOE Albuquerque, in cooperation with New Mexico State University.

Lepselter, Susan. 2005. "Why Rachel Isn't Buried at Her Grave: Ghosts, UFOs, and a Place in the West." In *Histories of the Future*, edited by Susan Harding and Daniel Rosenberg. Durham, NC: Duke University Press.

Lepselter, Susan. 2016. *The Resonance of Unseen Things: Poetics, Power, Captivity, and UFOs in the American Uncanny*. Ann Arbor: University of Michigan Press.

Lewontin, R. C., Ira Katznelson, Laura Nader, and Noam Chomsky, eds. 1997. *The Cold War and the University: Toward an Intellectual History of the Post–Cold War Years*. New York: New Press.

Liberace. 1973. *Liberace: An Autobiography*. New York: G. P. Putnam's Sons.

Liboiron, Max. 2020. *Pollution Is Colonialism*. Durham, NC: Duke University Press.

Lindee, Susan. 1997. *Suffering Made Real: American Science and the Survivors at Hiroshima*. Chicago: University of Chicago Press.

Lindqvist, Sven. 2001. *A History of Bombing*. New York: New Press.

Lindsay-Poland, John. 2003. *Emperors in the Jungle: The Hidden History of the U.S. in Panama*. Durham, NC: Duke University Press.

Loftus, Joseph A. 1961. "Kennedy Prefers Atomic Shelters for Large Groups." *New York Times*, November 25, A-1.

Lorey, Isabell. 2015. *State of Insecurity: Government of the Precarious*. London: Verso.

Los Alamos National Laboratory (LANL). 1994. *Institutional Plan, FY 1995–FY 2000: Science Serving Society*. Los Alamos: Los Alamos National Laboratory.

Luban, David. 2005. "Liberalism, Torture, and the Ticking Bomb." *Virginia Law Review* 91 (6): 1425–61.

Lumet, Sidney, dir. 1964. *Fail Safe*. Columbia Pictures.

Lutz, Catherine. 1997. "Epistemology of the Bunker: The Brainwashed and Other New Subjects of Permanent War." In *Inventing the Psychological: Toward a Cultural History of Emotional Life in America*, edited by Joel Pfister and Nancy Schnog. New Haven, CT: Yale University Press.

Lutz, Catherine. 2002. *Homefront: A Military City and the American Twentieth Century*. Boston: Beacon.

Lutz, Catherine, ed. 2009. *The Bases of Empire: The Struggle against U.S. Military Posts*. New York: New York University Press.

Lyman, Rick. 2001. "Hollywood Discusses Role in War Effort." *New York Times*, November 12.

Lyon, David. 2014. "Surveillance, Snowden, and Big Data: Capacities, Consequences, Critique." *Big Data and Society*, July–December, 1–13.

MacFarlane, Allison, and Rodney Ewing, eds. 2006. *Uncertainty Underground: Yucca Mountain and the Nation's High-Level Nuclear Waste*. Cambridge, MA: MIT Press.

Machta, Lester, and Robert J. List. 1960. "The Global Pattern of Fallout." In *Fallout: A Study of Superbombs, Strontium 90, and Survival*, edited by John M. Fowler. New York: Basic Books.

Machta, Lester, Robert J. List, and L. F. Hubert. 1956. "Worldwide Travel of Atomic Debris." *Science* 124 (3220): 474–77.

MacLean, Nancy. 2017. *Democracy in Chains*. New York: Viking.

Macrakis, Kristie. 2008. *Seduced by Secrets: Inside the Stasi's Spy Tech World*. Cambridge: Cambridge University Press.

Makhijani, Arjun, Howard Hu, and Katherine Yih, eds. 1995. *Nuclear Wastelands: A Global Guide to Nuclear Weapons Production and Its Health and Environmental Effects*. Cambridge, MA: MIT Press.

Makhijani, Arjun, and Stephen I. Schwartz. 1998. "Victims of the Bomb." In *Atomic Audit*, edited by Stephen I. Schwartz, 375–431. Washington, DC: Brookings Institution Press.

Marcus, George E. 1995. "Ethnography in/of the World System: The Emergence of Multi-sited Ethnography." *Annual Review of Anthropology* 24: 95–117.

Masco, Joseph. 2002. "Lie Detectors: On Secrets and Hypersecurity in Los Alamos." *Public Culture* 14 (3): 441–67.

Masco, Joseph. 2004. "Mutant Ecologies: Radioactive Life in Post–Cold War New Mexico." *Cultural Anthropology* 19 (4): 517–50.

Masco, Joseph. 2006. *The Nuclear Borderlands: The Manhattan Project in Post–Cold War New Mexico*. Princeton, NJ: Princeton University Press.

Masco, Joseph. 2008. "'Survival Is Our Business': Engineering Ruins in Nuclear America." *Cultural Anthropology* 23 (2): 361–98.

Masco, Joseph. 2010. "Bad Weather: On Planetary Crisis." *Social Studies of Science* 40 (1): 7–40.

Masco, Joseph. 2014. *The Theater of Operations: National Security Affect from the Cold War to the War on Terror*. Durham, NC: Duke University Press.

Mayer, Jane. 2007. "The Black Sites." *New Yorker*, August 13.

Mayer-Schonberger, Viktor. 2009. *Delete: The Virtue of Forgetting in the Digital Age*. Princeton, NJ: Princeton University Press.

Mayer-Schonberger, Viktor, and Kenneth Cukier. 2014. *Big Data*. Boston: Mariner.

Mbembe, Achille. 2003. "Necropolitics." *Public Culture* 15 (1): 11–40.

McEnaney, Laura. 2000. *Civil Defense Begins at Home: Militarization Meets Everyday Life in the Fifties*. Princeton, NJ: Princeton University Press.

McKinzie, Matthew B., Thomas B. Cochran, Robert S. Norris, and William M. Arkin. 2001. *The U.S. Nuclear War Plan: A Time for Change*. Washington, DC: National Resources Defense Council.

McNeill, J. R., and Peter Engelke. 2014. *The Great Acceleration: An Environmental History of the Anthropocene since 1945*. Cambridge, MA: Belknap.

McNeill, J. R., and Corinna R. Unger, eds. 2010. *Environmental Histories of the Cold War*. Cambridge: Cambridge University Press.

McPhee, John. 1973. *The Curve of Binding Energy*. New York: Farrar, Straus and Giroux.

Meinig, D. W. 1993. *The Shaping of America: A Geographical Perspective*. Vol. 2. New Haven, CT: Yale University Press.

Melillo, Jerry M., Terese Richmond, and Gary W. Yohe, eds. 2014. *Highlights of Climate Change Impacts in the United States: The Third National Climate Assessment*. Washington, DC: U.S. Global Change Research Program.

Melley, Timothy. 2012. *The Covert Sphere: Secrecy, Fiction, and the National Security State*. Ithaca, NY: Cornell University Press.

Metzl, Jonathan. 2003. *Prozac on the Couch: Prescribing Gender in the Era of Wonder Drugs*. Durham, NC: Duke University Press.

Miller, Richard L. 1986. *Under the Cloud: The Decades of Nuclear Testing*. New York: Free Press.

Mitman, Gregg. 2007. *Breathing Space: How Allergies Shape Our Lives and Landscapes*. New Haven, CT: Yale University Press.

Mitman, Gregg, Michelle Murphy, and Christopher Sellers, eds. 2004. *Landscapes of Exposure: Knowledge and Illness in Modern Environments*. Osiris, vol. 19. Chicago: University of Chicago Press.

Monteyne, David. 2011. *Fallout Shelter: Designing for Civil Defense in the Cold War*. Minneapolis: University of Minnesota Press.

Morton, Oliver. 2015. *The Planet Remade: How Geoengineering Could Change the World*. Princeton, NJ: Princeton University Press.

Moynihan, Daniel Patrick. 1998. *Secrecy: The American Experience*. New Haven, CT: Yale University Press.

Murphy, Michelle. 2006. *Sick Building Syndrome and the Problem of Uncertainty: Environmental Politics, Technoscience, and Women Workers.* Durham, NC: Duke University Press.

Murphy, Michelle. 2008. "Chemical Regimes of History." *Environmental History* 13 (4): 695–703.

Murphy, Michelle. 2017a. "Alterlife and Decolonial Chemical Relations." *Cultural Anthropology* 32 (4): 494–503.

Murphy, Michelle. 2017b. *The Economization of Life.* Durham, NC: Duke University Press.

Nadel, Alan. 1995. *Containment Culture: American Narratives, Postmodernism, and the Atomic Age.* Durham, NC: Duke University Press.

Nader, Laura. 1997. "The Phantom Factor: The Effect of the Cold War on Anthropology." In *The Cold War and the University: Toward an Intellectual History of the Post–Cold War Years*, by Noam Chomsky, Ira Katznelson, R. C. Lewontin, David Montgomery, Laura Nader, Richard Ohmann, Ray Siever, Immanuel Wallerstein, and Howard Zinn. New York: New Press.

Nagatani, Patrick. 1991. *Nuclear Enchantment.* Albuquerque: University of New Mexico Press.

Nagl, John A. 2002. *Learning to Eat Soup with a Knife: Counterinsurgency Lessons from Malaya and Vietnam.* Chicago: University of Chicago Press.

Nancy, Jean-Luc. 2015. *After Fukushima: The Equivalence of Catastrophes.* New York: Fordham University Press.

National Cancer Institute. 1997. *Estimated Exposures and Thyroid Doses Received by the American People from Iodine-131 in Fallout Following Nevada Atmospheric Nuclear Bomb Tests.* Washington, DC: National Institutes of Health. https://www.cancer.gov/about-cancer/causes-prevention/risk/radiation/i131 -report-and-appendix.

National Research Council. 2006. *Health Risks from Exposure to Low Levels of Ionizing Radiation: BEIR VII Phase 2.* Washington, DC: National Academies Press.

Nelson, Diane M. 2015. *Who Counts? The Mathematics of Death and Life after Genocide.* Durham, NC: Duke University Press.

New York Department of Health. 2014. *A Public Health Review of High Volume Hydraulic Fracturing for Shale Gas Development.* New York: New York Department of Public Health.

Nietschman, Bernard, and William Le Bon. 1987. "Nuclear Weapons States and Fourth World Weapons." *Cultural Survival Quarterly* 11 (4): 5–7.

Nixon, Rob. 2011. *Slow Violence and the Environmentalism of the Poor.* Cambridge, MA: Harvard University Press.

Nostrand, Richard L. 1992. *The Hispano Homeland.* Norman: University of Oklahoma Press.

Nyce, James M., and Paul Kahn. 1991. *From Memex to Hypertext: Vannevar Bush and the Mind's Machine.* San Diego: Academic Press.

Oakes, Guy. 1994. *The Imaginary War: Civil Defense and American Cold War Culture.* Oxford: Oxford University Press.

Odum, Howard T., and Eugene P. Odum. 1955. "Trophic Structure and Productivity of a Windward Coral Reef Community on Eniwetok Atoll." *Ecological Monographs* 25 (3): 291–320.

Olmsted, Kathryn S. 1996. *Challenging the Secret Government: The Post Watergate Investigations of the CIA and FBI*. Chapel Hill: University of North Carolina Press.

O'Neill, Dan. 2007. *The Firecracker Boys: H-Bombs, Inupiat Eskimos, and the Roots of the Environmental Movement*. New York: Basic Books.

Oreskes, Naomi, and Erik M. Conway. 2010. *Merchants of Doubt*. London: Bloomsbury Press.

Oreskes, Naomi, and John Krige, eds. 2014. *Science and Technology in the Global Cold War*. Cambridge, MA: MIT Press.

Orff, Kate, and Robert Misrach. 2012. *Petrochemical America*. New York: Aperture.

Orr, Jackie. 2006. *Panic Diaries: A Genealogy of Panic Disorder*. Durham, NC: Duke University Press.

Ortiz, Alfonso. 1969. *The Tewa World: Space, Time, Being, and Becoming in a Pueblo Society*. Chicago: University of Chicago Press.

Ortiz, Roxanne Dunbar. 1980. *Roots of Resistance: Land Tenure in New Mexico, 1680–1980*. Los Angeles: Chicano Studies Research Center and American Indian Studies Center, UCLA.

Paglen, Trevor. 2009. *Blank Spots on the Map: The Dark Geography of the Pentagon's Secret World*. New York: Penguin.

Parenti, Christian. 2003. *The Soft Cage: Surveillance in America from Slavery to the War on Terror*. New York: Basic Books.

Parenti, Christian. 2011. *Tropic of Chaos: Climate Change and the New Geography of Violence*. New York: Nation.

Paret, Peter. 1964. *French Revolutionary Warfare from Indochina to Algeria: The Analysis of a Political and Military Doctrine*. Princeton, NJ: Princeton University Press.

Parr, Joy. 2010. *Sensing Changes: Technologies, Environments, and the Everyday, 1953–2003*. Vancouver: University of British Columbia Press.

Peebles, Curtis. 1997. *The Corona Project: America's First Spy Satellites*. Annapolis: Naval Institute Press.

PEN American Center. 2015. *Global Chilling: The Impact of Mass Surveillance on International Writers*. New York: PEN American Center.

Peterson, Val. 1953. "Panic: The Ultimate Weapon." *Collier's: The National Weekly*, August 21.

Petraeus, David H. 2012. "Remarks by Director David H. Petraeus in In-Q-Tel CEO Summit." Central Intelligence Agency. https://www.cia.gov/news-information /speeches-testimony/2012-speeches-testimony/in-q-tel-summit-remarks.html.

Petryna, Adriana. 2002. *Life Exposed: Biological Citizens after Chernobyl*. Princeton, NJ: Princeton University Press.

Poitras, Laura, Marcel Rosenbach, and Holger Stark. 2014. "'A' for Angela: GCHQ and NSA Target Private German Companies and Merkel." *Spiegel Online*

International, March 29. http://www.spiegel.de/international/germany/gchq
-and-nsa-targeted-private-german-companies-a-961444.html.

Pontecorvo, Gillo, dir. 1966. *The Battle of Algiers*. DVD, Criterion Collection.

Poole, Robert. 2008. *Earthrise: How Man First Saw the Earth*. New Haven, CT:
Yale University Press.

Povinelli, Elizabeth A. 2012. "The Will to Be Otherwise/The Effort of Endurance."
South Atlantic Quarterly 111 (3): 453–75.

Povinelli, Elizabeth A. 2016. *Geontologies: A Requiem to Late Liberalism*. Durham,
NC: Duke University Press.

Powell, Dana E. 2018. *Landscapes of Power: Politics of Energy in the Navajo Nation*.
Durham, NC: Duke University Press.

Prados, John. 2013. *The Family Jewels: The CIA, Secrecy, and Presidential Power*.
Austin: University of Texas Press.

Project for the New American Century. 1997. "Statement of Principles." June 3.
https://web.archive.org/web/20050205041635/http://www.newamericancentury
.org/statementofprinciples.htm.

Project for the New American Century. 2000. *Rebuilding America's Defenses: Strat-
egy, Forces, and Resources for a New Century*. Washington, DC: Project for the
New American Century. https://archive.org/details/ProjectForANewAmerican
CenturyRebuildingAmericasDefenses.

Pulido, Laura. 1996. *Environmentalism and Economic Justice: Two Chicano Strug-
gles in the Southwest*. Tucson: University of Arizona Press.

Rafael, Vicente L. 1994. "The Cultures of Area Studies in the United States." *Social
Text* 41: 91–111.

Raffles, Hugh. 2002. *In Amazonia: A Natural History*. Princeton, NJ: Princeton
University Press.

Rainie, Lee, and Janna Anderson. 2014. "The Future of Privacy." Pew Research
Center, December 18. https://www.pewresearch.org/internet/2014/12/18/future
-of-privacy/.

Ralph, Laurence. 2014. *Renegade Dreams: Living through Injury in Gangland Chicago*. Chicago: University of Chicago Press.

Rand Corporation. 1958. *Report on a Study of Non-military Defense*. Santa Monica,
CA: Rand Corporation.

Reagan, Ronald. 1987. "Address to the 42nd Session of the United Nations General Assembly, September 21, 1987." https://www.reaganlibrary.gov/research
/speeches/092187b.

Rhodes, Richard. 1986. *The Making of the Atomic Bomb*. New York: Simon and
Schuster.

Rhodes, Richard. 1995. *Dark Sun: The Making of the Hydrogen Bomb*. New York:
Simon and Schuster.

Richelson, Jeffrey T. 2006. *Spying on the Bomb: American Nuclear Intelligence
from Nazi Germany to Iran and North Korea*. New York: Norton.

Richland, Justin. 2008. *Arguing with Tradition: The Language of Law in Hopi
Tribal Court*. Chicago: University of Chicago Press.

Riles Annelise, ed. 2006. *Documents: Artifacts of Modern Knowledge.* Ann Arbor: University of Michigan Press.

Rivkin, Mark. 2017. *Beyond Settler Time: Temporal Soveignty and Indigenous Self-Determination.* Durham, NC: Duke University Press.

Robin, Libby, Svenker Sorlin, and Paul Warde, eds. 2013. *The Future of Nature.* New Haven, CT: Yale University Press.

Robin, Ron. 2016. *The Cold World They Made: The Strategic Legacy of Robert and Albert Wohlstetter.* Cambridge, MA: Harvard University Press.

Robock, Alan, Allison Marquardt, Ben Kravitz, and Georgiy Stenchikov. 2009. "Benefits, Risk, and Cost of Stratospheric Geoengineering." *Geophysical Research Letters* 36 (19): L19703.

Rogin, Michael. 1988. *"Ronald Reagan," the Movie and Other Episodes in Political Demonology.* Berkeley: University of California Press.

Roitman, Janet. 2014. *Anti-crisis.* Durham, NC: Duke University Press.

Roman, Peter J. 1995. *Eisenhower and the Missile Gap.* Ithaca, NY: Cornell University Press.

Romero, Hilario. 1995. "Los Alamos, D.C.: Growing Up under a Cloud of Secrecy." *Race, Poverty, and Environment* 5 (3/4): 9–10.

Rose, Kenneth D. 2001. *One Nation Underground: The Fallout Shelter in American Culture.* New York: New York University Press.

Rosenbach, Marcel, Laura Poitras, and Holger Stark. 2013. "iSpy: How the NSA Accesses Smartphone Data." *Spiegel Online International*, September 9. http://www.spiegel.de/international/world/how-the-nsa-spies-on-smartphones-including-the-blackberry-a-921161.html.

Rosenbaum, Robert J. 1981. *Mexicano Resistance in the Southwest: "The Sacred Right of Self-Preservation."* Austin: University of Texas Press.

Rosenberg, Daniel. 2001. "No One Is Buried in Hoover Dam." In *Modernism, Inc.: Body, Memory, Capital,* edited by Jani Scandura and Michael Thurston. New York: New York University Press.

Rosenberg, David Alan. 1981. "'A Smoking Radiating Ruin at the End of Two Hours': Documents on American Plans for Nuclear War with the Soviet Union, 1954–1955." *International Security* 6 (3): 3–38.

Rosenberg, David Alan. 1983. "The Origin of Overkill: Nuclear Weapons and American Security, 1945–1960." *International Security* 7 (4): 3–71.

Rosenthal, Debra. 1990. *At the Heart of the Bomb: The Dangerous Allure of Weapons Work.* New York: Addison-Wesley.

Ross, Richard. 2004. *Waiting for the End of the World.* New York: Princeton Architectural Press.

Rothman, Hal K. 1992. *On Rims and Ridges: The Los Alamos Area since 1880.* Lincoln: University of Nebraska Press.

Ruffner, Kevin. 1995. *CORONA: America's First Satellite Program.* Washington, DC: Center for Study of Intelligence, Central Intelligence Agency.

Rumsfeld, Donald H. 2002. "Transforming the Military." *Foreign Affairs* 81 (3): 20–32.

Russell, Edmund. 2001. *War and Nature.* Cambridge: Cambridge University Press.

Sagan, Scott D. 1987. "SIOP-62: The Nuclear War Plan Briefing to President Kennedy." *International Security* 12 (1): 22–51.

Sando, Joe S. 1992. *Pueblo Nations: Eight Centuries of Pueblo Indian History*. Santa Fe, NM: Clear Light.

Savell, Stephanie. 2019. "Current United States Counterterror War Locations." Costs of War Project, Watson Institute for International and Public Affairs, Brown University. Graphic published in *Smithsonian*, January/February. https://watson.brown.edu/costsofwar/files/cow/imce/papers/Current%20US%20Counterterror%20War%20Locations_Costs%20of%20War%20Project%20Map.pdf.

Schlosser, Eric. 2013. *Command and Control: Nuclear Weapons, the Damascus Accident, and the Illusion of Safety*. New York: Penguin.

Schmid, Sonja. 2015. *Producing Power: The Pre-Chernobyl History of the Soviet Nuclear Industry*. Cambridge, MA: MIT Press.

Schmidt, Eric, and Jared Cohen. 2014. *The New Digital Age: Transforming Nations, Businesses, and Our Lives*. New York: Vintage.

Schmitt, Carl. 2007. *The Concept of the Political*. Chicago: University of Chicago Press.

Schneider, Stephen. 2008. "Geoengineering: Could We or Should We Make It Work?" *Philosophical Transactions of the Royal Society A* 366: 3843–62.

Schneier, Bruce. 2015. *Data and Goliath: The Hidden Battles to Collect Your Data and Control Your World*. New York: W. W. Norton.

Schwartz, Stephen I. 1995. "Four Trillion Dollars and Counting." *Bulletin of Atomic Scientists*, December, 32–52.

Schwartz, Stephen I., ed. 1998. *Atomic Audit: The Costs and Consequences of U.S. Nuclear Weapons since 1940*. Washington, DC: Brookings Institution Press.

Schwartz, Stephen I. 2012. "The Real Price of Ballistic Missile Defenses." *WMD Junction*, April 13.

Scott, David. 2014. *Omens of Adversity: Tragedy, Time, Memory, Justice*. Durham, NC: Duke University Press.

Secretary of Energy Advisory Board Task Force. 1995. *Alternative Futures for the Development of Energy National Laboratories*. Washington, DC: Department of Energy.

Security Resources Panel of the Science Advisory Committee. 1957. *Deterrence and Survival in the Nuclear Age*. Washington, DC: Government Printing Office.

Shapiro, Nick. 2015. "Attuning to the Chemosphere: Domestic Formaldehyde, Bodily Reasoning, and the Chemical Sublime." *Cultural Anthropology* 30 (3): 368–93.

Sharpe, Christina. 2016. *In the Wake: On Blackness and Being*. Durham, NC: Duke University Press.

Siegel, James T. 1998. *A New Criminal Type in Jakarta: Counter-revolution Today*. Durham, NC: Duke University Press.

Simmons, Kristen. 2017. "Settler Atmospherics." Member Voices, *Fieldsights*, November 20. https://culanth.org/fieldsights/settler-atmospherics.

Simmons, Marc. 1978. "History of the Pueblos since 1821." In *Handbook of North American Indians*, vol. 9, *Southwest*, edited by Alfonso Ortiz, 206–23. Washington, DC: Smithsonian Institution Press.

Simon, Stevens L., Andrea Bouville, and Charles E. Land. 2006. "Fallout from Nuclear Weapons Tests and Cancer Risks." *American Scientist* 94 (1): 48–57.

Simpson, Audra. 2014. *Mohawk Interruptus: Political Life across the Borders of Settler States*. Durham, NC: Duke University Press.

Singh, Nikhil Pal. 2017. *Race and America's Long War*. Berkeley: University of California Press.

Sloterdijk, Peter. 2009. *Terror from the Air*. Los Angeles: Semiotext(e).

Sloterdijk, Peter, and Hans-Jürgen Henrichs. 2011. *Neither Sun nor Death*. Los Angeles: Semiotext(e).

Slotkin, Richard. 2000. *Regeneration through Violence: The Mythology of the American Frontier, 1600–1800*. Norman: University of Oklahoma Press.

Snead, David L. 1999. *The Gaither Committee, Eisenhower, and the Cold War*. Columbus: Ohio State University Press.

Sourcewatch. n.d. "The Long War." Center for Media and Democracy. https://www .sourcewatch.org/index.php?title=The_Long_War.

Starosielski, Nicole. 2015. *The Undersea Network*. Durham, NC: Duke University Press.

Steffen, Will, Åsa Persson, Lisa Deutsch, Jan Zalasiewicz, Mark Williams, Katherine Richardson, Carole Crumley, et al. 2011. "The Anthropocene: From Global Change to Planetary Stewardship." *Ambio* 40 (7): 739–61.

Stewart, Kathleen. 1994. "Bitter Faiths." In *Technoscientific Imaginaries*, edited by George E. Marcus, 381–98. Chicago: University of Chicago Press.

Stewart, Kathleen, and Stewart Harding. 1999. "Bad Endings: American Apocalypsis." *Annual Review of Anthropology* 28: 285–310.

Stoffle, Richard, and Michael J. Evans. 1988. "American Indians and Nuclear Waste Storage: The Debate at Yucca Mountain, Nevada." *Policy Studies Journal* 16 (4): 751–67.

Stout, David. 2003. "Former Top Russian Spy Pledges New Allegiance." *New York Times*, August 4. https://www.nytimes.com/2003/08/24/us/former-top-russian -spy-pledges-new-allegiance.html.

Streeby, Shelley S. 2018. *Imaging the Future of Climate Change: World-Making through Science Fiction and Activism*. Berkeley: Unversity of California Press.

Sullivan, Walter. 1961. "Babies Surveyed for Strontium 90." *New York Times*, November 25, A-2. https://www.nytimes.com/1961/11/25/archives/babies -surveyed-for-strontium-90-ratio-to-calcium-in-bones-is.html.

Tallbear, Kim. 2013. *Native American DNA: Tribal Belonging and the False Promise of Genetic Science*. Minneapolis: University of Minnesota Press.

Taussig, Michael. 1999. *Defacement: Public Secrecy and the Labor of the Negative*. Stanford, CA: Stanford University Press.

Taylor, Astra, dir. 2005. *Zizek!* Zeitgeist Films.

Teller, Edward. 1960. "We're Going to Work Miracles." *Popular Mechanics* 113 (3): 97–103.

Teller, E., W. K. Talley, G. H. Higgins, and G. W. Johnson. 1968. *The Constructive Uses of Nuclear Explosives*. New York: McGraw-Hill.

Thomas, Bob. 1987. *Liberace: The True Story*. New York: St. Martin's.

Thomas, Deborah A. 2019. *Political Life in the Wake of the Plantation: Sovereignty, Witnessing, Repair*. Durham, NC: Duke University Press.

Titus, Constantina A. 1986. *Bombs in the Backyard: Atomic Testing and American Politics*. Las Vegas: University of Nevada Press.

Trujillo, Michael. 2009. *Land of Disenchantment: Latina/o Identities and Transformations of Northern New Mexico*. Albuquerque: University of New Mexico Press.

Tsing, Anna, Heather Swanson, Elain Gan, and Nils Bubandt, eds. 2017. *Arts of Living on a Damaged Planet*. Minneapolis: University of Minnesota Press.

Tuck, Eve, and K. Wayne Yang. 2012. "Decolonization Is Not a Metaphor." *Decolonization: Indigeneity, Education and Society* 1 (1): 1–40.

Turchetti, Simone, and Peder Roberts, eds. 2014. *The Surveillance Imperative: Geosciences during the Cold War and Beyond*. New York: Palgrave.

Turner, Fred. 2006. *From Counterculture to Cyberculture: Stewart Brand, the Whole Earth Network, and the Rise of Digital Utopianism*. Chicago: University of Chicago Press.

Turner, Fred. 2013. *The Democratic Surround: Multimedia and American Liberalism from World War II to the Psychedelic Sixties*. Chicago: University of Chicago Press.

United Nations. 1968. *Treaty on the Non-proliferation of Nuclear Weapons*. New York: United Nations.

United Nations. 2017. *Treaty on the Prohibition of Nuclear Weapons*. New York: United Nations.

U.S. Air Force. 1958. *The Power of Decision*. https://archive.org/details/AirForceSpecialFilmProject416powerOfDecision.

U.S. Army Marine Corps. 2007. *Counterinsurgency Field Manual*. Chicago: University of Chicago Press.

U.S. Defense Intelligence Agency. 2004. *Intelligence Law Handbook*. https://www.aclu.org/files/assets/e012333/DIA/Intelligence%20Law%20Handbook%20Defense%20HUMINT%20Service.pdf.

U.S. Department of Defense. 2002. *Nuclear Posture Review*. http://web.stanford.edu/class/polisci211z/2.6/NPR2001leaked.pdf.

U.S. Department of Defense. 2018. *Nuclear Posture Review*. Washington, DC: Office of the Secretary of Defense.

U.S. Department of Energy. 1995. *Dual Axis Radiographic Hydrodynamic Test Facility: Final Environmental Impact Statement*. 2 vols. Washington, DC: Government Printing Office.

U.S. Department of Energy. 2000. *United States Nuclear Tests July 1945–September 1992*. Washington, DC: Government Printing Office.

U.S. Department of Energy. 2013. *Fiscal Year 2014: Stockpile Stewardship and Management Plan*. Washington, DC: Government Printing Office.

U.S. Department of Energy. 2018. *Fiscal Year 2019: Stockpile Stewardship Management Plan—Biennial Plan Summary to Congress*. Washington, DC: Government Printing Office.

U.S. Department of State. 2009. *U.S. Government Counterinsurgency Guide*. Washington, DC: Government Printing Office.

U.S. General Accounting Office. 1995a. *Department of Energy: National Laborato-ries Need Clearer Missions and Better Management.* GAO/RCED-95th-10th ed. Washington, DC: Government Printing Office.

U.S. General Accounting Office. 1995b. *Security Clearances: Consideration of Sexual Orientation in the Clearance Process.* Washington, DC: GAO.

U.S. Joint Chiefs of Staff. 2000. *Joint Vision 2020.* Washington, DC: Government Printing Office.

U.S. National Security Agency. 2010. "Hardening Tips for Mac OS X 10.6 'Snow Leopard.'" Fort Meade, MD: Systems and Network Analysis Center, National Security Agency. Accessed September 12, 2014. https://www.nsa.gov/ia/_files /factsheets/macosx_10_6_hardeningtips.pdf.

U.S. National Security Council. 1993. "NSC 68: United States Objectives and Pro-grams for National Security (April 14, 1950)." In *American Cold War Strategy: Interpreting NSC 68,* edited by Ernest R. May. New York: St. Martin's.

U.S. Privacy and Civil Liberties Oversight Board. 2015. *Recommendations Assess-ment Report.* Washington, DC: Government Printing Office.

U.S. Senate Select Committee on Intelligence and U.S. House Permanent Select Committee on Intelligence. 2002. *Joint Inquiry into Intelligence Community Ac-tivities before and after the Terrorist Attacks of September 11, 2001.* Washington, DC: Government Printing Office.

Vanderbilt, Tom. 2002. *Survival City: Adventures among the Ruins of Atomic America.* Princeton, NJ: Princeton Architectural Press.

van Wyck, Peter C. 2004. *Signs of Danger: Waste, Trauma, and Nuclear Threat.* Minneapolis: University of Minesota Press.

Verdery, Katherine. 2014. *Secrets and Truths: Ethnography in the Archive of Roma-nia's Secret Police.* Budapest: Central European University Press.

Vine, David. 2015. *Base Nation: How U.S. Military Bases Abroad Harm America and the World.* New York: Metropolitan.

Virilio, Paul. 1989. *War and Cinema: The Logistics of Perception.* London: Verso.

Voyles, Traci Brynne. 2015. *Wastelanding: Legacies of Uranium Mining in Navajo Country.* Minneapolis: University of Minnesota Press.

Walsh, Lawrence E. 1993. *Final Report of the Independent Counsel for Iran/Contra Matters.* Washington, DC: United States Court of Appeals for the District of Columbia Circuit. http://www.fas.org/irp/offdocs/walsh.

Waters, Colin N., Jan Zalasiewicz, C. Summerhayes, Anthony Barnosky, Clément Poirier, Agnieszka Gałuszka, Alejandro Cearreta, et al. 2016. "The Anthropo-cene Is Functionally and Stratigraphically Distinct from the Holocene." *Science* 351 (6269): 137–47.

Weart, Spencer. 1988. *Nuclear Fear: A History of Images.* Cambridge, MA: Harvard University Press.

Weart, Spencer. 2008. *The Discovery of Global Warming.* Cambridge, MA: Har-vard University Press.

Webb, Ellen, S. Bushkin-Bedient, A. Cheng, C. D. Kassotis, V. Balise, and S. C. Nagel. 2014. "Developmental and Reproductive Effects of Chemicals Associated with Unconventional Oil and Natural Gas Operations." *Review of Environmental Health* 29 (4): 307–18.

Weigle, Marta, ed. 1975. *Hispanic Villages of Northern New Mexico: A Reprint of Volume II of the 1935 Tewa Basin Study, with Supplementary Materials.* Santa Fe, NM: Lightning Tree.

Weiner, Tim. 2012. *Enemies: A History of the FBI.* New York: Random House.

Welsome, Eileen. 1999. *The Plutonium Files: America's Secret Medical Experiments in the Cold War.* New York: Dial.

Weston, Kath. 2012. "Political Ecologies of the Precarious." *Anthropology Quarterly* 85 (2): 429–56.

Whissel, Kristen. 2014. *Spectacular Digital Effects: CGI and Contemporary Cinema.* Durham, NC: Duke University Press.

White, Josh, and Ann Scott Tyson. 2006. "Rumsfeld Offers Strategies for Current War." *Washington Post*, February 3.

White House. 2005. "President Discusses Patriot Act." June 9. https://georgewbush-whitehouse.archives.gov/news/releases/2005/06/20050609-2.html.

Whyte, Kyle Powys. 2019. "Way Beyond the Lifeboat: An Indigenous Allegory of Climate Justice." In *Climate Futures: Reimagining Global Climate Justice*, edited by Kum-Kum Bhavnani, John Foran, Priya Kurian, and Debashish Munshi, 11–20. London: Zed.

Willis, C. Scott, dir. 2007. *Astrospies.* Nova Productions.

Wills, Gary. 2010. *Bomb Power: The Modern Presidency and the National Security State.* New York: Penguin.

Winiarek, Victor, Marc Bocquet, Yelva Roustan, Camille Birman, and Pierre Tran. 2014. "Atmospheric Dispersion of Radionuclides from the Fukushima Daichii Nuclear Power Plant." Centre d'Enseignement et de Recherche en Environnement Atmospherique. http://cerea.enpc.fr/fukushima/index.html.

Wittner, Lawrence S. 1993. *One World or None: A History of the World Nuclear Disarmament Movement through 1953.* Stanford, CA: Stanford University Press.

Wittner, Lawrence S. 1997. *Resisting the Bomb: A History of the World Nuclear Disarmament Movement, 1954–1970.* Stanford, CA: Stanford University Press.

Wittner, Lawrence S. 2003. *Toward Abolition: A History of the World Nuclear Disarmament Movement, 1971 to the Present.* Stanford, CA: Stanford University Press.

Wittner, Lawrence S. 2009. *Confronting the Bomb: A Short History of the World Nuclear Disarmament Movement.* Stanford, CA: Stanford University Press.

Wolfe, Patrick. 2006. "Settler Colonialism and the Elimination of the Native." *Journal of Genocide Studies* 8 (4): 387–406.

Wolfsthal, Jon B., Jeffrey Lewis, and Marc Quint. 2014. *The Trillion Dollar Nuclear Triad.* Monterey, CA: James Martin Center for Nonproliferation Studies.

Woodruff, Wayne. 1967. *Nuclear Operation: Project Gasbuggy.* Livermore, CA: Lawrence Livermore National Laboratory.

Wray, Matt. 2006. "A Blast from the Past: Preserving and Interpreting the Atomic Age." *American Quarterly* 58 (2): 467–83.

Wylie, Sara Ann. 2018. *Fractivism: Corporate Bodies and Chemical Bonds.* Durham, NC: Duke University Press.

Zaretsky, Natasha. 2018. *Radiation Nation: Three Mile Island and the Political Transformation of the 1970s.* New York: Columbia University Press.

Zerriffi, Hisham, and Arjun Makhijani. 1996. "The Stewardship Smokescreen." *Bulletin of the Atomic Scientists* 52 (5): 22–28.

Zuboff, Shoshana. 2019. *The Age of Surveillance Capitalism.* New York: Public Affairs.

Zulaika, Joseba. 2009. *Terrorism: The Self-Fulfilling Prophecy.* Chicago: University of Chicago Press.

Zulaika, Joseba, and William Douglass. 1996. *Terror and Taboo: The Follies, Fables, and Faces of Terrorism.* New York: Routledge.

danger, nuclear: climate change and, 10, 29,
  252–54, 257, 261–64, 355–56, 360–62,
  369; existential, 9, 201, 342–43, 354–59,
  362, 369
DARHT (Dual Axis Radiographic Hydrodynamic Test Facility), 75–76, 378n22
DARPA (Defense Advanced Research Projects Agency), 323–24
data collection: Defense Department on,
  326–27; NSA, 325–28, 332–38, 386n2,
  386n4; TIA, 323–26, 330, 386n2
data storage, 327–28, 331–33
death, collective, 187–90, 194
declassification. See classification, declassification and
deep geology, 229, 232
Deepwater Horizon oil spill, 358
Defense Advanced Research Projects
  Agency (DARPA), 323–24
Defense Intelligence Agency, 326–27,
  386n4
del Toro, Guillermo, 237, 240
Department of Defense, 200, 364–65; *The
  Battle of Algiers* screened by, 265–67,
  270; on counterinsurgency, 265–67,
  270–71; Cybercommand securing, 325;
  on data collection, 326–27; environmental science and, 19–20, 30, 354; *Exercise
  Desert Rock* documentary produced by,
  201–6, 210, 213; *Joint Vision 2020* of,
  272–73; Rumsfeld at, 271–72, 317, 384n6;
  spending on, 273, 367, 384n4
Department of Energy (DOE), 58, 376n7;
  black budget of, 384n4; DARHT project
  of, 75–76, 378n22; Native American
  nations and, 65–66; nuclear complex
  modernization plans of, 78, 356, 358;
  nuclear facilities map of, 24–27; on
  nuclear waste, 79, 95, 98–99, 104; nuclear
  weapons meetings sponsored by, 335
Department of Homeland Security (DHS),
  301, 330; civil defense advertisements of,
  173–76; spending on, 367, 384n4; television show on, 316–17
Department of State, 276
Derrida, Jacques, 13, 194
desert modernism: Area 51 and, 100, 103;
  conspiracy theories and, 103–6; of Las

Vegas, 44, 83–84, 106–9; of Liberace, 83,
  106–12; masculinity in, 84–86, 108–9; of
  NTS, 44, 85–86, 93–95, 100, 106, 108–9,
  111; of Yucca Mountain Project, 95,
  99–100, 106
DHS. See Department of Homeland
  Security
D.H.S. (television show), 316–17
DISHFIRE program, 334
distanced viewer, 198
Dixon, Ivan, 277
documentary film. See film, documentary
DOE. See Department of Energy
*Dr. Strangelove, Or: How I Learned to Stop
  Worrying and Love the Bomb* (film), 153,
  159
Dual Axis Radiographic Hydrodynamic
  Test Facility (DARHT), 75–76, 378n22
duck-and-cover drill, 152

Earth, images of planet, 23, 181, 184
East Germany, 338
Eden, Lynn, 382n3
Edwards, Paul, 29, 144, 346
Eisenhower administration, 141, 167, 173,
  190
Elba, Idris, 238, 240
election cycle, 2016 U.S., 334
embassies, Soviet and U.S., 306–7
emergency alerts, 1–6
emergency powers, Bush, G. W., invoking,
  272–73
emulsion, film, 229, 232
encryption, 333
endangerment, 6
enemy combatants, 275
Enola Gay, 49–50
environment: Cold War militarization of,
  346; geographical engineering impacting, 223–26, 229; Ivy Mike detonation
  impacting, 25, 28–29, 33, 234, 344–46;
  lag in, 33; LANL impacting, 62–65, 74,
  118–19; LTBT and, 348–50; plutonium
  impacting humans and, 56–57, 66–67,
  104, 159, 166, 234–35; public concern
  about nuclear testing and, 23, 62–65,
  344, 347–49
environmental futurity, 383n3

kaiju (giant monsters), 237, 239, 242

Kalugin, Oleg, 286; CI Centre tour given by, 302–9, 313–14; International Spy Museum lecture of, 309–15; on McCarthy era, 307–8; U.S. citizenship given to, 301–2

Kant, Immanuel, 188, 192, 194

Kennedy, John F.: assassination of, 86, 103, 109, 314; Cold War masculinity and, 108–9; on fallout shelters, 150, 347; on LTBT, 348–49; missile gap and, 131, 141, 190

KGB: CIA and, 301, 304, 315; in International Spy Museum, 310; Kalugin of, 286, 301–15

Khrushchev, Nikita, 348

Kilcullen, David, 276

King, Martin Luther, Jr., 282, 307

Kissinger, Henry, 304

Koselleck, Reinhart, 340–41

Kubrick, Stanley, 153, 159

lag, 12; environmental, 33; in fallout, 5, 20, 33, 373n2; politics of, 5, 10

LASG. *See* Los Alamos Study Group

Las Vegas, Nevada: desert modernism of, 44, 83–84, 106–9; Liberace in, 106–12; NTS and, 106, 108, 111

Lawrence Livermore National Laboratory, 86, 229, 233

LeMay, Curtis, 247–48

Lennon, John, 295

Libby, Scooter, 384n6

Liberace, 83; nuclear testing compared with, 109, 111–12; sequins of, 106–8, 110, 112; sexuality of, 108–9; toxic costume of, 109–10

Liberace Museum, 106

lifeboat, figure of, 257–58, 383n3

Limited Test Ban Treaty (LTBT), 23, 200, 262; environment and, 348–50; Kennedy on, 348–49; media politics and signing of, 343, 348–49

List, Robert J., 28–31, 344

Little A'Le'Inn Café, 100, 102–3

Little Boy, 46–47, 49

Lookout Mountain Laboratory: Air Force and, 200–201, 212–17; *Special Weapons Orientation*, 201, 212–17

Los Alamos, New Mexico: Bradbury Science Museum in, 47; indigenous resistance around, 44; in *The Nuclear Borderlands*, 8

Los Alamos National Laboratory (LANL), 86, 319–20; antinuclear activists on, 57, 62, 75–77, 378n22; DARHT project of, 75–76, 378n22; employment at, 67–69, 74, 116; environmental impact of, 62–65, 74, 118–19; in geopolitics, 58–62; maps of, 26, 59; Native American nations and, 52–55, 57, 62–67, 76, 81, 377n18, 377nn15–16; Nuevomexicanos and, 53–55, 57, 67–69, 74, 76, 81; in plutonium economy, 57–69, 74, 116; in post–Cold War era, 58, 60–62, 366–67; Pueblo nations and, 53, 57, 62–67, 76, 81, 377n18, 377nn15–16; secrecy at, 116; technoscientific community of, 61, 65; virtual cave simulation at, 290

Los Alamos Scientific Laboratory, recruiting advertisements for, 68, 70–73

Los Alamos Study Group (LASG): billboard campaign of, 44, 114–23; citizens' inspection team sponsored by, 117–18; DARHT fought by, 75–76, 378n22

LTBT. *See* Limited Test Ban Treaty

Machta, Lester, 28–31, 344

Malcolm X, 282

manga, 238

Manhattan Project, 8, 189, 289, 363; commemorations of, 46–47; government secrecy and, 76, 377n16; Native Americans and, 64, 377n16; on shake, atomic, 287–88

Mars, 38

Marshall Islands: biomedical studies of, 30, 346; Ivy Mike detonation in, 25, 28–29, 33, 212, 234, 344–46; nuclear testing in, 25, 28–30, 33, 159, 200, 212, 214, 226, 234, 290, 344–46

masculinity: bunker and, 153; in desert modernism, 84–86, 108–9; Liberace and Cold War, 108–9; NTS and, 85–86; in *Plowshare*, white, 219

McCarthy era, 307–8, 310

McDonald's, 255, 352

vibration, 287–91

Vietnam, U.S. war in, 368; activists opposing, persecution of, 282; counterinsurgency in, 266, 270; KGB and opposition to, 314; in *The Spook Who Sat by the Door*, 280

Viking Fund, 347

virtual nuclear testing, 289–90, 356

Walker, John, 303, 311

War on Terror: accountability lacking in, 13–14; activism in, 299; *Battle of Algiers* and, 265–67, 270; big data and, 324–25, 328–30; blowback and, 276–77, 283; bunker in, 153–55; under Bush, G. W., 9–10, 116, 119, 154–55, 173, 239–40, 271–77, 282–83, 316–17, 365, 384n9; catastrophe in, 239–40; Cheney in, 153–54, 316; civil defense in, 173–76; Cold War compared with, 9–12, 47, 134–36, 153–55, 173, 176, 272, 286, 299, 316–17, 338, 356; cost of, 367–68; counterinsurgency in, 265–67, 270–77, 281–83, 302, 328, 384n9; counterintelligence in, 308; cybersecurity in, 324–25, 329; domestic counterterror political strategy of, 201; domestic covert actions in, 282; existential danger in, 9, 343; FOIA under, 322–23, 385n1; full-spectrum dominance in, 272–74; future of, 369–70; global resistance to, 276–77; as GWOT, 274; health in, 158, 173, 176–77; in LASG billboard campaign, 116, 119–23; as new normal, 154, 239–40, 316–17; nuclear fear in, 9–10, 173, 272; *Pacific Rim* and, 239–40; preemption in, 12, 114, 200, 271, 316, 322, 325–26; Project for the New American Century and, 273–74; race and, 281–83; rendition program in, 154, 274–76, 283; security state, regeneration of, and, 316–17; settler colonialism and, 282; surveillance in, 154, 275, 282, 308, 322–39, 385n1, 386n2; technoscience of, 13; torture in, 267, 275–76, 283; U.S. citizens and, 277; U.S. power demonstrated in, 271–72; WMD in, 9, 12, 119–23, 131,

185, 187, 191, 239, 272, 343, 356. *See also* Bush, George W.; National Security Agency

waste, nuclear: DOE regulations on, 79, 95, 98–99, 104; Native Americans and storage of, 66–67, 79; in New Mexico, map of, 75; from NTS, 87, 89, 94; ten-thousand-year safety plan for, 79, 95, 98–99, 104; Yucca Mountain storage site for, 95–100, 106, 378n4

Watson Institute, 367–68

weapon of mass destruction (WMD): as Iraq War rationale, 119–23, 131, 185, 187; in War on Terror, 9, 12, 119–23, 131, 185, 187, 191, 239, 272, 343, 356

welfare state, decline of, 340–42, 355–56

Wenner-Gren, Axel, 347

White Sands Missile Range, 45, 54

white supremacy, 280–82, 368

Whyte, Kyle, 383n3

WMD. *See* weapon of mass destruction

Wolfowitz, Paul, 384n6

Works Progress Administration, 116

World Court, 76, 378n23

world-making, 7, 232; nuclear nationalism as, 14–15; positive, 15, 362; radioactive, 11–12, 374n9

World War II, 363; espionage in, 304–6, 310; Pearl Harbor attack in, 2, 247, 249

worm program, software, 325

Wyden, Ron, 332

XKEYSCORE program, 334

Yahoo, 333–34

Yucca Mountain, 96; controversies over, 98, 378n4; desert modernism of, 95, 99–100, 106; rock bolts of, 98–100; ten-thousand-year safety plan for, 95, 98–99; touring, 95, 97–100; tunnels in, 97–98

Yugoslavia, former, 80

Yurchenko, Vitaly, 304

Žižek, Slavoj, 259–60

Zuboff, Shoshana, 331

Zuckerberg, Mark, 330–31